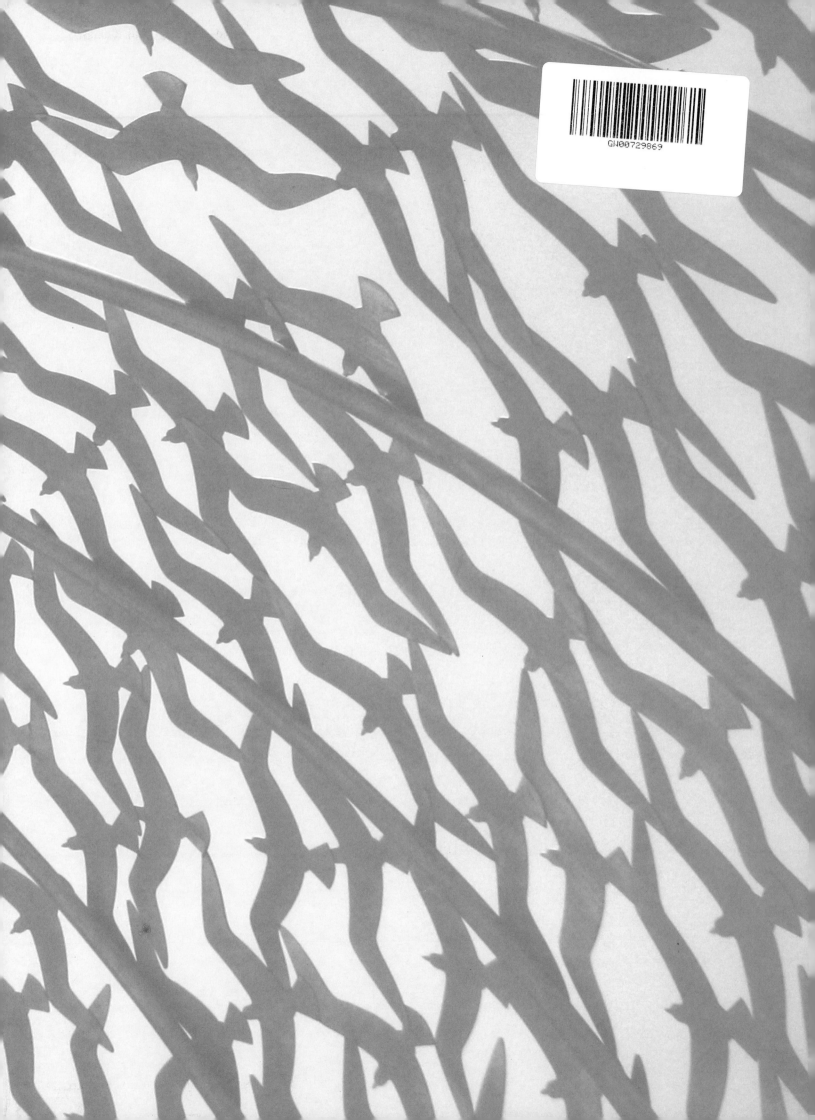

The Search for the

SYDNEY

DAVID L. MEARNS

HarperCollins*Publishers*

To Simon

Best Wishes

David

HarperCollins_Publishers_

First published in Australia in 2009
by HarperCollins_Publishers_ Pty Limited
ABN 36 009 913 517
www.harpercollins.com.au

HarperCollins_Publishers_
25 Ryde Road, Pymble, Sydney, NSW 2073, Australia
31 View Road, Glenfield, Auckland 0627, New Zealand
1–A, Hamilton House, Connaught Place, New Delhi – 110 001, India
77–85 Fulham Palace Road, London W6 8JB, United Kingdom
2 Bloor Street East, 20th Floor, Toronto, Ontario M4W 1A8, Canada
10 East 53rd Street, New York, NY 10022, USA

National Library of Australia Cataloguing-in-Publication data:

Mearns, David L.
The search for the Sydney / David L Mearns.
ISBN 9780732288891
Includes index.

Sydney. (Cruiser: 1934–1941)
Kormoran (Raider)
Australia. Royal Australian Navy—History.
Cruisers (Warships)— Australian—History.
Shipwrecks—Indian Ocean.
Underwater exploration—Indian Ocean.
World War, 1939–1945—Naval operations, Australian.
World War, 1939–1945—Naval operations, German.

940.545994.

Cover and internal design by Matt Stanton
Cover CGI Model by Thomas Schmid, 3DHistory
Back cover photograph courtesy Australian War Memorial
Author photograph by John Perryman
Typeset in 10.75/16pt Bembo by Matt Stanton
Reproduction by Graphic Print Group, South Australia
Produced in Hong Kong by Phoenix Offset on 157gsm Chinese Matt Art
Printed in China

09 10 11 12   10 9 8 7 6 5 4 3 2 1

For Sarah, Sam, Alexandra and Isabella

On 19 November 1941, a fierce battle which was unprecedented in the annals of naval warfare took place in the Indian Ocean, far from the coast of Western Australia. This book is dedicated to the memory of the 645 men from HMAS Sydney and seventy-nine men from HSK Kormoran who perished as a result.

CONTENTS

•••

PROLOGUE

...

The loss of a legend

When HMAS *Sydney* (II) succumbed to battle damage inflicted on her by the German raider *Kormoran* on the night of 19 November 1941 and disappeared beneath the surface of the Indian Ocean, the short but distinguished career of Australia's most famous fighting ship came to an end. The loss of this great warship and her entire complement of 645 officers and men sent a shock wave throughout the Australian nation. It also set in train a series of events that would span two generations before her final resting place was found and her crew laid to rest.

Sydney's loss heralded what was to be the beginning of a particularly dark period for the Royal Australian Navy (RAN) during World War II. In a single afternoon its champion, and all that she represented, was gone, leaving the Australian population feeling vulnerable and exposed to a very uncertain future.

Within a fortnight of *Sydney*'s sinking, the sloop HMAS *Parramatta* was torpedoed and sunk by a German U-boat in the Mediterranean while escorting a convoy to Tobruk. In March 1942, *Sydney*'s sister ship *Perth* was sunk following a desperately fought action against an overwhelming force of Imperial Japanese Navy cruisers in the Battle of the Sunda Strait. Within days of *Perth*'s loss, the sloop *Yarra* was sunk when her captain valiantly placed her between the small convoy he was escorting and a superior force of Japanese cruisers and destroyers. By December 1942 the heavy cruiser *Canberra*, destroyers *Vampire*, *Voyager* and *Nestor,* and corvette *Armidale* had all joined the RAN's rapidly growing list of wartime losses.

The demise of so many ships and men during such a short period left a deep wound in the heart of the Australian nation and came at a time when its naval forces were needed more than ever to protect its own shores and sea lines of communications. Gradually, following a further three years of fighting alongside its Commonwealth and American allies, Australia's fortunes changed, and its warships were among those present in Tokyo Bay on 2 September 1945 to bear witness to the formal surrender of the Imperial Japanese Forces, bringing an end to the second great conflict of the twentieth century.

Left: HMAS Sydney *(II) slides stern first down the slipway 22 September, 1934.*

With the cessation of hostilities came renewed hope for a war-weary Australia. Its armed forces were undergoing mass demobilisation and its fighting men and women were returning to the civilian work force, where they looked forward to the future and more prosperous and peaceful times. Thoughts of war were gradually pushed to the back of people's minds as they strove to put painful memories of armed conflict and lost loved ones behind them. While this was true for the most part, there remained one episode in Australia's war at sea which sat uneasily in the consciousness of the Australian people … and that was the loss of *Sydney*.

By then, four years had passed since her disappearance in 1941, and although numerous other Australian and Allied warships had been lost to enemy action during that time, it was the magnitude of *Sydney*'s loss, the circumstances surrounding her disappearance, and the great affection felt for this ship that continued to resonate throughout Australia. Relatives and friends of those lost in *Sydney* began to call on the navy and government for an explanation as to how such a capable, modern and well-armed warship could be sunk with all hands by what was, to their minds, little more than a crudely armed merchant ship. How was it that 317 Germans had survived the encounter, yet not one of *Sydney*'s crew lived to tell the tale?

Over the years the discussion concerning the fate of the RAN's most famous ship intensified rather than abated, keeping the story of *Sydney* alive through successive generations, to the point where it has, arguably, become folklore in Australian history. With the passing decades, advancements in sonar technology have led to the almost miraculous discovery of some of the world's most notable deep-water shipwrecks. *Titanic*, *Bismarck*, *Hood* and *Derbyshire* are just a handful of the famous ships that have been found lying at the bottom of the world's oceans, and by 2005 it became apparent to even the most casual observer that the Australian public was desperate to see the name *Sydney* added to this esteemed list.

HMAS *Sydney* (I)

To fully appreciate the widespread affection felt for *Sydney* (II) it is necessary to look back to 9 November 1914 when the first RAN ship to carry the name *Sydney* engaged and destroyed the German cruiser *Emden*. This event won for the infant RAN its first naval victory and the enduring admiration of the citizens of Australia. Moreover, the deeds performed by the crew of *Sydney* on that day laid the cornerstone for a legacy of distinguished service that would follow in three successive ships to carry the name of Australia's largest city.

Sydney's story began on 1 November 1914 when she sailed from Albany, Western Australia, as part of the escort for the first ANZAC troop convoy bound for the Middle East. On the morning of 9 November, the convoy intercepted wireless signals originating from the nearby Cocos Islands group, raising the alarm that a 'strange warship' had been sighted at the harbour entrance of Port Refuge. *Sydney*, under the command of Captain John Glossop, RN, was immediately detached to investigate and within a few hours sighted the notorious German raider *Emden*.

Emden had been at large in the Indian Ocean for months and during that time had sunk an estimated £2 million worth of British shipping, as well as a Russian cruiser and French destroyer during an audacious raid on Penang Harbour on 28 October 1914. She had sailed to the Cocos Islands to land a shore party to destroy the international cable and wireless station on Direction Island and to take coal from her attendant collier, *Buresk*. The captain of *Emden*, *Fregattenkapitän* Karl von Müller, soon realised that the appearance of *Sydney* posed a very real threat to his ship and, leaving his raiding party behind, he steamed out to meet her.

Although *Sydney* was faster than *Emden* and possessed superior firepower, Müller opened the engagement with rapid and accurate long-range fire, attempting to inflict as much damage as possible from the outset. He soon scored hits on *Sydney*'s control platform and rangefinder located on the upper bridge, killing four ratings and wounding several others.

Above: The RAN light cruiser HMAS Sydney *(I) in 1927.*

Glossop, however, used his ship's advantage of superior speed and armament to good effect and registered hits on *Emden*. Forty minutes later, *Emden*'s fire control positions, forward funnel and foremast were gone and she was burning fiercely fore and aft. Realising that *Emden* was at *Sydney*'s mercy, Müller ran his ship aground onto the reef at North Keeling Island in order to save the lives of his surviving crew. Glossop then broke off the engagement to pursue the *Emden*'s collier *Buresk*, which had been sighted during the action. By

the time *Sydney* had overhauled *Buresk*, the German crew had taken steps to scuttle her, ensuring that Glossop would not seize her as a prize.

On returning to North Keeling Island, Glossop observed that *Emden* was stuck fast on the reef but had not struck her battle ensign to indicate capitulation. He signalled *Emden*, seeking her formal surrender, but *Emden*'s ensign continued to fly defiantly from her mainmast. Reluctantly, Glossop fired several further salvos at the raider before a sailor was seen to climb aloft and haul the ensign down. This act heralded the end of Australia's first decisive naval engagement and etched *Sydney*'s name into the annals of the RAN.

Above: Early drawing of HMAS Sydney *(II) at sea.*

News of this victory was quickly communicated to the Australian mainland where it was received with great jubilation. On the other side of the world, the London *Times* recorded: 'We are glad to know that the distinction of disposing of the German cruiser *Emden* has fallen to the King's Australian Navy, and the greatest city in the Commonwealth will be proud of the success of the ship which bears her name.'

Indeed, the city of Sydney was very proud of her success. *Sydney*'s crew was rewarded with a special silver commemorative medal produced from a haul of captured Mexican dollar coins found on board the *Emden*. Following *Sydney*'s decommissioning in 1928, her tripod mast was removed from the ship and erected at Bradley's Head in Sydney Harbour as a permanent memorial to her. Other ship fittings, such as the teak from her decks, were used to make official mementos which were then offered for sale to the public. Many of these items have now become family heirlooms and are keenly sought by collectors.

HMAS *Sydney* (II)

On 8 July 1933 the ship that would become *Sydney* (II) was laid down as HMS *Phaeton* in the shipyard of Swan, Hunter and Wigham Richardson, at Wallsend-on-Tyne in England. The following year she was purchased, still under construction, by the Australian Government and renamed *Sydney*, in memory of her namesake and the capital city of New South Wales. She was launched on 22 September 1934 by Mrs Ethel Bruce, the wife of Mr Stanley Bruce, MC, the Australian high commissioner to Great Britain and former Australian prime minister.

Sydney was one of three British modified *Leander* class light cruisers acquired by the RAN in the years immediately preceding World War II. Her sister ships were *Perth* and *Hobart*, and they were sometimes referred to as *Perth* class light cruisers.

In January 1935 Commander J.A. Collins, RAN, arrived at Wallsend-on-Tyne to take up the appointment of executive officer in *Sydney*. Collins, a gunnery officer, was a graduate of the inaugural entry of the Royal Australian Naval College and although he did not know

it at the time, it would be under his leadership that *Sydney* would later reach the pinnacle of her career during the hard-fought Mediterranean campaign of World War II, which was now just four years distant.

Sydney was completed on 24 September 1935 and following acceptance trials she was commissioned under the command of Captain J.U.P. FitzGerald, R.N. With a steaming party embarked, she made the short voyage to Portsmouth where the balance of her Australian ship's company was waiting to join her. These men had been standing by in Portsmouth, having sailed there in the obsolete light cruiser HMAS *Brisbane*, which had been sailed to England for disposal.

The crew of *Sydney* liked what they saw before them. Her longest surviving officer, Lieutenant Commander John Ross, recalled in his memoirs: 'It was an exciting and proud moment for us as we watched this brand new ship — the last word in cruiser design — come gliding in, her new paintwork shining and her deck snow-white in the morning sunlight.'[1] *Sydney* was undeniably a modern, handsome-looking ship with sleek businesslike lines. With an overall length of 555 feet, a beam of 56 feet 8

inches and a standard displacement of 7,250 tons, she was much larger than her predecessor. Her main armament consisted of eight 6-inch Mark XXIII guns, housed in four Mark XXI twin turrets. The two forward turrets were designated 'A' and 'B' respectively, while the two after turrets were designated 'X' and 'Y'.

Her secondary armament consisted of four 4-inch quick-firing Mark V anti-aircraft guns and she was also equipped with eight 21-inch QR Mark VII above-water torpedo tubes arranged in quadruple (QR) mountings. These mountings when loaded housed Mark IX torpedoes, each of which carried a 750-pound warhead. Her close range weapons comprised of twelve 0.5-inch Vickers machine guns, sited on three Mark II quadruple mountings.

Sydney had a wartime complement of 645 men, which included six members of the Royal Australian Air Force (RAAF) who maintained and operated her amphibious catapult-launched aircraft. She also carried four civilian canteen staff.

With her full complement now embarked, the ship spent the next month undergoing trials (working up)

Left: HMAS Sydney *(II) in the dry dock; right top: Commander J.A. Collins with Billy Hughes; middle:* Sydney *(II)'s official launch party, 1934; bottom: HMAS* Sydney *(II) passing the mast of her namesake mounted at Bradleys Head, Sydney Harbour.*

in cold and blustery weather. At the end of this period *Sydney*'s band led a contingent of men on a march through London to the famous Guildhall. There, the Lord Mayor of London hosted a farewell luncheon for the Australian sailors before they returned by train to Portsmouth to make preparations for *Sydney*'s voyage to Australia.

On 29 October *Sydney* steamed out of Portsmouth with her crew's spirits high. World events, however, were to soon have an impact on the newly commissioned warship when Italy invaded Abyssinia. Sanctions were quickly imposed on Italy and *Sydney*'s voyage home was interrupted with orders to proceed to Gibraltar to reinforce the Royal Navy's Second Cruiser Squadron. The time spent working with the Royal Navy in the Mediterranean served her well and she continued to hone her war-fighting skills. An unfortunate outbreak of rubella among her crew, followed by mumps, then caused the ship to be placed under a quarantine order, preventing her crew from going ashore until the illness passed.

In March 1936 *Sydney* joined the heavy cruiser HMAS *Australia* in Alexandria, Egypt, as part of the First Cruiser Squadron. During the next four months the two Australian vessels continued to participate in numerous fleet exercises before finally sailing for home on 14 July.

Sydney's first Australian port of call was Fremantle, Western Australia. There she was warmly received by more than 800 well-wishers, many of whom had fond memories of *Sydney* (I)'s last visit in May 1927. Stopping only for a day, she was soon steaming east, bound for Melbourne, Victoria, where she arrived on 8 August. The citizens of Melbourne turned out in droves to see the RAN's new light cruiser and the ship received 18,000 visitors when she was opened for inspection at Princes Pier.

On 11 August *Sydney* made her long-awaited entry through Sydney Heads and into Port Jackson, where her arrival was viewed from the shore by thousands of citizens

Above: HMAS Sydney *in her peacetime paint scheme departing Farm Cove, Sydney.*

who had turned out to see her. As she slowly made her way through the channel to a buoy off Garden Island she was saluted with the sound of ferry whistles. Once again the citizens of Sydney had a ship that they could call their own and Australia a cruiser worthy of the lingering affection and esteem held for HMAS *Sydney* (I).

Prelude to war

In July 1937 Captain J.W.A. Waller, RN, succeeded Captain FitzGerald as *Sydney's* commanding officer. The following month Commander Collins was also relieved, having spent almost three years as her executive officer. Between 1937 and the outbreak of war, *Sydney* was kept busy exercising, mostly operating in Australian waters. It was with increasing apprehension that Australians watched Germany's and Italy's threats to peace in Europe steadily materialise. The Munich crisis of 1938 saw the partial mobilisation of Australia's naval forces; however, they were later stood down when it appeared that war had been averted.

In August 1939 it became apparent that the situation in Europe had again deteriorated, and on 30 August the Commonwealth Government reaffirmed that it would place the ships of the RAN and their personnel at the disposal of the British Government in the event of war. The government did, however, find it necessary to stipulate that no ships (other than HMAS *Perth*) should be taken from Australian waters without concurrence of the Australian Government.[2]

Commencement of hostilities with Germany

When the declaration of war came on 3 September 1939, *Sydney* had already taken up her war station at Fremantle. There she received a draft of an additional 135 ratings from the Fremantle Division of the Royal Australian Naval Reserve (RANR) and several additional officers to boost her complement to its war footing. The cruiser then commenced a rigorous series of gunnery and torpedo exercises off the West Australian coast and began patrol and escort duties.

On 16 November, Captain J.A. Collins, RAN, returned to *Sydney* to relieve Captain Waller, RN, as her commanding officer. With three years' experience under his belt as *Sydney's* executive officer, Collins's selection as the first Australian officer to command the vessel was seen as a logical choice and one which was popular with many of the cruiser's 'old hands', who were pleased to see him return.

Patrol work in the Indian Ocean continued for the remainder of 1939 before the cruiser was ordered to return to Sydney for docking and Christmas leave. Work-ups followed early in the new year, and on completion *Sydney* returned to Western Australia where she arrived on 8 February 1940. For the next few months she continued the now familiar pattern of patrol and escort work, which stretched from Bunbury in the south to Carnarvon in the north. She also conducted patrols well out into the Indian Ocean. Throughout this time she had become a familiar sight to the residents of Fremantle and Perth who, with many of their own kith and kin serving in her, had all but adopted the ship as their own.

On 1 May *Sydney* was returning to Fremantle from escort duties when she received orders to proceed to Colombo at best speed. These orders were the instrument that would see *Sydney* leave the Australian Station and later win fame in the Mediterranean Sea. Taking passage via Singapore to refuel, *Sydney* arrived in Colombo on 8 May. Her time there, however, was short and she was soon directed to proceed to Alexandria, where she joined the Royal Navy Mediterranean Fleet on 26 May.

The Mediterranean

In early June 1940 *Sydney* participated in a series of exercises as part of the Seventh Cruiser Squadron and it did not take her long to establish a reputation as an efficient and happy ship. On 10 June, with France about to fall and with Britain's future looking precarious, Italy entered the war on the side of Germany. It was now clear to the men of *Sydney* that the balance of power in the Mediterranean could easily shift and that the struggle for control of the sea there was about to begin in earnest.

Right: Australian War Memorial's tribute to RAN sailors.

Within hours of Italy's war declaration, the British fleet, under the command of Admiral Sir Andrew Cunningham, RN, sailed on its first patrol sweep in the early hours of 11 June. Hostilities commenced almost immediately and first blood was drawn that night at 2330 when the destroyer HMS *Decoy* reported sighting a submarine on the surface, which she attacked. At dawn the next morning, an oil slick two miles long was detected, although it was not known whether the submarine was destroyed. The enemy also struck quickly. On 12 June the cruiser HMS *Calypso* was torpedoed by a submarine off Crete and sank with the loss of one officer and 38 ratings.

The fleet completed its patrol sweep and returned to Alexandria two days later where it was forced to make a cautious entry due to the presence of minefields which had been laid by enemy submarines off the harbour entrance. The war in the Mediterranean had erupted swiftly and for the young Australian sailors in *Sydney* it was a sobering introduction to battle at sea in the northern hemisphere.

On 22 June France signed an armistice with Germany, the terms of which called for French naval units deployed abroad to return to France where they would be demobilised under the supervision of the Axis forces. As feared, the balance of sea power had indeed shifted and the British Government resolved that under no circumstances should the French fleet be permitted to fall into the hands of the enemy. It was a matter which was eventually settled by extreme measures on the one hand, and considered diplomacy on the other.

In the Western Mediterranean the majority of the French fleet was in the port of Mers-el-Kebir at Oran. There the French admiral in command was given an ultimatum by the British. He could order his ships to sail to Britain or to the United States where they would be interned; he could demilitarise them in situ; or he would face annihilation by units of the Royal Navy. Tragically, with no positive response forthcoming, the majority of the fleet was neutralised with force.

In Alexandria, where *Sydney* was berthed, the situation was similarly tense, with many French naval units present in the harbour and now under the guns of the Commonwealth warships. There, Admiral Cunningham insisted on negotiating with his French counterpart, Vice Admiral Godfroy, who up until the signing of the armistice had been operating alongside the Allied warships. Through Cunningham's diplomacy, tragedy was averted when Godfroy agreed to demilitarise his ships, keep them in port and reduce their crews to 30 per cent. With great relief *Sydney*'s menacing guns were trained back to the more benign fore and aft positions and unloaded.

Throughout June *Sydney* participated in numerous patrols and took part in a major shore bombardment of Bardia later in the month. During this bombardment *Sydney*'s amphibious *Seagull* aircraft was launched to assist in coordinating the cruiser's fire. The RAAF aircrew who manned the aircraft had no sooner begun their task when they were set upon by fighters which seemed intent on shooting them down. They put up a spirited defence in the lumbering aircraft before the aggressors broke off their attack, leaving the *Seagull* full of holes and barely airworthy. Her pilot, Flight Lieutenant T.M. Price, RAAF, force-landed at a British airfield some miles away but the plane was so badly damaged that it was written off. Price was awarded the Distinguished Flying Cross for his courageous performance and credited his crew's survival to the slow speed of his aircraft, which caused the speeding enemy fighters to over-shoot their intended target.

On 28 June *Sydney* was involved in the pursuit of three enemy destroyers detected by aerial reconnaissance. They were engaged at long range. One of them, the *Espero*, was crippled and Collins was ordered to finish her off and pick up any survivors. As he approached the stricken Italian vessel it opened fire with guns and torpedoes in a last brave act of defiance. *Sydney*'s response was swift and final, with her 6-inch guns soon reducing the destroyer to a burning wreck. The *Espero* then healed over and sank.

Captain Collins immediately ordered his boats away and the next two hours were spent rescuing survivors in the gathering darkness. When it became too dangerous for *Sydney* to remain in the area any longer, Collins instructed that one of his boats was to be fully provisioned and left behind to ensure that any crew they had missed were

Above: HMAS Sydney's *triumphant return to Alexandria.*

given a sporting chance of survival. Those recovered were well cared for, to the extent that when it came time for them to disembark in Alexandria, many requested that they remain on board as *Sydney*'s prisoners rather than go to a prisoner of war camp.

On 30 June the Seventh Cruiser Squadron came under several aerial attacks from Italian bombers during its return passage to Alexandria. This was to be the first of many that *Sydney* would emerge from unscathed, and in the weeks that followed she earned the reputation as a 'lucky ship'. Later, in July, during a particularly virulent attack, Admiral Cunningham observed that *Sydney* completely disappeared 'in a line of towering pillars of spray as high as church steeples'. When *Sydney* emerged, Cunningham signalled: 'Are you all right?' to which came the rather dubious reply from that stout-hearted Australian, Captain J.A. Collins, 'I hope so.'[3]

Action off Calabria

The fleet next sailed from Alexandria late in the evening of 7 July and the following day came under intense air attack from the Italian Air Force. During one of these raids the cruiser HMS *Gloucester* was hit by a bomb which killed her captain and seventeen others. Later that evening a reconnaissance aircraft reported sighting two enemy battleships steering south about 100 miles north-west of Benghazi. These capital ships were supported by six cruisers and seven destroyers, and were later observed to alter course to the north. Cunningham immediately determined to manoeuvre his force between the enemy fleet and their base at Taranto to try and cut them off and bring them into action.

The following day planes from the aircraft carrier HMS *Eagle* relocated the Italian ships and Cunningham's fleet closed them rapidly. At approximately 1500 hours HMS *Neptune,* part of the vanguard of four cruisers which

Left: Painting of HMAS Sydney *in action in the Mediterranean, by John Alcott.*

included *Sydney*, reported sighting four Italian cruisers, and shortly afterwards the entire enemy fleet came into view, consisting of two battleships, twelve cruisers and numerous destroyers.[4] The vanguard, greatly outnumbered, quickly found itself in action when the Italian heavy cruisers opened fire on them at 1514 hours.

Cunningham, in HMS *Warspite,* came to the assistance of the beleaguered cruisers and the battleship's fire forced the enemy to retire under the cover of smoke, after which there was a lull in the action. By this time, the battleships HMS *Malaya* and *Royal Sovereign* were also approaching the scene of action as were the British destroyers which were concentrating for an attack.

Shortly before 1600 hours, at a range of roughly thirteen miles, *Warspite* opened fire on the two enemy battleships and succeeded in straddling them. Moments later the Italian flagship, *Guilio Cesare*, was hit by a 15-inch shell from *Warspite*, causing the Italians to turn away under a dense screen of smoke.

Meanwhile, the Allied cruisers had rejoined the action and were attempting to close the enemy destroyers. By 1640, however, the engagement was all but over, and while it did not culminate in the much anticipated full-scale fleet action, *Sydney* had again been in the thick of it and survived relatively unscathed with no casualties and only a few of her signal halyards shot away. During the action she expended more than 400 rounds of her 6-inch ammunition and by the time she returned to Alexandria she had expended her entire outfit of 4-inch anti-aircraft ammunition in beating off air attacks.

These attacks came as the battle fleet chased the Italians to within 25 miles of the coast of Calabria before breaking off the pursuit and altering course for a position south of Malta. The Allied fleet continued to be harassed from the air as it made its way back to Alexandria where it arrived on 13 July. There *Sydney* docked briefly for hull maintenance and to take on ammunition before her next patrol.

Back in Australia, *Sydney*'s exploits in the Mediterranean were followed with fervour and within weeks she was to make headlines that would see her become a household name.

Victory off Cape Spada

On 18 July *Sydney* sailed from Alexandria in company with the destroyer HMS *Havock*, bound for the Gulf of Athens. Together they had orders to support Commander H. St L. Nicolson's destroyer flotilla consisting of HMS *Hyperion*, *Hero*, *Hasty* and *Ilex* in the Aegean Sea. Nicolson was to intercept any Italian shipping attempting passage to or from the Dodecanese and also carry out an anti-submarine sweep from east to west along the north coast of the island of Crete.

Collins, realising that Nicolson's westward sweep might expose him to enemy attack in the restricted waters of the Aegean, adjusted his course and speed so that he was better

Above: The defeated Bartolomeo Colleoni *on fire.*

placed to provide support if required. In pre-radar days, dawn was often the most dangerous time of day, as daylight could reveal the presence of previously undetected enemy ships or aircraft, and on 19 July this proved to be the case when Nicolson, at the western end of his sweep, sighted two enemy *Condottieri* class cruisers which soon opened fire on his destroyers. With little choice other than to turn and run, and not knowing that *Sydney* and *Havock* were closing their position, Nicolson made an enemy contact report and began a speedy retiring action towards what he believed to be a far distant *Sydney*. Collins, hundreds of miles closer than anyone realised, prepared his ship for action but maintained strict communications silence so as not to alert the enemy to his presence. At 0820 the two Italian cruisers were sighted and eight minutes later,

with tension mounting, *Sydney* hoisted her battle ensigns and opened fire at a range of approximately ten miles. Both the enemy and the fleeing British destroyers were taken by surprise at the sudden appearance of *Sydney* and before long hits were registered on one of the enemy cruisers, the *Giovanni Delle Bande Nere*.

By now Nicolson's destroyers were in wireless contact with *Sydney* and the two groups joined forces north of Cape Spada. *Sydney* had scored hits on both enemy cruisers and it became apparent to Collins that they were attempting to retreat towards the Antikithera Channel under cover of smoke. The enemy gunfire become sporadic at this point of the action and one of the cruisers, later identified as the *Bartolomeo Colleoni*, was seen to be on fire and losing way, before coming to a complete stop. Two of Nicolson's destroyers, *Hyperion* and *Ilex*, were subsequently ordered to finish her off and pick up survivors. They were later relieved by *Havock*, which remained in the area until she came under the threat of enemy air attack. In all, some 550 Italians, including the cruiser's captain, were rescued by the destroyers.

Meanwhile, Collins continued to chase the remaining cruiser, the *Giovanni Delle Bande Nere*. At 1025, by which time *Sydney* was low on ammunition and coming within range of Italian bomber aircraft, Collins broke off the pursuit. During the action *Sydney* sustained just one hit to her forward funnel, which caused only minor damage and no casualties.

Intent on retribution, the Italian air force was soon on the scene and doing its best to sink the *Sydney*, which continued to lead a charmed life, escaping several very near misses. These attacks prevailed throughout the afternoon and *Havock*, now bound for Alexandria, was damaged in one of them, although not seriously. At 1100 hours on 20 July *Sydney* entered Alexandria harbour with the Australian national flag flying proudly from her foremast and to the rousing cheers of the men of the Mediterranean fleet. The Commander-in-Chief, Admiral Cunningham, boarded *Sydney* from his barge to personally congratulate Captain Collins and his crew. He was to recall in his memoirs: 'For this fine, brisk action which showed the high efficiency and magnificent fighting qualities of the Royal Australian Navy,

**H.M.A.S. SYDNEY OFFICERS
DECORATED:**

Captain J. A. COLLINS
(who was previously awarded the
honour of C.B.)

Lt.-Commander M. SINGER, D.S.C.

Commander T. HILKIN, D.S.O.

Commander L. DALTON, D.S.O.

and

Lt.-Commander E. THRUSTON, D.S.O.

Captain J. A. COLLINS, C.B.

**RATINGS AND PETTY OFFICERS
DECORATED:**

Chief-Petty-Officer A. P. PRIOR,
D.S.M.

Chief-Petty-Officer S. G. SILK,
D.S.M.

Chief-Ordnance-Artificer
W. J. KEANE, D.S.M.

Chief Stoker J. N. BEAUMONT,
D.S.M.

Able-Seaman G. ROSEVEAR,
D.S.M.

Stoker E. EVANS, D.S.M.

Above: Following the Colleoni*'s defeat, the men of* Sydney *were decorated.*

Captain Collins was immediately awarded the Companion of the Bath, by His Majesty, a well-deserved honour.'[5] His report to the Admiralty concerning the action was similarly flattering: 'The credit for this successful and gallant action belongs mainly to Captain J.A. Collins, C.B., R.A.N., who by his quick appreciation of the situation, offensive spirit and resolute handling of H.M.A.S. "Sydney," achieved a victory over a superior force which has had important strategical effects. It is significant that, so far as is known, no Italian surface forces have returned into or near the Aegean since this action was fought.'[6]

Throughout Australia news of *Sydney*'s victory dominated the newspapers. The Melbourne *Herald* of 20 July 1940 reported in its evening edition that: 'Once again the Australian Navy has shown the splendid fighting quality and efficiency of the last war. "Sydney" outfought and destroyed the famous "Emden" and now her younger sister writes another page of naval history that will thrill the civilized world.' And thrill it did. Newspapers in London and New York enthusiastically acknowledged

Sydney's victory over the two superior Italian cruisers, while the *Sydney Morning Herald* of 22 July 1940 announced that: 'Flags will be flown on all Government buildings throughout New South Wales today in honour of a great naval exploit.'

With this victory, *Sydney*'s aura of invincibility became cemented in the minds of the Australian people. On the other side of the world she had survived intense air attacks, taken on the might of the Italian Navy and snatched a decisive victory through a combination of initiative and bravado in the face of overwhelming odds. Her exploits were now becoming legendary. Almost every Australian community had one of its own serving in the cruiser and as she continued to add to her already impressive war record, so their pride in the ship, which Admiral Cunningham had dubbed a 'stormy petrel', continued to grow.

Throughout the remainder of 1940 *Sydney* participated in further patrols, anti-submarine sweeps, convoy escort duties and shore bombardments in the Mediterranean and Adriatic. In January 1941 she received orders recalling her to Australia and as she departed Alexandria she received many farewell signals from the ships which she had

fought alongside throughout 1940. Admiral Cunningham expressed his deep personal regret over her departure but also conveyed his hope that 'your countrymen will give you the reception you deserve'.

During *Sydney*'s passage home she passed through the Suez Canal and escorted several small convoys through the Red Sea before entering the Indian Ocean. There she conducted a sweep past Mogadiscio (present-day Mogadishu) looking for Italian vessels before proceeding independently to Fremantle where she arrived on 5 February to be greeted by a large contingent of the media, photographers and well-wishers. Disappointingly for the West Australians on board, the visit was short-lived as she sailed the same afternoon for Sydney, having taken on stores and fresh provisions as well as embarking a small group of reporters and their cameramen.

Sydney arrived in her namesake harbour shortly before midnight on Sunday, 9 February 1941, anchoring in Watsons Bay. The following morning she weighed anchor and slowly made her way down the harbour towards her berth at Circular Quay, amid an escort of dozens of motor launches carrying excited relatives and friends.

Admiral Cunningham's hope that the men of *Sydney* would 'get the reception they deserved' was certainly fulfilled, for when the cruiser arrived at the quay she was met by a huge crowd of people who had come to greet her. Many VIPs had also assembled to welcome *Sydney* home, including the Governor-General, Lord Gowrie; the Minister for the Navy, Billy Hughes; and the First Naval Member, Sir Ragnar Colvin. Following addresses from them, the crew of *Sydney* went ashore where they were embraced by their friends and families. News of *Sydney*'s arrival home dominated the newspapers, which devoted the next three days to covering her triumphant return in great detail.

On Tuesday, 11 February, the Premier of New South Wales, Mr Mair, and the City of Sydney Lord Mayor, Alderman Crick, came on board the cruiser to present a plaque to the ship commemorating her victory over the *Bartolomeo Colleoni* on behalf of the citizens of Sydney. The plaque consisted of two large cast medallions mounted on oak and was affixed to the gun housing of 'Y' turret below the sighting ports. With the unveiling of the plaque completed, the crew was fallen in on the quay side behind *Sydney*'s band and they marched through the streets of Sydney to a civic reception which had been arranged for them at the town hall.

Thousands of people turned out to watch the men parade through the city and children were given the day off school so that they too could enjoy the celebration. At the town hall, each member of *Sydney*'s crew was presented with a smaller medallion of the same design as that awarded to the ship, all of which were individually inscribed with the recipient's personal details. As with the medals fashioned from the Mexican dollars captured from *Emden* and awarded to the crew of the first HMAS *Sydney*, so too was the crew of *Sydney* (II) similarly feted.

For many of those present it was a day never to be forgotten. The victorious *Sydney* had come home at a time when the threat to Australian shipping in both the Pacific and Indian oceans was increasing. Evidence that German raiders had been active around the Australian coastline was also mounting — indeed, Bass Strait and the entrance to Port Phillip Bay had both been mined by raiders — and pressure had been brought to bear on the government to bring the RAN's big ships home to deal with the mounting threat.

Sydney's return was both timely and symbolic. The government had not only heeded the call, but had brought home the battle-hardened *Sydney*. In the eyes of the Australian public, all would be well now that *Sydney* was home … none would have believed that in less than a year she would be gone, taking all those on board with her.

The Australia Station

With the excitement surrounding *Sydney*'s return abating, and with censorship reapplied to her movements, the Australian Navy turned its attention towards more practical matters, putting *Sydney* into dry dock for maintenance while her crew was sent on leave.

On 28 February, with her docking completed, the cruiser sailed for Fremantle where she began a period of routine convoy escort duties operating off the West Australian coast. In April she returned to the eastern seaboard escorting the troopship *Queen Mary* to Jervis Bay before undertaking a high-speed passage via Fremantle to Singapore to carry the First Naval Member to a high-level Allied conference. While in Singapore it was decided that Captain Collins would be appointed the Australian Naval Representative to the Commander-in-Chief China (based in Singapore) Vice Admiral (Sir) Geoffrey Layton.[7]

And so it was that in Fremantle on 15 May 1941, 'Colleoni John', as he had been nicknamed by his crew, handed over command of *Sydney* to Captain Joseph Burnett, RAN. In later years, following a long and distinguished career in the RAN, Collins reflected: 'To me there has never been before nor will there ever be again, a ship quite to compare with the cruiser *Sydney* of World War II.'[8]

Like Collins, Joseph Burnett had attended the Royal Australian Naval College as one of the original entry of cadets in 1913. He was rated cadet-captain in 1914 and went on to specialise in gunnery. He served in HMAS *Australia* during World War I and a number of Royal Navy vessels between the wars, which included service abroad during the Spanish Civil War. Promoted to captain in 1938 he was serving in England when war broke out and returned home in late 1939 to take up the appointment of Assistant Chief of Naval Staff.

Burnett took his new command to sea for the first time between 17 and 21 May to conduct routine patrols and exercises in the Indian Ocean. On 26 May *Sydney* relieved HMAS *Hobart* as the escort for the troopship *Zealandia*, which was making passage from Melbourne to Singapore via Fremantle. After a short stopover in Fremantle the two vessels continued their voyage on 31 May and arrived in the vicinity of the Sunda Strait on 6

Right: Captain Joseph Burnett.

June. There *Sydney* was relieved by HMS *Danae* before returning independently to Fremantle, where she arrived four days later.

Zealandia was to become a familiar sight to the men of *Sydney* as her next assignment was to provide escort for the troopship during her return passage from the Sunda Strait to Fremantle later in the month. On 24 June *Zealandia* was again under *Sydney*'s watchful eyes as part of a small convoy designated FS 1 taking passage across the Great Australian Bight bound for Melbourne and Sydney respectively.

A change of scenery came in July when Captain Burnett and his crew escorted the *Berwickshire* and *Gleniffer* to New Zealand before conducting a resupply run to Noumea. She returned to Sydney on 25 July to escort convoy US 11B to Melbourne, and after a brief docking in early August was again crossing the Tasman Sea bound for Auckland, New Zealand, as escort for the *Awatea*. Following a three-day stopover, the two vessels sailed on 14 August for Suva, where they arrived a few days later. *Sydney* returned home independently on 28 August, having escorted the *Awatea* beyond Samoa.

Meanwhile in the far distant Indian Ocean there had been a number of disturbing developments. Reports of spurious wireless signals coupled with the unexplained disappearance of several merchant ships had raised concerns that there might be a raider at large. This was indeed the case.

The German Navy's largest auxiliary cruiser, the *Kormoran*, now disguised as the Dutch merchant ship MV *Straat Malakka,* had entered the Indian Ocean some months previously and was making her presence felt throughout the region. Adept at subterfuge and with a well-drilled and disciplined crew, she was more than a match for any unsuspecting merchant ship. Her captain, however, had no desire to encounter a warship from what he termed Australia's 'grey funnel' line.

On 4 September *Sydney* sailed from Port Jackson in company with the large troop transport *Queen Mary*. Picking up the *Queen Elizabeth* en route, the three vessels later rendezvoused with HMAS *Canberra*, which assumed responsibility for their safe passage to Fremantle.

Sydney then called at Melbourne to refuel and make good minor defects.

Her next voyage, escorting convoy US 12B to Fremantle, would see *Sydney* leave the eastern seaboard for the last time. Never again would she sail through Sydney Heads, never again would she pass the mast of her forebear and never again would she be feted by the citizens of the city whose name she carried. As she shepherded her convoy west, her date with destiny was fast approaching as the *Kormoran* slowly made her way east towards the West Australian coast.

Sydney arrived in Fremantle on 25 September and three days later continued with US 12B on the now familiar route to the Sunda Strait where she was relieved by HMS *Glasgow*. Many of *Sydney*'s crew viewed this work as being a 'milk run' in comparison to the high-tempo operations in the Mediterranean, yet there were subtle signs starting to appear, leading Captain Burnett to believe that things may not be as benign as they appeared.

One of these signs came on the evening of 3 October when *Sydney* sighted an object floating on the sea, which on investigation appeared to be a large gunnery target. The wooden structure was recovered by one of *Sydney*'s boats and hoisted on board, where it was examined and dismantled. Captain Burnett reported the discovery to Naval headquarters in Melbourne stating that it was 'difficult to find an explanation of this large structure which fitted all the facts'. He went on to express 'that there is just a possibility that it may have been dropped by a raider'[9].

In the early hours of the morning of 6 October an unidentified vessel was sighted by HMAS *Yandra* eight miles from Rottnest Island. The vessel melted into the darkness and in spite of an air search, no trace of it was found. Speculation concerning the identity of the vessel became the subject of considerable attention in the Naval Intelligence summaries over the next few days, which again raised the possibility that a raider may have been operating in the area.[10] As a precaution, minesweepers were ordered to operate ahead of *Queen Mary* and *Sydney*, both of which were due to arrive in Fremantle,

Left top: Sydney*'s crew marching through the streets of Sydney in 1941 and (bottom): the Governor-General addressing the ship's company.*

with each visit the bonds between the cruiser and the citizens of Western Australia were further strengthened.

On 1 November *Sydney* sailed from Fremantle to again rendezvous with *Zealandia*, which was on passage from Melbourne with HMAS *Adelaide* as her escort. *Sydney* relieved *Adelaide* off King George Sound, Albany, before escorting the troopship to Fremantle where they arrived on 9 November. Two days later *Sydney* sailed with *Zealandia* on the familiar 'milk run' to the Sunda Strait, signalling shore authorities before she sailed that she would return to port in the afternoon of Thursday 20 November.

Sydney's passage to the Sunda Strait was without incident and at noon on 17 November she rendezvoused with HMS *Durban*, which assumed responsibility for escorting *Zealandia* on to Singapore. Relieved of her escort duty, *Sydney* reversed course and resumed the now well-worn navigational track that would take her back to Fremantle.

As she disappeared over the horizon, none of those watching in *Zealandia* or *Durban* suspected that they would be among the last to see her and that it would be a further 66 years before friendly eyes once more gazed upon the pride of the Royal Australian Navy.

LIEUTENANT JOHN PERRYMAN,
CSM, RANR
2009

while anti-submarine patrols were maintained during daylight hours.

Over the next few weeks *Sydney* engaged in exercises off the West Australian coastline and conducted short visits to Geraldton and Bunbury. Throughout 1941 she had become a familiar sight in West Australian waters and

INTRODUCTION
...

The shock of *Sydney*'s loss was enormous and felt deeply all across the nation. Australians believed that they had lost the bravest of men fighting on the Australian Navy's best and most famous ship. Sadness and anger was quickly replaced by disbelief and intense questioning. How was it possible that *Kormoran*, this seemingly inferior converted freighter, was able to defeat and sink the glorious *Sydney*? What had transpired between these two clear enemies that brought them into such dangerously close contact before the battle? But most disturbingly, why were virtually no traces of *Sydney*, or any of her men, ever found during the exhaustive air and sea searches that followed when the sea was practically littered with life rafts and boats full of German survivors who were ultimately rescued and in relatively good condition? With no Australian eyewitnesses alive to tell their story, could the German accounts of the incredible battle and their improbable victory be trusted?

More than 60 years after *Sydney* and *Kormoran* violently crossed bows on that tragic afternoon in late November 1941, much of Australia still feels that these questions remain unsatisfactorily answered. This is despite the informal naval investigation into *Sydney*'s loss at the time[1] (as opposed to a more official and formal board of inquiry), the official RAN history by George Hermon Gill which describes the battle in considerable detail,[2] a full-blown cross-party parliamentary inquiry into the loss conducted in 1998–99[3] and the production of roughly two dozen books on the subject. Nothing, it seems, has been able to prevent this sad event from being transformed from Australia's greatest naval loss to Australia's greatest maritime mystery.

To solve the mystery once and for all, it was absolutely clear that the wrecks of *Sydney* and *Kormoran* would have to be found. Their hulls, in whatever location and condition, would be the final truthful witnesses to the events of 19 November 1941. Preserved by the stillness of the deep, the wrecks with the scars from their battle, would lay bare the

Left: Manning one of Sydney's 4-inch guns.

testimony of *Kormoran*'s commander, Theodor Detmers, for all to see and cross-examine. The great challenge of this quest, which became my challenge when I agreed to lead the search for the wrecks, was how to use the information left by Detmers to find them. This would be the same information that was believed by many to be highly questionable at best and at worst totally false.[4]

In my professional opinion as a shipwreck hunter, the risks were stark. If Detmers had indeed lied, then the wrecks would never be found. On the other hand, without Detmers's information no search for the wrecks could possibly proceed because his were the only navigational coordinates that existed for the battle. In my mind the success or failure of the search would come down to this crucial question: was Captain Detmers's account honest and accurate? On a personal level I would be putting my reputation on the line in what was gearing up to be an extremely high-profile and eagerly anticipated search. The fact that the search was being mostly funded with $4.8 million from the public purse granted by the Commonwealth and state (WA and NSW) governments only increased the stakes. To put it bluntly, a lot of money, careers and the hope of millions of Australians would be riding on the account of one man, and I was betting big that he was right.

A chance encounter

As the *Hilfskreuzer* (HSK) *Kormoran* steamed up the coast of Western Australia on the afternoon of Wednesday, 19 November 1941, heading just east of due north on her 352nd continuous day at sea, no one on board — from her commanding officer, the experienced and battle-hardened *Fregattenkapitän*[5] Theodor Detmers, to the lowest engine room rating — knew how the events of the next several hours would forever change their lives and plunge an entire nation into a deep shock and questioning that would persist for the next 66 years. *Kormoran*, an auxiliary cruiser or merchant raider of the German *Kriegsmarine*[6] now disguised as the Dutch merchant freighter *Straat Malakka*, was about to cross paths with its worst nightmare.

Freshly resupplied with fuel and provisions from her recent rendezvous with the supply ship *Kulmerland*, Detmers had *Kormoran* making her way up the coast in the hope that a new area might bring better luck than they had had in the Indian Ocean to date. *Kormoran*'s tally of sunk or captured ships was stuck on eleven ships totalling 68,274 tonnes, of which only three ships had been taken in the Indian Ocean in the preceding seven months. This return, while not poor, did not reach the ambitious target Detmers had personally set for himself and his ship, and he was keen for new conquests. At the same time, Detmers knew that the only way to increase his total was to remain at sea for as long as possible and to do this meant steering clear of enemy warships.

HMAS *Sydney*, the *Perth* class light cruiser that had become the glory ship of the young Royal Australian Navy due to her famous exploits in the Mediterranean, was heading south-east on an intercepting course. *Sydney* was much faster and more powerful than *Kormoran*. Her top speed was 32 knots to *Kormoran*'s 18 knots and on paper *Sydney* was a deadlier ship with better guns, fire control systems and protective armour. She was exactly the type of superior naval enemy that Captain Detmers was ordered to avoid at all costs. While *Kormoran*'s job was to disrupt Allied merchant shipping, sinking as many ships as she could or taking them back to Germany as prizes when possible, she was not under any circumstances to do battle with naval ships like *Sydney*,[7] or as Detmers called them, ships of the 'grey funnel' line.[8]

Raider captains such as Detmers were purposely given the freedom and autonomy to decide where and when they took their ships to inflict maximum damage and disruption. Before he left Germany, his instructions from Grand Admiral Erich Raeder, leader of the *Kriegsmarine*, were simple: 'The world is your oyster, go where you like, Arctic or Antarctic, but get results.'[9] In contrast, *Sydney* was on specific orders, returning to Fremantle after escorting the Australian troopship *Zealandia* north to the Sunda Strait without incident. As per routine procedure, however, *Sydney* was observing strict radio silence and her exact whereabouts were also unknown.

What happened next, well beyond 100 nautical miles from the nearest stretch of virtually uninhabited coastline, has been vividly described by historians as Australia's greatest wartime naval loss.[10] In excess of one thousand men — 399 on board *Kormoran* and 645 on board *Sydney* — were pitched into a fierce battle that took place at the naval equivalent of point-blank range. By the time their blazing guns were silenced, some 75 minutes later, the damage these two ill-fated combatants had inflicted on each other would lead to the loss of both ships and 725 of the men.

The outcome of the battle, fought in isolation and not part of a larger campaign or strategic initiative, would by itself have limited significance with respect to the global picture of World War II in late 1941. Just eighteen days later, on 7 December, Japan's apocalyptic attack on the United States Navy fleet based at Pearl Harbor would set off the Pacific War and drag America headlong into the fight alongside the Allied forces, including Britain and Australia. The war was rapidly escalating and spreading to all corners of the globe and the events on Japan's 'day of infamy', as Roosevelt put it, would overshadow the loss of *Sydney* and the entire ship's company of 645 men. Australia, however, would never forget.

The sighting and pursuit

At 1555 hours on 19 November alarm bells began ringing throughout the 8,736-tonne displacement auxiliary cruiser *Kormoran*, alerting her crew of 395 German sailors and four Chinese prisoners turned laundrymen[11] that their lonely voyage northwards along the coast of Western Australia was being interrupted.[12] For the first time in twelve days since *Kormoran* allowed an American steamer to pass them by untroubled, the raider was going to have some unwelcome company.

Before Captain Detmers was able to get up from the mess table where he was having his afternoon coffee a steward came to him with the news that a ship, probably a sailing vessel, had been sighted just off on the port bow. As a ship with sails was unlikely to cause any difficulties for the large and stoutly built *Kormoran*, Detmers's initial calm reaction was in direct contrast to the siren blaring loudly enough to make normal conversation difficult. However, by the time Detmers himself made it to the bridge for a look at the unknown vessel, the situation was rapidly changing.

Lieutenant Rudolf Jansen, the lookout perched in the crow's-nest high up on *Kormoran*'s foremast, was updating his original identification of the ship coming over the horizon towards their position. In quick succession the sailing ship resolved itself in Jansen's powerful binoculars to be two sailing ships; then several vessels possibly in convoy; then two columns of smoke that to Detmers was a sure sign of a military escort. Knowing that Jansen had served with the Norddeutscher Lloyd shipping line before the war[13] and that his experience at sea prepared him to be an excellent lookout, Detmers wasted no time in giving the orders: 'Pull down the crow's-nest and get into your battle stations. Turn port 260 [to] draw away full speed ahead.'

The promoted Kapitän zur See *Theodor Detmers wearing the Knight's Cross he was awarded for sinking the* Sydney.

Above: Steiermark *before she became* Kormoran.

Detmers's swift action in turning *Kormoran* into the sun, and away from the menacing hull belching increasing amounts of smoke, couldn't have been made a second sooner. With *Kormoran* cruising at 11 knots and the mystery ship travelling at a shade more than 20 knots in nearly the opposite direction, their combined closing speed was close to 30 knots and the gap between them would have been bridged in just 30 minutes without this manoeuvre. As soon as Detmers was able to have a close look at the ship, using the sighting telescope of a gunnery control point on the signal deck,[14] he knew his decision to run was the correct one. The ship obviously wasn't a harmless sailing vessel but an Australian light cruiser of the *Perth* class and was increasing its speed to close on *Kormoran.*

Barely five minutes had passed since *Kormoran's* alarm first sounded but Detmers already knew that this encounter was going to be far more precarious than anything he and his crew had faced during their previous year operating in the Atlantic and Indian oceans. Detmers

had been to Australia before, in 1933, while serving as an *Oberleutenat zur See* on board the German cruiser *Köln* and had the pleasure of being entertained in the heavy cruiser HMAS *Canberra* moored in Sydney Harbour, so he had some first-hand knowledge of RAN ships to draw upon in assessing the fighting power of this potential enemy. He knew all too well that in just a couple of hours his ship would be up against a faster, better armed opponent with belts of armour protecting its hull and engine room in places where *Kormoran* had none. His only possible advantage, set against this string of serious disadvantages, was that Detmers knew who the enemy was and the full extent of the Australian cruiser's superiority. It wasn't much, but could this knowledge be enough for Detmers to extricate *Kormoran* from this tight spot?

The outcome depended on what the opposing commander, and his staff, on the bridge of the cruiser knew about the ship they were pursuing. The columns of smoke the cruiser was making when sighted was a clear indication that they were bringing extra boilers on line to increase their speed. What Detmers didn't know, however, was that in a wartime footing Australian warships were forbidden from making any more smoke than necessary to avoid detection by the enemy.[15] Detmers may have hoped to slip away undetected, but in reality the excess smoke indicated that the cruiser probably sighted *Kormoran* first and had decided to raise her speed to investigate this mysterious freighter before *Kormoran* altered course.[16] The worst scenario for Detmers would have been for the cruiser to have suspected, or even known, that the ship fleeing into the late afternoon sun was an enemy raider.

Detmers's decision to turn west, rather than east, was aimed at making it harder for the cruiser to see *Kormoran* in the blinding glare of the afternoon sun. He also knew that a neutral or Allied merchant ship would do exactly the same, and he requested his engineers to increase to full speed to buy him additional time. At best *Kormoran* running flat out on all four engines could do 18 knots. But this top speed didn't take into account the thick layer of slowing marine growth that had accumulated on her bottom, nor the troublesome No. 4 engine that was about to break down at the most inopportune time, frustrating Detmers's plan. Fourteen knots was the most the engine room could produce while they repaired the overheated piston causing all the problems. Detmers, his hand forced by his ship's pedestrian speed and uncooperative engines, had no option but to play a waiting game and hope the cruiser lost interest or, even more unlikely, made a mistake that handed him the advantage. Until then Detmers would have to rely on their disguise as the Dutch freighter *Straat Malakka* to conceal *Kormoran's* true identity.

If the cruiser's intention wasn't clear to Detmers at the outset it certainly became clearer when she began signalling *Kormoran* by flashing light. The first signal 'NNJ'[17] went unanswered because no one on *Kormoran* knew what it meant or was asking, but the next signal was unmistakable: 'What Ship?' The cruiser was asking *Kormoran* to identify herself. The battle of wits between Detmers and those guiding the cruiser had begun.

Rather than reply by light to this straightforward question Detmers cunningly directed his chief signalman, Erich Ahlbach, to answer slowly by flag as if he was a merchant-navy greenhorn of the type that were often found on ships like the *Straat Malakka*. Detmers's strategy was becoming clear. With escape impossible, and surrender out of the question, he knew that he would have to fight the cruiser but that his only chance of survival was to nullify the warship's clear advantage in a long-range gun battle fought at a distance beyond the 12,000-yard range of his own guns but within the 22,000-yard maximum range of the cruiser's. He needed to carefully draw the cruiser closer without raising the slightest suspicion of his true identity.[18]

By projecting the appearance of a cooperative, albeit bumbling, merchant vessel Detmers thought he could perhaps lure the cruiser in — basically tricking the enemy

Below: Detmers on parade leading navy cadets through the Brandenburg Gate during the 1936 Olympics.

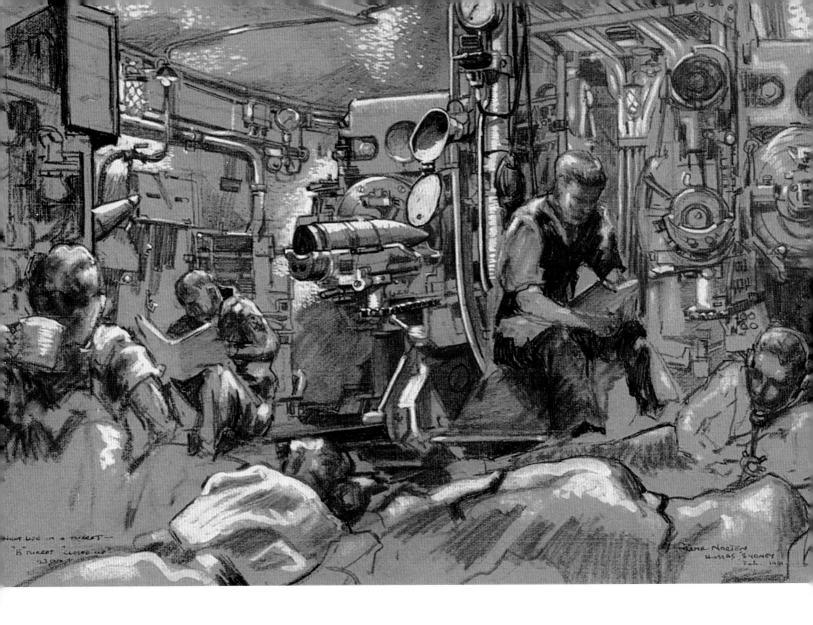

Above: Life in 'A' turret on board Sydney*, as depicted by artist F. Norton.*

into dropping its guard. It was a classic, and legitimate *ruse de guerre* that was used by the Royal Navy during the Napoleonic Wars and was at the heart of the German Navy's use of armed raiders such as *Kormoran* in both world wars. *Kormoran*'s disguise as the unthreatening *Straat Malakka* was the starting point for the ruse but it was up to Ahlbach to completely 'sell' it with his fumbled and deceptive signals, and evidently he was more than up to the challenge.

By the time Ahlbach had hoisted the signal flags for the international call sign of the *Straat Malakka* (PKQI) at 1605 hours,[19] as ordered by Detmers, a pattern was developing in communications between the two ships now about 15,000 metres apart. While the cruiser was efficiently asking questions by signal lamp, Ahlbach was deliberately labouring with his flags to such an extent that

the cruiser was forced to repeat its signals and must have thought the merchantman's signaller incompetent. Flags were sent up incomplete, twisted, taken down and hoisted back up again.

The cruiser's next question was where the freighter posing as *Straat Malakka* was bound for. Detmers's answer, conveyed by yet more sloppy flag work by Ahlbach, was Batavia. Another question followed: what cargo was she carrying? The answer 'piece-goods' revealed even less useful information. What impact this mangled exchange had on the cruiser's intentions was hard to tell, other than the fact she kept closing and the distance between the ships at 1635 hours had diminished to about 8,000 metres. *Kormoran* had been using its main three-metre rangefinder to range the cruiser but now withdrew it in favour of the smaller anti-aircraft unit that was portable and could be operated from the bridge without being spotted.

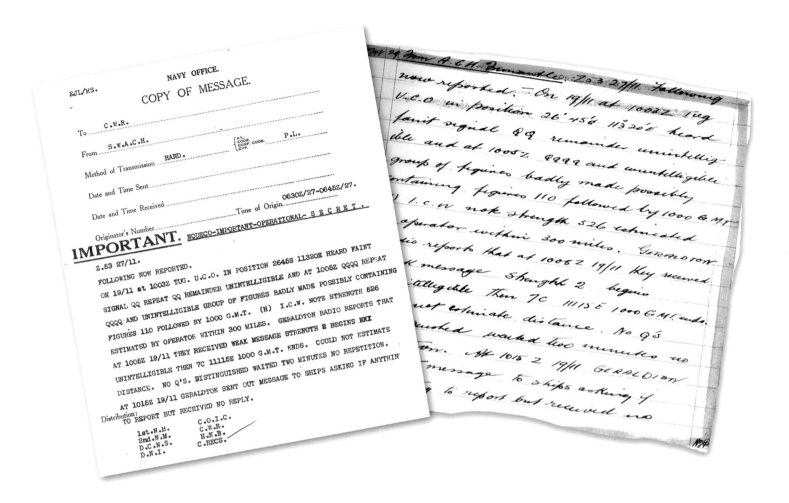

At this time, Detmers was informed that the No. 4 engine was repaired and again available on eight cylinders, but he dared not increase speed as the *Straat Malakka* ruse appeared to be working well. Up to this point the cruiser, while clearly curious, showed no outward signs of being suspicious and actually seemed to be quite tolerant of the merchantman's inefficient signalling. Detmers was not taking any chances, however, and decided to unleash his next ploy. The Dutch flag was hoisted on the stern ensign staff and a 'QQQQ' signal was sent out (twice) in wireless transmissions that identified the ship as the *Straat Malakka* and gave its position as 111° East 26° South. The 'QQQQ' signals, the Royal Navy's distress call for a ship suspecting it was under attack by a German raider, were meant to further convince the cruiser that it was dealing with an innocent merchantman.

The first 'QQQQ' signal was sent out at 1703 hours, followed by a repetition two minutes later.[20] By this stage

Above: Reports of Kormoran's *'QQQQ' signal, which were received eight days too late.*

the cruiser was approximately 3,000 metres astern of *Kormoran*, and showing a narrow silhouette. Oddly, the catapult to launch the Walrus aircraft, whose engine was running and propellers turning, was rotated back inboard. Any plans the cruiser had for making a reconnaissance flight over *Kormoran*, which would have seen through her disguise, appeared to have been aborted.

Nor did the cruiser demand that *Kormoran* stop in order to be searched, something Detmers fully expected but was surprised and delighted the order never came. In his mind, and in those of his officers watching from the bridge, it could only mean that the cruiser truly wasn't suspicious about their ship. At the least it was obvious that the cruiser did not know that *Kormoran* was not the *Straat Malakka*. Perhaps the ruse was so perfectly executed the

Above: Sydney *and* Australia *viewed from HMAS* Hobart.

cruiser would send *Kormoran* on her way without a shot being fired. Lieutenant Heinz Messerschmidt, the mines officer and Detmers's adjutant, could hear Detmers saying over the telephone linking the bridge to the gunnery control station and all the gun positions, 'Our camouflage is excellent. He has no suspicion. Maybe they will say good voyage and let us go!'[21]

By 1715 hours the cruiser had virtually drawn level with *Kormoran* and was stationed just abaft her starboard beam at a distance Detmers estimated to be 900 metres. The cruiser had also slowed to match *Kormoran*'s 14 knots. The two ships were as close as strangers on the high seas would probably ever approach each other, and those watching on *Kormoran*, including Lieutenant Messerschmidt who was stationed on the open deck above the bridge (the monkey island) hiding behind covers alongside the artillery officer Fritz Skeries, could easily see 'men walking very slowly and a lot of officers in white caps on the bridge looking very easy going'. This remarkable scene wasn't without a hint of menace,

however, as all four of the cruiser's twin-gun turrets in addition to the port-side quadruple-mounted torpedo battery were firmly trained on *Kormoran*.

Waves of apprehension and fearful expectation rolled over *Kormoran*'s crew as the seconds passed and they waited for the cruiser's next signal. They were surprised that the ghost-like nature of their own ship, with all hands hidden behind camouflage and not a single soul visible on any of *Kormoran*'s decks, did not raise suspicion inside the cruiser.[22] The seconds turned into minutes as the two ships nervously eyed each other. Surely the end of this cat-and-mouse game was near.

Finally, the signal that Detmers feared would ultimately trip him up came. 'Show your secret signal' flashed the cruiser.[23] Detmers turned to his senior wireless officer, Reinhold von Malapert, and put the question directly to him. 'Do we know the secret call for the *Straat Malakka*?'[24] Malapert shook his head, no, which was no great surprise to Detmers; nor did it really affect his thinking because his decision to fight had already been made.

Earlier during the chase he turned to his first officer, Lieutenant Commander Kurt Foerster, and asked him,

'Shall we scuttle or fight?' to which Foerster replied, 'We can only die once, Captain'.[25] The big question for Detmers therefore was not if to fight, but when. And now that the two ships were running at the same speed virtually parallel to each other at a distance of only 900 yards, the time was ripe for Detmers to reveal his true colours and open fire.

The cruiser had made the mistake Detmers was praying for and relinquished all her superiority in speed and gunnery. The distance between the two enemies had narrowed to the naval equivalent of point-blank range such that whichever ship fired first would surely cause devastating damage on the other and gain a huge advantage. Detmers waited just a few more minutes to be sure the cruiser's course was unchanging and then ordered signalman Ahlbach to 'pull down the neutral flag and set the war flag'. After the report came back that the German colours were flying just behind the bridge Detmers gave a general order that was chilling in its simplicity and deadly intent. 'Entarnen! Feur Frei!'

In the space of a mere six seconds Kormoran's crew sprung into action with all the speed and skill they had gained from constant training and preparation for exactly this situation. Detmers had ordered them to 'de-camouflage' and 'fire free' with all guns and torpedoes! It was 1730 hours on 19 November 1941, and an event that would forever be seared into the minds of millions of Australians was starting as the sounds of war shook this remote coastline from its peaceful tranquillity.

The action

Kormoran's first shot from a single 15-cm gun fell short and the second, also a single shot according to artillery officer Skeries, went over.[26] Even if these misses gave the cruiser a few seconds to recover from the swiftness of Kormoran's surprise attack, they had virtually no time at all to react to the raider's powerful 3.7-cm PAK anti-tank gun, which had found the correct range straightaway and scored immediate hits on the cruiser's unarmoured bridge directly opposite its concealed position. Because the enemy was so close, Kormoran's 2-cm C/30 anti-aircraft machine guns also had sufficient range to reach her and they burst into action raking the cruiser's bridge, port torpedo battery and 4-inch gun deck with a vengeance.

Observing the fall of shot from their first two misses, Kormoran's gunners adjusted their range to 1,500 metres and immediately scored with a salvo of 15-cm hits, causing massive destruction to the cruiser, most crucially on her bridge. Anyone not wounded or killed by the initial 3.7-cm shell hits would certainly have been by the much heavier 15-cm shell as it completely destroyed this vital command centre. Barely twenty seconds had elapsed since Kormoran raised her battle flag and already the cruiser's captain and some of his key officers — who would have been just realising that the quiet and bumbling ship on their beam was not the innocent Dutch freighter Straat Malakka but a deadly and committed enemy — were most probably all dead.

The speed with which Kormoran was able to de-camouflage and transform from an ordinary-looking freighter to a warship with weaponry equivalent to the surprised cruiser was achieved through a combination of engineering and skill gained during many months of practice and successful actions against Allied ships. During her conversion to an auxiliary cruiser, Kormoran[27] was fitted with a system of camouflage, concealment and screens which was simple in design and operation, but more importantly extremely fast to uncover or drop. Deck railings were folded down; covers over the twin 15-cm guns on the bow and stern flew upwards, sprung by counterweights; hatch coamings concealing the other two big guns mounted in the centre of the false cargo holds No. 2 and No. 4 were hydraulically lowered at the push of a button like guillotine blades; light covers over the smaller guns were simply pulled away; the forward 2-cm machine guns were hydraulically raised from under the forecastle deck; and a thin plate covering the opening for the twin torpedo mounts either side of the main deck also flapped upwards sprung by counterweights.

To make the camouflage system work as efficiently as possible, however, Detmers constantly drilled the men. Encounter training sessions were held every week, on

Above: The freighter Steiermark *being converted to* Hilfskreuzer Kormoran.

Thursdays, and Detmers was insistent his men knew their respective targets when faced with the enemy. Heinz Messerschmidt recalls how Detmers drilled leading seaman Jakob Fend. 'Every week he asked Fend, "Where do you aim at?" He said, "At the bridge, Captain".'[28] Possibly of greater importance, the officers and crew of *Kormoran* had been tested in previous actions and proven themselves in sinking, or taking as prizes, eleven ships in their year together at sea before this chance encounter with the cruiser. Detmers's men knew their jobs well and needed no instructions once the order to fire was given.

For Detmers the speed of their initial reaction was all-important, especially if they were to ever encounter a warship. Once, when they had finished resupplying a U-boat in the Atlantic Ocean, the captain of the U-boat did a rapid dive and ascent and said to Detmers, 'Can you do that?' Detmers asked him to do it again. As the U-boat dived Detmers gave the order '*Entarrnen*' to his

Previous page: Sydney *as she would have looked to* Kormoran's *gunners when she veered to port and crossed the raider's stern.*

men. When the U-boat resurfaced *Komoran*'s camouflage was down and all its guns were pointing at the U-boat. Detmers then said to the young U-boat captain, 'Can you do that?'[29]

Once *Kormoran*'s gunners found their targets they poured overwhelming fire on the cruiser as fast as they could, determined to destroy their enemy and in the process save their own lives. *Kormoran*'s 15-cm guns, firing independently, began hitting the cruiser with sickening regularity. According to Detmers every shell fired was a direct hit. During this opening phase the cruiser fired a full salvo which sailed over the *Kormoran* without inflicting any damage. Had any of the cruiser's eight 6-inch shells hit *Kormoran* the outcome of the battle might have been very different. As it transpired, these were the only shells to be fired from the cruiser's forward turrets. Designated 'A' and 'B', they fell forever silent following direct hits to them and the central gunnery control tower located above the bridge.

As the cruiser's crew regrouped from the loss of half her main armament, *Kormoran* was able to fire five salvos from her 15-cm guns at about six-second intervals unimpeded by incoming fire. Lieutenant Fritz Skeries had given the order '*Gut, schnell*' and was directing the gunners to aim at specific targets on the cruiser, although as the target was directly in front of them aiming was not a problem. Further devastating hits were scored on the cruiser's bridge, director control tower, 'A' and 'B' turrets, engine room and aircraft.

Although the aircraft was specifically targeted by *Kormoran*'s No. 4 gun, commanded by boatswain's mate Karl Reidt, Skeries admitted in testimony afterwards that he felt the direct hit was a lucky shot. There was a terrific explosion when the aircraft was hit, which would have been devastating for the aircrew or any of the

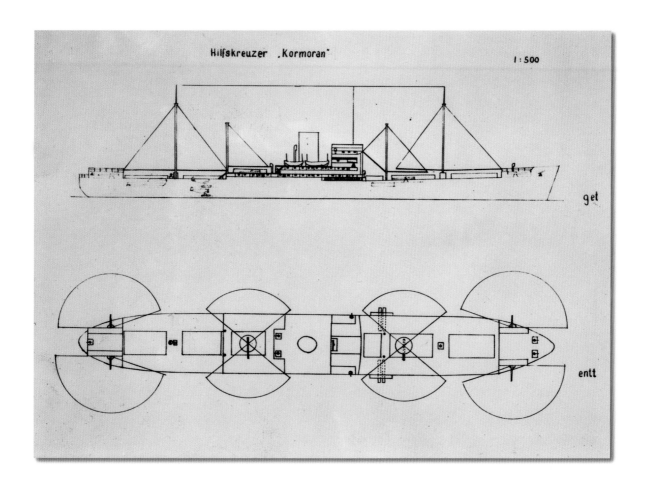

Above: Kormoran's *six 15-cm gun emplacements and their firing arcs.*

cruiser's personnel caught up in the fire ignited by the fuel escaping from the aeroplane. For them the hit was anything but lucky.

The fate of any crew caught on the cruiser's exposed upper decks would have been similarly dire. *Kormoran* had three 2-cm anti-aircraft machine guns firing at the cruiser from different directions, making it virtually impossible to find safe shelter. The primary objective for these guns was to prevent any men reaching the cruiser's port torpedo battery or 4-inch guns, either of which if manned and allowed to fire could have changed the course of the action with drastic consequences for *Kormoran*. With a rate of fire of up to 120 rounds per minute, the biggest problem for these gunners would have been keeping the guns loaded with fresh magazines, cooled and unjammed. Despite the terrible carnage they could see their shells causing they refused to let up, knowing that the fight boiled down to a question of kill or be killed.

At the same time that Skeries's men were pouring withering fire into the cruiser, Detmers, a torpedo specialist, was altering course slightly to bring his above-water torpedo tubes to bear on the enemy's bow. Two torpedoes in the starboard battery would have been standing by ready to fire, having already been swung outboard as soon as the cover concealing them was lifted. With the two ships travelling roughly parallel and the torpedo battery fixed at a 90° angle it was simply a matter of manoeuvring *Kormoran* onto the perfect heading that would let the torpedoes run squarely onto the cruiser's bow after adjusting for her speed of 14 knots.

Detmers and his officers were surprised and relieved that there was no reaction from the cruiser — other than the opening salvo — and that the fight up to this point was overwhelmingly one-sided. The action was less than a minute old but at the rate *Kormoran* was hitting the cruiser she was not going to last very long. Suddenly the cruiser's aft turrets, designated 'X' and 'Y', burst into life and began firing again in solitary defence of their ship. Because of the apparent loss of central gunnery control

Above: HMAS Sydney *as seen from the deck of an Allied warship.*

the aft turrets had to switch to local control and vital seconds were lost in the transition. Remarkably 'X' turret was immediately effective in hitting *Kormoran* with fire that Detmers described as 'good and quick'.

The first 6-inch shell from 'X' turret ripped clean through *Kormoran*'s large funnel before harmlessly exploding in the sea. Although a number of men were killed and wounded by splinters that scattered throughout the bridge superstructure,[30] this hit would have been relatively innocuous had it not been for the complex design of *Kormoran*'s funnel. The funnel was double-walled with a centre cavity that housed pipes containing oil pumped up from the engine room for it to be heated inside the funnel before being sent back down to the four diesel-electric engines. The use of heated oil was more efficient for *Kormoran*'s engines and meant the ship could carry less

oil. However, what was an advantage for *Kormoran* in her former life as the merchant vessel *Steiermark* was without doubt her Achilles heel as an armed raider, because the flaming oil from the holed funnel cascaded down into the engine room and set it alight with disastrous consequences for the men working there and for the ship itself.

Several more shells from 'X' turret hit *Kormoran*. One, apparently a dud, hit close to the No. 3 gun, killing one man and injuring another although this did not stop the remaining gun crew from continuing to fire on the cruiser. Another of *Sydney*'s shells penetrated *Kormoran*'s unarmoured engine room and tore the forward tank bulkhead, causing a thick jet of burning oil to pour into the room, filling it with opaque smoke. Shell fragments punctured the main fire extinguisher pipes on either side of the engine room, putting this vital system out of action along with the foam extinguisher plant. In a final fatal blow, an explosion on *Kormoran*'s starboard side rendered the electrical transformers unserviceable, thereby cutting off supply for the main generators and propulsion motors.[31]

'Y' turret also fired two or three salvos at *Kormoran* but these all fell wide. Despite the heavy damage inflicted on the cruiser, and surely the loss of many officers and men, the crews that remained closed up in the aft turrets were desperately trying to mount a spirited fight-back against *Kormoran*. They had done extremely well to get on target so quickly and had just the briefest of chances to severely damage the raider and possibly reverse the outcome of the battle. Without warning, and much to their horror, however, a tremendous explosion erupted beneath the cruiser's bow that sent shock waves reverberating throughout their ship and heralded the beginning of its end.

The explosion was caused by one of *Kormoran*'s torpedoes, fired by torpedo officer Greter about 55 seconds previously, that slammed into the cruiser with deadly effect just forward of 'A' turret while the second torpedo narrowly missed its bow. The impact of the torpedo, and its 280-kg hexanite warhead,[32] was immediately apparent as the cruiser first rose with the force of the explosion and then sank down from the tons of seawater flooding through the gaping wound on her port side. Shortly after, the bow of the cruiser was seen to be almost entirely submerged and her speed was dropping rapidly. The battle was less than two minutes old and *Kormoran* had delivered a fatal blow from which the cruiser would never recover.

Mortally wounded, the cruiser suddenly veered to port and crossed *Kormoran*'s stern in a manoeuvre that was thought to be an attempt to ram her but in actuality was probably due to a momentary loss of steering and control. At the same time the roof of 'B' turret was seen to be blown away along with the entire roof and gun housing of 'A' turret by the impact of several 15-cm shells. For a brief moment there was some respite for the cruiser as she was passing the stern of *Kormoran*, whose forward gunners could not shoot backwards nor see through the thick black smoke pouring out of the funnel from the fire in her engine room. However, this did not prevent *Kormoran*'s 15-cm guns on the stern from joining the fray.

Lieutenant Wilhelm Brinkman, who was the officer in charge of the 2-cm anti-aircraft guns which could no longer reach the cruiser because of its increasing range, was told by Skeries to run aft and begin directing the fight from there. The cruiser's range had opened up to 4,000 metres and her starboard side, untouched in the action so far, was about to take concentrated fire from the *Kormoran*'s 15-cm stern guns that had a clear line of sight to their target. The combination of the cruiser's reduced speed, now about 5 knots, and the favourable angle as she limped passed *Kormoran*'s stern, made it easy for her No. 5 and No. 6 guns to hit the cruiser virtually at will. The cruiser was now completely defenceless to this devastating onslaught as her 6-inch guns were silent and pointing in the wrong direction, while her 4-inch guns were unmanned, having been swept clean by the murderous anti-aircraft fire.

Realising the advantage over his stricken enemy, Detmers was preparing to turn to port to 'fully destroy the enemy' when it was reported that the revolutions of *Kormoran*'s engines were falling rapidly and that contact with the engine room was lost. Simultaneously, Detmers claimed to see the wake of four torpedoes coming towards them so he held their course steady to let them pass safely by the stern. Other officers, including Lieutenants Messerschmidt and Joachim von Gösseln in particular, whose position on the stern gave them the best possible view, privately doubted this claim as neither of them saw any torpedo tracks.

The initial indication that *Kormoran*'s engine room was experiencing problems was confirmed shortly after when severe vibrations shook through the raider as her engines raced at high speed. Lieutenant Rudolph Lensch, who was on the bridge relaying messages from the engine room, reported that the 'engines and all fire-fighting equipment are completely out of action'. With the loss of her engines *Kormoran* would soon be dead in the water and at great risk if the cruiser was somehow able to recover from her own desperate situation and mount a counterattack. Lensch was sent back to the engine room by Detmers with firm instructions to do everything possible 'to get at least one engine to work'. Meanwhile,

Kormoran's merciless shelling of the cruiser continued with the only let-up coming when some of its smoking gun barrels needed to be cooled down with fire hoses.

At 1750 hours, about twenty minutes from the start of the action, the cruiser was still moving away from the now stationary *Kormoran* on an approximately southern course. Skeries was back in control of *Kormoran's* big guns and was using four of them (Nos 2, 3, 4 and 6) to continually hit the cruiser with salvo after salvo of the high-explosive and armour-piercing shells. The cruiser's guns had been silent for some time and Detmers must have sensed that the battle was probably won as he observed his enemy's critical condition: 'Forecastle lies deep in water. Front of bridge to after [sic] funnel burning.'

Whether they were operating on huge doses of adrenalin or because they still felt vulnerable stopped as they were like a sitting duck, Detmers and his men continued to try to finish the cruiser off and sink her. A further single torpedo was fired at the stern of the cruiser which missed and they continued firing with their big guns until Detmers finally ordered 'cease fire' at 1825 hours. The final gun range was noted by Skeries to be 10,400 metres with the cruiser on a bearing of 225° relative to *Kormoran's* heading.

The battle between the *Perth* class cruiser and *Kormoran* lasted approximately 55 minutes and killed many men outright on both sides. This was an incredibly fierce fight, especially in the first couple of minutes when the enemies were squared off against each other and the truly telling blows were struck. Naval engagements at close, personal quarters such that it was possible for both sides to the see the tragic consequences in horrific human terms were extremely rare in the age of the modern warships.

In extremis

As their ship drifted aimlessly in the wind and current completely without electrical or propulsive power, Captain Detmers and the crew of Kormoran began to take stock of their situation. Lieutenant Skeries reported that his gunners expended a total 450 15-cm shells, of which 50 were nose-fuse shells and the remainder were base-fuse (armour-piercing) shells, in their barrage of the enemy cruiser, which was badly on fire and no longer a threat as she was slowly limping away in the opposite direction.[33] The fire that most concerned Detmers, however, was in his own engine room, which was located dangerously close to the after cargo holds fully stocked with mines. His situation was by now precarious, to say the least.

All contact with the engine room had been lost and everyone sent there to determine the extent of the fire and the well-being of the crew came back reporting that it was 'impossible to get through to the engine room'. The last contact with Chief Engineer Hermann Stehr, when Detmers was pleading with him to get at least one engine running, also made it clear that he had permission to evacuate his crew if necessary. That was the last communication heard from Stehr and every attempt to put out the fire enveloping *Kormoran's* mid-section was failing, in large part because all the ship's fire-fighting and foam extinguisher equipment had been damaged beyond repair during the battle.

Detmers was quickly running out of options to save his ship. His No. 2 reserve generator room, located just forward of the bridge, had escaped damage but the generators there were not big enough to drive the ship and therefore were simply useless. If they could not put out the midship fires it was just a matter of time before they spread to the nearest mines, separated by only one transverse bulkhead, and triggered an explosion that would simultaneously detonate all of the 340 mines and 106 tons of explosive charges they contained. A constant watch was set up to monitor the mine deck but Detmers knew he had only one realistic option left and that was to abandon ship and scuttle the *Kormoran*.

After calling all his officers to the bridge Detmers gave his final order to his first officer, Lieutenant Commander Kurt Foerster, for 'all boats and life saving equipment to be launched'.

Over the next five hours, under the constant threat of fire, smoke and *Kormoran's* huge cache of mines exploding, Detmers and his men made what could be

Above: Sydney *in action off Cape Spada, as painted by artist F. Norton.*

fairly described as Herculean efforts to launch by hand every lifeboat and raft that was not damaged by gunfire and was still seaworthy. This included several large wooden lifeboats that were taken from the merchant vessels sunk by *Kormoran* and two of *Kormoran*'s own steel lifeboats, weighing about a ton each, that had to be manhandled out of the forward hold using conventional block and tackle because the derricks and electric winches were no longer working.

Without the use of davits or derricks the boats had to be simply pushed over the side with the men praying they would land right side up and not be too damaged by the free-fall drop. The situation for the men trapped on the quarterdeck was far more desperate as they were cut off from all the boats by the fire and had to resort to throwing overboard absolutely anything they felt could support the weight of a man in water, including a wooden kennel painted green that was home to the ship's pet Alsatian dog named Senta.[34] Many men had little choice but to jump into the water and cling to these feeble pieces of flotation until they were rescued by one of the lifeboats the following day.

Nothing, however, could save the 60-odd men who were lost when the first and largest rubber raft that was launched broke away from *Kormoran* in the worsening weather and sank when the wooden stiffeners in the floor of the raft collapsed. It seems likely that this raft was seriously overloaded in the rush to get the first boats away. To compound the tragedy most of the men placed in this raft were wounded and were unable to save themselves when suddenly pitched into the increasingly treacherous seas.

As the lifeboats were filled one by one, the men who looked in the direction of the cruiser could see it off in the distance marked only by the glow of the large fire that continued to blaze in several places. At about 1900 hours Detmers estimated the range to the cruiser at 16,000 metres and its course as 150° true. The last to see the burning cruiser were those who stayed with *Kormoran* until the bitter end, including Detmers, and could see furthest from her higher deck level. No clear explosion was heard or seen by anyone. One minute the cruiser was there shining in the darkness far away on the horizon and the next minute she was simply gone. As Detmers described, 'all was blackness'.

With all the lifeboats in the water, the last act for Detmers was to scuttle his own ship to prevent her from falling into enemy hands and to have the German war flag retrieved. *Kormoran* had been a good ship and a happy ship but she had served her purpose and was no longer of any use to Detmers or his men. The mechanic Willy Rotzin had the dangerous job of venturing aft on the ship past the funnel and through the fire that had been spreading out from the engine room in order to reach the mainmast from where the war flag still flew. His only protection from the heat and flames were mattresses he wrapped around his body, but he returned safely clutching the flag tightly to his breast before helping Heinz Messerschmidt

initiate the scuttling charges that had been prepared on two of the forward oil tanks.

The fuses had been timed for twenty minutes, which would have given Rotzin and Messerschmidt a safe margin to meet Detmers on the forward deck before all three boarded the last lifeboat. There was no time to waste, however, as the smoke filling the mine deck was getting thicker. For reasons known only to himself, Detmers lingered before stepping off the *Kormoran*. Perhaps he was running through a mental checklist of his final responsibilities as commander of *Kormoran*, or was this pause a hint of uncharacteristic sentimentality about leaving his ship for the last time in circumstances he could not have predicted earlier that day?

Ten minutes after Detmers's lifeboat cast off from *Kormoran* the scuttling charges set off bang on schedule. As it was only a matter of time before the mines began exploding the men handling the three oars started pulling the lifeboat, loaded with 61 in total, away from the abandoned ship with all the might they could muster from their tired bodies. Detmers, who never liked having so many highly explosive mines on his ship and referred to mine laying as 'the devil's business', probably did not appreciate the irony of having the same mines they carried for nearly a year finish off his own ship.

At 0035 hours on 20 November the tremendous explosion that Detmers and everyone else were expecting came and it did not disappoint. The simultaneous explosion of *Kormoran*'s mines turned the ship into a huge fireball that shot several hundred metres high into the night sky and lit the scene for all those survivors who cared to watch the final destruction of their ship. The last image they would have had, of the bows lifting up and sliding back into the oily sea, surely indicated that *Kormoran*'s hull had been broken in two and all that was left for her was the final death plunge and race to the seabed thousands of metres below.

As Detmers began contemplating the long and uncertain journey to safety his mind no doubt would have raced ahead to how others — mainly the enemy seeing that he was still in Australian waters — would view his version of their improbable victory. The cruiser was well out of sight, perhaps already sunk herself, but a number of questions would have been at the forefront of Detmers's mind. The first obvious question was: which of Australia's three *Perth* class light cruisers had they fought? Despite the close quarters of their battle Detmers did not know the answer. While Detmers would have been grateful for the advantage the cruiser's commander handed him by coming so close he would have also wondered, like everyone else he imagined, why they had chosen to do so.

Finally, the fate of the cruiser and her men was possibly the biggest question. Had they managed to keep their ship afloat and on the course last observed? Had they managed to head back to port for repairs as a number of other Allied ships had been able to do under similar circumstances? Or were the hundreds of enemy sailors in the same predicament as them — scattered in boats and rafts and drifting at the mercy of winds and currents — just a long way further south? In fact neither Detmers nor anyone else could possibly have imagined the intense and prolonged questioning that was soon to begin and continue unabated, and largely unanswered, into the next century.

CHAPTER ONE
...

The original search

In all, 317 (two of whom later died at sea) of the 395 German crew of *Kormoran* and three of the four Chinese prisoners turned laundrymen were able to safely abandon the ship and get under way in various lifeboats and rafts before she exploded and sank in the early morning of 20 November.[1] The men were scattered among seven craft made up of two pneumatic rubber life rafts, one wooden and four steel lifeboats, all of which were dangerously overloaded and required continuous bailing to keep afloat. Detmers's lifeboat — a steel one — had only four inches of freeboard to keep the sea out so it was constantly shipping water. In one of the other boats the men lined up on the gunwales shoulder to shoulder with their backs to the sea to keep the waves from pouring in.

An effort was made to get officers with small boat experience distributed into every craft but this only went so far as some of the boats and not the rafts, which were generally manned by the youngest and most inexperienced ratings. Through the first night and following morning a number of the craft managed to stay in close proximity but thereafter they separated on differing tracks determined in part by their ability to be propelled with either sails or oars, and in part by the men's own desire to reach the safety of land as quickly as possible.

Kormoran was no longer a ship of 399 men unified by the command of a singly authoritative captain. It was now a small fleet of boats and rafts dispersed on the high seas whose courses were dictated by the vagaries of the winds and currents and, in the case of the boats, the will of the fleet's occupants.

The pneumatic rafts, which were actually German army rafts and not designed for open ocean voyages, were by far the worst equipped. They had no sail, no oars, no rudder and no sea drogue to deploy when the seas turned rough.[2] At least one of these rafts capsized (as did one of the lifeboats) and the men had to scramble back on board as quickly as possible for fear of being taken by the sharks that periodically appeared out of the deep blue water to harass them. Quite simply, the men were powerless to control the movement of their rafts and were drifting downstream at the mercy of the wind and

Left: The wake of HMAS Sydney.

Above: HSK Kormoran.

currents like any of the other flotsam that was ripped from *Kormoran* when she was violently scuttled.

Before abandoning *Kormoran* Detmers made a point of assembling his officers and informing them of their position relative to land. Some crew would have been more precisely informed than others, in particular the navigators and wireless operators, but in general most would have known that they were roughly 120 nautical miles from the coast and would have to head east to make landfall. The journey to safety, therefore, was going to take more than a few days and those in command would need to ration their provisions accordingly unless they were lucky enough to be rescued by a passing ship. The count of each passing day and night, which every one of the men would have kept track of in his own personal way, reached three before one group of the men did indeed get lucky.

At 0600 (Zone 'H' time) on the morning of 23 November, a Sunday, the Cunard liner *Aquitania*, converted by the RAN to transport troops from Sydney, spotted one of *Kormoran*'s life rafts filled with 26 sailors. Captain G. Gibbons of the merchant navy had *Aquitania* slowly circle the suspicious raft before stopping to retrieve the men who, except for three who were wounded, 'scrambled on board like cats'.[3] A photo taken of the raft shows the men packed like sardines and sitting precariously on the inflated tubes not much more than a foot or two from the surface of the sea. The raft was also towing a smaller

raft that was used to carry the injured Petty Officer Fritz Knoll, who climbed back into the main raft before being taken on board *Aquitania*.[4] The position was 24°35' South, 110°57' East.[5]

Rather than question them himself, Captain Gibbons turned over the men to the staff captain, who made his interrogation with the help of a German-speaking passenger, and the *Aquitania* immediately resumed its transit south at approximately 20 knots. The hatbands of the men identified them as coming from the *Kriegsmarine* and they did not hide the fact that they had been in battle with a cruiser which had been hit and was last seen on fire. Despite these ominous signs, Captain Gibbons decided to act strictly by the book and maintain complete radio silence because 'There had been no distress signals, no enemy action signals, no Raider, no Submarine, no Aircraft signals, or anything hostile that I could clear myself with breaking Wireless silence … Furthermore, I had no reason to suppose that anything out of the ordinary had happened, beyond the vital fact that a Cruiser had sunk an enemy raider.'[6]

Unbeknown to Captain Gibbons, serious concern had been mounting within the RAN hierarchy about the fate of an overdue and missing cruiser. The cruiser in question was none other than HMAS *Sydney* and she was about three days late from her scheduled ETA into Fremantle after completion of her most recent escort duties.[7] Later that evening, after *Sydney* failed to answer a request to break radio silence and report an amended

ETA, the wheels started turning to step up the action to locate her. The following morning, on Monday 24 November, the RAAF ordered and organised an air search for *Sydney* covering her likely position on approach to Fremantle. As more radio calls to *Sydney* during the day went unanswered, an incoming wireless (W/T) signal was relayed from the Commander in Chief China to the Australian Commonwealth Naval Board with the first piece of news to possibly explain *Sydney's* delayed arrival.

S.S. 'TROCAS' REPORTED AT 0700Z 24TH NOVEMBER BEGINS 'PICKED UP 25 GERMAN NAVAL MEN FLOATING RAFT REQUIRE GUARD IMMEDIATELY. POSITION 24°06' SOUTH 110°40' EAST'[8]

Was *Sydney* somehow connected with this discovery of 25 Germans floating in a raft 100 nautical miles out to sea? The Navy Office and the Central War Room in Melbourne obviously thought so because they immediately began to reorganise the air search for *Sydney* and instructed a handful of merchant vessels to pass through the position reported by *Trocas*. Meanwhile, an urgent message was sent to *Trocas*: 'Request report on details of engagement & name of ship from which survivors received.'[9]

As night fell on 24 November without any word or sign about the location of *Sydney* and her crew of 645, senior officers of Australia's armed forces began to privately fear the worst. Rear Admiral John G. Crace, RN, Commander of Australian Squadron (RACAS) and a member of the Naval Board, wrote in his diary that he had 'Heard from N.B. that they are very worried about *Sydney* … N.B. think there is a possibility that a Vichy S/m [submarine] escorting a Vichy ship has torpedoed her'.[10]

The W/T signal received from *Trocas* early the next morning on 25 November provided little in the way of new information other than that the 25 German seamen they picked up were 'from Comoron [sic] sunk by cruiser'.[11] While there was confusion over the identity of the German ship due to the misspelling of *Kormoran*, it was becoming increasingly clear that the other vessel — a cruiser — was most certainly *Sydney*.

The air and sea search centred on the *Trocas* position was now in full swing and by the end of the day three more lifeboats, two having made it to the coast north of Carnarvon, had been spotted from the air. The pilots reported the lifeboats to be full of men and either buff or brown in colour, which was not a good sign as *Sydney's* lifeboats were painted naval grey. It was left to the Admiralty to suggest the explanation that perhaps no one in Australia wanted to face: 'That the raider torpedoed "Sydney" before being sunk.'[12]

A total of 103 men had landed in the two lifeboats about 50–55 nautical miles north of Carnarvon. Hans Linke, a wireless operator who spoke good English, was taken ahead of the other men — now prisoners — to Carnarvon as he was happy to volunteer information about what had happened. The account he told his interrogators must have chilled them to the bone. The cruiser approached their ship to within half a mile before *Kormoran* opened fire and its first salvo silenced the cruiser's guns. Their ship was on fire and blew up but the crew escaped in boats. The cruiser vanished over the horizon burning amidship and astern and was believed to have sunk.[13] This action had taken place on 19 November, meaning that HMAS *Sydney* has been lost for at least six days — far longer than anyone in the Australian Navy had previously imagined. The position given by Linke for the action was 026°S 111°E.

There could be little doubt that *Sydney* had been in a serious action with an enemy raider and most probably had been sunk as a result. This realisation put even more pressure on the air and sea search that was now entering its third day. New instructions were issued for the aircraft to attempt to establish the nationality of the men in the lifeboats and the Commander in Chief Netherlands East Indies Naval Forces was asked to have an air search cover the possibility of *Sydney* proceeding at slow speed to Singapore or Surabaya, Java, for repairs in case the German reports were wrong.

Several more sightings of lifeboats were made on 26 November which ultimately led to a boat with 31 men being picked up by the State Shipping Service vessel *Koolinda* at 1950 hours, while another with 61 men in it was taken in tow by the liner *Centaur* at 2220 hours. Walter F. Dark, captain of the *Centaur*, did not want to risk taking on enemy prisoners so he continued to tow the lifeboat into Carnarvon until an armed guard was taken on board. Dark had been torpedoed twice previously, so he was in no mood to be accommodating with such a large number of potentially dangerous prisoners.[14]

When the men were finally allowed on board the *Centaur* later the following day it was learned that *Kormoran*'s captain, Detmers, was one of the prisoners along with a number of other senior officers including Kurt Foerster, Fritz Skeries and Heinz Messerschmidt. Lieutenant Commander James L. Rycroft, a reserve officer who had flown to Carnarvon with an interpreter to begin preliminary interrogations of the German prisoners amassing there, found Detmers on board the *Centaur*. Detmers's testimony, the first of many to come, confirmed the previous reports about the action and added the new information that it took place at latitude 26°31' South longitude 111° East and that *Sydney* had fired two torpedoes which had missed.[15]

It was Rycroft who first informed Detmers that the cruiser they attacked was in fact HMAS *Sydney*. The moment he was alone with Foerster, Detmers was able to show his immense pride in having defeated a superior and more powerful warship. He knew that he had made naval history by defeating a cruiser with an armed merchant ship in open battle and that his victory would be seen in Germany as revenge for the previous *Sydney*'s victory over the German light cruiser *Emden* in 1914. Detmers might have lost his ship and with it the chance to reach 100,000 tons of shipping — the magic figure a raider captain would have to achieve in order to be awarded the Knight's Cross[16] — but in claiming what would certainly be considered a famous victory over *Sydney* his reputation as one of the great raider captains would be assured.

Detmers also knew, however, that his tactics in the battle would be questioned and that he would undergo intense scrutiny by his Australian captors. His skill and that of his men had played a major part in their survival,

alongside luck, but would the Australian Navy accept his version of the action or think that there was some hidden truth to their improbable victory? Whatever the case, an enemy court martial was to be expected.

The search for any trace of *Sydney* and her men continued for two more days. Another German lifeboat was found with 72 men in it, making a total of 315 Germans and three Chinese rescued from five lifeboats and two rafts. Meanwhile, *Aquitania*, now off Wilsons Promontory en route to Sydney, had finally reported by visual signal her rescue of the 26 Germans recovered on 23 November. Similarly, two late reports also came in from the tug *Uco* and a W/T station in Geraldton, both of which had received the two 'QQQQ' signals transmitted by *Kormoran* at 1803 hours and 1805 hours on 19 November before the battle began.

The fact that information of such critical importance came to light days after it was of any use to the search effort was undoubtedly frustrating for the RAN. Nothing, however, could compare with the frustration experienced by the search teams as they combed the seas endlessly with no positive news about *Sydney*. When two life belts and an empty Carley float identified as belonging to *Sydney* were finally plucked out of the sea on 27 and 28 November their discovery and condition only reinforced the heartbreaking but inescapable conclusion that all hope of finding any survivors from *Sydney* was gone. It was left to the Naval Board to issue the final secret message on 29 November at 2054 hours that formalised this conclusion.

THE N.B. REGRET THAT AFTER INTENSIVE AIR AND SURFACE SEARCH OF THE AREA NO EVIDENCE OF H.M.A.S. 'SYDNEY' HAS BEEN SIGHTED EXCEPT TWO R.A.N. LIFE BELTS AND ONE CARLEY FLOAT BADLY DAMAGED BY GUNFIRE. IT IS CONCLUDED THAT 'SYDNEY' SANK AFTER THE ACTION AND FURTHER SEARCH HAS BEEN ABANDONED.

Australia had just lost its most famous ship along with 645 men, making this the worst naval tragedy in its history.

Above: Seventy-two of the Kormoran *survivors in a lifeboat being rescued by* Yandra.

The search for survivors was over. It was now up to the Australian Navy and the Commonwealth Government to inform the next of kin and public in a manner that would reassure them that despite this horrible loss Australia was still safe from the enemy and that the people could trust the government to protect them.

The controversy begins

The first official announcement of the loss of *Sydney* was made by Prime Minister John Curtin on the evening of Sunday 30 November, a full eleven days after the battle took place. Curtin's written statement, which was intended for press publication the following day but forbidden from radio broadcast for a further 48 hours, gave only the briefest details of the action itself.

HMAS Sydney has been in action with a heavily armed enemy merchant raider, which she sank by gunfire. The information was received from the survivors of the enemy vessel, who were picked up some time after the action. No subsequent communication has been received from HMAS Sydney, and the Government regrets to say that it must be presumed that she has been lost.[17]

In violation of government censorship orders prohibiting speculation, the press, working on a combination of rumours, leaks and reports from civilians involved in the interrogation of German prisoners, painted a far more detailed and worryingly vivid picture of the loss. The papers variously wrote about there being a second raider or warship involved — even going as far as naming the battleship *Tirpitz*; about the likelihood that *Kormoran* opened fire before showing the German war flag — a violation of international law; and that two machine-gunned *Sydney* lifeboats were found on the coast of Western Australia[18] — suggesting that a serious war crime under the Geneva and Hague conventions might have occurred if the Germans had actually fired upon *Sydney*'s survivors.

The purpose of prohibiting the broadcast of the news for an additional 48 hours was for security reasons; to prevent this vital information falling into the hands of the German Navy. The Naval Board was itself wondering whether a second raider or supply ship was involved in the action and did not want to alert it and thereby lose the opportunity of detecting it. The RAN would have obviously liked nothing better than to find and sink a second German vessel, if one actually existed, and if it still happened to be lurking in Australian waters.

The fact, however, was that there was no second German vessel involved and the German Navy had known that *Kormoran* had been in some sort of battle since 24 November when B-Dienst, their code-breaking organisation, intercepted and decrypted the urgent signal to *Trocas* requesting her to report by W/T the details of engagement and name of ship from which survivors were rescued.[19] *Kormoran* was the only raider operating in this part of the world at the time so the unnamed ship had to be her.[20] A subsequent signal from the Admiralty intercepted by B-Dienst on 26 November and decrypted on 30 November identified *Sydney* as the cruiser that sank the enemy raider.

Enormous press and public pressure was building on the government to release more details about *Sydney*'s loss, which it eventually did in the form of a second statement by Prime Minister Curtin issued on 3 December to the afternoon papers and this time for radio broadcast as well. The carefully worded statement was broadly in step with the story being told by the *Kormoran* survivors: *Kormoran* was officially named for the first time as the German raider disguised as a merchant ship; *Sydney* did not make use of her reconnaissance aircraft; the raider's opening salvo struck *Sydney*'s bridge and started a fire that lasted throughout the action; *Sydney* crippled the enemy with a direct hit in the engine room causing the ship to be abandoned and to blow up; torpedoes fired by the raider might have struck *Sydney* and caused her to sink; fires on *Sydney* possibly destroyed the lifeboats and Carley floats;

there was no evidence of *Sydney* blowing up; and the last evidence of *Sydney* was of her disappearing, still afloat, over the horizon.

For some unknown reason, however, the RAN and Prime Minister Curtin gave the position of the engagement in the statement as 300 miles west of Carnarvon, also adding that *Sydney* was on patrol duties in this area. Exactly why the RAN allowed this obviously incorrect position to be released has never been revealed or fully understood. It was well aware that *Sydney*'s normal transit route to Fremantle was a long way east of this position — by approximately 170 nautical miles — and also that the various coordinates given by Detmers and his fellow officers agreed with this eastern location. On top of this, all the floating debris recovered during the search was found in the general vicinity of *Sydney*'s normal transit route 120–130 nautical miles from the coast, not 300 nautical miles. The question still remains: what was behind this misleading position?

In the absence of any documentary evidence one can only guess. Perhaps the intention was to avoid alarming the public with news that a German raider was within reach of the West Australian coast so they reported a position much further offshore. Or is it more likely that the 300 nautical mile figure originated from the receipt of *Kormoran*'s 'QQQQ' signal by the tugboat *Uco*, whose operator estimated the sender was within 300 miles of their position near the coast? The 300-mile figure was rarely ever mentioned again and then it was simply derived from Curtin's original statement. The original source of this position never came to light nor was it corroborated by any new independent source. Whatever its origins, this original position put out by the RAN and the government sowed the first seeds of confusion and doubt about where the battle took place, and anyone trying to make sense of this position (including me) was left to struggle with the question why the most senior political and naval figures in the country with complete access to every piece of classified information could get it so wrong.

The West Australian interrogations

The questioning of Detmers and his crew began virtually as soon as they were captured and by 10 December each of them had been thoroughly interrogated with the exception of two ratings undergoing amputations in hospital. Key figures such as Detmers, Chief Signalman Ahlbach, W/T operator Hans Linke, Lieutenant Wilhelm Bunjes, engineer Rudolph Lensch and other officers were interrogated multiple times because they would have known better than anyone the inner workings of *Kormoran* and, in particular, how the battle with *Sydney* was conducted. A number of junior crewmen, such as assistant navigator Otto Jöergensen, AA gunner Hans Köblitz, torpedo mechanic Philipp Bernhardt and signaller Ehrhardt Otte, were also called up by the interrogating team[21] a second time for the simple reason that they spoke good English and were willing to talk at length about what they knew and saw.[22]

Captain Charles Farquhar-Smith, the District Naval Officer Western Australia, submitted his detailed report on the interrogations to the Naval Board on 16 December, which was followed on 21 December by an interim report of the investigation into the loss of HMAS *Sydney*[23] by Commander Emile F.V. Dechaineux DSC, the Director of Operations Navy Office, who was coordinating the interrogations on behalf of Naval Intelligence. At the top of a list of lessons learned, Dechaineux's report stated that 'Captain of "Sydney" was deceived and placed himself in a tactically unsound position. The contributory cause of this is the admitted inefficiency of Merchant Ships in challenge and reply procedures'. One of the three recipients of Dechaineux's report, either the Chief or Deputy Chief of Naval Staff or the Director of Naval Intelligence (DNI), apparently disagreed with the second sentence on the contributing cause and crossed it out.

Another comment in Dechaineux's report — 'The necessity of Commanding Officers to regard all ships as suspicious' — also inferred blame on Captain Burnett, although he stopped short of mentioning him by name. Dechaineux may have been working with Naval Intelligence at the time but he was no desk-bound analyst. He had served as commanding officer (CO) of the destroyers HMS *Vivacious* and *Eglinton* while in Britain during the war, winning the Distinguished Service Cross in July 1941, and thus had his own first-hand understanding of the crucible of command.[24] Nevertheless, Dechaineux's pointed remark about the need for COs to be suspicious of all ships apparently didn't make it past his superiors as it was not on the final list of recommendations the Naval Board signalled to Admiralty two days later.

While Dechaineux was clearly critical of Burnett he was also equally clear about his belief in the veracity of Captain Detmers and his men, saying that: 'The Captain of the sunken raider Fregatten Kapitän Dettmers [sic] and other prisoners have frankly told the story of the action, and there is every reason to believe the authenticity of their story.' Dechaineux was not alone among the interrogating team in putting his critical views on the record. In a remarkable private letter to Admiral Crace dated 11 December, Commander Victor Ramage wrote that 'I think it is desirable that though most N.O.'s [Naval Officers] probably realise that SYDNEY was taken by surprise, the details should be confined to as few as possible.' For Ramage, the important lesson was that the Germans, even when faced with unfavourable odds, knew 'the value of bluff and surprise' and in this instance it was the 'QQQQ' signal sent out by Detmers that allayed Burnett's suspicions.

Dechaineux and Ramage's criticisms could be viewed as being overly harsh to Captain Burnett, especially as they only had one side of the story on which to base their deductions. Burnett was killed along with everyone else from *Sydney* and could neither defend himself nor explain the reasons for his actions. He was being judged solely on the testimony of the enemy and this must have been an uncomfortable situation for some in the RAN. Dechaineux tacitly acknowledged the preliminary nature of his report by proposing that the DNI sift and prepare a final report that should be studied to 'extract all benefits and further lessons learnt'. He clearly felt that his report should not be the final word on the loss of *Sydney*. But

Above: The imprisoned crew of Kormoran, *who named their POW camp after a German cult hero, Klaus Störtebeker.*

The Murchison interrogations

A second opportunity to probe the stories of Detmers and his men came when the prisoners were transferred to Victoria and were interned at the Murchison prisoner of war camp. Much of what we know from this round of interrogations comes from the private diary of Captain John Leslie Hehir of Military Intelligence, Southern Command. Hehir, an army signals intelligence expert and linguist who was fluent in Italian and competent in German, French and other languages,[25] arrived at Camp 13 in Murchison on 28 December for the purpose of investigating the destruction of *Sydney* and was teamed

with Lieutenants Yarra and Harwood and Sergeants Thompson and Caminer. In order to ensure its complete confidentiality Hehir wrote his diary in Italian.

On his first entry in the new 1942 diary, Hehir lists the four methods they planned to use to extract the true story of the battle between *Kormoran* and *Sydney*: '(1) special preparations in the hospital enclosure, (2) censorship & other documents, (3) interrogation of Captain Detmers by hospital officers, (4) interrogation of sailors.'[26]

There was nothing unusual in these methods, except for the 'special preparations' which turned out to be listening devices secretly planted in new hospital quarters that was set aside solely for the crew of *Kormoran*. The idea for bugging this room apparently came from Dechaineux himself, who learnt of its value while in England.[27] All the while the Germans were together in this 'secret room' and speaking freely among themselves their conversations were being surreptitiously monitored for any information that was either new or contradicted their earlier stories. Hehir referred to the Germans as their 'caged birds' and appeared upset when two young women were introduced to the secret room, calling it 'superfluous'. When he

Wednesday 7

*Il maggiore McQuie ha fatto oggi
un grande interrogazione del Com. Dettmers
chi ha detto tutta la storia dell'inffondamento
e del'azione, ed io, dalla mia
parte, credo chi'è la verità.*

Maj. McQuie today made a major interrogation
of Cdr Detmers who told him the full story of the
sinking and the action and I, for my part, believe
he told the truth.

*Above: An extract from Captain John L. Hehir's personal
diary, with a translation by his daughter.*

addressed the question to his superior, Major Walker, he
was told 'it's necessary…to cover every eventuality'. No
further explanation was provided.

Their other trick was to engage the prisoners in
casual conversation, hoping that this would encourage
them to drop their guard and divulge something new.
Kormoran's doctor, Siebelt Habben, was a particular
target of Lieutenant Yarra, who was intent on gaining
his confidence by teaching him English. The lessons
continued every morning and while Dr Habben, the
pupil, was learning rapidly, so were the teachers.

Every method seemed to pay dividends. An intercepted
airmail letter was found to contain a map of *Kormoran*'s route.
A major interrogation of Detmers on 7 January yielded
the full story of the action and the sinking, which Hehir
believed was the truth. Dr Fritz List, a doctor of economics
whose role on *Kormoran* could be described as either a
war correspondent or a propaganda officer depending on
one's view, was pressured to explain the sketch he made on

toilet paper of two caves near where the lifeboat he was
in landed at Red Bluff, north of Carnarvon. The sketches
were believed to conceal shorthand characters that made
sense to Hehir and encouraged him to enlist the help of an
expert, a Swiss/German national named Hermaine Kevin,[28]
who spent hours with him trying to make sense out of
the squiggly lines that were drawn to depict the outside
of the two caves. These squiggles have been interpreted by
various people to mean various things, including mention
of some sort of Japanese attack, but Hehir's diary throws no
further light on the subject.

By Friday 16 January the Murchison interrogations
were over and the five intelligence officers were leaving
to return to their normal 'signals' work. Hehir capped this
section of his diary with a flourish. Writing in Pitman's
shorthand he began his entry with the words 'And this is the
story of the sinking of the *Sydney*'. Recounting a version
of the battle that was very close to Detmers's, he offered
his own conclusion: 'From all men under investigation I
am convinced that the Commander of the *Sydney* made a
fatal mistake in coming in too close and that the story as
told by Commander Detmers is what happened.'

The Eldridge report

After the Murchison interrogations were concluded Dechaineux's earlier proposal that the DNI compile a report on the loss of *Sydney* was finally taken up. However, rather than consume any more of their senior officer's valuable time the DNI delegated this unenviable task to F.B. Eldridge, Esq, MA, a senior master at the Royal Australian Naval College. In addition to the material gathered during the West Australian and Murchison interrogations, Eldridge had the benefit of two conferences with Captain Hehir, the first on 20 January when Hehir made his verbal report to the Naval Office. Nevertheless, it was a significant amount of information for any one person to absorb in a short period of time and the commendation that Eldridge received from the Naval Board for the work was an indication of how grateful they and the DNI were that he voluntarily took on this arduous, and seemingly unwanted, job.

Eldridge's report, dated 28 January 1942, ran to 27 pages in total, including appendices, track charts, a photo and simple drawing of *Kormoran* and other documents.[29] The main body of the report covered much the same

Previous page: The Walrus flying away from HMAS Sydney.

ground as the previous reports by Farquhar-Smith and Dechaineux, although it was more coherent and better organised. Unfortunately, without being able to interrogate any of the prisoners himself or initiate any new inquiries, Eldridge was left to merely collect all the information handed to him.

To his credit, Eldridge compiled the most detailed account of the action to date by incorporating all the disparate pieces of information that came out during the interrogations. He shied away from offering his own opinions or making conclusions; however, at the outset he does write that:

> *The story of the action between the Sydney and the Raider was frankly told by the Captain, Fregatten Kapitan Detmers and other prisoners, and the story told seems to ring true, though there is no explanation on the surface as to why the 'Sydney' came so close, or why she came so close before attempting to launch her aircraft.*

Not surprisingly, Eldridge's account is virtually identical to the account told by Detmers and his men during the interrogations. However, when this account is compared with Detmers's own personal account which he kept secretly hidden during his time in the prisoner of war camp, an intriguing difference is revealed about the signalling from *Sydney* just before the battle began. Eldridge writes that 'Detmers mentions an order to stop immediately before the signal by searchlight in plain language to give the secret call.' The original source of this statement is the first interrogation of Detmers that was conducted on 1 December. It is the only time Detmers ever mentions this signal to 'Stop' and it is uncorroborated by Chief Signalman Ahlbach, who later stated that the 'Cruiser did *not* signal "Proceed" or "Stop"'.[30]

If Detmers's comment about being ordered to stop is true, and on the face of it there is no reason to say it is not, it would indicate that *Sydney* was clearly intent on stopping *Kormoran* to verify her true identity. She

Historical reassessments

remained suspicious and was not about to let *Kormoran* go and bid her good voyage as Detmers had hoped. For his part, Detmers was ready to fight so there was no way he was about to stop and hand the advantage he had won so cleverly back to *Sydney*. The denouement of the chase then came down to *Sydney*'s final signal for *Kormoran* to give *Straat Malakka*'s secret call, which they did not have and thus opened fire. At that point *Sydney* was already too close to an enemy whose firepower was unexpectedly lethal.

Eldridge's report was forwarded to the Admiralty on 12 February 1942 in duplicate, as per a standing requirement by the Admiralty for all Boards of Inquiry into the loss or damage of His Majesty's ships, which included Australian ships. Although it was apparently treated as such by both the RAN and Admiralty, Eldridge's report was *not* a Board of Inquiry by any stretch of the imagination. The first essential element of a Board of Inquiry is that it is conducted by a board, generally of three senior naval figures (captains and above) with one acting as president. The board takes evidence from eyewitnesses in a court-like setting; they assess the evidence and then report their findings and conclusions in a formal document. Eldridge did none of these things.

The first in-depth historical reassessment of the battle between *Sydney* and *Kormoran* was written in 1957 by George H. Gill as part of his official World War II history of the RAN.[31] As no truly new information had come to light in the intervening years Gill's account of the action was essentially the same as the account compiled by Eldridge some fifteen years earlier. However, where Eldridge and the others before him made only the briefest comments about where they felt Captain Burnett had erred in his decision-making, Gill was clearly far less constrained in making a full critical assessment of Burnett and his actions.

Gill suggested that Burnett's inexperience in a recognised war zone might have left him to be less cautious than he should have been. Burnett had spent the first years of the war on an appointment in the Navy Office and he took command of *Sydney* only in May that year with his time on board spent mostly on escort duty. Gill posed a number of reasonable questions that were undoubtedly asked by others behind closed doors, but in this instance they were being put forward in arguably the most important and influential historical review of the Australian Navy's role in fighting World War II: 'Why Burnett did not use his aircraft, [why he] did not keep his distance and use his superior speed and armament, [why he] did not confirm his suspicions by asking Navy Office by wireless if *Straat Malakka* was in the area?'

Knowing that these questions could never be answered, Gill offered some possible explanations of the factors that might well have influenced Burnett to act the way he did. Gill cited the example of the commanding officer of HMAS *Canberra* (Captain Farncomb), who had been criticised for expending 215 rounds of 8-inch ammunition at the extreme range of 19,000 yards in the successful sinking of the German supply ships *Coburg* and *Ketty Brovig*. Burnett would have been aware of these circumstances. Although Farncomb was credited with avoiding the possibility of being torpedoed by maintaining a prudent range, he was criticised at the same time for being overcautious and not closing the enemy faster. In the view of at least two admirals, Farncomb's action, while ultimately successful, came at the expense of wasted ammunition and this was just not good enough. Gill suggests that the implied criticism of Farncomb might have influenced Burnett's thinking as he was faced with deciding how fast and how near he might approach *Kormoran*. Gill also raised the possibility that the impending nightfall was a factor in Burnett's calculations. In deciding to close *Kormoran* faster and confirm her identity before darkness set in, was Burnett relying too much on the superiority of his own firepower trained menacingly on the suspect ship?

Whatever the case, Gill concluded that Burnett courted disaster with his risky tactics and even if *Sydney* had prevailed over *Kormoran* she would have been badly damaged and suffered casualties unnecessarily. For those sympathetic to Burnett, and the memory of a good and capable man no longer alive to defend himself against his critics, Gill's criticism of Burnett was incorrect and unfair. One of those who strongly felt this way was Michael Montgomery, the son of *Sydney*'s navigation officer, Lieutenant Commander Clive Montgomery.

Michael Montgomery is an Oxford-educated author who was just four years old when his father, a Royal Navy officer on loan to the RAN, was lost with *Sydney*. His 1981 book, *Who Sank the Sydney?*, was every bit as provocative as the question its title posed and it is fair to say that Montgomery's sensational claims set the controversial tone for debates about the loss of *Sydney* that raged for the next quarter-century. At every turn Montgomery attempts to discredit Detmers and his account. In its place he offers his own dramatic version of events that has Detmers and *Kormoran* illegally defeating Burnett and *Sydney* with the help of a Japanese *I* class submarine that fires the final fatal torpedo to sink *Sydney*. He then suggests that it brutally machine-gunned the Australian survivors before setting fire to the slick of oil enveloping them in order to destroy all evidence of their evil deeds.

If Montgomery is to be believed, *Kormoran* was inexplicably stopped in the water when she first sighted *Sydney* and was flying a Norwegian, not Dutch, flag. Knowing he could not outrun the faster *Sydney*, Detmers had his crew pretend that *Kormoran* was in distress and on fire, and signalled this with an SOS, prompting Burnett to stop *Sydney* and lower a boat to lend assistance. With *Sydney* stopped and at cruising stations unprepared for action, Detmers saw his chance for a surprise attack and, according to Montgomery, then opened fire at the defenceless cruiser with *Kormoran*'s hidden underwater torpedo tube while flying a neutral flag (Norwegian) in breach of the Geneva Convention. Montgomery also believed that at some point *Kormoran* made a formal signal of surrender to *Sydney* but reopened fire on her afterwards in another breach of international law. Although his book offered nothing in the way of real proof, Montgomery's speculations and claims constituted a serious indictment of German and Japanese collusion in the illegal sinking of *Sydney* and the cold-blooded murder of any men who might have survived.

Montgomery's claims didn't stop with just Detmers and the Japanese Imperial Navy, though. He also finds the Australian Naval Board and Intelligence Division to be equally culpable in the cowardly concealment and cover-up of the unbelievable version of events he sets out as the truth. Montgomery's basic thesis in all this is that the RAN knew the essential facts of the German and Japanese

Above: The real Straat Malakka.

misdeeds but suppressed the story because they wanted to avoid a full-scale inquiry into the Naval Board's handling of the affair. In his attack on the RAN, Montgomery goes so far as suggesting that Naval Intelligence planted false information into their own reconstruction of the action (Eldridge's Report) in order to give credibility to the story of Detmers and his officers.[32] Finally, Montgomery aims his last salvo at the politicians; he claims that Prime Minister Curtin personally informed Winston Churchill of the suspected Japanese involvement in the sinking of *Sydney* and that Churchill conveyed the same to US President Roosevelt *before* the Japanese attack on Pearl Harbor. In keeping with the cloak of conspiracy and cover-up cast by Montgomery, it should surprise no one that he concludes that the telegrams which could prove his allegations have been either withheld or destroyed.

As the son of *Sydney*'s navigator, who would have been on the bridge alongside Burnett during the action, Montgomery's motivations are perfectly understandable. In his vigorous defence of Burnett, whom he sees as a scapegoat and refers to as a 'lonely, conveniently silent figure', Montgomery was the first of numerous authors to follow who castigated their own naval establishment and government for real or perceived faults but, in the end, reserved their most vitriolic attacks for Burnett's opposite number: Captain Detmers. *Who Sank the Sydney?*, and the release of newly declassified documents that had been kept closed for 30 years after the war, effectively opened the floodgates for a prolonged national debate by men and women who argued their points of view with an

intensity and passion that often spilled over, ending in acrimony and a deep divide.

While every imaginable aspect of the battle was picked apart and put under the microscope of historical review, the central and most important questions boiled down to the decisions and conduct of the two captains. Did Detmers pull off the most perfect, and legal, *ruse de guerre* in *Kormoran*'s defeat of *Sydney* as per his account, or did he illegally trick Burnett into dropping his guard with a signal of distress and/or surrender as speculated by Montgomery and his followers? In Burnett's case the key questions surround his decision to take *Sydney* as close as he did to a clearly suspicious ship, irrespective of the flags or signals being shown by *Kormoran*. Was Burnett at least partially taken in by Detmers's ruse in allowing *Sydney* to be lured into such dangerously close range, or was he planning his own pre-emptive strike and capture of a suspected raider or supply ship only to underestimate the firepower of his enemy? Underlying these questions about how Burnett handled his first direct contact with the enemy was whether his relative inexperience as a wartime commander led to an overconfidence that proved to be fatal. The question of Japanese involvement in the sinking of *Sydney* also gained momentum and took on a life of its own.

The first book to directly challenge Montogomery's controversial claims and the many 'ill-informed, emotional and extravagant rumours' that spread about the loss of *Sydney* was the expertly researched *H.M.A.S. Sydney — Fact, Fantasy and Fraud* by Barbara Winter.[33] Winter, who studied in Germany and knew the language, was the first to make use of German naval documents in her research that also covered a wealth of material in the Australian archives and interviews with a good number of surviving *Kormoran* officers and crew. In enormous detail Winter traces the history of both ships and their respective captains, including information and insights that could only come from those who actually lived the events. But arguably Winter's most important contribution was her painstaking dissection and debunking of more than 40 vexing rumours — ranging from the claim that *Sydney* sent W/T signals during the action to whether it was a Japanese submarine which finally sank her — that spurred her to set the record straight.

The next major investigation of the subject was by one of the RAN's own sons, Tom Frame, who entered the RAN as a cadet midshipman in 1979, served as a research officer to the Chief of Naval Staff in 1988, then earned his doctorate in history before leaving the navy as a lieutenant in November 1992 to join the Anglican priesthood. Frame's 1993 *HMAS Sydney — Loss & Controversy* is another thoroughly researched book that wades deep into the controversy about what is the true version of the battle. Like Winter, a lot of his effort is dedicated to exposing the alternative theories of the authors and researchers who came before him as baseless ideas sprouting from the seeds of hearsay, speculation and wild imagination. In their place Frame offers his own reconstruction, which he believes 'makes better use of all the available evidence and embodies a more sceptical approach to the German evidence'.[34]

While Frame accepts Detmers's account to a point, he believes that it is false in a number of very important areas. To begin with, Frame picks up on Detmers' admission during interrogation that *Sydney* ordered *Kormoran* to stop; however, he believes this occurred at a safe range for *Sydney* at or beyond 14,000 yards rather than at the close range of 900 metres implied in Detmers's testimony. Most importantly, Frame suggests that *Kormoran* heeded *Sydney*'s order and did indeed stop, or come practically to a standstill. This crucial point, if true, would change the entire nature of the ensuing battle and would condemn as liars all the Germans who gave testimony to the contrary. Frame also finds conflict with

Detmers on the type of torpedo with which *Kormoran* hit *Sydney* at the start of the battle, suggesting that it was fired from the single underwater torpedo tube on the starboard side and not from the twin above-water torpedo tubes as made clear in the German testimony. Finally, Frame again raises the possibility, first postulated by Montgomery, that Detmers indicated his intention to surrender, which Burnett took as a clear signal that his enemy was not about to fight and would readily capitulate to be boarded or agree to abandon ship. Much of Frame's faith in his alternative reconstruction of the battle is derived from his surprising belief that just Joachim von Gösseln and Petty Officer Otto Jurgensen were on the bridge with Detmers at the time and that they, in addition to signalman Ahlbach and Detmers himself, were the only ones to witness *Sydney* ordering *Kormoran* to stop and *Kormoran*'s signal of surrender, however it was supposedly made. Frame argues that with so few members of the crew in the know about this information it 'could be successfully and permanently concealed'.[35]

The unknown and the unknowable

In his final chapter, entitled 'The Unknown and the Unknowable', Tom Frame quotes Barbara Tuchman about the challenge for historians 'to recapture the truth of past events and find out what really happened'. As if to prove how difficult that challenge can be, especially with as controversial a subject as the loss of HMAS *Sydney*, he goes on to point out, perhaps a bit harshly, the deficiencies and shortcomings of his fellow historians Gill, Montgomery and Winter. For his own part, Frame knows that the reconstruction of the battle he proposes can only be one of a number of possible reconstructions as an alternative to the German/Detmers's account, which has been largely adopted as the 'official' account of the action. Frame concludes that 'In the case of *Sydney*, we will never know how it really was.

Above: Captain Detmers's POW service and casualty form.

Those with an interest in the loss of this proud Australian ship must learn to live with the unknown, and the unknowable.'

It is easy to understand the hope that Frame had in 1993 for his book to 'diminish further speculation about the loss of Sydney'. By then the controversy had rumbled on for more than 50 years and the recent expeditions to successfully locate the wrecks of *Titanic* and *Bismarck* by Dr Robert Ballard and his team from the Woods Hole Oceanographic Institute that made headlines around the world inspired yet more intense debate about where a possible search for the wrecks of *Sydney* and *Kormoran* should start and who should fund it. Finding the wrecks and filming their remains was undoubtedly the one last hope to shed new light on the subject and to put to bed, once and for all, the nagging and painful questions about what really happened in the battle. The problem, however, was that no one could agree where off the coast of Western Australia the search should start. Even the world's top expert, Dr Ballard, having been contacted by the Western Australian Maritime Museum for his help, was forced to decline this request on the basis that a search for *Sydney* couldn't even be described as the proverbial search for a needle in a haystack because the correct haystack had yet to be found.[36]

For the families and friends of *Sydney* crewmen it must have seemed that Tom Frame was right. They would have to learn to live with the disappointment and empty feeling left by never knowing the final resting place of their loved ones, despite having their hopes raised countless times by the release of some new promising historical information or yet another 'expert' who supposedly knew where *Sydney* had been lost. Sadly, as the calls for *Sydney* to be found intensified and more and more people weighed in with differing opinions about where the search should commence, it only acted to highlight the serious level of disagreement among historians and researchers that made it virtually impossible for the RAN or the government to back a search. For nearly two decades the technical capability to locate the wreck of *Sydney* has existed but the main stumbling block has been an uncertainty about where to search and finding someone with the skills, experience and courage to take on this impossibly difficult challenge.

CHAPTER TWO

...

A fateful meeting

I can remember very well the first time I heard about the story of HMAS *Sydney* and the great mystery surrounding her final resting place. It was late January 1996 and I was in London attending a conference on the protection of underwater cultural heritage, which is another way to describe ancient shipwrecks and their cargoes. The meeting was being held at the International Maritime Organisation and the purpose was to bring together experts from around the world to discuss a UNESCO convention that was being drafted in order to safeguard historically important shipwrecks. This was the second meeting of its type and while it was mostly attended by archaeologists and lawyers — I was one of the few token experts invited to represent the marine salvage industry — I was getting to know some of the attendees better, having met most of them the previous year. One in particular was the Australian maritime archaeologist Graeme Henderson, who at the time was a director with the Western Australian Maritime Museum in Fremantle.

At the first meeting Graeme hardly said a word but I was told by someone that he carried a lot of influence in the South-East Asian and Pacific regions and for that reason I thought perhaps he was in the luxurious position of not having to say too much. Graeme was also unforgettable because he wore a very thick beard and moustache, so he perfectly fitted the mould of a salty (and silent) sea-dog. Even though I was meant to be advocating for the rights of salvage companies, and thus was literally and figuratively sitting on the opposite side of the table from Graeme, he was someone I thought I should get to know.

My chance came during a coffee break at the International Maritime Organisation's meeting the following year and I started talking to Graeme about the ultra-deep-water shipwrecks my company, Blue Water Recoveries Limited, had recently found. One of the major concerns of Graeme and his colleagues was that advances in subsea technologies had made it possible to reach virtually any depth in the oceans, thereby placing a whole new frontier of shipwrecks potentially at risk of being unlawfully disturbed. Fortunately, Graeme had no reason to view our achievements with concern

Left: Sydney's *stowed aircraft and 4-inch gun deck viewed from above.*

because the wrecks the UNESCO convention wanted to protect were 100 years and older, while the wrecks Blue Water Recoveries was primarily interested in were much younger.

Graeme must have understood this because he immediately showed an obvious interest in our deep-water search capabilities and said to me: 'If you can find shipwrecks that deep then you need to come out to Australia and find HMAS *Sydney*.' As I didn't know the story of *Sydney* at the time I asked Graeme to tell me all about her, which he proceeded to do with unusual emotion for such a naturally quiet man. It was clear from the way Graeme spoke about *Sydney*, and her men, that this was no ordinary shipwreck story and that the memory of *Sydney* held a very special place in the hearts and minds of Australians. It was also very clear that finding the wreck of *Sydney* would be no ordinary challenge. From what Graeme said I formed the distinct impression that *Sydney* was truly an impossible wreck to find because no one, it seemed, knew where to start looking.

There was no need for me to take notes while Graeme spoke or even write down *Sydney*'s name, for the story he recounted was so unbelievably tragic and mysterious that I knew it would be forever etched in my mind. Our discussion was one of those rare moments in life for me where I instinctively knew that some day I would take up this great challenge being put to me. I had no idea when or how or on what basis I would ever seriously consider mounting a search expedition for *Sydney* but I knew that one day fate would draw me back to her incredible story.

Starting out

One question I am often asked about my work is how I came to be a professional shipwreck hunter. I think my story is probably atypical, but then again I don't really know what would be the typical path for a shipwreck hunter to have taken since it is such an unusual and rare profession to have.

I wasn't born by the sea unless the Hudson River between New York City and New Jersey, where I lived, counts. Nor did I have an early interest in ships, or history or any of the things I do today in pursuit of finding shipwrecks. Those interests came much later in life. However, the one passion I have had throughout my life that has always attracted me to water, be it sweet or salty, is fishing. Unfortunately, growing up in Union City, New Jersey — infamous for being the most densely populated city in the United States — did not afford me many opportunities to fish. To fish — in fact to see anything green or natural and not made of concrete — I had to travel the 100 miles or so to the small town in rural Pennsylvania where my mother was raised and my uncles still lived.

One hundred miles is certainly not far to travel but to me it was an entirely different world that I absolutely adored. I could fish every day with my uncles and when I was not fishing I was wading through the narrow creek behind my grandmother's house looking for crayfish. Left to my own devices I would have stayed out all day and night completely lost in exploration of the rivers and lakes until the search parties arrived. This magical time I spent with my uncles Pete, Vince and Lawrence had such an impact on me that by the time I was sixteen and thinking about going to university I had firmly decided that I would choose a course and career that would allow me to work outdoors and, ideally, close to the sea.

When it came to selecting a university I was very lucky that there was a good private one called Fairleigh Dickinson University within commuting distance from where we lived and that happened to offer a BSc in marine biology. While commuting every day on the notoriously unattractive highways of New Jersey to Teaneck wasn't exactly my idea of being close to the sea, the course did include a half-year semester at the university's own private laboratory in St Croix, US Virgin Islands. So without doubt, the three and a half years of hard study was worth the life-transforming experience of being able to be taught in such a beautiful environment, especially since half our time was literally spent learning underwater.

Even though I chose my degree course at a relatively young age I knew before the end of my last year that I had picked the right field for me and that I wanted to further my education with another degree. The only question was whether I was going to remain a marine biologist or whether I should switch to marine geology, which I found to be far more stimulating because of the field research that I did in St Croix. I was again fortunate to have been accepted into the MSc program at the University of South Florida, whose Marine Science Department in St Petersburg had just been made a state-wide Center of Excellence. Finally, I was at a campus right on the water of Tampa Bay and docked out back were coastal research vessels that would take us throughout the Gulf of Mexico and Bahamas Islands on scientific cruises lasting up to two weeks.

It took more than a year but I ultimately made the transition to marine geology and was lucky that an upcoming and respected assistant professor named Al Hine was willing to take me on as one of his graduate students. Al had a growing reputation as a talented sedimentologist specialising in shallow carbonate environments, but most importantly, he was a proper sea-going scientist, meaning I would have plenty of opportunities to go to sea myself and get hands-on experience with the high-resolution geophysical instruments that were his tools of the trade. Al believed in taking all his graduate students to sea and giving them full responsibility for operating the expensive and scientifically powerful equipment. On my first training cruise with Al he put me in charge of a high-frequency side-scan sonar system that we used to image the sea-floor geology and it was without question an experience that transformed my life forever.

The sonar was an old, disused EG&G 259-4 unit that was in such bad shape I had to spend a week breaking it down and repairing it just to get it working to about half its rated capability. The 259-4 was one of the earliest commercially available side-scan sonars and difficult to operate, but when I finally got it working and it started to produce sonar images of the West Florida continental shelf as we slowly steamed away from the coast I immediately knew that operating this type of equipment was what I

wanted to do for the rest of my life. The images of sand waves and rocky outcrops, even taking into account their relative poor quality, were an absolute revelation to me. I felt this was probably the most perfect mix of science and underwater exploration that I could ever hope to experience. What I found particularly powerful was the ability of the sonar to scan wide strips of the sea-floor that could reveal geology that was either millions of years old or sedimentary patterns that were created by the storm that passed just the week before. Before our short cruise was finished I had already decided to learn everything I could about this amazing technology and become an expert in its use.

Learning the trade

In order to fulfil my ambitions to become an expert sea-going geophysicist I joined every single scientific cruise that I possibly could during my years at graduate school. One way or the other I managed to go away to sea on ten different cruises that totalled about three months in duration, enabling me to become a proficient equipment operator. The high-resolution geophysical gear that we used included acoustic profilers, sparkers and air-guns but my main interest was always the side-scan sonar. I quickly became the department's resident 'expert' and by the end of my tenure at the university Al Hine was having me give the lecture on the theory and use of side-scan sonar to the new geology students.

As Al's field research was primarily focused on the continental shelf we were generally working in fewer than 200 metres water depth. I had no deep-water experience to speak of so when I got the opportunity to join one last cruise that happened to be leaving from our dock to study a newly discovered community of cold-seep clams and tube worms found at the base of the west Florida escarpment I jumped at the chance. This cruise appealed to me for a number of reasons. First, the co-principal investigator was the legendary Dr Fred Spiess of the Scripps Institute of Oceanography who pioneered the use of deep-tow instruments for scientific mapping of the deep seabed. Second, the research vessel was going to be the RV *Knorr* that had hit the headlines just the previous year when she was used to find the wreck of the *Titanic*. And finally, the study area was at a depth of 3,600 metres, which meant I would be exposed to a whole new set of instruments and methodologies.

I couldn't dream of a better way to cap off my graduate school career, which had just finished with the successful defence of my MSc thesis. This was an incredible opportunity to take part in cutting-edge deep-water research and to work with some of the best scientists in the world on the biggest and best ship I had ever embarked upon. Probably of even more importance was that I had run out of money for food and rent, and was living on a friend's sofa while I waited to hear if I was going to be offered the job at Eastport International for which I had recently been interviewed. So I could easily add self-preservation to the list of benefits in joining a three-week cruise that offered a bunk and plenty of food.

As I had imagined, the cruise was an unforgettable experience and I learned an enormous amount. I walked away with a new understanding of how to deploy and use side-scan sonars in the deep ocean and with the confidence that I was ready for my career to move on to the next challenge. Partly out of necessity, and partly as a tactic, I gave Eastport a deadline on the possible job offer, which meant they were going to have to call me at sea by an expensive shore-to-ship connection one way or another. While I know that the radio office of the *Knorr* had been the scene of some extraordinary calls over the years, especially when Dr Robert Ballard announced they had found the *Titanic*, I can't imagine that many people have used it, either before or since, as the place to receive their first serious job offer. Eastport wanted me to grow their geophysical survey and search business and I was delighted to accept their offer. I was also greatly relieved to know when the *Knorr* docked back in St Petersburg that I would be moving on to a new and exciting life and not back to my friend's sofa.

Diving into the deep end

From my first day at Eastport International I knew that I had been given a marvellous opportunity to excel at a seriously cool and exciting company, but that I would also need to work extremely hard to get up to speed at a technical level. Eastport's main business at the time was as a contractor for the US Navy Supervisor of Salvage (SUPSALV), maintaining and operating its deep-water remotely operated vehicles (ROVs) which were often called on in emergencies to recover US Government assets lost at sea. The 80-person company was full of engineers, mechanics, electronics technicians and operators that pilot the ROVs — all highly skilled technical experts. My background as a scientist certainly impressed the management and helped get my foot in the door but among the guys I would be going to sea with it was only a curiosity. To earn their respect and become a valued member of the team I needed to know my stuff, backwards and forwards, and prove myself where it counted: offshore.

When I joined Eastport in September 1986 its forté was the recovery of downed aircraft from deep water. The company operated a SUPSALV ROV called Deep Drone 6000 that could dive to a depth of 1,800 metres and either pick up small bits of aircraft wreckage with its two manipulator arms or attach lifting lines to recover an entire Chinook helicopter if necessary. Together the navy and Eastport had recently completed recovering wreckage of the ill-fated space shuttle *Challenger*, which exploded in spectacular fashion shortly after take-off, killing all seven of its crew members, including Christa McAuliffe who was poised to become the first schoolteacher in space. The accident, caused by a failed O-ring on the right solid rocket booster, was a horrific tragedy witnessed on TV by millions of Americans, including me, watching the skyline from the opposite side of Florida.

The recovery of *Challenger* was an enormously difficult project because the wreckage was spread over a huge distance, owing to its explosion in mid-air, and pieces of the problematic solid rocket booster sank in the deep, swift-moving waters of the Gulf Stream. The salvage teams coped with the difficult conditions but afterwards the navy decided it needed a deeper, more powerful ROV that could handle the worst-case combination of high currents and great depth to a maximum of 6,000 metres. No ROV had ever dived so deep, so the development of this new controllable underwater remote vehicle, called CURV III, also turned out to be a race against another US Navy R&D centre over who would take the honours in reaching this important milestone first. Because of my background in marine science the first assignment of my new job was to compile a worldwide database of surface and subsurface currents and worst-case current profiles that would establish the key performance criteria for this new CURV. It would have never occurred to me as I watched the vapour trails of *Challenger's* debris fall to earth on that sad day in late January 1986 that in a way I would owe my first job to that horrible scene.

Dealing with deadly accident scenes was obviously something I was going to have to get used to. Objects that need to be found and recovered from the bottom of the ocean only really get there because some accident has occurred. Sometimes we were tasked to recover unmanned objects such as test torpedoes that failed to float to the surface at the end of their run or live Tomahawk cruise missiles that never reached their intended target. But mostly, they were helicopters or jet aircraft and in those cases the chance that someone lost their life in the accident was generally quite high. I guess that everyone had their own coping mechanism although it wasn't a big topic of discussion offshore. For me I found it helpful to remember that the job we were doing to assist the accident investigation teams was vital in the prevention of future accidents.

After the first couple of years at Eastport I began to take on bigger and more complicated projects. The company was growing nicely and new milestones were being achieved, including winning the race for CURV to be the first ROV to dive below 6,000 metres, beating the other navy-funded ROV to the record by less than one week, and setting a new depth record for aircraft salvage (4,500 metres) with recovery of a South African 747 jumbo jet that crashed while on fire into the Indian

Above: The Challenger *lifting off and (below) the wreckage.*

Ocean. However, we still hadn't achieved our objective of improving our side-scan sonar search capability to the same deep-water standards as our ROVs had attained. In the summer of 1990 that was about to change virtually overnight when we were controversially awarded the contract by an Austrian Criminal Court to find the wreck of the MV *Lucona*.

The search for the *Lucona*

The *Lucona* affair, as it is known throughout Austria and Germany, is a story of insurance fraud and political cover-up that revolved around the sinking of an ordinary cargo

Above: Me with my trusted EG&G 259-4 sonar recorder.

ship and the premeditated murder of some of its crew. The man at the centre of the affair was Udo Proksch, a well-connected businessman who owned the famous Viennese confectioners Demel and the social Club 45 upstairs. In 1977 Proksch and his business partner Hans Peter Daimler — a relation of the famous Daimler-Benz family — organised the shipping of a valuable cargo of uranium-processing equipment they supposedly owned from Italy to Hong Kong on board the freighter *Lucona*. The cargo, well insured for $20 million, was anything but valuable., however. In truth it was nothing more than worthless scrap metal and a coal-mining plant freshly polished and painted to look the part. Proksch and Daimler's criminal plan was to sink *Lucona* and fraudulently collect the insurance payment of $20 million. Hidden in the cargo by Proksch's hand-selected cargo master was a container of explosives — a bomb — timed to go off during *Lucona*'s voyage east, somewhere over the deep waters of the Indian Ocean. Proksch visited the vessel himself

while the bomb was being loaded in Italy and presented the crew with one of Demel's famed chocolate tortes, of which the prosecution lawyers said 'the cake was not a travel provision but an executioner's meal'.

The explosion that ripped *Lucona*'s hull in two, obliterating her bow and causing the ship to sink in less than one minute, was so shocking to the captain, a man who had been a seaman since the age of fifteen, and his wife, who was also on board, that he vowed never to return to sea. Of *Lucona*'s crew of twelve, six went down with the ship while the others, who were incredibly lucky to have survived the rapid sinking, were rescued from their dinghy later that evening by a passing ship. Proksch's claim for his cargo loss was rejected by the Austrian insurance company Bundeslander, which hired a private detective to uncover Proksch's plot. Over the course of the next eleven years an investigation was started; Proksch and Daimler were arrested, then freed by Austria's foreign minister; a journalist broke the case wide open with publication of a best-selling book on the affair;[1] and finally the federal attorney called for a probe which sent Proksch into hiding for good.

With Proksch reportedly hiding in the Philippines at the palace of his friend Ferdinand Marcos, a parliamentary inquiry was launched into the affair which ultimately led to sixteen politicians, lawyers and top officials being removed from their posts, including the interior and foreign ministers who had allegedly been involved in the plot. A dozen more people involved were mysteriously killed. Proksch disguised his appearance with plastic surgery and a toupée but it was not enough to prevent him from being recognised by a customs official when in 1989 he stupidly passed through Vienna's airport on a connecting flight. In custody at last, Proksch was placed on trial charged with insurance fraud and six counts of premeditated murder. Knowing that the government's case hung mostly on circumstantial evidence, however, Proksch and his lawyers claimed that he could not be convicted unless the wreck of *Lucona* was found. Proksch famously stood up in open court and demanded 'Where is this *Lucona*! Find the *Lucona*!'

Remarkably, this is exactly what the primary judge hearing the case decided to do when he ordered a search for the wreck and turned to the deep-ocean search industry for help. The competition for the high-profile search project was intense so it was a major surprise when Eastport won the tender over far more experienced companies. After all, our search experience was limited to a few small shallow-water projects of no great significance and most importantly the company did not own any deep-water search equipment or ROVs that could reach the extreme depths to which *Lucona* was believed to have sunk. Everything would have to be built from scratch in just five months and shipped out to Singapore and then loaded onto a support vessel before the end of the year. The other surprise was that the judge himself would be joining the expedition along with a naval architect and two explosive experts.

I was part of a small operations team handpicked by my boss, Don Dean, who creatively came up with the innovative technical solution that won Eastport the contract. Rather than conduct the project in two separate phases — side-scan sonar search followed by ROV video investigation — as was the normal approach by our competitors, Don worked out an ingenious way we could perform both phases from the same vessel without having to return to port for a second costly and time-consuming mobilisation. Because the key to the project's success would be the initial search phase I was given the job of project manager, which also carried the added responsibility of being an expert witness — under oath — to the Austrian Court.

The build-up to the search was incredibly intense with enormous pressure on the whole team, although I felt as if the weight was entirely on my shoulders. Everything was run to the last minute, including the sea-trials for our brand-new deeptow search sonar, named the Ocean Explorer 6000. We were forced to conduct the essential trials during the transit from Singapore to the Maldives. The sonar had failed every single test dive during the transit, until the absolute last one conducted within sight of Male harbour, where we were collecting the judge and his expert assistants. The experience was nerve-racking for me, especially when Don, Eastport's president, Craig Mullen, and the two engineers who built

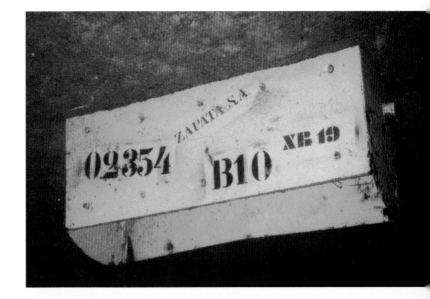

Above: The wreckage of Lucona, *including labels which conclusively tied the cargo to Udo Proksch.*

the sonar stepped off the support vessel and said, 'It's all up to you now.'

I was still very anxious about our untried equipment when we began the search on 23 January — exactly fourteen years to the day *Lucona* disappeared — under almost identical conditions. I remembered thinking this was a good omen and allowed excitement to start replacing my nervous feelings. Seven days later, after covering 450 square nautical miles of seabed and on our last line through the search box (the designated area of the search), a cluster of sonar targets began to light up our screens. I was instantly in no doubt that we had found *Lucona* but neither I, nor anyone else on board, had the experience to be 100 per cent sure, so we had to wait for the ROV video to confirm my interpretations of the sonar images.

When we finally got our new ROV, called Magellan 725, working on the seabed at a depth of 4,200 metres it wasn't long before we were able to confirm that the wreckage was from a shipwreck, and that the shipwreck was indeed *Lucona*. Despite the catastrophic damage suffered in the explosion it was possible for us to see that the remains of the ship matched exactly the plans and photographs the judge and his experts had of *Lucona*. The clinching proof, however, turned out to be Proksch's fraudulent cargo that was now strewn all over the seabed of the Indian Ocean. It was stamped in bold red lettering with the name of his Swiss front company — ZAPATA — and the project code number XB19 which was assigned to him by the Austrian defence minister who authorised his shipment. The pictures we took of the cargo and Proksch's unique identification marks were as good as being able to lift his fingerprints from the scene of the crime.

Our next objective was to determine whether explosives ripped the ship apart and where they might have been placed inside the cargo hold. A massive explosion seemed to be the obvious cause, based on the twisted and torn hull structure scattered throughout the dense debris field, but the judge still needed conclusive video footage to prove this in court. When the proof came it was stunningly clear. An explosion had sheared the ship in half, clean across her double bottoms just forward of the midship derrick, and left the side plating splayed outwards like a tin can. The explosive experts calculated that the bomb must have contained at least 100 kilograms of TNT, which was roughly the same amount Proksch had been given by the defence minister, who was a partner in Proksch's company that owned the cargo, a year before *Lucona* sank.

The evidence from the expedition was so conclusive that less than three weeks later Proksch was found guilty of all charges. He was originally sentenced to twenty years in prison, which he foolishly appealed, only to have this sentence increased to a lifetime term. Proksch's sentence did indeed turn out to be life as he died in 2001 during heart surgery while still a prisoner. For his part, Daimler was separately tried in Germany in 1997 and convicted of six counts of aiding murder for which he received a fourteen-year jail term.

The *Lucona* scandal inspired a 1993 feature film, starring David Suchet as Proksch's character, and more recently became the subject of a Vienna musical called *Udo 77*. The trial, because of the enormous costs of the search expedition, turned out to be the most expensive in Austrian history. Fortunately, I was not needed to testify as an expert witness because the video footage we shot spoke volumes itself. For Eastport, and me, the project was a huge success and put us right up there with the best deep-water search companies and firmly on track for a lot more interesting projects.

Success breeds success

The success of the *Lucona* search led directly to a series of deep-water search and investigation projects that followed on immediately and kept us busy with work for the next eighteen months. The main project was the search and recovery of an Itavia Airlines DC-9 that crashed in the Tyrrhenian Sea off Italy in 1980 under mysterious circumstances which matched the *Lucona* affair for political intrigue and possible criminal activity. While the aircraft recovery at a depth of 3,600 metres was a return to work we knew very well, there were also other opportunities to work on deep-water shipwrecks.

The SS *John Barry*, a US Liberty Ship that was sunk by a German U-boat in 1944 and rumoured to be carrying a large cargo of silver bullion being shipped to India as part of the US lend-lease program, had already been found off the coast of Oman at a depth of 2,600 metres but the extensive wreckage field needed to be mapped by side-scan sonar and an ROV video investigation conducted. This project wasn't the same challenge as with *Lucona* since the wreck was previously located but I still felt we gained valuable experience in the high-resolution mapping and video investigation of a shipwreck debris field and were adding to our track record of successful projects.

I was especially looking forward to the next shipwreck project because it was another proper search and because it was on behalf of a Lloyd's of London insurance syndicate that suspected the owners who were claiming an insurance payout had actually scuttled the ship. I was very keen for this project to go well as I believed we could solve a lot more suspicious shipwreck losses for Lloyd's insurers and this was our chance to show that important industry what we could do. This time it was my job to study the navigational clues as to where the ship might have sunk and set out the search box and sequence of sonar tracklines to find it as quickly as possible. Looking back this wasn't a particularly difficult search problem because the clues were of good quality, but at the time I was still proud to have found the wreck at a depth of 1,800 metres in less than 26 hours of searching. The important thing, I felt, was that I was learning so much with each project and that we were building a reputation one successful project at a time. That reputation was going to be seriously tested in our next major shipwreck search.

The search for the *Derbyshire*

The bulk carrier *Derbyshire*, which sank in 1980 during a typhoon off the coast of Okinawa, Japan, with total loss of life, was declared by news headlines at the time to have been 'lost without trace'. There was no mayday call from the ship, no survivors and no sign of any wreckage other than an empty lifeboat found six weeks later drifting 700 miles from *Derbyshire*'s last reported position. The question that everyone was asking, especially the families of the ship's crew, was: how could a 91,655-ton ship — the largest British ship ever to have been lost at sea — just disappear without trace? With virtually no evidence to go

on, the UK Minister for Trade decided that there would be no formal investigation of the loss.

Suspicions persisted, however, that *Derbyshire* sank because of a design flaw in the alignment of her main longitudinal girder at Frame 65, which along with the use of poor quality steel, led to total structure failure of the hull. The families of the 42 crew members[2] continued to push for a formal investigation into the loss, which was finally held in 1987 after several of *Derbsyhire*'s sister ships suffered serious cracking in the suspect Frame 65 area, leading to a second vessel sinking. Unfortunately, the formal investigation could only conclude that the ship 'was probably overcome by the forces of nature in Typhoon Orchid'. The lack of any factual evidence was highlighted as the reason a firmer finding could not be supported.[3]

Despite this gut-wrenching setback, the families, now organised as the Derbyshire Families Association and supported by Britain's three main transport unions — the National Union of Rail, Maritime and Transport Workers, National Union of Marine, Aviation and Shipping Transport Officers, and the International Transport Workers Federation (ITF) — stepped up their campaign in order get the factual evidence that was missing. They called for the wreck of *Derbyshire* to be located and began consulting undersea exploration experts to see whether that was feasible. Dr Robert Ballard, famed for finding the wrecks of *Titanic* and the German battleship *Bismarck*, was the first expert to be asked. His answer, however, was not what the families association had hoped to hear. Ballard flatly ruled out a search for *Derbyshire* saying, 'There just isn't enough data available to locate the area the ship went down closely enough. I think that given the lack of data, the cost of finding the *Derbyshire* would just be prohibitive.'[4] Coming from a man of Ballard's expertise and credentials, this news was devastating to the association.

The key campaigners of the association were made of strong stuff, however, and they were not about to walk away because of one or two disappointments.

On 23 March 1993 they placed an advertisement on the front page of *Lloyd's List* seeking qualified search contractors, which immediately made its way to my

Above: The combination carrier Derbyshire *(originally* Liverpool Bridge*).*

desk. I replied the same day and thus began a tortuous fourteen-month journey working to win the confidence of the association, the ITF (which ultimately agreed to fund the search), and some people in my own company (which had gone through an ownership change) that this was an important project worth taking a risk on.[5]

A lot of the doubt was whether we could find a wreck that Ballard thought couldn't be found. The reason for my confidence was that contrary to the 'lost without trace' scenario there was some information from the Japanese search and rescue teams that I believed was actually a very good clue to the location of the wreck. The information was sightings of oil variously described as either floating or welling up to the surface in the days immediately following the sinking. The oil was clearly floating up from the wreck but the big question was how far it would drift laterally while rising from more than 4,000 metres deep through the Kuroshio current, which is the world's second strongest ocean current after the Gulf Stream. One study predicted the lateral displacement could be as

much as ten nautical miles,[6] but I intuitively felt it would be much less.

The budget the ITF had allocated for the search would only fund about eight days on site leaving virtually no margin for errors or uncertainty, so I made a point of leaving no stone unturned in my analysis of the loss clues. In addition to my own manual analysis, I used two different computer-based search probability programs to define the most likely sinking location and flew to Japan ahead of the operations team to verify the Japanese data on the oil sightings and the Kuroshio current. The extra effort in Japan turned out to be invaluable as it allowed me to eliminate one rogue position for the wreck more than 21 nautical miles away and get much better information on the ocean currents. In addition to freeing up more time to search my preferred high-probability area, the trip to Japan also taught me a valuable lesson for the future: be wary of any second- or third-hand information and, most importantly, *always* verify primary source information yourself.

Our transit to the search area was going to take three days so I had plenty of time to revise my search box, which encompassed 172.5 square nautical miles —

less than the search box for *Lucona* but more than the 100-square nautical mile area searched during the 1985 location of *Titanic*. The only real worries I had were that the seabed terrain might be particularly rugged and that the annoying tropical depression that was moving in our direction might make for an uncomfortable transit.

Although we arrived on site ahead of time, and the tropical depression had petered out overnight, the weather conditions were still too rough to launch the Ocean Explorer sonar. Contingencies are always made for rough weather but I never want to lose time at the start of a project because it increases the pressure on everybody from the outset. After waiting two days for the weather to pass we launched the sonar towfish and eagerly anticipated the first images to start scrolling down our screens. My concerns about the seabed terrain were justified — it was very rocky in many areas and there was a large sea-mount just outside the search box that was going to be a serious hazard when turning the towfish around. However, about two-thirds of the way down our first sonar trackline we detected two targets that were square in shape and thus unlikely to be geology. These targets were the one bright spot in a fairly poor start to the search.

The second sonar trackline yielded nothing so we turned onto the line adjacent to the first line, frantically clearing the top of the sea-mount by just seventeen metres, so we could see what was on the other side of the two square targets. Sure enough there was a huge cluster of very hard targets covering an area 1,300 metres long by 900 metres wide. There wasn't anything in the image that directly suggested a shipwreck but the targets were also unlike the surrounding geology. *Derbyshire* may have broken in one or two sections but, as one of the biggest ships in the world at 294 metres long, we were expecting to see very large pieces of intact hull, not hundreds of individual pieces in a tight cluster. In the absence of anything conclusive we decided to continue our prearranged search and return to image the cluster in high resolution if no other targets turned up elsewhere.

Searching in deep water can be an agonisingly slow and tedious process. Because the sonar towfish is being

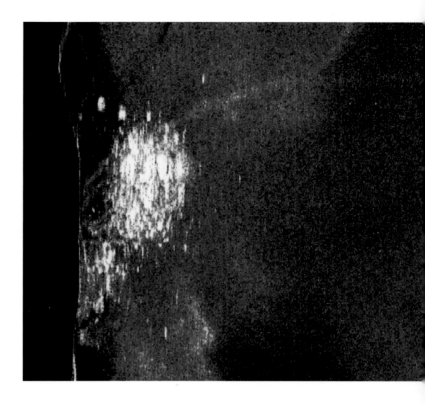

Above: The initial sonar detection of Derbyshire's *obliterated wreckage.*

towed at the end of ten-kilometre steel cable with huge drag forces building up as the cable is pulled through the water, the speed of the support vessel is limited to roughly 2.5 knots or about average walking speed. Our screens displaying the sonar images are even slower. They update only once every four seconds in step with the rate our low-frequency sonar emits each sonar ping. And to top it off, the turns we have to make to get from the end of one sonar trackline to the start of the next can take eight to ten hours or more, every second of which is effectively unproductive downtime. So by the time we completed two more tracklines and turns with nothing found we were all champing at the bit to get back to the strange cluster of targets and see exactly what its true nature was.

In high-resolution mode the Ocean Explorer sonar is towed closer to the seabed, the ping rate is increased to once per second and the images are 'magnified' by about four times, allowing individual targets to be better resolved. As the sonar approached the target area, small pieces of debris started coming into view. Soon after, we

hit the first large target showing an acoustic shadow and by now it was fairly obvious we were beginning to pass over the top of a very large field of wreckage. This was completely unlike the patterns of geology we had come across earlier in the search. What we saw over the next 30 minutes, as each ping filled our screens with yet more pieces of wreckage, left us all stunned. This was *Derbyshire* all right, but in a state none of us expected. The hull was literally shattered into thousands of individual pieces. The only thing that we could compare to this scene of total destruction was what a jet aircraft looks like when it hits the water surface at high speed and is torn to shreds.

As professionals we were used to seeing the aftermath of a ship that was destroyed, but if these images shocked us we could only imagine what kind of impact they would have on the people waiting in Britain to see our results, especially the *Derbyshire* families. We knew we would have to get pictures of the wreckage to reinforce my interpretation of the sonar images and to prove that the wreckage was indeed *Derbyshire*'s. Although we were contracted by the ITF to conduct only the sonar search, we donated the use of our Magellan ROV to film the wreckage. There was time for just one short dive of about six hours on the bottom, which would give us very little opportunity to safely negotiate the debris field and find a piece of wreckage that would conclusively identify it as *Derbyshire*. I plotted a course through several large pieces towards the largest single piece of wreckage which I suspected might be the bow because of its shape and dimensions, and will never forget the moment the lights of Magellan illuminated the white lettering on the starboard bow: DERBYSHIRE.

Our finding of *Derbyshire* set in motion a series of events that finally brought the Derbyshire Families Association and the ITF the answers they demanded and a global focus on the appalling history of bulk carrier losses over the previous twenty years that resulted in the deaths of hundreds of seafarers. A return expedition was organised by the British Government to confirm my

Previous page: The reassembled fuselage of the wrecked Itavia DC-9.

sonar interpretation that the stern section of *Derbyshire* was also in the debris field and that the break was very close to the suspect Frame 65 area. Following on from this, a major £2 million investigation of the wreckage was conducted by the government, which wrongly concluded that crew negligence was a contributing factor in the loss.[7] This terrible injustice for the association was finally put right when the formal investigation into *Derbyshire*'s loss was reopened and after 54 days of expert testimony an Admiralty court concluded that the crew wasn't at fault after all. The true cause of the loss was the sequential collapse of *Derbyshire*'s forward three hatch covers by the large waves whipped up during the typhoon.[8] The hatch covers were exposed to the full force of the waves because *Derbyshire*'s bow was already low in the water when it became flooded as numerous ventilators were ripped away from the unprotected forecastle deck during the storm. The misalignment of Frame 65 was found not to be a factor in the loss, but there were clearly problems with the structural design of bulk carriers that are now being put right and will never be repeated as a result of the *Derbyshire* investigation. If I had to choose one aspect of my work with shipwrecks of which I am most proud, it is this.

The search for the *Hood*

An unusual thing I have noticed about being a professional shipwreck hunter is that the first question people ask after you have successfully found one ship is: 'What are you going to find next?' When the question was put to me during a transmission party for the broadcast of an award-winning documentary on the *Derbyshire* search I answered without hesitation: 'HMS *Hood*'.

In 1995, the year following our locating the *Derbyshire*, I moved to England to take up the position of Research and Search Director for Blue Water Recoveries Limited. In terms of refining my skills as a researcher and shipwreck hunter I couldn't have dreamt of a better position. Instead of searching for one big wreck every couple of years or so, I was going to have full responsibility for conducting more than a dozen searches in my first two years on the job. It was an amazingly pressure-filled but fun period, especially when we were successful. There are very few things in life that can match the sheer excitement, unbridled joy and deep satisfaction you feel when a long-lost wreck is found. Fortunately, I had a very good string of successes with Blue Water Recoveries so there were plenty of opportunities to experience those exhilarating feelings. My one personal dream, however, was for HMS *Hood* to bring out that feeling in me one more time.

After many years of false dawns the opportunity to mount a search expedition for the British battle cruiser *Hood* finally came my way. The British television broadcaster Channel 4 was keen to produce a major event program in 2001, and by being in the right place, with the right idea and at the right time, I was commissioned to search for *Hood* on the sixtieth anniversary of her famous battle with the German battleship *Bismarck*. It certainly helped that I had spent the previous six years conducting all the necessary historical research on her sinking and gaining the support of the HMS *Hood* Association, the sole living survivor Ted Briggs, the Royal Navy and other veterans' groups. For such a major investment, however, I had to virtually guarantee that some underwater footage of a shipwreck would be included in the documentary. While I couldn't guarantee that I would find *Hood*, I could guarantee that I would find the ship that sank her. *Bismarck* had already been located by Bob Ballard and his team in 1989[9] so I knew the wreck was findable as long as I did all the research work needed to define her probable sinking position. Telling the story of both combatants during the course of a single deep-water search expedition hadn't been tried before so that concept gave Channel 4 the major television event it was seeking.

I had only four months to put the entire expedition together from scratch in order to get the best of the narrow North Atlantic weather window. Fortunately,

Above: HMS Hood.

I was able to reunite with my former workmates from Eastport, now Oceaneering Technologies, and hire the Ocean Explorer sonar and Magellan ROV for the project. This expedition was different from all the others I had led in that instead of a team of investigators we had on board a documentary film team and a journalist, who in a first for British television news was going to report live from our ship by way of a special satellite-based broadcast system. We also had an ambitious plan to stream live ROV video footage directly onto the Channel 4 expedition website — something that had never been tried before.

Despite losing the first two days of the expedition to a Force 10 storm in the Bay of Biscay, the search for *Bismarck* went exactly as I had planned. With the knowledge that Ballard had found the wreck at the base of an extinct underwater volcano at a depth of 4,700 metres, I was able to locate *Bismarck*'s wreckage on the first line of search after just three hours. The footage of the wreck was also spectacularly clear and compelling. *Bismarck* may have lost her superstructure and all four of her gun turrets when she turned over as she sank but her

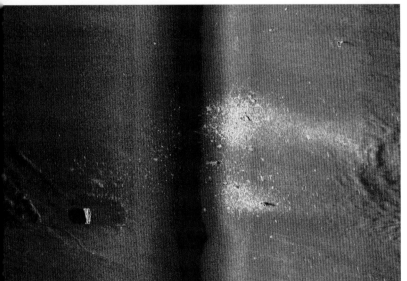

hull still retained its beautiful lines. Making the most of the gin clear water and the manoeuvrability of Magellan, we were able to show for the first time the full extent of the damage the British shells and torpedoes had inflicted on her. The gunnery of the British home fleet moving in for the kill was devastating in its intensity and accuracy. *Bismarck* never had a chance. The only question remaining was whether the end would come at the hands of the attacking quartet of British ships or would *Bismarck*'s crew seal her fate themselves with scuttling charges. The archival and physical evidence I was able to collect pointed to the former, and led me to conclude in 2001 that 'while the British guns made *Bismarck* a wreck, it was the torpedoes that sank her.'[10]

I had no illusions that finding *Hood* would be as easy as relocating *Bismarck*. I was going to be the first to attempt the search, which was going to be covered in nightly news bulletins on Channel 4, guaranteeing huge public interest in our progress. I had compiled every scrap of historical information about where the battle took place and had spent months plotting and re-plotting my navigational analysis to determine where to place my search box, which wound up encompassing 600 square nautical miles — the second largest I had ever used. I had counted on the full search taking at least eight days; however, I also had my own personal hunch about the most probable sinking position and prioritised the search tracklines to cover that area first.

One of the most exciting things about searching for shipwrecks is that you never know when a wreck will appear on your screens. The realisation that you have found your wreck can be a painfully long and drawn-out process as it was with *Derbyshire*, or it can literally happen in seconds, as it did with *Hood*. Only a handful of scan lines had scrolled down my screen before I knew I was looking at the wreck of HMS *Hood*. The search had taken a mere 39 hours. Sadly, *Hood* had been ripped apart by a magazine explosion, which left her badly broken up into several large pieces with two distinct debris fields indicating the possibility of a second magazine explosion. It hurt me to see *Hood* in such a condition but those feelings were soon replaced by the joy of knowing that she was found and that Ted Briggs, the sole living survivor from *Hood*'s crew of 1,418, would soon be on board with us to share the occasion and lay a memorial plaque on the wreck in honour of his shipmates.

Ted had always wanted to return to the site where *Hood* was lost to bid one last farewell to his friends, and it was an immense honour for me to help make his dream come true. Ted likes to say that I 'laid a ghost' in finding the wreck of his ship. Perhaps he is right. I know that for many years of his life Ted did feel burdened by his unbelievable luck in surviving *Hood*'s sinking when so many others didn't. Whatever the case, I am very proud that Ted and I were able to stand together and pay our respects to the men entombed below us in the watery grave that is forever marked with their names.

What to find next?

I didn't have another shipwreck in mind after *Hood* and *Bismarck*; such was my focus on that project it was impossible for me to look further ahead. I also knew that I would be busy for the next couple of months writing a book and advising the production company on the television documentaries that were scheduled to air at the end of 2001. Then, out of nowhere, I got an email in early November from someone in the ROV industry based in Fremantle congratulating me on finding *Hood* and suggesting that I should think about HMAS *Sydney* as my next search project. Coincidentally, my company owned a survey vessel that was scheduled to dock in Fremantle at the end of November. It was the simple matter of these two unconnected events clicking in my mind that led me to begin investigating the latest status about the ongoing search for *Sydney*.

A quick internet search turned up the 1998 Parliamentary Inquiry Report and the fact that a wreck location seminar was going to be held at the Western Australian Maritime Museum in Fremantle on 16 November. Dr David Stevens, the Director of Naval Historical Studies, was organising the seminar, so I contacted him and asked if I could help. David got back straight away and asked me a few questions about the realistic sizes of search boxes and ball park costs for such a search, which I was happy to answer.

The following week David wrote, telling me that while the seminar went well he was disappointed that there was no consensus on either the search area or methodology. David promised to send me a copy of the seminar proceedings when they were printed and that was that.

I was intrigued by what I had read in the parliamentary inquiry report and impressed that politicians in Australia were taking on the serious job of investigating *Sydney*'s loss. There were obvious parallels between the project I had just completed and the idea of mounting an expedition to find both *Kormoran* and *Sydney*. In addition to the simple fact that two ships would have to be searched for and found, it was also clear that *Sydney*, like *Hood*, was a much loved ship and the shock of her loss with all hands was deeply felt across the entire country. I thought the historical research would be interesting, especially as it would allow me to explore the battle from both the German and Australian perspectives. Most of all, however, I was attracted to the challenge of finding a wreck that many people thought could never be found. I had spent the past eleven years learning and perfecting my craft on dozens of shipwreck searches and felt I had all the skills to take on this massive challenge. Nearly six years had passed since Graeme Henderson first planted the seed of finding *Sydney* in my head, and I was beginning to believe it was time to have a go at it.

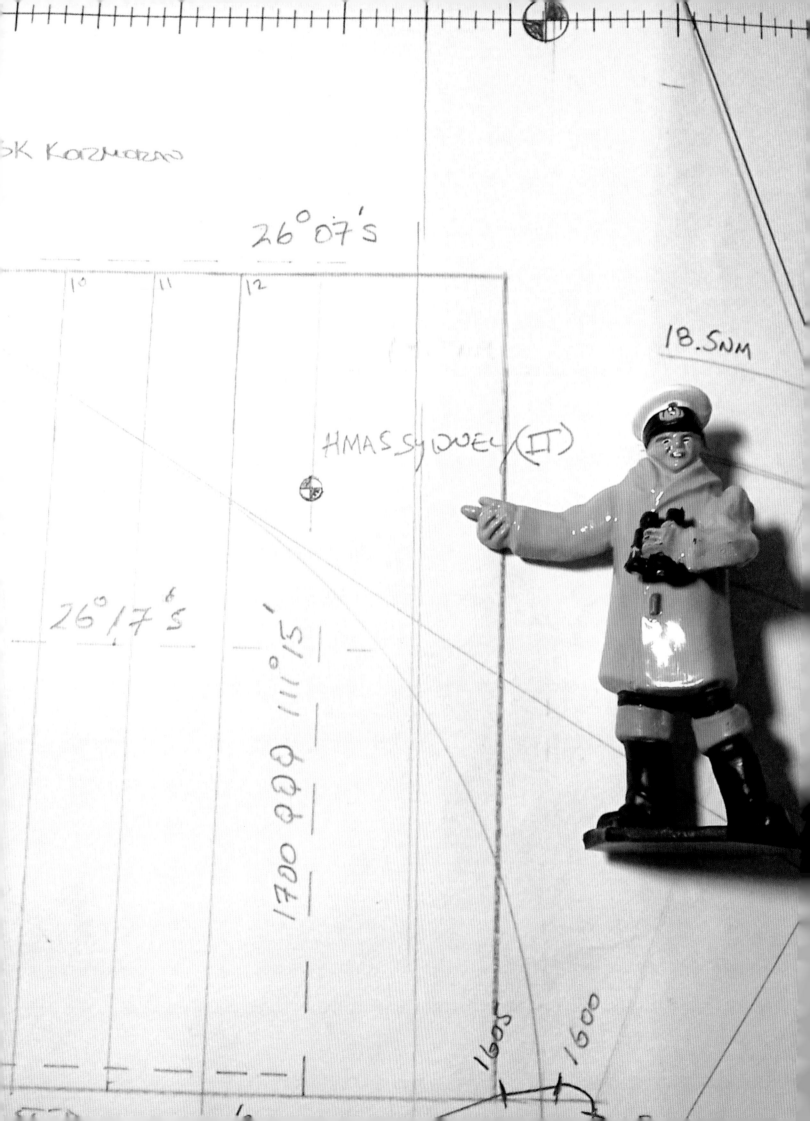

SK Karmann

26°07'S

18.5NM

HMAS SYDNEY (IT)

26°17'S

111°15'

1700 000

1700 000

SK Karmann

1605   1600

CHAPTER THREE
...

The challenge

Finding the wreck of HMAS Sydney and solving the mysteries behind her loss have been invariably described as almost impossibly difficult challenges. The reasons for this are as simple as they are tragic.

First and foremost, there is absolutely no reliable physical or historical evidence about where and when *Sydney* sank. None of the German survivors actually saw *Sydney* slip beneath the waves. Darkness had fallen, the sea conditions were worsening and they had to look to their own survival. All Detmers and the others could really say was that one moment *Sydney* could be seen blazing away on the horizon and the next moment she was gone. Whether that was because *Sydney* sank at that precise moment or because she had moved over the horizon no one knew. If it was the latter then *Sydney* could have sunk virtually anywhere and deciding where to start a search would be pure guesswork.

When *Sydney* did finally sink she apparently took with her the lives of virtually the entire ship's company. With all 645 men from *Sydney* killed there was no Australian witness to pinpoint exactly where the country's most loved naval ship went down. Only one body, found months later drifting in a damaged Carley float off Christmas Island nearly 1,000 nautical miles from where it was launched, has proven to be from *Sydney*. There has been speculation by some researchers that *Sydney* was able to send a distress or mayday signal by radio during her final moments afloat but no reliable evidence has been offered to prove this belief.

In fact, the uncertainty about the precise time that *Sydney* sank means that there was no way of knowing for sure whether the vessel went down on 19 November 1941 (the day of the battle) or sometime the following day. Given that the most basic question about *Sydney*'s loss — which day did it occur on — is unknown, it makes it easier to understand the view of an expert as esteemed as Dr Ballard, the finder of *Titanic* and *Bismarck*, who advised the RAN that it would be impossible to locate the wreck because the search area was not sufficiently defined.[1] Even Dr Michael McCarthy of the Western Australian Maritime Museum, one of the earliest and most influentially vocal supporters

Left: Our mascot, a watch-keeping officer, pointing to the charted location of Sydney's *wreck.*

of a search for *Sydney*, suggested that the probability of success was just 10 per cent.[2]

The most important opinion, however, and the one that really mattered, was that held by Vice Admiral David Shackleton, who was Australia's Chief of Navy in 2002. Following an evaluation of the proceedings of a wreck location seminar held on the sixtieth anniversary of the battle the previous November, Vice Admiral Shackleton decided that a suitable basis did not exist for an official (that is, government-sponsored) search for the wreck of *Sydney*. The problem, as made clear in the Defence statement outlining the reasons for his decision, was that 'it remains the case that there are no eyewitness accounts of *Sydney's* sinking and hence no direct evidence to provide a search datum for the wreck'. Another key factor behind the Australian Navy's lack of support for a search was the general level of disagreement among researchers.

This conclusion is based on the lack of consensus among historians and researchers as to where the wrecks might be, and hence the huge size of any potential search area. Until this area can be significantly reduced in a credible manner, I do not consider that a search can be justified, because of the low probability of success, the large costs that would be involved and the open-ended nature that any such commitment would entail.[3]

The RAN undoubtedly knew that this was going to be an unpopular decision, especially as the aim of the wreck location seminar it sponsored was to define a potential search area for the wrecks by seeking a consensus among researchers. The seminar was one of the tangible results that rose directly from the 1998 parliamentary inquiry into the loss of *Sydney*, so it was seen as a major disappointment and step backwards that it failed. Afterwards some of the participants privately speculated that this was all part of a cynical master plan of the RAN to structure the seminar in a way that it exposed and exacerbated the differences between researchers. Irrespective of the RAN's motives, a big opportunity was missed by everyone involved.

Months later, when I read a copy of the seminar proceedings sent to me by Dr David Stevens I was able to see for myself why Vice Admiral Shackleton decided against a search. Of the five formal papers presented, only two really dealt with the question of where to search for the wrecks. The opening paper by Glenys McDonald, a researcher and one-time resident of Port Gregory, Western Australia, used the oral histories of eyewitnesses living in the area to support her passionate belief that the battle, and the eventual sinking of *Sydney*, took place off the north-west coast from Port Gregory. McDonald recommended a shallow-water grid search of a very small area that incorporated her research findings. The second paper by Wes Olson, a locomotive driver and author of an important book on the loss of *Sydney*, made the case based on the archival record of documents that the German accounts were essentially accurate and that the area to be searched for *Kormoran* should be centred on the position 25°58' South 110°56' East. Olson proposed that after *Kormoran* was found the wreck of *Sydney* would be found within fifteen nautical miles away.[4]

The two papers could scarcely be more different in their methodology and widely scattered search areas. McDonald's location was in about 50 metres of water less than 30 nautical miles from the coast while Olson's location was approximately 185 nautical miles distant and much further offshore in water depths of 2,700 metres. Both papers were well presented and the authors were not alone, as others shared their opinions; however, it posed a very difficult problem for the navy and neutral observers to decide which paper was more plausible; clearly the large disagreement between them meant that only one could be right. Even a third paper by Dr John Bye, which considered the oceanographic factors involved, was unable to judge between the two. Faced with this stark choice, and the divided opinions and controversy that coursed throughout the seminar, the navy decided it could not recommend using public funds for a search that had an obviously high risk of failure.

While I initially regretted not being able to attend the seminar to lend my expertise, given the final outcome I was glad that I didn't. From my experience with the *Derbyshire* search I knew how strong the emotions could run when the public and relatives are engaged in a project

Above: Vice Admiral David Shackleton, Chief of the Navy, 2002, Wes Olson and Glenys McDonald.

like this. When Peter Lambert, aged nineteen, died along with 41 of his shipmates and two wives travelling with their husbands in the tragic loss of *Derbyshire*, his older brother Paul vowed that he would get to the bottom of the mystery behind its sinking. Putting his own life on hold for many years, Paul campaigned relentlessly for the wreck to be found and then for a formal inquiry into *Derbyshire*'s loss to be reopened. After we found *Derbyshire*'s wreckage I had to break the news to Paul that I believed that the accommodations superstructure of the ship, where his brother's body was probably entombed, was sitting in the wreckage field. This was a completely unexpected finding and I will never forget the grimace of pain, followed by shock that descended over Paul's face as he took in what I was telling him. In one sense Paul's fourteen-year fight to find his brother and reveal the cause of his death was vindicated, but in the process he gave up so much of his own life and was never able to truly let go of *Derbyshire*.

The seminar proceedings more than hinted at a strong undercurrent of acrimony and the clashing of egos that would have been a bit daunting for someone walking in unprepared. I felt that I learned two important things from the seminar and the navy's subsequent decision. The first was that the field of *Sydney* researchers was already a very crowded space and that I should expect some people would not take kindly to me elbowing my way in. The second was that the key to making any progress in the hunt for *Sydney* was that I would have to reverse the navy's thinking about the chances of finding the wreck before any prospective government support and funding could be triggered. This is exactly what I set out to do.

Searching the archives

Although a number of expertly researched books had already been published about the battle between *Sydney* and *Kormoran*, I made a conscious decision to focus my research on original primary source documents held in archives before reading other people's work. My reasoning was that I wanted to come at the problem with a completely open mind and without being swayed by someone else's conclusions or prejudices. What happened in the battle was far less important to me than where it happened. If I was to have any hope of finding the wrecks I would have to focus 100 per cent on the navigational clues about where the battle took place. I couldn't let myself get sidetracked by the dozens of other unsolved questions that dominated debate between researchers. For me, the research needed to be all about location, location, location.

Above: Peter Hore.

The documentary information that interested me most was anything which would allow me to replot the final tracks of the ships up to, during and after the battle. This included courses, speeds, ranges, bearings, positions in latitude/longitude, and any sort of observation of the wind and sea conditions. All this information had to be referenced in a common timeframe, which was a little tricky as the two ships kept time differently — *Kormoran* kept time in Zone G (GMT plus seven hours), while *Sydney* kept time in Zone H (GMT plus eight hours). It was also extremely important to me that the information was from *original* primary source documents created or based on the direct testimony of well-placed eyewitnesses. Copies, facsimiles, printed accounts or transcriptions were simply not acceptable. I was absolutely committed to this principle and would leave no stone unturned in my efforts to find the documents I felt were essential.

Before starting the research I wrote to the Chief of the Navy, Vice Admiral Chris Ritchie, to give him my views on the seminar proceedings and to offer my help on a formal basis. I told Ritchie that Wes Olson's report 'was a balanced and well-reasoned analysis of all the factual information available' and that Olson's conclusion on the most likely position for the wreck of *Kormoran* 'swings largely on the analysis that the position reported by Detmers of 26° 34' South 111° East was actually the noon time position of *Kormoran* and not the position at the time of the action or sinking'. As this analysis was of such fundamental importance to any chance of finding the wrecks I felt that every effort must be made to ensure whether it was correct, or not. The Australian archives had been scoured by researchers for years and the RAN had recently commissioned an exhaustive search of the British archives conducted by retired Royal Navy Captain Peter Hore,[5] so I agreed with Olson's recommendation for the German archives to be re-examined and offered to do this on behalf of the RAN. Ritchie's reply turning down my offer didn't surprise me as I had half expected it. I was still determined to continue with this research but at least now the Australian Navy would know my plans.

To help me plough through all the previous archival research I was very fortunate to be given a leg up by Wes Olson and Peter Hore. Both men had written excellent books on *Sydney* and were keen to help me focus on the question of the wrecks' locations. Wes started sending me the key primary source documents from Australia while Peter provided good advice on where I might unearth fresh documentary evidence about the battle. We all felt that potentially crucial documents were still to be found and analysed. Peter coined a timely phrase for this research — the search for the 'factual ground zero'. Part of our plan was also to make new translations and decodes of known German documents in order to double-check the original versions made by intelligence agencies during the war. Actually finding the wrecks on the seabed wouldn't have occurred to anyone in the 1940s so it was possible they might have overlooked or been a bit less careful with navigational clues.

At the start of 2003 I was planning my first foray into the archives. Before turning my attention to Germany I wanted to check a few items in the Naval Historical Branch in London that piqued my interest. In particular, I wanted to make sense of a reference number written on a document from the National Archives of Australia shown to me by Peter Hore. The document was an Australian intelligence memorandum on the cipher used by Captain Detmers to conceal the action report that was found on him when he briefly escaped from his prisoner of war camp in January of 1945.[6] What confused me was that I recognised the number (PG/11875/NID) as a British registration number from the preface 'PG', which stands for 'Pinched from the Germans' and which the British gave to all the documents they captured from the German Navy in April 1945.[7] So why was a British 'PG' number being used in connection with a document that originated in Australia? Was Naval Intelligence in Australia required to register confiscated documents with the 'PG' preface too, or did this indicate that the British had their own, different copy of Detmers's action report? Whatever the case I had a hunch that following this line of research would pay dividends.

An interesting side story to these documents goes back to when they were originally captured from Tambach Castle by the famous 30 Assault Unit (30 AU). The unit was created specifically to operate in advanced positions in order to swiftly capture intelligence information and operated directly under the Director of Naval Intelligence. The Germans had previously moved their naval archives, contained in some 600 medium-sized wooden crates, to the castle beginning in March 1941 where they were housed in the west wing and on the second storey.[8] The assault unit had been searching for Tambach after discovering a document listing Germany's intelligence establishments, including one they didn't know existed. Upon finally locating the correct Tambach they were astonished to find that it was a very big record depository and was staffed by no fewer than three admirals! When presented to the senior admiral, the commander of the 30 AU team asked to see the files of the cruiser *Sydney*, knowing that she had been lost under mysterious circumstances. When the complete file was produced, he knew that it was proof they had found the official German naval archive.[9] After the war Ian Fleming, the spy novelist who came up with the idea of 30 AU and was its planner, used his experiences with the unit and his colleagues there as inspiration to create the characters of James Bond and Miss Moneypenny.

I'll never forget the day I walked into the Naval Historical Branch at Great Scotland Yard to start my research. It was a cold, grey January morning made gloomier by this usually busy central London street being deserted because of building works. Normally I would be met by an archivist and taken directly to a desk to view the documents I ordered, but this time I was surprised to be ushered into the head of the Naval Historical Branch's office. My first thought was that he wanted to congratulate me on finding the wreck of HMS *Hood*, which he did do, but only after showing me something far more exciting. In the lap of the archivist sitting next to us was box file No. 274 with '*KORMORAN*' written in large black letters down its spline. The archivist began by explaining to us how this box, containing papers confiscated from nine of *Kormoran*'s crew, including Captain Detmers, during their return voyage to Germany after the war, came to be sitting in the basement for decades. It had been waiting to be catalogued before its contents could be added to the archive's open collection. The only lead to the uncatalogued box were some old notes left by a former archivist which the present archivist decided to consult when she was unable to find any documents relating to the PG/11875/NID reference number I asked her to check.

I struggled to take in her explanation but the sight of the box and the name *Kormoran* were just too tantalising for me to concentrate on anything but the prospect of finding important new information inside it. It was one of those rare moments researchers dream about when a hunch pays off and they come across fresh documents they know no one else has laid eyes on for many years. Either by fate or pure luck, I had hit the jackpot on my very first day in the archives. Despite all previous efforts to uncover every single document related to the battle between *Kormoran* and *Sydney* in official government archives, here was a box full of potentially significant information, probably unseen since 1947, which might shed new light on the events of 19 November 1941. It was an important find which delighted me, as it justified my decision to head back into the archives in our search for the 'factual ground zero'.

All the researchers I have ever spoken to can recount the moment they were hooked by the story of the loss of *Sydney* and became determined to find out what really happened. Finding these 'missing' documents was mine.

Verifying Detmers's account

When the documents I found at the Naval Historical Branch were finally made available for me and Peter Hore to study, after they were first properly catalogued, scanned and a copy provided to the RAN's own Sea Power Centre, we were delighted to find that they did indeed contain new information.[10] Most importantly, in terms of location, the documents included two new positions for *Sydney* and *Kormoran* that had never been revealed before. Both positions — one reported by stoker second class Thurow as the 'last position' of *Kormoran* at 26° South 111°21' East and the other by the shipwright second class Hartmann as the apparent sinking position of *Kormoran* at 26° South 111°40' East — provided some measure of corroboration of Detmers's testimony about where the action and sinkings took place.

Another equally remarkable document found in the box was a diagram of the battle drawn by Lieutenant Wilhelm Bunjes, one of the prize officers (whose job was to capture valuable enemy cargo to send on to Germany) on *Kormoran* who relieved Lieutenant Rudolf Jansen in the crow's-nest soon after *Sydney* was first sighted. Bunjes's hand-drawn diagram captures the entire action in four different scenes that depict the initial sighting, the pursuit by *Sydney,* the broadside fighting and launch of two torpedoes by *Kormoran,* and finally *Sydney*'s retreat while on fire and her last salvo of torpedoes fired in desperation at *Kormoran*'s stern. Bunjes's diagram of the action, by far the most detailed from the hand of a direct eyewitness, also corroborates Detmers's account right down to the Dutch flag giving way to the German battle ensign before the fight.

As exciting as these documents were, the trophy amongst them from my point of view was a new, typed account of the battle in plain German entitled *Gefechtsbericht* (Action Report) that was confiscated from Captain Detmers himself. At the time the Australian DNI was satisfied with the analysis that 'whilst no new information has resulted from research carried out on the documents they have confirmed previous information held.' Despite this view, Peter and I were excited by the prospect of now having a second account created by Detmers to compare forensically, on a character by character basis, against the coded account that had been found on Detmers during his escape more than two years earlier. The unexpected appearance of this account was an encouraging sign to me that other missing accounts might still be found.

The account I was most keen to find had only been seen by Barbara Winter in 1991 after she had already completed and published her book. It was first described to me by Wes Olson as the 'master copy of the encoded report, which was recorded in a dictionary using dots under letters'. The 'master' copy of any account is always of great interest simply because having been recorded closest to the actual event in time it generally reflects the earliest and truest memory of the author. Furthermore, if this account also proved to be written in some sort of code, as Wes implied, a reasonable assumption would be for it to be an honest account as it would stretch the imagination to believe that Detmers went to such great lengths to secretly create, and hide for many years, a false account that only he would ever see.

Via Wes, Barbara Winter provided the name of Detmers's nephew, Dr Hans-Günther Jantzen, who was living in Hamburg, whom she believed might have the dictionary, given that Detmers's widow Ursula had passed away. Armed with Barbara's tip I asked a naval friend in Hamburg if he could help locate Dr Jantzen. Everything was moving very fast but I still couldn't believe my luck when barely a fortnight after finding the box of documents at the Naval Historical Branch I was speaking with Hans Jantzen, who did indeed have his uncle's precious dictionary, with the account hidden inside; fortunately, he was happy to allow us to study it.

From my point of view the box of *Kormoran* documents was clearly important new information that needed to be thoroughly assessed in terms of its validity and accuracy, and I was hoping the RAN would agree and reconsider its decision to support our research. I fired off another letter to Vice Admiral Ritchie highlighting the new documents, the rediscovered Detmers's dictionary and the work needed to translate and independently check all these

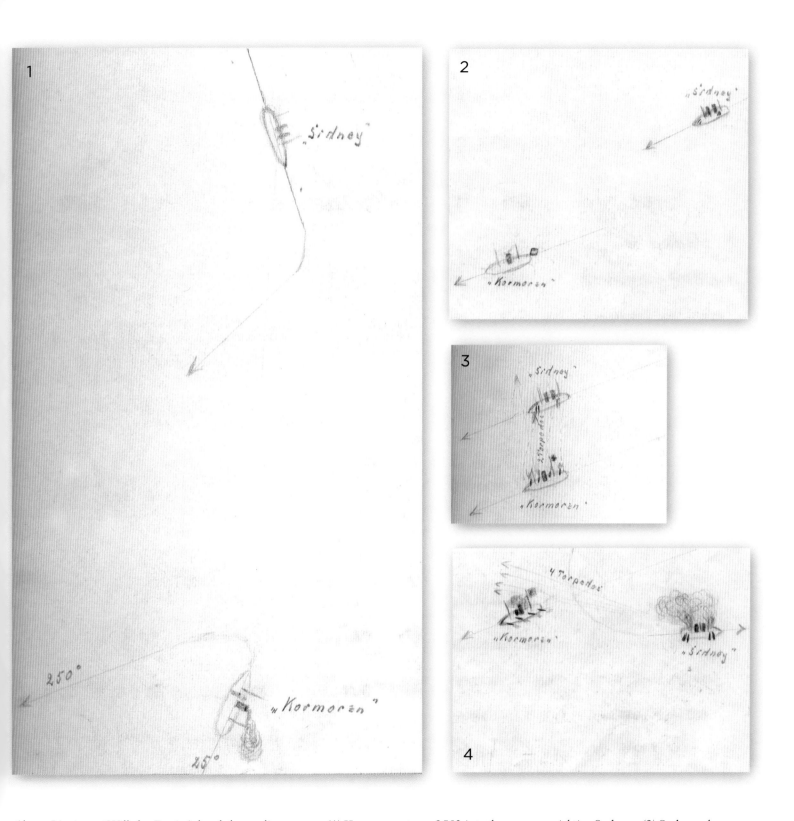

Above: Lieutenant Wilhelm Bunjes's hand-drawn diagrams — (1) Kormoran *turns 250° into the sun upon sighting* Sydney; *(2)* Sydney *chases* Kormoran, *which is showing the Dutch flag; (3)* Kormoran *raises her war flag and fires on* Sydney; *(4)* Sydney, *fatally damaged and on fire, turns behind* Kormoran *and launches torpedoes.*

documents. Ritchie's reply was polite and encouraging, but in the end other operational commitments took priority. Instead, he intended 'to have the documents translated and analysed internally to determine whether they contain any significant new evidence'.

Faced with this second RAN rejection, Peter and I continued to work on our own, with help from Wes, and began making plans to visit Hans Jantzen in Hamburg. In the meantime, Peter began developing a comparative analysis of the different Detmers's accounts and translations using advance copies of the dictionary pages Hans had sent to me, while I drafted my first plot of *Kormoran*'s dead-reckoning track from the course and speed information included in Detmers's account. My plot also included all the positions where the life rafts, lifeboats and floating debris were picked up after the battle, in addition to *Sydney*'s previous tracks through the area in June and October 1941 whilst Captain Burnett was in command and Montgomery was the navigating officer on board.[11]

Although my initial plot was preliminary and I knew that it would have to be revised many more times as new information came to light, I was able to draw a number of immediate conclusions. Firstly, that *Kormoran* would have been in the right position to have sighted *Sydney* assuming that she was following more or less the same course Burnett and Montgomery had set during her previous transits to Fremantle.[12] Secondly, that the floating debris picked up days after the battle was roughly in the right location given the prevailing winds and current in that part of the world had it entered the water near to *Kormoran*'s nominal sinking position of 26° South 111° East. Thirdly, that the cluster of positions reported by the Germans, including Detmers, wireless operator Hans Linke, the navigator Henry Meyer, Thurow and Hartmann, while not tight, did indicate a measure of agreement and corroboration that was believable. Finally, and most importantly, the detailed navigation and gunnery information provided by Detmers, when plotted, was entirely consistent with his account of the position and movement of both ships. If any single piece of this detailed interconnected information provided by

Detmers was fictitious then my plot wouldn't join up and the incorrect information would be readily apparent.

By the time May rolled round and we were able to travel to visit Hans Jantzen, Peter had discovered what Barbara Winter already knew: that the account Detmers hid in his dictionary was actually recorded in more or less plain German and was not coded as many people had mistakenly believed. The dictionary, the second volume of a German and English dictionary published by Cassell and Company in 1939, was bound in a plain cloth cover that belied the historical importance of its secret contents. One look at the two sections[13] in which the action and engine room reports are recorded told me why Detmers needn't have worried about using a cipher to hide his account. The pencil dots Detmers placed under individual letters to spell out his account were so small and slightly made they would easily escape detection by anyone not knowing where to look. To be absolutely sure about some of the dots it was necessary to hold the page up to the daylight to see the tiniest of indentations that confirmed the mark was made by Detmers's pencil point. As an American, it reminded me of the farcical scenes during the 2000 presidential election between George W. Bush and Al Gore when election officials in Florida had to inspect thousands of punch card ballots to detect the indentations, or 'dimpled chads' as they were famously called, to discern each voter's intent. Peter and I weren't electing a US president but we knew how significant one incorrect letter or digit could be in changing Detmers' account and we were determined to get it perfectly right.

The really hard work began as soon as we returned from Hamburg. Peter threw himself into 'dedotting' the dictionary account and increasing his comparative analysis to cover all three of Detmers's primary source accounts (the dictionary account; the *Gefechtsbericht* account found in the Naval Historical Branch; and the coded account found on Detmers when he escaped) and various translations. Peter hated the damned dots, which nearly drove him mad and ruined his eyes. It was painstaking work, made more difficult by the fact that although the dictionary account wasn't coded it contained numerous substitutions, abbreviations and misspellings and no punctuation or spacing to indicate when one word ended and the next began. With assistance from Hans, Peter ultimately completed a reliable English translation of the dictionary account that was a major step forward from Barbara Winter's cursory effort in 1991.

At the same time, Peter also tackled a fresh translation of the coded account, incorrectly referred to in the archives as Detmers's Diary,[14] which was originally decrypted and translated in 1945 by the Fleet Radio Unit Melbourne, a signal intelligence unit jointly operated by the RAN and US Navy. Although the actual coded account and the first page of the transcription were missing from the archives, the remaining fifteen pages of the transcribed cipher were available to be transcribed and translated anew.[15] This work revealed serious errors in the 1945 translations that appear to have misled historians for decades. For example, Detmers's observation that *Sydney* turned her Walrus aircraft engine off just before the fight began has been incorrectly translated as 'cruiser stops engines', as the translator inexplicably inserted the word 'cruiser' into the statement even though it doesn't exist in the cipher or decrypted versions. Another significant error was the addition of a zero in the range *Sydney* was seen to open out on the starboard beam from *Kormoran* at 1715 hours, which wrongly increased the distance between the ships at this critical juncture in the action from '9 hm' (900 metres) to '90 hm' (9,000 metres).[16]

Counting his book on *Kormoran*, which features several chapters on the battle with *Sydney* and its aftermath, we now knew that Detmers was directly responsible for creating four separate accounts of the action over the space of some seventeen years. By dissecting and comparing the accounts we were able to reasonably conclude the correct chronology of their creation. It was our opinion that the original, or master account, was the one hidden by Detmers in the dictionary and probably created by him in early 1942, not long after he arrived at the Murchison prisoner of war camp in Victoria.[17] It was the shortest account of the four and contained mistakes suggesting that it was created quickly. The coded account would have been made next, prior to Detmers's escape in

Above: Dr Hans Gunther Jantzen, Detmers's nephew, with his uncle's dictionary in Hamburg, and (bottom) the grave of Theodor Detmers and his wife.

January 1945, while the *Gefechtsbericht* account appears to have been typed on a German typewriter after Detmers was moved to the Tatura camp in November 1945. Each successive account, ending with his book published in 1959, included a bit more detail to round out the story but they were all essentially identical with regards to the common navigation and battle information they contained.

Although other researchers disagreed with me, I was very impressed by the consistency of Detmers's accounts despite the fact they were created under very

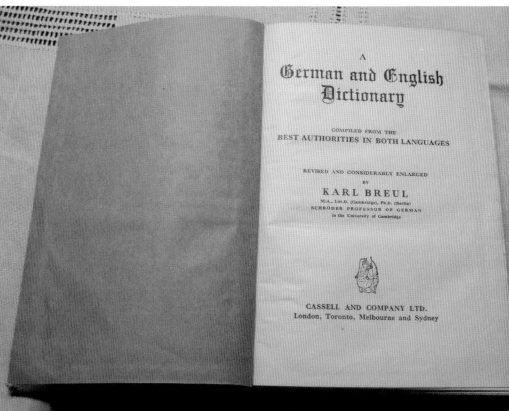

𝕭

𝕭, 𝕭, B, b; B-flat (*Mus.*); *a mark depressing the note before which it is placed a semitone lower (b-flat)*; das Quadrat 𝕭, or 𝕭-Quadrat, *a mark* (♮) *rendering the note to which it is prefixed natural*; das Stück geht aus —moll, —dur, *the piece is in the key of B-flat minor, in the key of B-flat major*; *for abbreviations see Index at the end of the German-English part.*

𝕭

𝕭, 𝕭, B, b; B-flat (*Mus.*); *a mark depressing the note before which it is placed a semitone lower (b-flat)*; das Quadrat 𝕭, or 𝕭-Quadrat, *a mark* (♮) *rendering the note to which it is prefixed natural*; das Stück geht aus —moll, —dur, *the piece is in the key of B-flat minor, in the key of B-flat major*; *for abbreviations see Index at the end of the German-English part.*

Above top: Theodor Detmers's dictionary; bottom: (l) Detmers's hidden account spelt out with pencil dots under letters, and (r) the relevant letters marked in red.

different circumstances over such a relatively long time span. I felt this spoke volumes about Detmers's credibility, in particular with regards to his testimony about how the battle was conducted and where it took place. As a shipwreck hunter it was enormously important to me that the position recorded by Detmers in each of his personal accounts (26°34' South 111° East) never varied. There was still a lot of work to do to try to determine whether that position referred to *Kormoran*'s noon position or the action position, but I firmly believed that Detmers's account could be trusted and was a true version of what

really happened. Certainly all the documentary evidence was stacking up that way. In my mind, Detmers had taken extraordinary measures to keep these accounts hidden from his captors and had absolutely nothing to gain from holding onto a fictitious account. I also felt that there was no logical reason or motivation for Detmers to knowingly lie about the position where the action took place.

Any lingering doubts I might have had about Detmers's account were completely washed away after reading the official German version of the battle, known as *Book 10 — The Voyage of the Auxiliary Cruiser Ship 41*.[18] This 'most secret' history was put together by the German Navy in December 1943 and the section on the battle is based largely on the account relayed by Dr Siebelt Habben, one of two doctors on board *Kormoran* who was repatriated to

Germany sometime after May 1943 as part of a prisoner exchange scheme. Habben, who was working below decks in the first-aid room treating injured seamen, was not an eyewitness to the battle and thus in no position to be the primary source of the considerable amount of detailed information included in *Book 10*. Clearly, the primary source was not Habben, but Detmers, and he was using Habben as a messenger to deliver his action report to his superiors in the German Navy at the time when the historical context suggested Detmers had no reason to make anything up, as explained by Peter Hore.[19]

> *Since it was written for internal consumption and at a time when many Germans still believed that they were winning the war, there would seem to be no reason to lie or fabricate within Volume 10, which may therefore be considered a reliable witness of the events which it describes.*[20]

The occurrence of the *Book 10* account was proof of Detmers's absolute determination to fulfil his final obligation as commander of *Kormoran* and report the loss of his own ship. Unsurprisingly, this account was identical in all important details with the other four accounts we know Detmers wrote. While some researchers continued to doubt the veracity of Detmers it was impossible for them to base their opinions on any inconsistency in his accounts, as none existed. If consistency was one of the tests upon which Detmers's truthfulness was to be judged then in my opinion he was passing with flying colours.

Convincing Australia

Having completed my initial research and analysis into the most probable sinking positions for *Kormoran* and *Sydney* I decided it was time to fire off another letter to Vice Admiral Ritchie. There was no request for funds this time. This was a detailed letter that explained the key findings and conclusions I had made, with the help of Peter and Wes, over the past year, culminating with my definition of two search boxes for the wrecks. In addition

to the archival research, my summary, which ran to five pages, also spoke about an initial drift analysis on the life raft recovered by the troopship *Aquitania*, which was consistent with *Kormoran* sinking in the general area of the German positions.

At the same time I also issued a press release on the sixty-second anniversary of the battle that announced the unearthing of the new archival documents pointing to the location of the wrecks and called upon the RAN to reconsider its decision not to support a search for *Sydney*. I was publically throwing my hat into the ring by voicing my professional opinion that the wrecks could be found and my desire to be the person to lead the search for them.

> *After a year of concentrated research and analysis I am now 100 per cent certain that the battle took place in a northern location near to the position originally reported by the German survivors. More importantly, we have been able to significantly reduce the size of the search area to the extent that mounting a search is now technically and economically feasible. Based upon the new information I was very fortunate to find, I believe that the probability of success for finding KORMORAN is now of the order of 80 per cent to 90 per cent, and only slightly lower for finding SYDNEY. We can finally offer some real hope to the relatives of SYDNEY's crew that the wreck can be found and marked as a war grave to be honoured and protected.*

The following month our paper on the comparative analysis of the various Detmers accounts was published in the *Australian Navy History Review*. Peter purposely opted for a bold title: 'HMAS *Sydney* — an end to the controversy', but I don't think he really believed that this one paper would end a controversy that had been simmering for decades and was beginning to show signs of boiling over. Because of the recent press coverage, more and more researchers were learning about my work and a number were strongly opposed to the faith I was placing in Detmers and his account. Wes Olson warned me from the start that the atmosphere between rival researchers was not good and that I should expect my views to be strenuously challenged. I certainly didn't mind having to defend my conclusions to other researchers but the last thing I wanted was to engage in petty arguments or turf wars. So I decided to adopt a simple policy in dealing with others. I would entertain ideas and questions from anyone so long as the discourse was friendly and collegial, but in the end I would make up my own mind about what to believe.

Michael Montgomery (the son of Sydney's navigator) and Warren Whittaker were the first to make contact with me in August 2002. Michael's views of Detmers were already well known. In short, he thought that Detmers was not to be trusted, that his account was duplicitous and that he ordered all his men to tell the same deceitful story when interrogated. Despite the fact that we had polar opposite views on Detmers, Michael was always very helpful and generously shared his research and thoughts with me. I later learned that Michael was sent copies of some of the Kormoran Box 274 documents by the Naval Historical Branch in 1991, twelve years before I 'rediscovered' them.[21] Unfortunately, this did not include the Thurow or Hartmann papers and Michael discounted the action diagram drawn by Bunjes because he believed that Bunjes was acting as the appointed 'survivors' spokesman' with the clear implication that he was promulgating Detmers's deceit. For obvious reasons Michael also ignored Detmers's Gefechtsbericht account.

In the end the one account that Michael effectively passed on to other researchers in Australia, by sending a copy to the Western Australia Maritime Museum, was the eight-page handwritten diary by wireless officer Reinhold von Malapert. Malapert's papers, which were most certainly written after the event, included his daily account of their five-day lifeboat journey complete with courses, wind conditions and distance travelled. On the face of it, this information looked like it could be used to confirm the sinking location of Kormoran by reverse calculation of the lifeboat's daily progress from its landing point on the beach at Red Bluff, north of Carnarvon, backwards to where the boats left Kormoran.[22] This

methodology of backtracking an object's journey through water, whether by sail or passive drift, has proved successful in pinpointing the sinking position of shipwrecks in the past. I had used this method to help define the search box that led me to finding HMS Hood, so I could understand how Malapert's lifeboat diary was seized upon as possibly the missing clue to where the wrecks sank. Unfortunately, in this case, I believed that people were badly mistaken.

The fundamental problem wasn't the methodology: it was the imprecision and incompleteness of Malapert's navigation information, together with a lack of reliable information about the prevailing wind and sea conditions, which made it absolutely impossible for anyone to pinpoint Kormoran's sinking position with even the slightest degree of accuracy. Because there was far more that was unknown about the lifeboat journey than was known, researchers were free to come up with their own set of assumptions to fill in the blank spots in Malapert's diary and to make guesses about important factors such as current speed and direction. Naturally, there was no consensus of opinion and the range of different positions was enormous. It appeared to me that this subject, more than any other, dominated the debate among researchers and led to a fragmentation of opinion which contributed to the failure of the 2001 symposium.

The list of researchers boasting an array of professional qualifications and life experience that tried to tackle this impossible problem was impressive. It included Commander Reg Hardstaff, the former Deputy Hydrographer of the RAN; Mr Sam Hughes, a search and rescue expert from the Australian Maritime Safety Authority; Dr Kim Kirsner, a professor of psychology from the University of Western Australia; Fugro Survey Pty Ltd, a professional hydrographic survey company; Ean McDonald, a former lieutenant commander who actually served as a signalman on Sydney up until 1939; former Lieutenant Colonel Warren Whittaker, OBE,

Right: My initial renavigation plot of Kormoran *and* Sydney's *tracks, as published in 2003, superimposed against the final search boxes.*

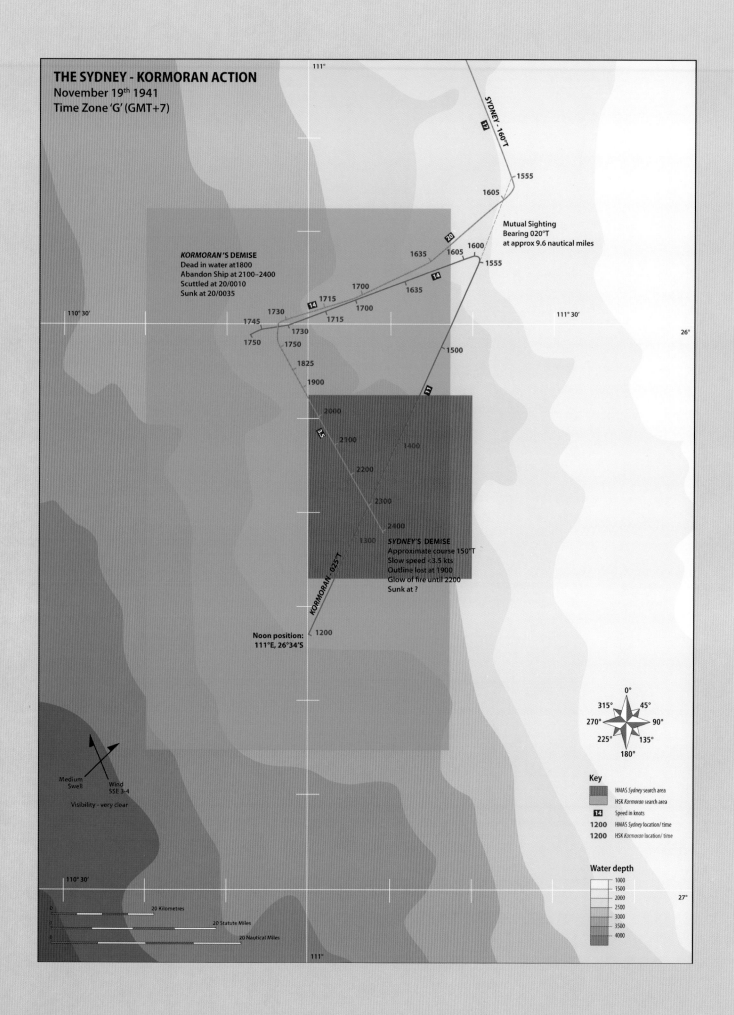

THE SYDNEY - KORMORAN ACTION
November 19th 1941
Time Zone 'G' (GMT+7)

SYDNEY - 160°T

— 1555
1605 —

Mutual Sighting
Bearing 020°T
at approx 9.6 nautical miles

KORMORAN'S DEMISE
Dead in water at1800
Abandon Ship at 2100–2400
Scuttled at 20/0010
Sunk at 20/0035

1635
1605
1600
1555

1635
1700
1715
1745
1730
1730
1750
1750
1715
1700
1825
1900

1500

2000
2100
2200
2300
2400
1300

1400

KORMORAN - 025°T

SYDNEY'S DEMISE
Approximate course 150°T
Slow speed <3.5 kts
Outline lost at 1900
Glow of fire until 2200
Sunk at ?

Noon position:
111°E, 26°34'S

1200

Medium
Swell
Wind
SSE 3-4

Visibility - very clear

0°
315°   45°
270°   90°
225°   135°
180°

Key

	HMAS *Sydney* search area
	HSK *Kormoran* search area
14	Speed in knots
1200	HMAS *Sydney* location/ time
1200	HSK *Kormoran* location/ time

Water depth
1000
1500
2000
2500
3000
3500
4000

0   20 Kilometres
0   20 Statute Miles
0   20 Nautical Miles

Above: A page from Reinhold von Malapert's eight-page diary.

who had devoted many years of his life trying to find *Sydney*; and Lieutenant Commander David McDonald (son of Glenys McDonald), a sub-specialist navigation and surface warfare officer who was one of the RAN's senior navigation instructors. I disliked pouring cold water on the work of so many well-intentioned people, but my honest opinion was that this line of research was a complete red herring and was leading people to believe that the route of Malapert's lifeboat was a reliable and scientifically sound basis for determining where to search for the wrecks.

One of the most vocal and persistent proponents of using the Malapert lifeboat journey to pinpoint the wreck locations was Warren Whittaker, an octogenarian navigator who had created his own website (no longer available on the internet) to spread his unwavering belief that the battle took place just seaward of the Abrolhos Islands, west of Geraldton. Although his favoured spot was some 200 nautical miles south-east of the nominal German position (26°South 111°East), Warren had a band of supporters, including Ean McDonald, who argued long and hard with him that any prospective search should be conducted at a group of positions that became popularly known at the 'southern location'. The difference between other researchers and Warren was that while everyone else was hoping to find *Kormoran* and *Sydney* where their research indicated, Warren and his friend, the late Lindsay Knight, had actually conducted a search from an aeroplane and believed that they had already found *Kormoran* and probably found *Sydney* as well. The only problems were that Warren and Lindsay had no proof of this nor could they explain the scientific principles behind the seemingly magic black-box device they used to supposedly make these miraculous discoveries.[23] That didn't deter Warren, however, who despite his advancing age was fond of sending repeated emails that he had irrefutable evidence that the battle took place off the Abrolhos and that it was *impossible* for the Germans' positions to be correct.

Warren and his supporters were dead-set on ensuring that public and government attention was drawn to the southern location even at the cost of trying to derail growing support for a search at the northern location. The debate had become polarised between the southern and northern locations, and the often bitter argument threatened any chance of getting a search under way. It was a classic stalemate that was getting a full airing in the press. Like other researchers, Warren used the Malapert lifeboat journey to support his case but it was obvious to me that, unknowingly or not, the set of assumptions he was using were incorrectly skewing the results in favour of the southern location. Because all the other researchers were free to make their own assumptions it was very difficult for anyone to make the case that Warren was wrong and their solution was right. Even the RAN's Sea Power Centre was drawn into the debate when, at Warren's urging, Vice Admiral Ritchie agreed for the centre to establish a workshop made up of four RAN experts to evaluate Warren's theory and to come up with their own backtrack solution to where the lifeboat journey began.[24]

Not surprisingly, the RAN experts came up with yet another novel position for the lifeboat journey starting point (that is, where *Kormoran* sank) located between Detmers's position and Warren's southern position. This only proved my point that every new attempt at this analysis yielded another new position that was different from previous ones. I was pleased, however, that at least the centre independently reinforced my view in their letter to Warren:

> *However, given the limited and contradictory data that led to the requirement for pre-analysis assumptions, the actual position of the battle cannot be narrowed sufficiently to confidently suggest the resting place of the KORMORAN wreck. No matter how precisely the available data is analysed the data will always be imprecise due to the gaps in available knowledge. There will also always be endless alternative interpretations for a variety of potential influences; some are unknowable and most are certainly unverifiable. Were a different set of assumptions to be used a different starting point for the lifeboat voyage could be attained. For these reasons neither Detmers's position nor your position can be definitively ruled out at this time.*

No matter how hard I tried to counter each of Warren's arguments in the flood of emails he sent me, I knew he wasn't going to change his unshakable stance, and neither was I about to change mine. The only redeeming aspect of our otherwise futile debate was that it was conducted in a friendly manner entirely without rancour.

Fortunately, neither Warren nor Ean nor any of the other researchers who were vehemently opposed to my plans were the people I had to convince I knew where the wrecks were and how to find them. My task was to convince Vice Admiral Ritchie, and despite the fact that I had already struck out twice with him, I was cautiously optimistic that my latest letter and research summary would turn him around. A couple of months passed by, but then the reply I was hoping for finally arrived in late January 2004. Ritchie started by congratulating me on my persistence and he agreed that I had found some interesting information. More importantly, he indicated a willingness to reconsider the RAN's position on supporting a search for *Sydney*, although he stopped short of offering direct financial assistance. His letter also made it clear that he considered it advantageous for the various interested parties who were beginning to plan search operations to be seen to be cooperating.

At last I had made a real breakthrough with the RAN, although I knew there was a lot more work to do to completely convince Ritchie. His letter was very important because it was a crystal-clear indication that the RAN was not looking to hide from the *Sydney* issue as other people suspected. This was exactly the encouragement I needed to plough on with my research and analysis in the face of the stiff opposition I began to experience from other Australian researchers. I didn't think it was possible to get an expedition under way in 2004, but perhaps this would be the year that a search for *Sydney* would finally get the green light the relatives and public longed for.

Unseren gefallenen Kameraden zum Gedenken- der tapferen Besatzung von „H.M.A.S.Sydney" in ehrender Erinnerung!
Die überlebenden Besatzungsangehörigen des deutschen „Hilfskreuzers Kormoran" Hamburg, 19. November 1991

CHAPTER FOUR

...

Meeting Ted Graham

When Vice Admiral Ritchie mentioned in his last letter to me that he wanted the various parties interested in organising a search for *Sydney* to be seen to be cooperating I knew precisely with whom he wanted me to be working. HMAS *Sydney* Search Pty Ltd (HMA3S) was a not-for-profit Perth-based company that was set up in February 2001 by Ted Graham, Dr Don Pridmore and Dr Kim Kirsner with the sole objective of finding the wreck of *Sydney* and commemorating its crew. The three founding directors had no personal connection to the RAN, *Sydney* or its crew; however, they all had been drawn to the story and tragedy of *Sydney*'s loss and had the right type of skills between them to mount a search for the wreck.

HMA3S wasn't the first company set up to find *Sydney*. Two previous companies collapsed after failing to make any headway;[1] however, the common element in all three was Ted Graham, a determined businessman who spoke and dealt with people in a blunt, straight-to-the-point manner made even more forceful by his large physical presence. Ted can trace his interest in *Sydney* back to the early 1980s by way of an unsuccessful search for another of Australia's missing ships: the SS *Koombana*. It was his background in marine survey and long service as a senior manager with Fugro Survey, one of the world's leading marine survey and geotechnical companies, which gave him the requisite practical understanding about how to conduct a deep-water shipwreck search. However, it was Ted's God-given drive that would be most crucial in seeing *Sydney* found.

Ted's co-founding directors also had a long-term interest in finding *Sydney* and brought vital skills to the table. Don Pridmore has a PhD in geophysics and was the director of an airborne magnetic survey company involved in the investigation of suspect magnetic anomalies off the Western Australian coast in the mid-1990s. Kim Kirsner was a naval history buff who became fascinated with the subject after reading Montgomery's and Winter's books. Along with Dr Michael McCarthy of the Western Australian Maritime Museum, he organised the first forum of researchers held at the museum in 1991 on the fiftieth anniversary of *Sydney*'s loss. Kim's background as a cognitive scientist gave him an

Left: A 1991 drawing in memory of Kormoran *crew killed in action, from the survivors.*

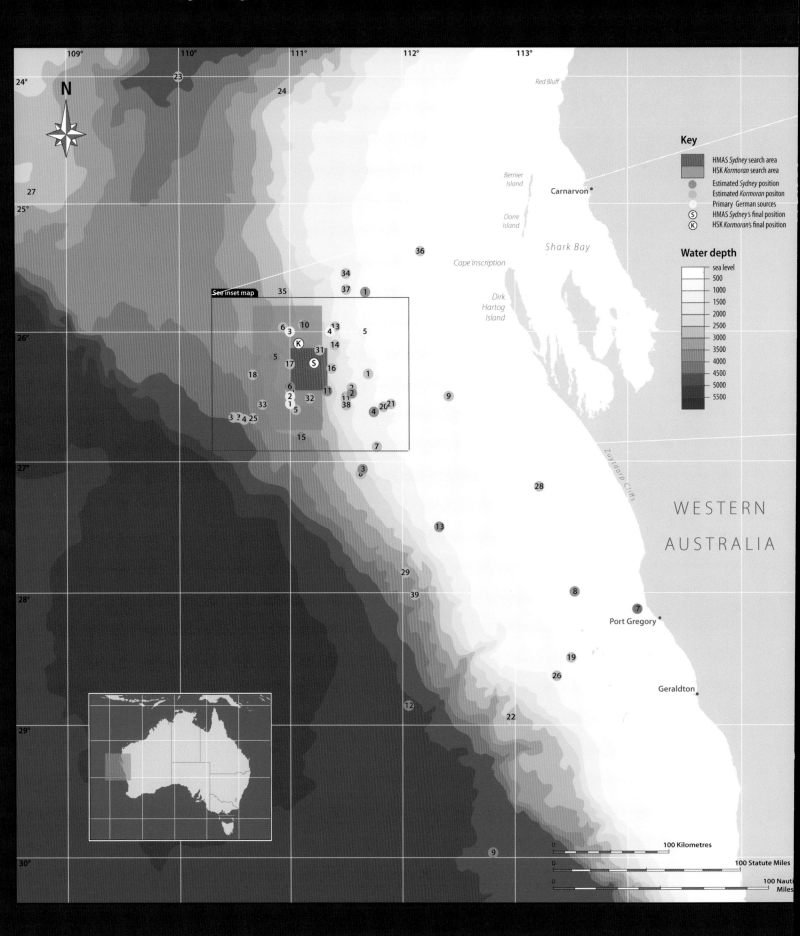

The possible locations of HMAS *Sydney* and HSK *Kormoran*

Key

- HMAS *Sydney* search area
- HSK *Kormoran* search area
- Estimated *Sydney* position
- Estimated *Kormoran* positon
- Primary German sources
- Ⓢ HMAS *Sydney*'s final position
- Ⓚ HSK *Kormoran*'s final position

Water depth

- sea level
- 500
- 1000
- 1500
- 2000
- 2500
- 3000
- 3500
- 4000
- 4500
- 5000
- 5500

Red Bluff

Bernier Island

Carnarvon

Dorre Island

Shark Bay

Cape Inscription

Dirk Hartog Island

Zuytdorp Cliffs

WESTERN AUSTRALIA

Port Gregory

Geraldton

See inset map

100 Kilometres

100 Statute Miles

100 Nauti Miles

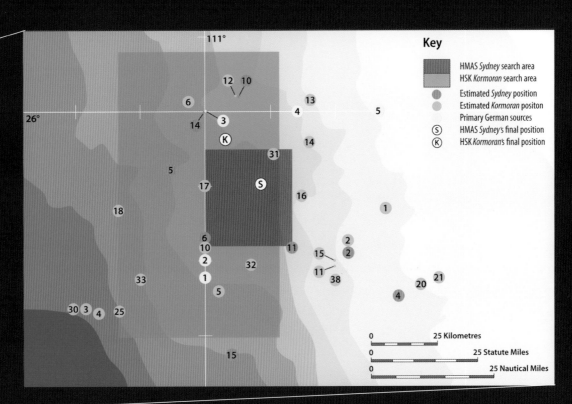

Key

- HMAS *Sydney* search area
- HSK *Kormoran* search area
- Estimated *Sydney* position
- Estimated *Kormoran* positon
- Primary German sources
- Ⓢ HMAS *Sydney*'s final position
- Ⓚ HSK *Kormoran*'s final position

0 — 25 Kilometres
0 — 25 Statute Miles
0 — 25 Nautical Miles

Estimated Positions of HMAS *Sydney*

#	Source	Lat	Long
1	Bathgate, G.	25°46′S	111°40′E
2	Hardstaff, R. (a)	26°28.4′S	111°32.6′E
3	Hardstaff, R. (b)	27°06′S	111°38′E
4	Laffer, G. & Hardstaff, R.	26°37′S	111°45′E
5	Kirsner, K. & Hughes, S.	26°12′S	110°52′E
6	Kirsner, K. & Dunn, J.	26°25′S	111°00′E
7	McDonald, G. (a)	28°08′S	114°05′E
8	McDonald, G. (b)	28°00′S	113°32′E
9	Whittaker, W. & Knight, L. (KDLS1)	29°58.5′S	112°48.3′E
10	Jackson, G. & Francis, J.	25°57′S	111°07′E
11	Brown, N., et al.	26°27.5′S	111°23.8′E
12	Brown, N., et al.	28°52.0′S	112°03.4′E
13	Montagu, J.	27°30′S	112°20′E
14	O'Sullivan, B.	26°00′S	111°00′E
15	Templeton, A.	26°49′S	111°06′E

Estimated Positions of HSK *Kormoran*

#	Source	Lat	Long
1	Fugro Survey Pty Ltd (a)	26°19.6′S	111°41.8′E
2	Fugro Survey Pty Ltd (b)	26°26′S	111°33′E
3	Gill, G.H.	26°40′S	110°32′E
4	Olson, W. (a)	26°41′S	110°35.5′E
5	Olson, W. (b)	26°36′S	111°03′E
6	Olson, W., et al.	25°58′S	110°56′E
7	Hardstaff, R. (a)	26°38.7′S	111°41.9′E
8	Hardstaff, R. (b)	26°53.4′S	111°46.3′E
9	Hughes, S. (a)	26°30′S	112°25′E
10	Hughes, S. (b)	26°30′S	111°00′E
11	Hughes, S. (c)	26°31′S	111°30′E
12	Kirsner, K. (a)	25°57′S	111°09′E
13	Kirsner, K. (b)	25°58′S	111°24′E
14	Kirsner, K. (c)	26°06′S	111°24′E
15	Kirsner, K. (d)	26°30′S	111°30′E
16	Kirsner, K. & Hughes, S.	26°17′S	111°22′E
17	Kirsner, K. & Dunn, J.	26°15′S	111°00′E
18	Dunn, J. & Kirsner, K.	26°20′S	110°40′E
19	Bye, J.	28°30′S	113°30′E
20	Laffer, G.	26°35′S	111°50′E
21	Laffer, G. & Hardstaff, R.	26°34′S	111°54′E
22	McDonald, E.	28°57′S	112°58′E
23	Montagu, J. (a)	24°00′S	110°00′E
24	Montagu, J. (b)	24°07′S	110°56′E
25	McCormack, M. & Steedman, R.	26°40′S	110°40′E
26	Whittaker, W. & Knight, L. (KDLS3)	28°38.2′S	113°22.2′E
27	Eagles, J.	24°54′S	108°42′E
28	King, D.	27°11.7′S	113°12.9′E
29	McDonald, D.	27°51.5′S	112°01.5′E
30	Penrose, J. & Klaka, K.	26°40′S	110°30′E
31	Brown, N., et al. (a)	26°10.6′S	111°14.8′E
32	Brown, N., et al. (b)	26°30.9′S	111°10.3′E
33	McLennan, B.	26°34′S	110°45′E
34	Bathgate, G.	25°33′S	111°30′E
35	O'Sullivan, B.	25°41′S	110°56′E
36	Barker, M.	25°22′S	112°10′E
37	Shepherd, P.	25°40′S	111°30′E
38	Templeton, A.	26°34′S	111°30′E
39	RAN SPC Workshop	28°01.5′S	112°06.5′E

Primary German Sources

#	Source	Lat	Long
1	Detmers, T.	26°34′S	111°E
2	Meyer, H.	26°30′S	111°E
3	Linke, H., et al.	26°S	111°E
4	Thurow, W.	26°S	111°21′E
5	Hartmann, E.	26°S	111°40′E

Final Wreck Sinking Positions

	Source	Lat	Long
Ⓚ	HSK *Kormoran*	26°05′46″S	111°04′33″E
Ⓢ	HMAS *Sydney*	26°14′31″S	111°12′48″E

Adapted from lists compiled by the late Cmdr R. J. Hardstaff

interesting insight into the testimony of the *Kormoran* survivors based on how their memories were affected by the passing of time.

Within days of my name first being connected with a search for *Sydney* in August 2002, Ted was in touch by email to introduce himself and HMA3S and to express his interest in working together. Nine months later, a very weary Ted Graham dropped into my office during a brief layover in London to discuss the basis upon which we could join forces on the project. While the meeting was short owing to Ted's extreme jet lag, it was clear that we shared the same philosophy on some key issues, including that the wrecks, if found, were not to be disturbed and that any investigation of them would occur on the same 'look but don't touch' basis we adopted for the filming of *Hood* and *Bismarck*.

Although lost and shipwrecked for more than 60 years *Sydney* and *Kormoran* remain the property of the Australian and German governments and are afforded special protection under international maritime law to prevent unauthorised disturbance. We also had a very strong moral obligation to respect the grave site of so many men.

It was also very important to Ted that the search was seen to be operating under the umbrella of HMA3S as an Australian venture, rather than as a project conducted by foreign interests. So long as everyone involved was suitably qualified, I had no problem with this as I, or Blue Water Recoveries, was not about to run such a complex and high-profile project from the other side of the world. We decided to continue exploring a working arrangement but that it was best for me to remain independent from HMA3S.

The lifeboat conundrum

After I publicly announced the finding of the *Kormoran* documents and Peter's and my paper was published in the December 2003 issue of *Australian Naval History Review*, the

Above: Ted Graham.

debate among a handful of researchers went into overdrive. What started as a trickle of emails from Australia soon turned into a flood and I found myself spending the first two to three hours each day composing lengthy replies to defend our work. It was an eye-opening experience for me which revealed the passion the subject generated and the long-held beliefs people had about where the battle actually took place. The debate largely centred on whether Detmers was a liar, or not, and where the wrecks would be found. Warren Whittaker and Ean McDonald were leading the charge for the southern location, while Kim Kirsner and I were defending the northern location and the journalist David Kennedy was acting as *agent provocateur*. The exchanges were argumentative but friendly and I felt it was a good test for me to have to respond to other researchers' questioning, especially as in their eyes I was still the new kid on the block. There was clearly some resentment, however, from both sides of the debate that I hadn't 'paid my dues' with respect to the relatively short time I had spent researching the subject, but I wasn't going to allow this to bother me. Regardless of whether I had spent one year researching, or decades like some of them had, I knew that Peter and I were making an important historical contribution that deserved everyone's attention.

The debate was also livened up by a paper written by Lieutenant Commander David McDonald, RAN, the son of Glenys McDonald, who asked him to specifically look into the journey of the Malapert lifeboat to see if he could determine its starting point. At first glance David's paper was a navigational *tour de force* consistent with his impressive CV, which included stints as navigation officer in five RAN ships and being a senior navigation instructor and officer-in-charge of a RAN navigation faculty. It was an extraordinarily detailed work of more than 12,000 words and packed with two dozen tables and charts.[2] I was hard pressed to remember seeing a more professionally executed navigational analysis and there

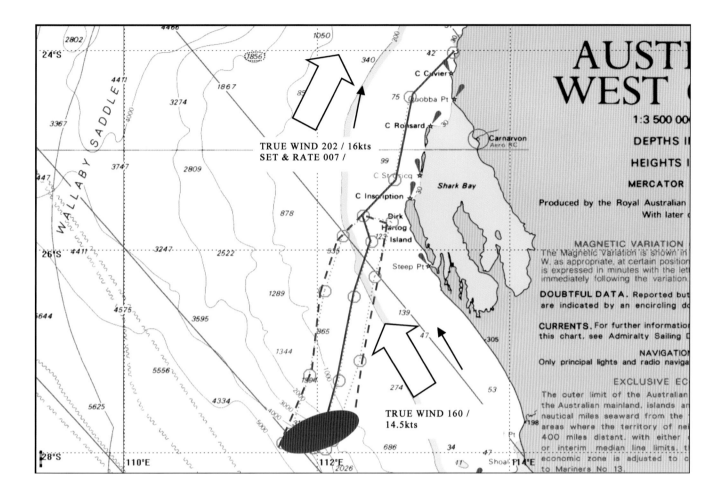

TRUE WIND 202 / 16kts
SET & RATE 007 /

TRUE WIND 160 /
14.5kts

Above: David McDonald's estimate of lifeboat drift suggested a sinking position for Kormoran *north-west from Port Gregory.*

was no doubt that David's effort was the best attempt at trying to solve this problem. However, despite David's hard work, the problem, in my opinion, was still impossible to solve because of all the unknowns, and David's solution was in fact no more accurate than any other.

I couldn't understand this long, and frankly futile, preoccupation with trying to retrace the course of the Malapert lifeboat, and asked David to instead look at the drift of the life raft loaded with 26 Germans that was recovered by the troopship *Aquitania* 82 hours after it left *Kormoran*. This life raft, and to a lesser extent the life raft loaded with 25 men recovered by *Trocas* the following day, was an infinitely better object for this type of analysis because it had no oars, rudder or functional sails and thus its voyage was purely a function of drift due to winds and currents, making it much simpler to estimate. A

second important advantage was that they were the first objects to be recovered after the battle. Because errors inherent in the estimating process compound with time, it is imperative to use the object that was drifting in the water for the shortest overall period. The clear suggestion here is that the Malapert lifeboat, which was at sea for approximately two days longer than the *Aquitania* life raft, is not the ideal object to use for such an analysis. Finally, both life rafts were picked up at sea by Australian vessels that were able to reliably report their position and time, thus eliminating any additional uncertainty.

My own initial estimate of the drift speed for these life rafts, taking into account their extreme loading and vulnerability in the rough open ocean, was roughly 1 knot. The life raft recovered by *Aquitania* would therefore have drifted north about 82 nautical miles during the 82 hours it was in the water after leaving *Kormoran*. My estimate was based on the same methodology developed by the US Coast Guard search and recovery planners that I

Above: Kormoran *crew cooling off in a make-shift pool that was once the hatch to cargo hold No. 3.*

had used a number of times in the past to locate other shipwrecks, including HMS *Hood*.[3] I knew that this was a much safer way of trying to backtrack to the sinking location of *Kormoran*, but I also knew that it still involved a fair amount of guesswork and at best might only help in deciding which of several possible locations was the most probable. Given what I considered to be our poor knowledge of the wind and current conditions after the battle, I believed that the error in any backtrack solution could be as great as plus or minus 25 nautical miles.

I was looking forward to receiving David's second paper, which he was preparing in response to my extensive comments on his first. His first attempt at a sinking position for *Kormoran* based on tracing the course of the lifeboat placed it at 28°15' South 112° 05' East, or 124 nautical miles south of the nominal German position. This implied an average drift speed for the *Aquitania* life raft of 2.5 knots, which I knew was much too fast. It would have taken gale-force winds on some days to push the life raft this fast and the resulting four- to five-metre seas would have surely caused the raft to come to grief, along with its 26 occupants who we all know survived in remarkably good condition. I expected that by asking David to focus on the *Aquitania* life raft it would lead him to a more realistic conclusion but

his revised position of 27°51.5' South 112° 01.5' East was another 24 nautical miles further south of his initial estimate! From this position the average speed of the *Aquitania* life raft would need to be 2.8 knots, meaning it would have had to cover an incredible 67 nautical miles per day, as the crow flies, for more than three and a half days in a row in order for David's estimate to be right.

I was dismayed by his conclusions and feared that this would be latched on to by someone in the RAN or government as yet another example of a lack of consensus among researchers. David had impressive credentials as a navigation specialist in the RAN so I was in no doubt that his paper and final conclusion would be taken seriously. He wrote:

I am even surer of the veracity of my proposed area of probability than I was with the last paper and am convinced that I have demonstrated that there is enough weight to this theory to give it the same level of credibility as a position based on the testimony of German survivors. To that end, I would recommend that the best approach to finally solving this mystery will be to search both probability areas — whilst the costs may be prohibitive, a search of one area only will not do the debate any justice.

Glenys McDonald was pleased with her son's work for obvious reasons. It validated her twin beliefs that the coastal sightings and oral testimony were accurate evidence that the battle took place off the north-west coast from Port Gregory and *not* where the Germans stated it did. Glenys also believed it supported her suspicion 'that Detmers gave a coded position which equated to deducting two degrees from the latitude and one degree from the longitude'.[4] I wasn't buying any of it, but I knew this would make it harder for the RAN to fully embrace my proposed search of the northern location. Glenys was at pains to distinguish her research and location off Port Gregory from Warren Whittaker's and Ean McDonald's locations off Geraldton, but to outsiders not conversant with the subtleties of the location argument her favoured spot was yet another in the group of southern locations that polarised opinion about where a prospective search should take place.

The *Rewind* documentary

In the middle of March 2004 a researcher working for a new ABC Television history series called *Rewind* contacted me about doing a documentary segment on the research documents I had located at the Naval Historical Branch and the rediscovery of Detmers's dictionary. The idea behind 'Rewind' was that it would provide a fresh perspective on the most fascinating characters and events in Australia's history. As that was exactly what we were trying to do with the loss of *Sydney* it seemed like our story was a natural fit. It was ultimately agreed that the filming would take place in early May at my office in West Sussex, at the Naval Historical Branch in London, and at various locations in Germany to be arranged. Peter Hore immediately got in touch with Peter Tamm to see if we could use his mansion on the banks of the Elbe River in Hamburg that housed the world's largest private collection of shipping and naval history, while the freelance journalist Graham Anderson put me in touch with Heinz Messerschmidt, the mines officer of *Kormoran* and aide-de-camp to Detmers, who was happy to be interviewed on camera and to give his recollection of the battle.

My hope for the *Rewind* segment was that it would reach a much wider national audience in Australia and provide a fuller background to this new research and the search proposals I was developing than had been previously seen in short news pieces. I was also very much looking forward to meeting Heinz Messerschmidt. Heinz was going to be the first *Kormoran* survivor I interviewed and I was hopeful he could provide fresh information or insights about *Kormoran*'s navigation on the day of the battle. An important question that Peter and I wanted to ask was where Heinz was during the battle, because some historians such as Tom Frame were indicating that there

were only one or two eyewitnesses to Detmers's strategy and actions. I had interviewed World War II veterans before and knew that the surroundings and atmosphere had to be perfectly relaxed to get the best results, so I was hoping for an uncomplicated shoot.

I was also hoping to use the documentary as an opportunity to make another rediscovery of a missing primary source account. Several months before, an envelope came in the post from Michael Montgomery that quite simply stunned me. It contained photocopies of twelve discoloured pages full of slightly blurred handwritten letters that were unrecognisable to me as a normal language. It took me several seconds to comprehend that what Michael had sent were copies of the actual notebook pages containing the coded account found on Detmers when he was recaptured following his week-long escape from Dhurringile officers' camp in January 1945. This important account was missing from the archives: all that the Australian National Archives had in its collection was the transcription and the decode of the account, but not the original. It was the last of the original Detmers's accounts that Peter and I knew existed but could not find anywhere. When Peter came to visit me later that same day we asked the same question of each other: where on earth did Michael get a copy of the coded account and where was the original?

It turned out that the source of the account was Maria Hehir, the daughter of Captain John Leslie Hehir, the army intelligence officer who coordinated the final round of observation and interrogations of the German prisoners at Murchison camp in January 1942. Hehir was later based at Dhurringile camp when Detmers was recaptured and this is when he would have come into possession of his copy of the coded account, which turned out to be a high quality photographic copy and not the original which is presumed lost. Fortunately these papers, including Hehir's personal diary of the interrogation period, survived the major Wangaratta flood of 1974 and Hehir's burning of most of his old papers when his family moved house in early 1985.[5] After Hehir's death in May 1987, Maria held on to the papers and sent Michael a copy of the notebook. As it was too late to include this information in his book and Michael had no expertise in cryptology, he could do nothing further with the account so he filed them in his large collection of papers where they stayed for years until he kindly mailed a copy to me.

The reason why Peter and I were so excited about having a copy of the original coded account, besides the fact that it completed our search for every known version of Detmers's primary source accounts, was because it would allow us to double-check the original decode performed by the Fleet Radio Unit Melbourne (FRUMEL) to ensure it was 100 per cent correct. As FRUMEL's 1945 translation of the decode contained some serious errors it was not out of the question that the decode was less than perfect as well. There was also the question of the missing first page of the FRUMEL transcription: did it include any information that might shed additional light on the big question of whether Detmers's 26°34' South 111° East position referred to the noon position or the action position?

I wanted to find Maria Hehir to get a better copy of the coded account than the one Michael provided and also to see whether she would be willing to donate it to the National Archives (NAA) where I felt it rightly belonged for the benefit of all researchers. I had been in touch with Steve Stuckey, the Assistant Director-General of the NAA, who confirmed that the whereabouts of the original notebook was not known and that the NAA was keen to have a copy of this 'extremely important document'. Michael did his best to locate Maria but when his inquiries proved fruitless I asked the *Rewind* researcher to see if he could help by employing the vast resources of the ABC, and within days they had found her. Maria was thrilled to be involved in our little project, so when I explained the historical importance of the coded account and how the NAA wanted a copy to complete

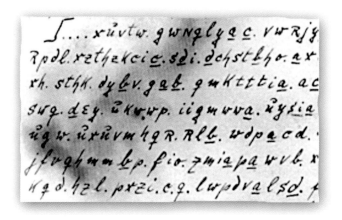

Above: Detmers's coded account.

their collection she generously agreed. Maria was yet another of the many Australians whose family history was intertwined with the loss of *Sydney* and who were still coming forward with new information to fill in blanks in the story.

The Peter Tamm Institute turned out to be an absolutely brilliant location for the meetings with Heinz Messerschmidt. Each floor of the large mansion was filled with boat models: from the first 1:1,250 scale miniature of a North Sea–Baltic coaster given to him by his mother when he was a boy of six (one of 36,000 miniatures in Tamm's collection) to the awesome eight-foot plus 1:100 models of *Hood* and *Bismarck* that were every visitor's favourites. It was arranged for us to meet Heinz in the room dedicated to the display of German auxiliary cruiser items after he had been involved in an already long day of filming. Heinz was incredibly accommodating with our questions, as well as the filming requirements of the ABC director. The TV interviews dragged on for longer than I liked and it was obvious to all that Heinz was getting tired. We really needed less distraction during the main interview we were planning for the next morning in order to get a clear understanding of Heinz's first-hand knowledge of the battle.

We all assembled the following day in the mansion's glass conservatory that overlooked the banks of the Elbe and grounds where Tamm kept a couple of small German submarines. To cut down on the distractions of the previous day I asked the documentary team to film from the outside looking in, which they reluctantly agreed to do. In addition to Heinz, Peter and myself, we were also joined by Detmers's nephew, Dr Hans Jantzen; Dr Diether Schmidt, curator of the Tamm Institute; and Dr Redelf Habben, the son of *Kormoran*'s doctor, who brought Heinz down from Kiel. With so many people involved the discussion was a bit chaotic but still very informative.

Heinz explained how he came directly to *Kormoran*'s bridge when *Sydney* was sighted and the siren sounded to call all crew to action stations. He then moved a deck above to the monkey island, which served as the signalling deck/operations centre where he was to man the telephone that connected him to Detmers and the artillery officer, Fritz Skeries. Standing alongside Skeries, where they both watched the entire battle unfold before their eyes under the cover of a canvas tarp, Messerschmidt also had the privilege of hearing Detmers's thoughts and commands down his telephone line. Heinz had no way of knowing about how the navigation was being kept but he was an excellent first-hand eyewitness to the battle and was able to confirm where the majority of officers were stationed. Contrary to Tom Frame's rather surprising belief that *Kormoran*'s bridge was empty of officers at such a critical moment, Heinz listed the names of those who were actually on the bridge with Detmers: navigation officer Meyer, officer of the watch von Gösseln, prize officer Diebitsch, and torpedo officer Greter. First officer Foerster also initially went to the bridge where he agreed with Detmers they would have to fight if necessary and then moved down to the decks to supervise operations there.

Through the glass windows of the conservatory I noticed the ABC cameraman zooming in as I started to lay my navigation charts out on the long patio table we were using. Although my charts facilitated our discussion of the battle and movement of the ships relative to each other, it was clear that Heinz was unaware of *Kormoran*'s real-world navigation and he could make no comment on the origin or accuracy of Detmers's position. However, Heinz did express surprise when I showed him the positions recorded by Thurow and Hartmann. He had no explanation for how either of these junior ratings came up with their positions and he was generally dismissive about their importance. I valued this input from Heinz, especially as he was in charge of the division of specialists that included Hartmann and would know better than

Above: Heinz Messerschmidt and me.

anyone whether he had access to this type of operational information.

Heinz was more than generous during the two days we were with him. Like other naval veterans I had interviewed in the twilight of their lives he had a natural desire for his story to be heard and was keen that history reflected it accurately. He was completely relaxed during the interview and answered every question, even the awkward ones, with openness and evident honesty. I knew there were a small number of researchers who were convinced that the Germans lied about many aspects of the engagement with *Sydney* and that their testimony should not be trusted, but there was nothing about Heinz's behaviour to suggest he was telling us anything but the truth as he remembered it. It also made no sense at all to me that Heinz, at the ripe old age of 85, would voluntarily subject himself to our probing questions if he had some dark secrets to hide.

Building momentum

The feedback from the *Rewind* documentary which aired in mid-September 2004 was mixed. The producers reported that it was very well received and the ratings were among the best for the series, so they were happy.

They had received calls from people wanting to donate to the search, and the historic shipwrecks officer at the Department of Environment and Heritage called to get in touch with me about my search plans.

The growing list of researchers I was corresponding with were less congratulatory. Kim Kirsner was disappointed because he did not believe we'd unearthed any new information with regard to the search area. Jim Eagles, who was writing to me for the first time, also felt that there was very little content revealed and that, in his opinion, the money spent on a search at Detmers's position would be money wasted.

Despite this less than enthusiastic response I sensed that the program served to move the debate forward as people were now discussing the prospect of a search in more realistic, rather than abstract, terms. In the run-up to the documentary I was able to obtain two important endorsements for my search plans and used the broadcast date to announce them in a press release. The first was official approval from the German Government for me to film the wreck of *Kormoran* on the same 'look but don't touch basis' that was agreed upon when we filmed the *Bismarck*. I was also extremely pleased to receive backing from the HMAS *Sydney* and Vietnam Logistic Support Veterans' Association and its president John Atkins, who wrote:

> *David Mearns' proposal to locate the wreck of SYDNEY and place a suitable memorial on its site received enthusiastic support from our national membership, which includes former crew members of SYDNEY and family members of those lost. Our Association is further convinced that a detailed recorded investigation of the damage will finally put to rest the critical historical and technical questions about her final moments, and will indeed give closure to not only the 645 families of loved ones but will achieve finality for one of Australia's most baffling wartime mysteries.*

Seeing that momentum was building for the wreck search to begin, I felt it was time to bite the bullet myself and travel to Australia for a series of meetings to kick-start the project. At the top of my agenda was a meeting with Ted Graham and his fellow directors of HMAS *Sydney* Search Pty Ltd, which included businessman Keith Rowe, project manager Bob King, barrister Ron Birmingham, QC, and retired RAN commodore Bob Trotter, in addition to Don Pridmore and Kim Kirsner. After the promising initial discussions with Ted about us joining forces everything seemed to slow down. The time difference between our locations and the fact that Ted and the other directors were all unpaid volunteers was an obvious constraint on our progress. Nevertheless, I was getting the distinct impression that HMA3S was keeping me at arm's length while it conducted its own internal due diligence and debate on me and my research. Other than one or two rare phone calls we corresponded by emails, which varied from being relaxed and friendly to very officious. One face-to-face meeting with Don Pridmore when he was on business travel in Britain in May 2004 was extremely productive, however, and convinced me that if I met with all the directors in one room at the same time we could quickly formalise our working relationship.

I was a bit concerned that the ongoing correspondence that Peter, Wes and I were having with Kim Kirsner about the search area for the wrecks was not leading to more agreement. There was absolutely no question at all between us that we should be looking in the 'northern location', but within that large area we had different ideas stemming from our different approaches to the problem. Kim's and his colleague Dr John Dunn's ideas were largely based on their analyses of the memory and recall of the German survivors, which they used to test each of the positions reported by the Germans. They didn't accept Wes's original idea, which I felt merited serious consideration, that Detmers's 26°34' South 111° East position might have been *Kormoran*'s noon position even though this would place the battle and sinking of *Kormoran* very close to the nominal 26° South 111° East position that in general we all agreed should be searched.

To me the argument was becoming overly academic and more about whose ideas were right or wrong. Kim

H.M.A.S. "SYDNEY"

Above: Signatures of Sydney *crewmen commemorating the victory over* Bartolomeo Colleoni.

had been involved with this research for more than a decade and had placed a lot of his academic credentials on the line. His views on where to search and what research information was reliable had evolved over the years, which was evident in the spread of different positions he had nominated in various papers. I thought his most recent work was very good but that his academic rejection of the validity of the 26°34' South 111° East noon position was weak and not based on solid evidence. His argument lacked the common sense and understanding of German naval navigation that was needed to see our point. A robust academic debate was all well and good, but at the end of the day I knew that if I was going to lead the search at sea it would be my responsibility to make real-world decisions about the search box and where to look first and regardless of whether we were successful or failed, the buck would stop with me.

Into the lion's den

I arrived in Perth on 16 November 2004, three days before I was to give a two-part lecture at the Western Australia Maritime Museum on the sixty-third anniversary of *Sydney*'s loss. Despite my long flight a meeting at HMA3S's office was scheduled for just a few hours after my arrival because Ted Graham was flying out that afternoon on a business trip and his availability was limited to just one hour. I was asked by Ted to start by giving a formal presentation of my company's background and the previous deep-water shipwreck searches I had conducted. All the directors were present with the exception of Kim Kirsner, who, unbeknown to me, had resigned from HMA3S the day before I arrived in Perth. I also brought my updated navigation charts to take everyone through a brief discussion of the possible search areas and operational challenges we would face. We quickly moved on to the subject of resurrecting our formal working relationship which had stalled over the past year. We agreed on the

main principles of the relationship and it was left for Ron Birmingham to take the lead on finalising the wording of a Memorandum of Understanding with me with the help of some outside lawyers who were donating their services. Keith Rowe was planning a number of social events for everyone to get to know me better, and that was about it. In less than two hours we had accomplished more than we had all year and the feeling of mutual respect in the room was excellent.

A few hours after the meeting broke up I was scheduled to have an early dinner with Glenys McDonald and her husband, Vic. I wanted to hear about Glenys's role in building the beautiful memorial to *Sydney* in Geraldton that featured as its central theme a dome of 645 seagulls to represent each of *Sydney*'s lost souls. Meeting Glenys was also part of my commitment to directly engage with all *Sydney* researchers, regardless of whether our beliefs were shared or not. I saw every researcher as possibly having valuable information to contribute and the experience of Michael Montgomery providing Detmers's coded account was proof of this. I liked Glenys and was impressed by her drive to see *Sydney* found and to bring comfort and closure to relatives. Judging from her work in getting the memorial funded she had an obvious talent in bridge-building and I left the meeting feeling that she was definitely a potential ally.

I was able to easily spend the next two days before the lecture meeting with other researchers in between interviews with local and national media. While the loss of *Sydney* and her men was felt all across the country, it is fair to say that it has lingered longest in Western Australia. There was no doubt about how much everyone wanted the wreck to be found. The front desk staff at the Esplanade Hotel in Fremantle where I was staying must have thought I was setting up my own business in their lobby as a steady stream of researchers arrived to meet me. First there was Phil Shepherd, a 74-year-old retiree who seemed to have spent his whole life either at sea or along the West Australian coastline. Phil handed me a thick envelope of archival documents to add to my growing

Previous page: HMAS Sydney *in her camouflage paint.*

collection. Next up was Commander Ian McGulkin, RANR. Ian wasn't a researcher: he was the RAN's representative in Western Australia on the *Sydney* issue, so I was grateful to meet him in advance of a briefing I was scheduled to give to Vice Admiral Ritchie the following week. I then met with Ean McDonald, who brought along Dr John McArthur. Ean actually served on *Sydney*, while, to earn his PhD, John had written his dissertation about her loss, so these men were experts. I wasn't expecting either of them to agree with my conclusions about the location of the battle but they graciously listened to my explanation and Ean even promised to buy me the best lunch in Australia if I found *Sydney*'s wreck.

My last meeting was with Wes Olson, who had been incredibly generous in sharing his research with me and seemed to have an encyclopaedic knowledge about *Sydney*. We had a good long discussion after which Wes gave me a large bundle of research documents that he used in writing his book. Wes was now working on a new book and felt that I could make better use of his archive in finding the wreck.

The lecture hall at the Western Australian Maritime Museum was full to the back rows in anticipation of my talk. There had been a lot of media coverage the day before and I could recognise all the researchers I had met previously dotted around the hall. I structured the talk into two halves: the first on the research and search areas, and the second on deep-ocean search technology and some examples of shipwrecks that I had found. I also taped a copy of my navigation chart onto a bulletin board so everyone was free to see it and give me their comments. I knew there was going to be people in the audience who disagreed with me and were coming to find fault with my conclusions, but I felt it was very important to take this criticism head on and answer all their questions.

Predictably, the questioning after I finished the first part of the presentation was intense and had to be curtailed because we were running well beyond schedule. As I began the second presentation I offered to skip through a whole series of shipwreck sonar images and photos to claw back some time but my offer was greeted with shouts of 'No, keep going' throughout the hall. This was the

Above: The volunteers of HMA3S: (back l to r) Bob Trotter, Ron Birmingham, QC, Ted Graham, Keith Rowe, John Begg, Tim Fischer, AC, and Don Pridmore; (front l to r) Pat Ingham, who lost her husband in Sydney, *Julie Bishop and Kim Kirsner.*

moment I knew that, despite the handful of opponents present, the audience were with me.

Funding the search

I left Perth and flew to Canberra for a meeting with the Chief of Navy, Vice Admiral Ritchie, confident that he would be pleased to hear of my newly consummated partnership with HMA3S. While it wasn't in the RAN's power to authorise funding for the search, it was clear that the first step in securing government approval for funds was to have Vice Admiral Richie provide affirmative advice that there was a consensus about where to start the search and that the group taking on the challenge was correctly structured and professionally managed. I gave

Ritchie and his staff, including Dr David Stevens, a much shorter version of my Maritime Museum presentation and showed him my navigation charts that outlined the likely areas to be searched. The atmosphere in the room was very positive and it was apparent that the RAN's view on supporting a search had shifted a great deal since Vice Admiral Shackleton's previous announcement of 'no support' following the failed 2001 symposium. I took it as a highly encouraging sign that Ritchie even offered his own opinion on how to interpret Detmers's position based on his experience commanding a ship. Although it would take many months before being confirmed, I left Canberra feeling that the RAN had crossed a threshold on the *Sydney* issue and now wanted to see her found as much as everyone else.

Even if government funds were to be provided for the search it was always envisioned that their contribution would only partially cover the costs and that corporate donations would make up the balance.[6] As our rough estimates of project costs ranged anywhere from $3.46 million to $5.58 million, depending on whether there was going to be just a sonar search for the wrecks or a combined expedition in which the wrecks were both found and filmed, the amount HMA3S would need to raise from the private sector was in the millions. Everyone was involved in the fundraising effort and a broad spectrum of companies and wealthy individuals were being approached. Our results, however, were very disappointing and discouraging. In the first seven months of 2005 not a single significant donation from the private sector was made. The public was donating cash in small amounts, but no Australian corporation seemed to share our vision that finding *Sydney* was of great national interest and a project worthy of their support. We all believed in what we were doing but were desperate for some positive indication that others believed as well.

That indication finally came on 14 August 2005 when Prime Minister John Howard announced that the Federal Government approved a $1.3 million grant to HMA3S to help fund the search for *Sydney*. While there was little warning of the announcement, and none regarding the amount, there was considerable activity behind the scenes to make this possible. Bob Trotter had met independently with Vice Admiral Ritchie to reinforce our consensus of opinion about where to conduct the search while Ted and the other directors were keeping up pressure on the politicians. We had hoped that everything we were doing would result in an announcement like this but until it was made, and we could see it in black and white, we couldn't be sure. The $1.3 million grant was a significant amount, but more importantly, the announcement was the first real proof that the government was ready to act to see that *Sydney* was found. Howard's statement, made to coincide with the sixtieth anniversary of the end of World War II, perfectly summed up our feelings about why finding *Sydney* was important to the country and relevant to all Australians: 'The finding of HMAS *Sydney* II would close a significant chapter in Australia's wartime history and bring a long awaited closure to the suffering of families, as well as allowing the proper recognition of the sacrifice made by the 645 crew.'

The government's announcement of the $1.3 million grant was exceptional news that triggered yet even more good news for HMA3S in the coming weeks. First, the West Australian Government announced that it too would contribute $500,000 to the search, followed shortly by a similar announcement from the New South Wales Government, which was prepared to make an additional contribution to the tune of $250,000. Within the space of six short weeks $2.05 million in funding had been garnered by HMA3S and it truly appeared that the long, long wait by relatives to see a search for *Sydney* get under way would soon be over. The rapid-fire announcements reminded me of that old joke about waiting forever for a bus and then having three come along at the same time. The difference here was that HMA3S was going to jump on each bus and make sure no others passed them by.

Back to the drawing board

Ted and his fellow directors had every reason to expect that the $2.05 million in federal and state grants would rapidly transform the project. The amount represented anywhere between 60 and 78 per cent of the initial funding required; the latter percentage was calculated on the possibility that a locally available vessel and equipment would be provided to the project by the current charterer at a significantly reduced rate in the form of a donation. Everyone also believed that the government's and the RAN's unequivocal declaration of support of my partnership with HMA3S would end the northern versus southern location debate once and for all and would ease the fears any potential donor might have that we would be looking in the wrong place for the wrecks. Sadly, we were badly mistaken.

It was very much a situation of being so near and yet so far. HMA3S was back to being deeply disappointed on every front in trying to raise the balance of funds required. The reasonable expectation that the other state governments would join Western Australia and New South Wales in making their own financial contributions towards the search was never realised.[7] The possible offer of a locally available vessel and equipment at reduced rates by an oil company never materialised. Numerous contacts and meetings with major Australian media companies who all wanted to be there the day *Sydney* was found never amounted to anything but a waste of time. Fundraising initiatives either never got off the ground or didn't raise enough money to justify their expense. A newspaper-led drive to help raise $1 million didn't get remotely close to its targeted amount. It wasn't as if nobody was donating, because some individuals and small companies were, and every cent they gave was gratefully appreciated. The reality, however, was that millions more were required and we were frustratingly short by a long way.

Despite this depressing backdrop in the provision of funding, progress was being made in other areas. In January 2006 Peter Hore and I were finally able to jointly organise a trip to Santiago, Chile, to meet with Reinhold von Malapert, *Kormoran*'s wireless officer and the last officer besides Heinz Messerschmidt still alive and willing to talk about his experiences. Malapert was 92 years old and quite frail so there was no time to waste. [8] We made the long trip to Santiago because we were hoping Malapert could tell us more about the 'QQQQ' wireless signals *Kormoran* transmitted about a half-hour before the fighting began. One of these signals was received by the tugboat *Uco* transiting south off the coast of the Zuytdorp Cliffs and by the wireless station in Geraldton, proving that they were sent at the exact time the Germans testified. This transmission was a potentially vital clue to the location of the wrecks as it is the *only* piece of documentary evidence referring to *Kormoran*'s position that can be directly tied to the date and time of the battle and has been independently corroborated. The problem, however, was that both *Uco* and Geraldton radio had trouble hearing the weak message and only Geraldton radio was able to record a partial and suspect position (7C 11115E). [9] It also didn't help that these signals hadn't come to light until eight days after the battle and the navy subsequently confiscated the original signal pads. Malapert was therefore the last remaining source of information that could give me an idea whether or not I could trust the longitude (111°15' East) fragment of the 'QQQQ' position.

We met with Malapert for three days straight, starting at 10.30 am when he was most alert, in his high-rise apartment along with Jauni, his dedicated private nurse. The interview was conducted mostly in Spanish, bar the times Malapert would revert to his native German. Peter did the conversing with Malapert while I took notes and fed Peter questions. When we got around to talking about the wireless operators and sending of the 'QQQQ' signal, Malapert explained that it was done as per their normal routine:

> *Sending the QQQQ signal was absolutely routine. Detmers would give the order verbally, either directly or by sound-powered telephone, on the bridge and I would have been standing at the radio room. In the radio room there was a method of knowing the navigation of the ship, a general operations chart that was kept. During the journey the radio room knew exactly where the ship was at all times. Henry Meyer was keeping a chart in the chart room and the radio operators were keeping their own chart and were up to date minute by minute with what was happening on the bridge.*

The detail about the wireless operators having their own up-to-date chart of *Kormoran*'s navigation was an extremely important piece of information for me. It meant that the wireless operators would have known *Kormoran*'s accurate position at the time and would have included it when transmitting the 'QQQQ' signal. As they were the *source* of the position it cuts down on the chance of an error being introduced had the position been provided to them from a different source (that is, the navigators). Most importantly, their chart would have been accurate to at least a minute of longitude and latitude. So although Hans Linke and Ernst Pachman testified that the position given in the 'QQQQ' signal was 26° South 111° East, I could now be 100 per cent certain that this was indeed a shorthand position as I had assumed. They may have forgotten the full position after their ordeal in the lifeboats or didn't think that level of precision was important to their interrogators. Whatever the case, whichever wireless operator actually sent out the 'QQQQ' signal, he would have been able to include *Kormoran*'s accurate and precise position.

In an indirect way, what Malapert told me gave me the confidence to safely accept the suspect longitude component in the 'QQQQ' signal as being genuine. This was an important conclusion that was going to help me define the eastern edge of the search box as the vessels travelled west from there before engaging and sinking.

Above: Peter Hore showing Reinhold von Malapert and his nurse, Juani, my chart of Kormoran's *navigation.*

Unfortunately, I had no such confidence about the latitude component (7C), which was clearly corrupt. Presumably the 'C' was supposed to be an 'S' for south, but the difference between 'C' and 'S' in morse code was so stark (dash-dot-dash-dot compared with dot-dot-dot) it is apparent that the Geraldton operator was not hearing this portion of the signal clearly. Given that the 'C' was corrupt and immediately before that the operator reported the signal as being 'unintelligible', I wasn't about to take the chance on the '7' being correct as just a single misheard dot or dash could easily turn it into a '6' or '8'.

As our search for *Sydney* was marooned on dry land another remarkable search was under way on Christmas Island for the body that washed ashore there in a Carley float months after the battle. The badly decomposed body had been buried in the white boiler suit he was wearing when found, in an unmarked grave in the Old European Cemetery on the island. Despite an early investigation by the Director of Naval Intelligence in 1949 that concluded that the Carley float, and thus the body, did not come from *Sydney*, most researchers were absolutely sure that he did. Unfortunately a search for the unmarked grave by the RAN in 2001 was unsuccessful, largely because the information about its location was imprecise and the search team ran out of time working in the difficult, overgrown and sloping conditions of the cemetery.[10] However, the re-emergence of an old photograph taken of the grave by Brian O'Shannassy when he was based on the island in 1950 led to a second search by the navy in October 2006. Armed with O'Shannassy's photograph as their guide, the navy expedition team of five, including an archaeologist and several forensic experts, had dug seven trenches by hand in the dense, rocky soil without success. They then noticed that the ground between two other graves was softer than everywhere else and resumed their digging. First, they came across some splinters of wood from the coffin and then unearthed a small foot bone that confirmed they had found 'Australia's Forgotten Son' — the name given to the Christmas Island body that would be coming home after 65 years.

The team eventually exhumed the entire, well-preserved skeleton and flew it back to Sydney for more detailed examination, where ongoing efforts have been aimed at individual identification of the body from *Sydney*'s crew of 645. The expedition was a stunning success for everyone involved and it marked a watershed moment for the RAN. Lieutenant John Perryman, the senior naval historical officer whose advice to the Chief of Navy led to the expedition being authorised, was from then on seen as someone who had an intimate understanding of the *Sydney* issue and was building a new relationship of trust and engagement with the relatives of those lost on her. Suddenly, *Sydney* had surrendered one of her secrets. Once viewed as seemingly impossible, the amazing discovery of the Christmas Island body began to change people's opinions, both inside and outside the RAN, about finally resolving the other great secrets of 19 November 1941.

Another major development in April 2007 was the elimination of one of the key 'southern locations' favoured by Warren Whittaker and named KDLS3 in recognition of it being discovered by Lindsay Knight using his magic locating device. The precise KDLS3 position off the Abrolhos Islands was surveyed using a vessel equipped with a hull-mounted multibeam echo sounder system which scanned a 2,000-metre swathe across the position in the highest possible resolution. The survey, donated to HMA3S by Perth-based survey company DOF Subsea Australia, showed that there wasn't even the slightest hint of wreckage at the site despite Warren's claims that we would find a shattered hull and debris scattered everywhere. In correspondence Warren was always very polite and it was impossible not to be impressed by his persistence, even if it was wrong-headed. However, Warren had begun writing letters to politicians and articles in newspapers actively trying to derail our search of the northern location on the basis it was going to be a waste of taxpayers' money. Warren and his KDLS positions had been a thorn in our side for years. It was a shame that a valuable donation had to be used this way to prove a negative, but it was the only way to effectively close the door on the southern location and get everyone focused on our search of the northern location.

A final push for funds

The elimination of the KDLS3 position was an important achievement, at no cost to the taxpayer, which needed to be made public and explained to the RAN and the government. It was also a critical time for HMA3S, which had been in existence for more than six years and had seen some changes in the ranks of its board of directors. Kim Kirsner and Ron Birmingham had already resigned for personal reasons by the time Glenys McDonald was drafted in as a replacement in November 2006. Glenys might have seemed an unusual choice given her firm belief in the Port Gregory sightings as a pointer to the battle and/or sinking locations, but she was always very open to a search of the northern position for the wreck of *Kormoran* and felt that the best way to achieve the aim everyone wanted was by working together rather than on opposite sides. Glenys provided a renewed enthusiasm and fresh outlook for HMA3S but cracks were beginning to show elsewhere, and at the beginning of June 2007 Bob King also resigned for personal reasons.

Bob was an integral part of all the technical discussions within HMA3S and I felt his resignation was a big loss. As just one example of his important contribution to the cause, he had recently completed a detailed status report on HMA3S's achievements and further intentions that was going to be sent to government ministers and the RAN. The report covered every aspect of HMA3S, including the recent elimination of the KDLS3 position. It also made a strong case for the government to step in immediately and provide the balance of funding required for HMA3S to conduct the search during the upcoming weather window of 2007–2008.[11]

The volunteer board of HMA3S and its associates had spent many years working to achieve its objectives, with only moderate success, and at the current rate of fundraising the next weather window was going to be missed. The primary reason for the low influx of donations was that while people in the private sector believed that finding *Sydney* was a worthwhile cause they also believed that the responsibility for funding the search should rightly fall on the government. Without additional government funding to enable the search to go ahead in the coming season there was a real risk that the HMA3S organisation might collapse. There was no denying the entire project had reached a critical juncture. In order to have a chance at conducting the search in the

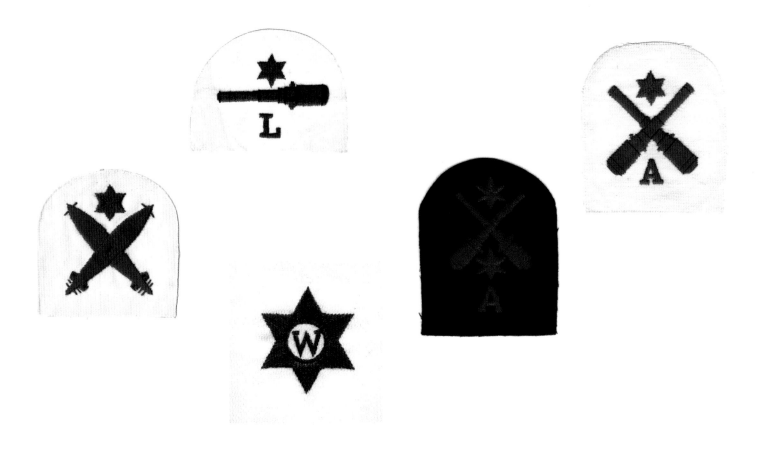

Above: HMAS Sydney *crew badges: (l to r) leading torpedoman; layer rating third class; anti-aircraft rating first class; writer; anti-aircraft rating second class; sick berth rating; quarters rating third class; ordinary signalman; visual signalman first class; leading wireless telegraphist; and stoker second class.*

2007–2008 season HMA3S would need to start issuing tender requests to subcontractors within the next two months, but without the full project funds in place this was a practical impossibility. Intervention was needed immediately and when it came it was from a completely unexpected source.

Lieutenant John Perryman, RANR, is the senior naval historical officer at the RAN's Sea Power Centre — Australia and works for Dr David Stevens, director at the centre. John had completed a 25-year stint in the RAN as a signalman and rose through the ranks to warrant officer before 'retiring' as a lieutenant to take up his dream job working in naval history. For the past several years he

had been spending an increasingly inordinate amount of his time answering letters to the RAN and government on the *Sydney* issue. John, therefore, knew better than anyone else what the HMA3S directors were going through. Crucially, he also believed that *Sydney* should be found, and could be found. So when John learned of Bob King's resignation he decided to act and sought approval to prepare a memorandum making the case for the government to provide its full support to HMA3S. John was sticking his neck way out on this one but he correctly sensed that it was now or never for HMA3S and the search for *Sydney*.

Fortunately, John's memo was well received by both the RAN and the government and it quickly set in motion a series of actions by Bruce Billson, MP, the Minister for Veterans Affairs and Minister Assisting the Minister for Defence. Billson and his chief of staff met with Ted Graham in Perth and Ted was able to give them a full briefing along the lines of the HMA3S status report

that was making the rounds within the government. The following day I received an urgent email from John requesting a paper detailing the precise search area I favoured and my reasons for favouring this area. John explained that he was drafting an urgent brief for the Chief of Navy and Minister Billson and that the right response could be worth $4.2 million to the search effort. That certainly got my attention and gave me all the motivation I needed to work through the night to get my response to John in time for his deadline.

With the hard work done the matter was now in the hands of the government as various briefing papers worked their way up to Prime Minister Howard for his final decision. We were all aware that an incalculable amount of work had been done by countless people, both inside and outside the HMA3S organisation, to get us this far. What struck me most, however, was how many times different people stepped into the breech at critical junctures to propel the project forward. Without doubt, however, the constant driving force was Ted Graham, who never relented in his determination to see a search for *Sydney* get under way and steadily pushed everyone forward towards this common goal. I was therefore particularly pleased that it was Ted who rang me with the good news, on my birthday no less, that the government was increasing its funding for the search to a total of $4.2 million. The long wait for HMA3S and me was over. Now it was going to be up to us to ensure that the far longer wait by the families of *Sydney*'s crew would also soon end.

CHAPTER FIVE

...

Sydney found?

I had grown accustomed to the surprises thrown up during my five years involved in the search for *Sydney* and thought I had seen it all. Nothing, however, prepared me for the phone call I received about an hour after Ted Graham rang me with the brilliant news that Prime Minister Howard had approved the increase in funding to HMA3S that would enable the search to go ahead. This phone call was also from Australia, from Peter Meakin, the director of news and public affairs at Channel Seven in Sydney, whom I had met before and stayed in touch with. I immediately thought that the good news had leaked out and he was calling me for a comment. Instead, Peter had unbelievable news that an amateur group of divers had actually found *Sydney* and had underwater pictures of the wreck!

This wasn't the first time that a similar claim had been made so my first reaction was incredulity. I was absolutely certain from my research that *Kormoran* and *Sydney* had sunk in deep water far out to sea, so if any group had been searching out there with an expensive ship and sonar equipment we would have heard about it on the grapevine. On the other hand, Peter Meakin was one of the country's most experienced news journalists so if he was ringing me on my mobile phone, late on a Friday evening, his time, there must be some substance to the story. He wanted me to see the underwater pictures to get my opinion and comment, and was sending them by email. Apparently the news was about to break with the entire front page of the following day's *West Australian* newspaper dedicated to the discovery and Channel Seven was preparing to show exclusive video footage of the wreck. I was going to be in London all day, away from my office, so it was going to be hours before I could look at any images. I urged Peter to be extremely cautious about this discovery as I had serious doubts and asked him to find out the names of the divers and call me back. Peter rang back in ten minutes with the name Phil Shepherd, and then the penny dropped.

Phil was one of the amateur researchers who had been in touch with me since 2003. We had also met twice before: in Fremantle at the time of my lecture at the Western

Left: Sydney's *Walrus aircraft returning to the ship.*

Australian Maritime Museum in 2004 and in my office in Midhurst when Phil was in Britain in 2006. Phil was one of the most helpful people and was constantly emailing me news clippings about *Sydney* from the local papers. He seemed to know everyone who worked on the water and was sort of like my 'eyes and ears' in Western Australia with regard to *Sydney*. Phil had also been writing to me for a number of months about a pair of seabed anomalies that had been discovered by a now deceased professional fisherman and Shark Bay pilot boat operator by the name of Marshall Hipper. The two anomalies were drop-offs — large rises or cliffs on the seabed that cause the sonar to just 'drop off' — in approximately 70 fathoms of water anywhere from 20 to 30 nautical miles seaward of Dirk Hartog Island and about 22 nautical miles apart from each other. Hipper fished this area exclusively and dared not reveal this valuable fishing spot to anyone, including Phil. However, the person who acquired Hipper's chart of the area after he died had just shown it to Phil and gave him the GPS coordinates of the two drop-offs. This got Phil very excited as he had known about these drop-offs for years and suspected at least one was a wreck because Hipper's sons had dredged up a copper bolt from the same location. Phil thought that if one drop-off was a wreck, perhaps the second drop-off was a wreck as well, and perhaps the two wrecks could be *Kormoran* and *Sydney*. Like many earnest amateurs before him, Phil's curiosity got the better of him and he decided, along with his son Graham and a diver named Ian Stiles, to mount his own mini-expedition to check out these drop-offs.

After returning from London I went straight to my office to look at the emails Phil had been sending me and, sure enough, the first one about the Hipper drop-offs included the GPS coordinates, which I immediately plotted. I was absolutely right to be doubtful because both positions were far too close to land and they didn't fit with where the lifeboats were found or the drifting debris had been picked up. The location of the three German lifeboats that hadn't reached land were actually found much further offshore than the two Hipper positions, which posed the question why on earth all three boats would choose to sail or row further out to sea and away from the safety of land. It made no sense and in my mind was the clincher that proved *Sydney* had not been found. I didn't know what wreck Phil and his team had filmed but I was convinced it couldn't be either *Sydney* or *Kormoran*.

As Peter Meakin forewarned, the headline in Saturday's *West Australian* trumpeted the discovery in large bold letters: 'FOUND, Local amateur historians say they have discovered HMAS *Sydney*, solving Australian's greatest military mystery.' A blurry, distorted picture that covered the entire front page supposedly showed the 'telltale bolts which held down the ship's timber decking' as proof of the discovery.

The timing of this breaking news couldn't be worse for the government and the RAN, as they had been planning to announce the increase in funding for the HMA3S search in a press conference the very next day from the deck of HMAS *Sydney* (IV). Everything was set for the Prime Minister to make the announcement, accompanied by Minister Billson, the Chief of Navy, Ted and Glenys. Now, with the whole country fixated on the claims that *Sydney* was found, the government really had no choice but to postpone the funding announcement until the identity of this wreck was confirmed one way or the other.

Later that day I received the still images of the wreck from Channel Seven. They were very poor quality and showed no distinctive features to positively identify what type of ship the wreck was; but it certainly wasn't *Sydney*. Where were the guns, the turrets, the lifeboats, the aeroplane, the torpedoes, the superstructure: anything that could identify the wreck as a warship of *Sydney*'s size? There were none of these things. The most telling negative clue was that the wreck, roughly measured to be 30 metres long, was just a fraction of *Sydney*'s overall length of 169 metres. I liked Phil Shepherd and knew that his heart was in the right place, but he and his team, and the journalists who rushed the story into print, had got it very wrong.

I was interviewed that night at home by a Channel Seven news crew and gave them my opinion that all that was found was an unidentified shipwreck, which I did not believe was *Sydney*. The headlines that *Sydney* was found were premature and irresponsible when you consider how this news will have falsely raised the hopes of so many families. I could not mention how this had scuppered the government's announcement regarding the increased funding. Because I came out quite strongly against the claim the media all wanted to get a comment from me. All that I could do in each interview was to stress the importance of getting this right and to urge that the wreck be properly examined as soon as it was possible to do so.

The next fortnight was quite frustrating, knowing that the wait for Shepherd's wreck to be ruled out was costing us precious time by delaying the start of the HMA3S search. The RAN had acted quickly and diverted one of their hydrographic survey ships, HMAS *Leeuwin*, to check out the unidentified wreck but they needed the GPS coordinates and Phil Shepherd did not immediately release them. Minister Billson was understandably frustrated and the whole situation degenerated into a sad and distressing slanging match between them. The *West Australian* had been stung by its mistake and was pilloried by its competitors in the national press for running the story the way it did. Against this backdrop of angst and recrimination Billson announced the government's decision to provide a further $2.9 million to HMA3S, on top of the $1.3 million grant already pledged, for a search of the northern location. The announcement of the government-backed HMA3S search, which everyone had wanted to be a triumphant moment and a cause for celebration, turned out to be a damp squib.

HMAS *Leeuwin* was eventually able to survey the wreck, with Phil Shepherd and his team watching from their chartered fishing-cum-survey boat just one kilometre away. The unidentified wreck, which Shark Bay locals suspected was a barge sunk just after the war, turned out to be far too small to be either *Sydney* or *Kormoran* and the *Leeuwin* found 'nothing of interest' in the areas surrounding the wreck's location. Phil's team also collected high-quality survey data that matched the findings made by HMAS *Leeuwin*, as well as some additional video footage that proved inconclusive. As far as the RAN and

the government was concerned the wreck was definitely not the *Sydney*, although Phil Shepherd was still clinging to the hope that it was.

This determination cleared the way for the government to reschedule its formal press conference, which was made as originally planned on board HMAS *Sydney* (IV). All five of the HMA3S directors travelled to Sydney to watch Minister Billson make the announcement of the extra funding which they had collectively worked many years to achieve. With the $4.2 million in funding the government was committing to support a large-scale search for the wreck of *Sydney* by HMA3S. The only downside on the day was that the Prime Minister was unable to attend. During the question and answer period one reporter asked the minister what would happen if *Sydney* wasn't found in the time budgeted, to which Billson replied to the effect that the government was committed to finding *Sydney* whatever it takes. The '*Sydney* Found' fiasco was unfortunate for its timing and for the upset it caused to the *Sydney* crew's relatives, but it seemed to have the effect of galvanising the government and the RAN into getting the job done once and for all.

Project kick-off

Now that the question of funding was settled our focus switched to the demanding schedule we were going to face to have any chance of conducting the search in the upcoming weather window. Statistically, the period of optimum weather at the search location starts in November and extends through April, although this also coincides with the height of tropical cyclone season. Cyclones were a risk we were going to have to accept in order to enjoy the smoother conditions that normally prevail at that time of the year. However, I had also been warned that the location was generally windy and to expect a good swell running from the Southern Ocean most of the time.

As preparations for the search, including the transportation of equipment to Australia, was going to take a minimum of four months we had to start working

Above: The Walrus aircraft on its extended catapult.

very quickly. Ideally, we hoped to be ready to start the search in early January but could easily live with starting in mid-February. I knew it was possible that the search could run the full 45-day period to find both wrecks, so I really wanted to avoid starting as late as March. My concern was that this would expose us to rough weather causing us to interrupt the search exactly at the most crucial time if we were still in the process of trying to find *Sydney*.

We needed a kick-off meeting with the navy, which was quickly arranged for the second week in September, to get the project started in earnest. John Perryman was flying in to Perth with Commander Fiona McNaught and legal adviser Kirk Hayden of the RAN for two days of meetings with me and all five HMA3S directors. Although John was now a civilian historian with the Sea Power Centre it was decided that in his capacity as an active member of the Naval Reserve he would be the RAN's uniformed observer on board the search vessel. Fiona,

who was the Director of Ministerials and Coordination at Navy Headquarters, was going to be looking after the entire project on behalf of the RAN and the government. The role of the RAN was to administer the funding and support the project where necessary, but not to run it. HMA3S would have full operational responsibility for the project with me directing the offshore search operations on its behalf.

The first matter of urgency was for Fiona to get the grant of funds approved through the many administrative hoops in the RAN's bureaucracy. This was normal for doing business with the RAN, but we were facing the added pressure that Prime Minister Howard was about to call for a federal election sometime within the next few weeks. If Fiona couldn't push the grant through the approval process before the election was called, and the government was put into caretaker mode, the funds wouldn't be available to HMA3S until the New Year, which would cause us to miss the optimum weather window. The meeting was just a few hours old and already there was a major challenge to overcome. Fiona was going to have to deliver, otherwise the search would be delayed another year. Despite this concern we all drew comfort from the fact that Fiona was obviously a very capable person and she made a point, along with John, of telling us how they were personally committed to the project and finding *Sydney*. It certainly helps when people's hearts are in the job they are doing.

The meeting was also used to achieve a consensus about a number of important policies regarding the media and public communications. Transparency at all times was the cornerstone of these policies. Our aim during the search would be to get factual information directly to the public on a timely basis and unfiltered by the press, the RAN or the government. The principal medium would be the HMA3S website, which would contain a search diary of the expedition; in this way people could log on at any time to see our progress. We had seen how an exclusive media arrangement could go wrong with the 'Sydney Found' fiasco and were keen to avoid making the same mistake. A policy of non-exclusivity was believed to be the fairest and most equitable way to provide information to the media. While a film team would be on board to make a factual documentary about the expedition, they were not there to report news but to provide background video footage which would be equally distributed to all television outlets. Finally, *all* the data and information collected during the expedition would be provided in the form of a final report to the RAN with copies sent to the Western Australian Maritime Museum for public viewing and study.

Fiona and Kirk needed to return to Canberra to start working on getting the grant moneys in place so we spent the second day alone with John Perryman discussing the project management and operational aspects of the search. As John was going to be the sole RAN/government representative on board the search vessel it was important that he was informed of every detail about how we were planning to conduct the search. A key issue I wanted to discuss with John was my plan to conduct a state-of-the-art oceanographic and weather analysis on the likely conditions that prevailed at the time of the battle and days afterward as the German life rafts drifted northwards before they were recovered.

This had been previously attempted back in 1991 but I believed there was a lot of improvement to be made using the latest scientific understanding of currents and winds based on recent advances in supercomputer and satellite sensor technology.[1] I explained to John how I intended to use these studies to conduct a fresh backtrack or drift analysis of the life rafts recovered by *Aquitania* and *Trocas*. The objective was not to come up with a single magical 'X' on a chart as others had tried before in what I felt were misguided attempts to pinpoint the position of *Kormoran*'s wreck. Even with the best possible information on currents and winds I knew the variability was still too great to do that. My approach was completely different. I planned to commission new scientific studies on the variability of current and winds and then use those results to determine the full scatter of possible sinking positions for *Kormoran*. Therefore, instead of a chart with just a single 'X' predicting one possible position for *Kormoran*, the final result of these studies would be a chart dotted with dozens and dozens of 'Xs' effectively outlining an overall area within which there would be a high degree of statistical likelihood the wreck of *Kormoran* would be found.

My decision about the precise area to search for *Kormoran* would come down to how the area outlined by the drift analysis overlapped with the positions provided by Detmers and other Germans such as wireless

Centre: HMAS Sydney *sweetheart brooch.*

operator Hans Linke and navigator Henry Meyer, keeping in mind, of course, the significant amount of uncertainty surrounding these positions. To compensate for the uncertainty I would need to apply large 'circles of error' around the German positions and to draw on my experience using exactly this type of information as I had done to locate shipwrecks in the past. With all the hard work done the final step would be to literally draw a box around all the possible areas where *Kormoran* might have sunk. If I did my job correctly, *and* the Germans had been truthful about their reported positions, then the chances of finding *Kormoran* inside my designated search box could be as high as 95 per cent.

Although I did believe the Germans, I also recognised that there were some niggling uncertainties I could never truly eliminate or compensate for with my scientific approach. We would have to live with these uncertainties and they represented a real risk of failure, which I knew was much greater than 5 per cent, and that is why I never quoted the overly optimistic figure of 95 per cent when asked what I thought my chances of finding *Kormoran* were. My standard reply to this question was always the same: an 80 per cent chance of finding *Kormoran* and once it was found the chance of finding *Sydney* would rise to 70 per cent. This was my honest estimate based on intuition and gut feeling, which I felt was important to stress for everyone to understand that, while we had a good chance of success, it was far from guaranteed.

The explanation of my approach to defining the search box was mainly for the benefit of John Perryman, but I also wanted the HMA3S directors to be aware that an ongoing refinement of my search box was just one of many tasks that needed to be done before the search could start. Although I had already put in years of research and analysis into where the wrecks sank, I would continue to look for new clues and ways to improve my analysis right up to the last minute. At the same time we needed to move quickly to choose the best available search contractor out of a handful of companies we had already pre-qualified and find a survey vessel from which the search would be conducted. This was to be an international selection process that would take me back to familiar ground.

The nuts and bolts of a shipwreck search

In deciding which technology and methods would work best in the search for *Kormoran* and *Sydney* I never had any doubts that the correct tool to use was a deeptow side-scan sonar. This technology had been pioneered in the 1980s and it was ideal for locating lost shipwrecks in the deep ocean, especially when the area to be searched was large. I had used this type of sonar in the past to locate much deeper shipwrecks, including *Lucona*, *Derbyshire* and *Hood*, as well as the SS *Rio Grande*, a German blockade runner that Blue Water Recoveries found at the mind-boggling depth of 5,762 metres and in doing so was awarded a Guinness World Record for discovering the world's deepest shipwreck. Nevertheless, while depth was a factor in our choice of equipment, it was actually the combination of extreme depth plus the enormous search area that made the search for *Kormoran* and *Sydney* a perfect candidate for using this rather unique search tool.

The use of sound waves to detect ships was first discussed by Leonardo da Vinci in 1490 and today there are many different types of sonars used for collecting data in the oceans and navigating ships. In its most general form a sonar can be thought of as a powerful underwater flashlight that uses sound waves, instead of light, to image objects on the seabed. Specifically, a side-scan sonar is one that is towed at the end of a long steel cable connected to a survey ship and can scan the seabed to either side of the ship's track to create a coherent two-dimensional map of the surface and objects lying upon it. Under the watchful eye of a skilled expert viewing and interpreting the sonar images as they are created in real time, a side-scan sonar is the surest way to detect shipwrecks whether their hulls are intact or shattered and even when the surrounding seabed is complicated by rugged geological formations.

A deeptow side-scan sonar is simply one that can operate very deeply, to a maximum of 6,000 metres.[2] At such extreme depths it is necessary to position the side-scan sonar close to the seabed otherwise all the energy in its sonar signal will be lost due to absorption and

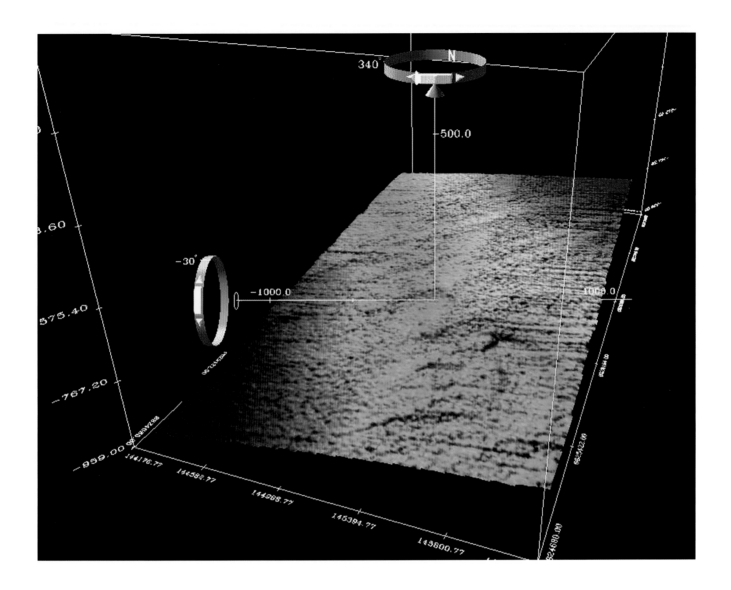

Above: The swathe bathymetry data of the KDLS3 location showed a smooth seabed devoid of any wreckage, allowing us to eliminate this area once and for all.

scattering effects as it travels long distances through sea water. Although towing a sonar this deep does have its drawbacks, there is an important benefit in that it results in the creation of 'acoustic shadows', which are formed like any normal shadow when a light shines on an object from a certain angle. Acoustic shadows can tell us a great deal of information about the height and shape of the object, especially as the basic two-dimensional nature of a sonar image means that an object's height is not directly apparent in the image and has to be inferred. The correct interpretation of acoustic shadows is important in being able to identify shipwrecks based on knowledge of their most prominent features like decks, masts and funnels.

Based upon the location of my provisional search box, I estimated that the water depths in the area would range from roughly 2,300 to 4,200 metres. By anyone's standards this was seriously deep water. In the US Gulf of Mexico, for example, where the world's deepest offshore natural gas platform *Independence* can be found anchored in 2,414 metres of water, the industry had to create a new term when oil exploration descended beyond the previous threshold for deep water. Any work in this new frontier below just 1,220 metres water depth is now considered 'ultra deep water'. Nevertheless, the greatest challenge posed by my search box was not the extreme depth; it was its enormous size.

Above: The unique SM-30 side-scan sonar.

My concern was that in the worst case we might have to search a box as large as 2,300 square nautical miles. That's an area equivalent in size to the cities of Perth, Adelaide and Canberra combined. More pertinently, it is over fifteen times larger than the area covered during the 1985 search for RMS *Titanic* — a search that took in excess of 40 days to complete. Our requirement to search such an enormous area, unprecedented in the short history of deep-water shipwreck hunting, was by far the single most important factor that drove our selection of the type of deeptow side-scan sonar we needed. We obviously wanted a sonar with good detection and resolution capabilities but its determining attribute had to be the ability to search large swathes of the seabed at a very rapid rate.

Specifically, I wanted a sonar that could search an area of seabed five to six kilometres wide and still be able to effectively detect shipwrecks the size of *Kormoran* and

Sydney, even in the unlucky situation of finding them lying on a surface of outcropping rock. Such 'wide-swathe' sonars were incredibly efficient and could cover anywhere between 70 to 100 square nautical miles per day while being towed behind a survey vessel at an average speed of 2.5 knots. With potentially 2,300 square nautical miles to search it was clear we needed to cover the seabed at similarly high rates, otherwise the search could take months to complete and prove to be too costly. The key technological feature of these sonars was the low frequency at which they operated: generally around 30 to 36 kilohertz. In simple terms, the lower the frequency of a side-scan sonar the greater its range or swathe. Although increased range generally comes at the expense of resolution, low-frequency side-scan sonars have surprisingly excellent detection capabilities because of a mechanical property of their transducers. If it sounds like these sonars were tailor-made for searching for deep-water shipwrecks, that is because they were. Unfortunately, that also makes them unique and very scarce. There were only a handful of these 'wide-swathe' sonars rated for deep-water operations in the world and even less were available to be commercially hired.

The search team

Everyone was immensely relieved when word came through from Fiona McNaught that HMA3S's application for the government grant had been officially approved by the RAN. Fiona had done a magnificent job in pushing through the application faster than anyone, including her, expected. The announcement of an election date that would send the government into caretaker mode was no longer a threat to the project and we could get on with the job of selecting the subcontractors who would make up the search team.

From the start of the selection process we knew that there were literally only a couple of contractors in the world who had the wide-swathe, deeptow side-scan sonar equipment and search expertise we needed, and they were both based in America. It would have been much more comfortable to have a larger pool of qualified companies to choose from, but this was the unique nature of this highly specialised field. After all, there is not a big call for firms that can find shipwrecks or downed aircraft at the bottom of the ocean and barely enough work for the two companies to share. I wasn't overly alarmed when our short list was reduced to one because the second contractor reported they had been hired for a different project at the same time and had to back out of the selection process. Both companies were eminently qualified and could rightly consider themselves world leaders in the field of deep-water searching so it wouldn't be an exaggeration to say that the one we chose — Williamson & Associates of Seattle, Washington — was the best available in the world.

For a small geophysical survey company with just 22 employees, Williamson & Associates punched well above its weight. Its clients ranged from the world's biggest and most demanding oil and gas and telecommunication

Above: (l) Carter Huynh Le and (r) Art Wright.

cable companies to the US Navy and other foreign governments around the globe. It first proved its shipwreck search credentials when it was hired to locate a famous treasure ship, the SS *Central America*, which was sunk in deep waters off the east coast of the United States during a ferocious 1857 hurricane with the loss of 452 lives. Three tons of gold coins and ingots worth more than $US100 million went down with the wreck and it became the focus of an underwater gold rush between three different groups of Americans looking to find and recover this amazing treasure. A team of scientists from the landlocked state of Ohio eventually won the race in 1986 when Williamson & Associates located the *Central America* for them after searching more than 1,200 square nautical miles of the ocean floor at depths of 2,600 metres using their 30-kilohertz deeptow side-scan sonar they called the SeaMARC 1A.[3]

I was forced to take notice of Williamson's technical triumph because my former company, Eastport International, had been hired by one of the other competing groups on the losing side of the race. Although disappointed not to be involved in such an exciting project, I was deeply impressed by Williamson's achievement and would have done anything to see for myself its equipment and its people at work offshore. My opportunity came two years later when I won a major contract for the oil giant Exxon for a side-scan sonar and swathe bathymetric route survey for a pipeline it wanted to run between several platforms offshore of Santa Barbara, California. Although I had devised the technical plan for this ground-breaking project, Eastport didn't have any of the special equipment required so I subcontracted Williamsons for the job. The contract was a huge responsibility for me — arguably too big for someone with only two years of industry experience — and at times I needed an older, more experienced hand to guide me through the difficult problems we encountered during the survey. That person turned out to be Art Wright, the Williamson party chief. In the end the Exxon survey was a big success and propelled everyone onto bigger and better things, but the lasting benefit in my mind was the start of a long professional relationship with Art.

Jumping forward nineteen years, the first name I wanted to see on Williamson's proposed crew list for the search was Art Wright's. Art might have been well beyond retirement age but he was incredibly fit and I knew that with him on board the Williamson team would work well under his leadership and be interested in only one thing: finding *Sydney*. It takes a rare blend of skills and character traits for someone to enjoy working at sea on small survey boats and to actually excel under highly stressful conditions. Generally, there is a mixture of both strong and silent characters in a team but invariably they all look to a leader they can trust and respect and who they know is knowledgeable. Art's background ticked all the boxes and then some: he had BS and MS degrees from the US Naval Academy, had been a captain in the US Navy, and was an expert in underwater acoustics. He was an authority with bags of experience and I could count on him to give me his honest opinion when needed.

The other key person I wanted to get to know was Carter Huynh Le, who had emigrated from Vietnam to take his electrical engineering degree at the University of Washington. Carter had been with Williamson & Associates for two and a half years and had worked extensively on their deeptow side-scan sonars to improve their electronic circuitry. If anything was to break offshore

Carter would be the only man capable of making the repairs to get us back on line, so the success or failure of the entire project could at some point fall on his shoulders. Communicating with Carter when I first met him wasn't easy as his English was poor and my Vietnamese non-existent. However, he seemed very conscientious and I liked the fact that he was confident around his equipment and that Art strongly vouched for his abilities.

With the search contractor selected, our focus switched back to Australia to find a suitable survey vessel to serve as the operating platform for the search and for Williamson's equipment. Although we had a slightly better choice of vessels than we had of search contractors it still came down to a question of availability and in the end only the SV *Geosounder* was freely available for hire during the period we needed it. The vessel was lying in Singapore but her new owners, DOF Subsea Australia, were keen to move her back to the west coast of Australia, which was ideal for us because it would allow the mobilisation to take place in Geraldton — the nearest port to the search area and the most economical in terms of saving time and fuel expended during transits. The *Geosounder* also happened to be the vessel that was donated by DOF earlier in the year to rule out the KDLS3 position so her capabilities as a survey vessel were well known to HMA3S.

We had four fundamental requirements of the survey vessel and the *Geosounder* comfortably met them all. She had more than enough deck space for the placement of Williamson's heavy towing winches; a large A-frame and crane for launching and recovery of the sonar towfishes; sufficient bunks for the entire marine crew and search team, which I estimated would total 31 people; and a dynamic positioning system to provide fine control of the vessel's propulsion, especially at slow speeds. The GPS-based survey systems on board were first rate and there was plenty of lab space in the bowels of the ship owing to her start in life as a Danish cargo vessel. On top of all this, there was the added bonus of a remotely operated vehicle (ROV) already on board and available for our use to film the wrecks if we were fortunate enough to find them during the search phase.

Above: The SV Geosounder.

It was a great advantage to have an ROV on board the *Geosounder* but I honestly didn't know if we'd ever get a chance to use it. To begin with, the ROV was limited to a depth of 3,000 metres and thus couldn't reach about 40 per cent of the area within my search box. If the wrecks were found a bit further west than the 111° line of longitude they would lie deeper than 3,000 metres. In that case I fully expected that the ROV phase would be put off until the following year while one of the few ROVs in the world that could dive deeper was transported to Australia. I had also mentally prepared myself for the search to take the entire 45 days we had estimated. While this would cause us to run out of funds and probably what remained of the good weather conditions, I honestly didn't care if it took us until the very last day to find the wrecks. Our primary objective was to find *Sydney* and the only thing that mattered was that she *was* found, not *when* she was found. I wanted everyone to have this same focus and not look beyond what we needed to achieve in the search phase. If fortune fell on us and *Sydney* was found, then diving on her with the ROV during this expedition would be like icing on the cake. But first we had to make the cake.

Refining the search box

Slowly but surely everything began to fall into place and a date for final mobilisation of the vessel in Geraldton was set for 27 February. HMA3S wisely took on a full-time professional project manager named Patrick Flynn to look after all the onshore management issues of the project, leaving me to concentrate on directing the offshore search. At times the project was a minefield of logistical problems that would have stopped us dead in our tracks had Patrick not skilfully steered around the dangers. Media and public interest in the search had also intensified and that brought its own pressures. It was simply impossible to expect the volunteer directors of HMA3S to handle such a big job. Patrick had been in charge of major offshore construction projects costing hundreds of millions of dollars so HMA3S was fortunate to have someone of his calibre running the show. For months leading up to the mobilisation Patrick, fuelled by a steady intake of flat white coffees, literally did the work of three people to keep the project on schedule and the RAN informed of our progress. Having Patrick as part of the team took a huge weight off my shoulders and freed my time to oversee the weather study and drift analysis I saw as the final attempt to refine my search box.

Above: Patrick Flynn.

When it comes to plotting the historical navigation information that I use to define the search box for any wreck, a process that is commonly referred to as 'renavigation', I eschew computers and rely on old-fashioned manual plotting on paper charts. I have always felt this gives me a better feel for how the captain was manoeuvring his ship in the moments preceding its loss. Computers are great and they have a definite role to play but they can lead to tunnel vision, whereas working on a chart gives me the expansive awareness I feel is needed to understand the overall picture of how and where the ship in question was lost. I also work strictly in pencil and for a difficult problem like this one, I generally create a couple of different renavigation plots that reflect my constant reassessment of the evidence and changes in thinking. In the years I was conducting my research I had made three different versions of the renavigation plot for the sinking of *Kormoran*. I had laboured over the first chart so much that it was badly frayed at the edges and falling apart at the seams. My plan was to bring a clean and unmarked chart with me to Australia to make one last final plot before starting the search.

In terms of documented information from the archives there was nothing new to plot that I wasn't already aware of from my own research or from other researchers. One last-ditch effort by Wes Olson, Glenys McDonald and John Perryman to get to the bottom of a reported sighting of oil by a pilot of one of the Catalina aeroplanes involved in the original search proved inconclusive. It was a potentially vital clue that could have actually pinpointed the location of *Kormoran*'s wreck but try as we might we were unable to corroborate it. If a clue didn't pass my strict test for corroboration then it didn't make it onto my final plot. I wasn't about to be swayed by speculative pieces of information.

I was reserving the unmarked chart to incorporate the results of a new and scientifically rigorous drift analysis of the life rafts recovered by *Aquitania* and *Trocas*, which I decided to commission. This idea came to me the year before when I learned about Dr David Griffin of the CSIRO Marine and Atmospheric Research Division based in Hobart and his applied research work on the surface currents at the site of the battle. Dr Griffin is a physical oceanographer and CSIRO's project leader for BLUElink, a government, RAN and CSIRO funded project that uses oceanographic and current data and advanced supercomputer technology to provide ocean forecasts around Australia. When I realised that the BLUElink database and computing power could be used to give us the first real measurements of the current field in this location I contacted Dr Griffin and asked for his help in finding the wrecks. Initially he was cautious because over the years he had been asked the same question many times before but was frustrated because the type of careful and concerted effort needed to produce results was never made. Nevertheless, as soon as I was able to convince him that I was serious and would see the analysis through to its conclusion, he generously volunteered his expertise and time to help me.

The ocean current data used by BLUElink is based on satellite radar altimetry that measures the height of the sea surface with such extraordinary precision that it is possible for powerful supercomputers to accurately estimate ocean currents. Although the satellites carrying accurate altimeters have been in orbit since 1992 — and collecting many years of data that is now available to BLUElink scientists — the supercomputing ability to estimate ocean currents from the sea surface altimetry is a more recent development. Officially, the BLUElink project was initiated in 2002. Before then physical oceanographers were more or less unaware of the complex dynamics of the ocean currents off the northern West Australian coast that featured large, swirling and unpredictable eddy currents.

The Search for the

SYDNEY

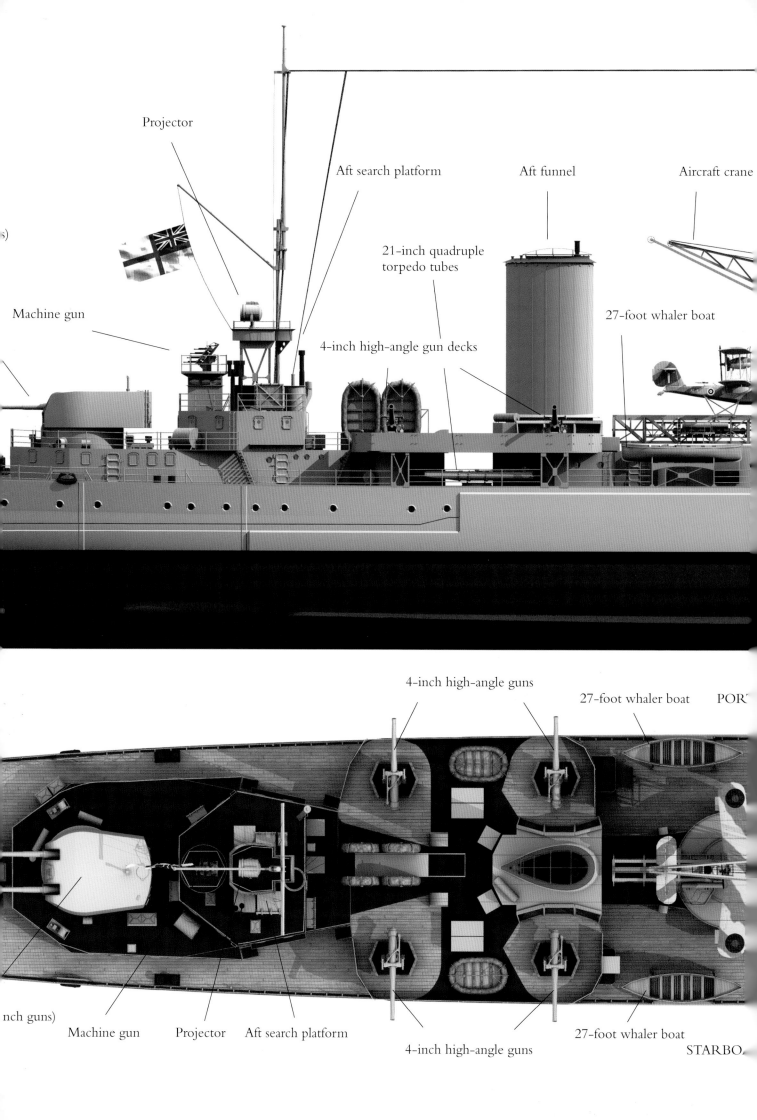

Projector

Aft search platform

Aft funnel

Aircraft crane

21-inch quadruple
torpedo tubes

Machine gun

27-foot whaler boat

4-inch high-angle gun decks

4-inch high-angle guns

27-foot whaler boat   POR

nch guns)

Machine gun   Projector   Aft search platform

4-inch high-angle guns

27-foot whaler boat

STARBO

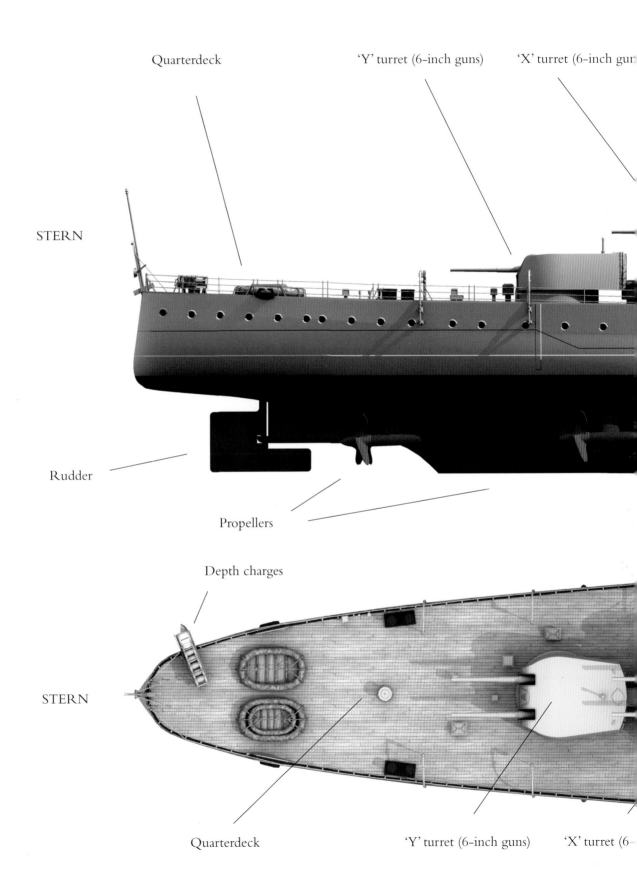

Quarterdeck

'Y' turret (6-inch guns)

'X' turret (6-inch gun

STERN

Rudder

Propellers

Depth charges

STERN

Quarterdeck

'Y' turret (6-inch guns)

'X' turret (6-

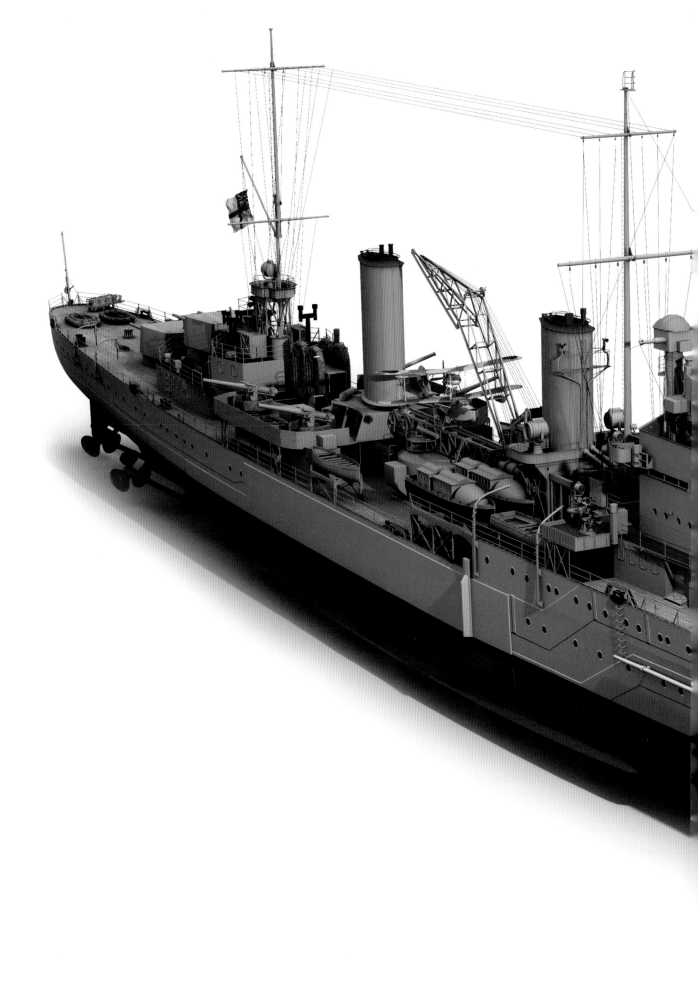

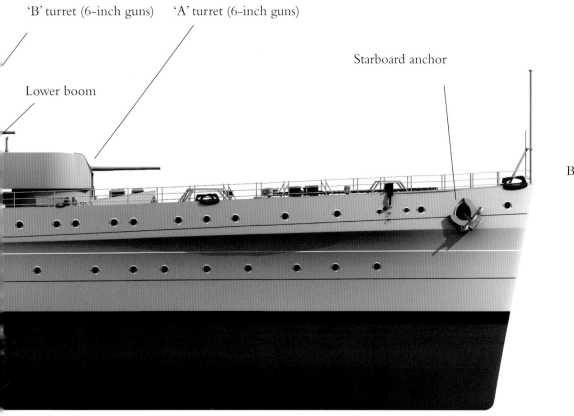

'B' turret (6-inch guns)   'A' turret (6-inch guns)

Starboard anchor

Lower boom

BOW/STEM

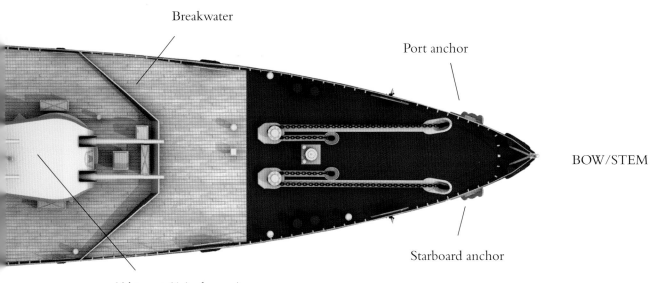

Breakwater

Port anchor

BOW/STEM

'A' turret (6-inch guns)

–inch guns)

Starboard anchor

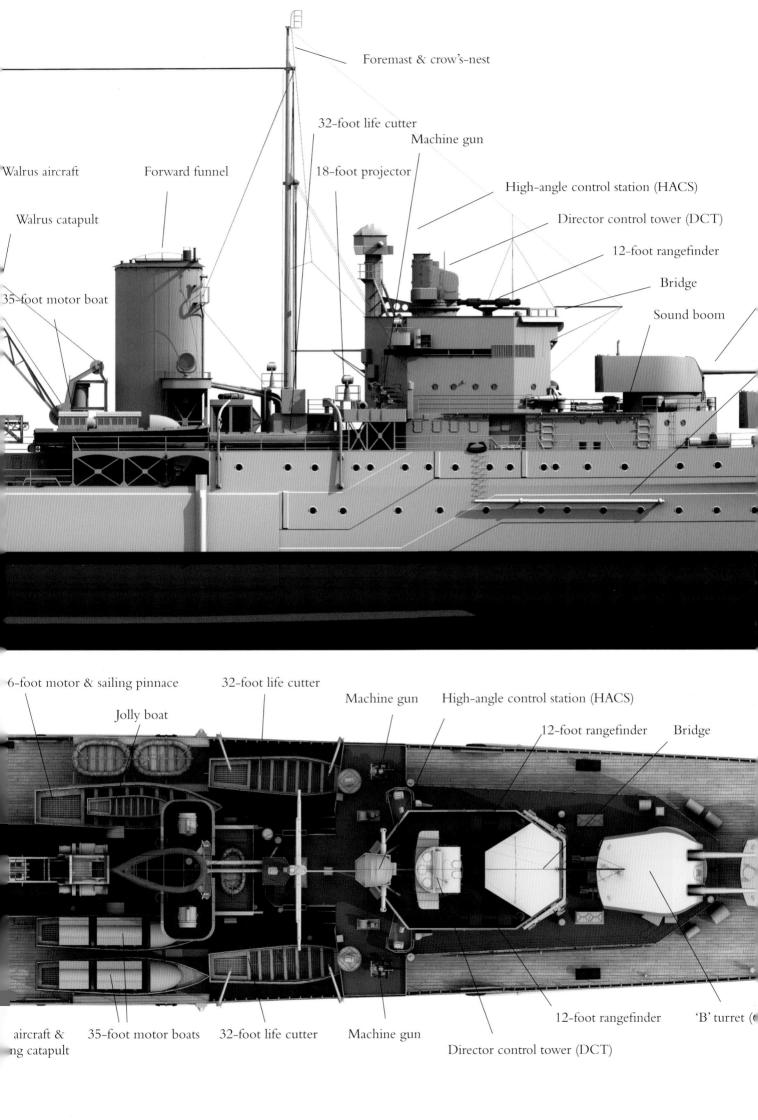

Foremast & crow's-nest

32-foot life cutter

Machine gun

Walrus aircraft

Forward funnel

18-foot projector

High-angle control station (HACS)

Director control tower (DCT)

Walrus catapult

12-foot rangefinder

Bridge

35-foot motor boat

Sound boom

6-foot motor & sailing pinnace

32-foot life cutter

Machine gun

High-angle control station (HACS)

Jolly boat

12-foot rangefinder

Bridge

aircraft &

ng catapult

35-foot motor boats

32-foot life cutter

Machine gun

12-foot rangefinder

'B' turret (

Director control tower (DCT)

SYDNEY

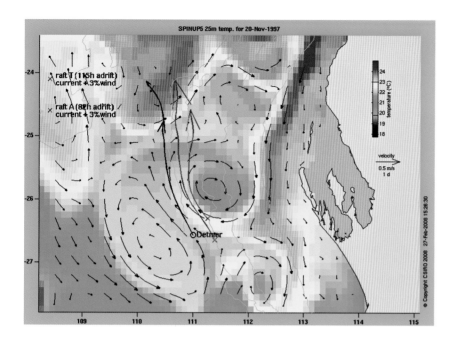

Above: The swirling arrows depict eddy currents. A scientific understanding of the currents was needed before we could determine the probable sinking location of Kormoran.

The earlier attempts by *Sydney* researchers to estimate the ocean current effect on the drift of the life rafts were based on an incorrect assumption that the prevailing currents were uniformly northward flowing. The possible presence of transient eddy currents that could flow in a multitude of directions made it impossible for anyone to know how they might have affected the drift of life rafts and debris in the aftermath of the battle. Any estimate of a probable sinking position for *Kormoran* based upon average current speed and direction that didn't take in the variability of the current field was bound to be invalid. This is why I cautioned researchers that the earlier attempts to precisely pinpoint the sinking position of *Kormoran* — in the form of an 'X' on a chart — based upon drift analysis were misguided. However, with BLUElink we had the potential missing link to solve this problem in a scientifically correct manner.

The first step was to commission a professional meteorologist to come up with a new and improved estimate of the historical wind conditions for the nominal battle location. This meteorological analysis of daily wind speeds and direction, or wind hindcast, was required for

Dr Griffin to determine how much of the total drift experienced by the two recovered life rafts was attributed to the winds and how much was attributed to the surface currents. Len van Burgel, formerly of the Australian Bureau of Meteorology, took on the seven-week assignment with the assistance of Grant Elliott, the regional manager of the bureau's Special Services Unit based in Perth.

Two different methodologies were employed by van Burgel and Elliott to estimate the historical wind conditions. One was based on an extremely careful reanalysis of the historical mean sea level pressure charts from November 1941, which were used to derive the pressure gradient and ultimately the wind direction and speed using the geostrophic wind equation. The second method, referred to as 'pattern matching', was based on matching the historical pressure gradients derived above against a computerised database of pressure gradients assembled for the period 1968–2007. The main benefit of this method is that because the matching is done by computers an extremely large 39-year database can be quickly scanned to come up with recent dates in which the pressure gradients most closely matched the historical conditions for 19–28 November 1941. Once van Burgel and Elliott had the matched dates they could go to three state-of-the-art sources of recent wind data and pick out the measured and computed wind conditions (direction and speed) and with a high degree of confidence they would closely match the historical conditions determined by the first method.[4]

A comparison of the estimates produced by the two methodologies indicated that absolute worst-case errors were plus or minus 4 knots for wind speed and 20 to 30 degrees for direction. This was a much better accommodation between the methodologies compared to the apparent differences between the two 1991 studies, and as the errors in this analysis are random they will tend to cancel out over the period in question. Estimating historical wind conditions over the open ocean without the benefit of actual observations is a task fraught with difficulty. There was no doubt, however, that van Burgel's and Elliott's analyses produced a very good set of data that was a considerable improvement over the estimates of wind speed and direction made in 1991.

It was also just in the nick of time. Mobilisation of the vessel in Geraldton was set to start in less than four days and I still had to check the data and get it over to Dr Griffin in Hobart for him to start the actual drift analysis. The software program he developed specifically for the analysis had never been used before so there was bound to be some debugging and fine-tuning required before he could send me the first set of reliable results. When I arrived in Geraldton I set up an area for plotting in my motel room and started work on my final renavigation plot by pencilling in all the German positions and the track of *Kormoran* as per Detmers's account. Patrick Flynn had everything well under control at the port ready for arrival of the *Geosounder*, leaving me free to complete the drift analysis with Dr Griffin.

The BLUElink dataset provided estimates of surface currents on a daily basis for a consecutive fifteen-year period up to 2006. We agreed to consider data from only the latter half of November to best match the period the life rafts were actually drifting. This yielded a total of 225 scenarios showing what the current field, including eddies, might have been in November 1941. Because we had good information that the coastal sea level was low in 1941 and this would have resulted in a weaker than normal southwards-flowing Leeuwin current, Dr Griffin included a variation of the same data for the years 1993–97, when the coastal sea level was also low. This increased the total number of scenarios available for the analysis to 300.

Dr Griffin's computer program produced a simulated trajectory of the possible drift tracks of the *Aquitania* and *Trocas* life rafts for each of the 300 scenarios in both back-tracking and forward-tracking modes. The program calculated the total drift as a vector sum of the surface current drift from the 300 scenarios and the leeway (wind) drift from an average of the wind conditions provided by van Burgel and Elliott. For the all-important leeway factor, which basically determines the leeway drift speed of the rafts taken as a percentage of the average daily wind speed in knots, I decided to consult one of the world's leading experts on leeway drift, Art Allen of the US Coast Guard's Office of Search and Rescue. Prior to asking his recommendation for an appropriate leeway factor to use, I gave Allen every piece of technical information I had about the life rafts, including a picture of the overloaded *Aquitania* life raft and details about its construction and drift voyage given to me by Kurt Meder, one of the its 26 occupants who I was able to track down in Germany. Allen's advice was that at the upper limit a 3 per cent leeway factor was reasonable, whereas at the lower limit it would be closer to 1 per cent at the times the life raft was swamped.

As Dr Griffin and I expected, the final results of the analysis revealed a very large spread of back-calculated launch points showing the possible positions where the two life rafts departed from *Kormoran*. We were also not surprised to see that the main orientation of the spread was in the north–south direction, indicating greater variability in drift speed versus direction. To help me visualise the overall result of the analysis Dr Griffin created a summary plot in which a single back-calculated launch point was plotted for each of the 20 annual late November periods he included in the sample size for both life rafts. When I opened this plot just before midnight at the end of the first day of the vessel mobilisation it revealed a clear pattern that would have an immediate impact on my search plans. In relation to Detmers's position of 26°34' South 111° East, only three of the possible 40 launch points were south of this; three more were approximately level with the latitude of Detmers's position; while the remaining 34 points were all well north of it.

The one conclusion I could draw from this analysis was unmistakable. While it was certainly possible that the life rafts could have been launched from Detmers's position, it was far more probable that the actual launch point was some way north of this position. What this meant was that Detmers's position was more likely to be the noon position rather than the action position of *Kormoran* on the day of the battle as Wes Olson first

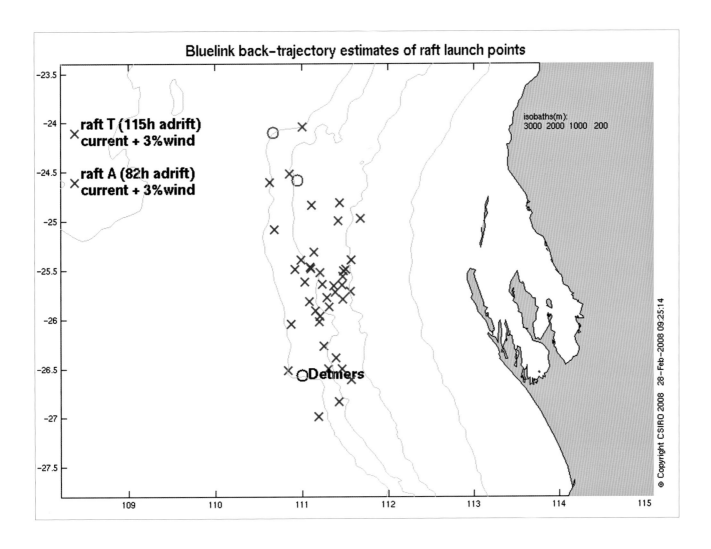

Bluelink back-trajectory estimates of raft launch points

raft T (115h adrift)
current + 3%wind

raft A (82h adrift)
current + 3%wind

isobaths(m):
3000 2000 1000 200

Detmers

© Copyright CSIRO 2008   28-Feb-2008 09:25:14

Above: Dr Griffin's summary plot showing thirty-seven of the forty projected launch points north of Detmers's noon position for Kormoran.

postulated in the 2001 seminar and I had been trying to prove ever since. I needed to be extremely careful how I used this result in refining my search box because there was still a lot of room for error. Nevertheless, this was a careful and scientifically sound use of trusted physical clues in conjunction with the best state-of-the-art data on currents and winds to narrow the most probable sinking position of *Kormoran*.

I had done everything I could possibly think of to make sure I was searching in the right place for the wrecks. True to a promise I made five years earlier, I had left no stone unturned in seeking clues to the wrecks' locations. I also pursued every idea imaginable to help narrow the search box and improve our chances of

success. All the hard work was done and now it was just a matter of completing the mobilisation and getting out to sea. At the press conference in Geraldton's town hall the next morning I felt very confident as I briefed the media and public about my search plans. I still needed a few hours of solitude to draw in the final search box on my renavigation chart, but I would have plenty of time for that during the transit to site. The long wait was over. The first, and hopefully last, search of the northern location for *Kormoran* and *Sydney* was about to begin.

CHAPTER SIX

...

False start

I checked my watch for what felt to be the thousandth time as I could feel the vibration of *Geosounder's* thrusters pushing her blue and white hull away from the quayside. It was 1612 local time on 29 February and following a string of frustrating delays we were about to leave behind the comfort of Port Geraldton and head out to sea to start the search. The local port pilot, Dave Murgatroyd, was on the bridge with *Geosounder's* captain, Blair Cliffe, ready to guide him through the protective breakwaters and entrance channel out to open water. I shot one last look at the people waving us farewell and noticed Patrick Flynn slip the last mooring line over the bollard that was holding us fast to land. Patrick had worked tirelessly to get the ship ready for departure so it was fitting he was the one releasing us to start what we all hoped and prayed would be a successful mission to solve the mystery of *Kormoran* and *Sydney*.

The last day of vessel mobilisations are typically pressure-filled events that wear down everyone's patience and this mobilisation proved to be no different. The day started fine and by 0610 hours a gang of welders were on hand to complete the modifications to the stern A-frame. It was supposed to be the last item holding up our departure, which I wanted to make as early as possible in order that the commissioning trials we had planned for the Williamson sonars at a shallow water location just seaward of the Abrolhos Islands could take place in daylight hours. At 0830 I chaired a meeting of all the contractors and vessel department heads to fix an estimated time for departure (ETD) and was encouraged when everyone nodded their heads in agreement to a 1000 ETD. However, within minutes of this meeting breaking up the first problem cropped up to dash these plans. An engineer had mistakenly cancelled the 0900 load test for the A-frame that had to be passed before it was certified safe for use. As an immediate call was made to get the test engineers down to the vessel straightaway I had no option but to push the ETD back to 1100.

This hiccup seemed to set the pattern for the day as it turned out to be the first of four ETD reschedules I was forced to make. The frustration of missing one departure

Left: The launch of Steiermark, *which would become* Kormoran.

slot after another was nothing compared to my concern about the problems causing these delays as they were serious enough to jeopardise the entire project. The first problem involved the primary 10,000-metre-long tow cable that the Williamson team was going to use to tow their sonars. The high-voltage electrical core of this tow cable was shorted at some unknown location along its full length, rendering this cable and winch combo unusable. Fortunately, Art Wright had brought a second winch and tow cable onto the vessel and this spare set-up would replace the broken primary one. Without a working tow cable no searching could take place so while I was relieved that Art had the foresight to bring the spare system it was disturbing that we had to use it on day one and were thus effectively starting the search without a spare.

The second problem was with Geosounder's satellite-based broadband internet system that had to be upgraded and reprogrammed to connect to a different satellite after the vessel's move from Singapore. Judging from the nervous look on the face of the engineer sent specifically to make these changes it wasn't as simple as it sounded and for the entire morning he seemed stymied. When I first started going to sea there was no internet or email or broadband communications, but with today's modern survey vessels these capabilities are no longer luxuries; they are necessities. On this project we needed them even more than usual for keeping the public and press informed and for sending the onshore TV production team the daily rushes of video documenting the search activities. This was a fundamental part of the HMA3S/RAN media plan to ensure that the progress of the search was as transparent to the public and press as practicable. HMA3S had revamped its website and the plan was for me to compile a daily report with associated images and send them to Patrick Flynn and Richard Sojka, the website's designer, for uploading.[1] This communication link was deemed essential, so we couldn't sail without it working and passing a test run.

For the fifth time that day the minutes ticked down to our departure deadline in what was now becoming an embarrassing and costly routine. Every hour lost in the delay was an hour less we could spend during the search. However, this time the engineers who greeted me with their status update all wore smiles of satisfaction and obvious relief. A sample of video successfully made the round-trip journey from the ship up to the satellite and back down to the production studio in Fremantle. We were finally cleared for departure.

As Geosounder moved steadily towards the breakwaters the cloud of anxiety that had hung over the ship throughout the day lifted in the fresh southerly breeze. Most of the search team had come up to the boat deck to watch a news helicopter buzz the ship in a series of increasingly close fly-bys and to catch one last glimpse of the Sydney memorial that overlooked the harbour. I was immensely relieved that we were on our way at last and there was a palpable sense of excitement and anticipation for what was to come over the next several weeks. Although I had the commissioning tests on my mind I decided to enjoy the moment and linger in the hot sun with Glenys and Carter as the pilot boat moved along our starboard side to retrieve Dave Murgatroyd after he handed command of the Geosounder back to Blair. I was told that the boy waving to us from the boat's wheelhouse was Dave's young son. He must have made this trip with his father countless times and seen much bigger ships out of Port Geraldton, but I suspect that like everyone else who showed up to wave us off he wanted to be part of the potentially historic event. I could just imagine him telling the story later on in his life of how he escorted the ship that found Sydney out to sea and I desperately wanted this dream to come true for him. Not a minute later the ship's loudspeaker shattered the mood by requesting my urgent presence on the bridge. I had only taken a few steps up the ladder-way but I could already tell something had gone wrong.

When I got to the bridge the anxious tone in Blair's voice confirmed my fears. Smoke was reported in the engine room and Blair had made an immediate decision to proceed to the nearest anchorage to stop and assess the situation. Smoke in a ship is an extremely serious concern, especially in the engine room where the risk of fire is greatest. As Blair and his second officer, Graham Cann, carefully manoeuvred the Geosounder past an area of

shoals, John and I stood by and provided some extra eyes to watch out for the floats and lines of crayfish pots and to monitor the echo sounder showing the depth of water under the keel. John had spent 25 years of his navy life on the bridge of ships in tense situations so the scene wasn't new to him, although I was sure he wasn't expecting such drama within minutes of our departure; nor was I.

By the time *Geosounder* was safely anchored in Champion Bay it was clear that everything was under control in the engine room and there was no immediate danger. The cause of the problem, however, was very serious. A hairline crack had opened in the bottom of the diesel fuel tank sitting directly above the main engine, which resulted in a stream of diesel fuel leaking down on the hot engine exhaust, causing the surrounding lagging to smoulder and fill the engine room with smoke. Although the crack was in a very bad location it was small enough that the engineers hoped they could seal it with some plastic metal. Later when I went down to the engine room to inspect the crack myself I could see that, as hard as the engineers had tried to seal it, their efforts were futile. Forced under the pressure of the 40 tonnes sitting in this tank, the fuel kept saturating the plastic metal and every few minutes a fresh stream would break out and douse the engineer below.

As much as I hated the idea of us limping back into port with our tail between our legs we had no other option but to go in to have the tank drained of all its fuel and its bottom repaired by welders. This problem was going to test the DOF vessel managers in getting their ship repaired and turned around as soon as possible, especially as we were coming back in during a holiday weekend. Fortunately, Patrick Flynn hadn't yet left Geraldton and would be on hand to assist. At best we were looking at a two- to three-day delay; it would be worse if we couldn't get the shore support we required because of the holiday weekend. This was a bad break that would only increase the pressure on our schedule and I struggled to find anything positive about it other than the fact it didn't happen much further from port. John was able to put the incident into perspective for me by recounting the tragic story of HMAS *Westralia* when an engine room fire in

Above: Repairing the crack in the diesel fuel tank.

1998 led to the deaths of four of her crew. That fire had a similar cause when a diesel fuel line ruptured and sprayed fuel on a hot engine igniting a deadly inferno. The horror of the *Westralia* incident made me rethink our situation; rather than us being unlucky that the fuel leak happened during our charter, the truth was we were actually lucky the incident wasn't more serious.

The search begins

Any worries I might have had about the holiday weekend getting in the way with the repairs to *Geosounder* disappeared as we arrived back in port and were immediately met by two road tankers to remove the 40 tonnes of diesel fuel and vent the tank of its dangerous gases. For once everything went like clockwork and the vessel was patched up and refuelled less than 30 hours later. It was a remarkable turnaround that was only slightly spoiled by having to wait until the following morning before a pilot was available to take us out again. This time we cleared the breakwater and entrance channel without drama and headed straight out into the Indian Ocean to a test site I had picked out just beyond the Abrolhos Islands where the water depths were about 350 metres. In addition to their low-frequency SM-30 side-scan sonar, Art Wright also brought Williamson's AMS-60 high-frequency (60 kilohertz) sonar on the expedition. This would be used in case any wreck-like targets were found by the SM-30 that required further scrutiny. The better quality imagery obtained by the AMS-60 would achieve this. The commissioning tests were successfully completed and the last sonar was finally brought on board at four in the morning after it was towed over to the lee of one of the islands for a recovery in calmer waters. With the sonars securely lashed down on deck, *Geosounder* got under way and proceeded north to the search box at 9.5 knots to start the hunt for *Kormoran* and *Sydney*.

A little more than nineteen hours later the *Geosounder* was in position south of the southern edge of my search box where I wanted the search to begin. Art Wright and his team of seven sonar technicians wasted no time in launching their SM-30 side-scan sonar towfish and the separate depressor weight, which is designed to minimise the negative effect that rough seas can have on the sonar imagery. The time was 2348 on 4 March as the SM-30 sonar disappeared beneath the inky black waves to begin its long descent to the ocean floor. It would be four hours before we could get our first glimpse of the sonar imagery that would tell us whether the seabed was going to be smooth and easy to search or rough and not so easy. I was worried about the possible type of geological formations we might find which could complicate the search. We might be faced with deep submarine canyons bisecting the search area or possibly find that the area was littered with fields of large boulders that had rolled down from the edge of the continental

shelf. I had information that suggested either was possible but we wouldn't be able to confirm this until the first search trackline was completed.

Initially, my heart sank when the first sonar images started to scroll down our screens. There was clearly quite a bit of geology present in the form of large boulders scattered about. I had found shipwrecks in far worse seabed conditions so I wasn't too alarmed but I also knew that everything would depend on whether the conditions improved or got worse as the sonar was towed into the search box proper. We had purposely started outside the search box to give the Williamson technicians ample time to 'tune in' the SM-30 sonar and for the bridge staff to find the best heading and speed to run the trackline. With a minimum of 7,000 metres of tow cable out and the *Geosounder* moving at an average speed of 2.8 knots, the sonar towfish was more than three nautical miles behind the ship at all times.

I was prepared for this first trackline, which we were running south to north through pretty much the heart of my search box, to serve as a practice/reconnaissance line; but we would have to run over this area again if the imagery didn't meet my high standard for quality and 100 per cent seabed coverage. In fact, the SM-30 sonar was having technical problems that made the image quality so poor that I requested Art Wright to recover the towfish after it reached the end of the trackline to determine what was wrong. No one knew for sure what exactly happened to the sonar to cause the imagery to degrade so soon after the successful commissioning test, but I couldn't allow another trackline consuming 21 hours of our time budget to be wasted.

My assessment of the first trackline was that no significant targets were detected and we only achieved about 70 per cent coverage due to a combination of problems. John was surprised to hear me say that one of the problems was actually because the water depths where we were searching were too shallow. To explain, I drew him a diagram that showed the spatial relationship between the depth of the SM-30 towfish and the sonar's maximum range, which is 3,000 metres or one-half of the total swathe. The fundamental problem we were

Above: Launching the SM-30 side-scan sonar…

facing was that, although most of the sonar's acoustic energy is directed downwards to the seabed, some of it also transmits upwards to the sea surface, such that when the physical depth of the sonar is less than the maximum 3,000-metre range it is possible for the sonar to 'see' the sea surface and for this surface image to mask the images of the seabed. In our case with the sonar towfish operating at a depth of roughly 2,200 metres, the sea surface returns were coming in on the imagery at 2,200 metres and effectively masking the outer 800 metres of seabed imagery on both the port and starboard channels. This is a common problem with all side-scan sonars to varying degrees and it is made worse when the weather is bad and breaking waves are injecting a lot of air — a very strong reflector of acoustic energy — into the surface waters.

The upshot of all this was that I decided to revise my original search plan by decreasing the spacing between

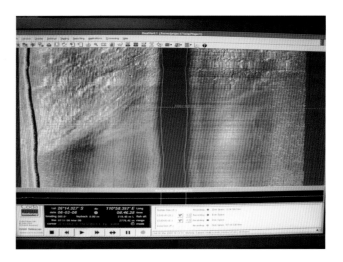

… which would send back the sonar imagery.

adjacent tracklines in order to solve the problem of the sea surface return masking the seabed imagery. The cost of this change would be an additional three or four days of search time to ensure that the search box for *Kormoran* was completely covered to my satisfaction. It was another painful hit to our schedule but I wasn't about to accept the risk that we could pass over the wrecks with the sonar but not see them because the imagery was being obliterated by the annoying surface return. No matter how small this risk, the consequences of possibly missing the wrecks was far too great for me to even contemplate taking this chance. I am normally a bit of a risk-taker but I wasn't about to take this one when so many people were counting on me to get it right.

Cyclone Ophelia

The final search box I mapped out for *Kormoran* measured 52 nautical miles (north–south) by 34 nautical miles (east–west) and encompassed a colossal 1,768 square nautical miles. This was the largest search box I had ever attempted by a very big margin and I knew this would put a lot of pressure on the search team and ship drivers. Each north–south trackline through the search box would take an average of 21 hours to complete during which everyone would have to be on constant alert to monitor

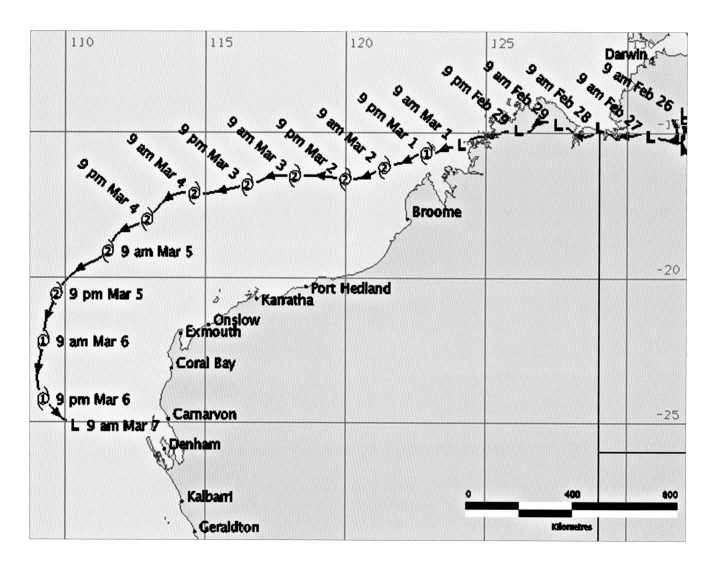

Above: The frustrating track of our nemesis Cyclone Ophelia.

the performance of the equipment, to keep *Geosounder* precisely on track and to watch out for sonar targets. The only time to relax even slightly was during the six hours it would take at the end of each completed trackline to turn the towfish around on to the next trackline. The search team was split into two shifts working twelve hours each but this still meant they would be spending the bulk, if not all, of their shift working on full alert. I also had an assistant named Robert Bruinsma to cover my opposite twelve-hour shift, although I knew the demands on my time meant I would be working more than eighteen hours a day.

It was going to be a brutal routine but it was designed this way to maximise our search productivity by reducing the amount of non-productive time spent in turns. The 30 days in our search budget might have seemed like plenty of time but I knew how quickly it could be eaten

up. My original estimate was that, including a moderate contingency for weather downtime, it would take at least seventeen days to entirely cover the *Kormoran* search box if there were no other losses of time because of technical issues. The mobilisation and fuel leak problems, which cost us nearly three and a half days before the search even began, showed this to be unrealistic. Taking into account the revision I had to make to the search plan because of the surface return problem, it now looked as though we would need 21 days to cover the search box with only 26.5 days remaining in our budget. This wouldn't leave much time to locate *Sydney* if the search for *Kormoran* went all the way to the last day. Adding to this pressure on the schedule was the fact that the SM-30 towfish appeared to be sick.

The dim flashing of a small light on the front of the SM-30 control panel on the ship indicated that there was an electrical ground fault (a type of short circuit) in the system and this was affecting the quality of the sonar imagery. The short could be located anywhere, but nine times out of ten it would be on the towfish in the form of a minute leak of water into any of the dozens of connectors or cables, including the main tow cable, which comprises the towfish. The problem would be more serious if the water was actually leaking into the pressure resistant housings, which protected the sensitive and high-voltage electrical components and left unchecked could result in catastrophic damage. The solution was to isolate the component causing the short and either repair or replace it. This was easier said then done, however, and Carter Le had his work cut out for him tracking down the underlying cause of the short. While Carter worked and the search was suspended, a new problem introduced herself to me.

The culprit was a tropical cyclone that had been harmlessly spinning her way into the Indian Ocean well north of our position before suddenly deciding to veer south towards us. The Bureau of Meteorology forecasters in Perth gave the cyclone what I thought was an enchanting name: Ophelia; although I couldn't help but think of Shakespeare's Ophelia who eventually drowns herself after being spurned by Hamlet. Ophelia's veer to the south as a Category 2 cyclone with maximum sustained winds of 100 kilometres per hour caught us slightly off guard as our focus was on solving the SM-30 sonar problems. At one point Carter thought he had solved all the electrical faults and the towfish was launched and on its way back down towards the seabed only for him to have one look at the imagery to see that the problems were still there. In the time the sonar was being worked on Ophelia had moved 180 nautical miles closer to our location and we were beginning to feel the force of her wrath. The winds had increased from 22 to 27 knots and Ophelia veered yet again, this time as if she was aiming directly for our position. Art Wright was inclined to leave the SM-30 in the water and ride the storm out but I wasn't keen on taking a chance if it increased the possibility of damage, or

loss, of the towfish. Even though Ophelia was weakening and her winds would only be gale force when catching up to us the Bureau of Meteorology meteorologists advised me we could still be hit with squalls and winds of 45 to 50 knots. This was no time to be taking a chance with Mother Nature, and her daughter Ophelia, so I made the call to have the towfish recovered.

The conditions for a night-time recovery of the towfish might have been marginal but Art Wright and his crew handled it smoothly and without incident. I talked through our options with the ship's master, Blair, and suggested we run to the north-east, which would keep us just ahead of Ophelia as she weakened while giving us the most comfortable ride into the three-metre swells. With the search suspended the most important thing now was to make things as easy as possible for Carter and Bill Heather to troubleshoot the sonar on a stable deck free from pitching and rolling, which was what they needed most. The *Geosounder* might have had a reputation as a good sea-boat but that was before we welded two heavy winches weighing 18.5 tonnes and 21.8 tonnes respectively to opposite sides of her deck. The pendulum effect caused by the placement of these two winches made the ship roll quite badly and sent anyone with questionable sea-legs scurrying to the rail or to their bunks.

Although I was getting increasingly frustrated by our poor start to the search I didn't want others to know the depth of my concern. Getting hit by Ophelia was plain bad luck and there wasn't anything we could do about that. My big worry was the ongoing technical problems with the SM-30 towfish, the cause of which seemed to be eluding Carter and Bill. The small white adhesive medicinal patch behind Carter's ear marked him as someone who suffers from seasickness and I was concerned how he was holding up in the less than ideal conditions. All that I could do was be optimistic and encouraging and keep my own worries to myself, although I saw that John was someone I could confide in. I constantly moved about the ship consulting with Blair about the weather or getting updates from Art and Carter about their progress. I also made frequent visits to the main deck to monitor the changing sea conditions.

Left top: Navigating Cyclone Ophelia; middle: Carter, with a seasickness patch behind his ear, repairing an electronic circuit board; bottom: Ophelia's wind blows the tops off waves.

Despite being unhappy with this weather-forced delay I enjoyed looking at the angry, windswept sea. In its own way it was a beautiful and exhilarating sight and it reminded me how much I loved being at sea under any conditions.

In total we had lost nearly 40 hours of search time before Carter was sure he had found and fixed the last of the SM-30 sonar's problems. What was left of Ophelia had moved past our location and was heading towards the coast to give Carnarvon a good soaking. The SM-30 had passed all its deck tests and we were about 40 nautical miles east of the start of the next search trackline. Everything was looking positive for a launch when we arrived on location as the winds had died down to 10 knots after being closer to 30 knots all day. Ten minutes later I was disheartened to watch the winds suddenly increase to 38 knots, with gusts to 45 knots, and the seas build back up in no time. The wave tops were being blown off and the sea was white with foam. Ophelia wasn't finished with us just yet; she had one last sting in her tail. The last entry in my logbook for another wasted day was 'W.O.W.' — waiting on weather.

Carter on the spot

It was early the next morning, at 0415 hours on 8 March, before the seas eased enough to safely launch the sonar and resume the search. I decided to search the trackline (No. 6 in our nomenclature) immediately to the west of the first trackline (No. 7) in order to cover the centre of my search box. This would allow us to concentrate thereafter on the north-eastern quadrant of the box, in case nothing was found, where the drift analysis indicated there was more likelihood of locating the wrecks. Everyone was anxious to see whether Carter had been successful in solving the problems which were ruining the sonar imagery.

Because the SM-30 transmits an acoustic ping only once every four seconds it takes a long time — at least 30 minutes — before there is enough imagery on our computer screens to judge its quality. This is one of the reasons why sonar operators like to say that their job is about as exciting as watching paint dry. Everything happens slowly, literally at the pace of a snail. However, it can also get incredibly exciting very fast when the first couple of pings from an obvious man-made target appear on their screens. Unfortunately, the sonar imagery hadn't improved. If anything, it was worse.

The imagery was still being plagued by excessive noise on the outer ranges, but now a problem with the new receiver card installed by Carter was limiting the range on both the port and starboard channels to well below the maximum 3,000 metres. When working properly the sonar's total swathe coverage should be 6,000 metres, but I reckoned the best we were getting was a total coverage of 5,450 metres. In addition, the starboard channel was suffering from dropouts — an annoying problem manifested as a blank line of no data across the imagery, which is generally caused by an electronic fault. Despite the hard work of the entire Williamson team, especially Carter, I felt we had taken a step backwards.

Another decision to make: did I make Art Wright immediately recover the sonar to start the troubleshooting all over again, or do I allow the search of this trackline to continue despite these problems? On the one hand, I had every right to demand that the sonar was operating at full performance. But on the other hand, I knew that suspending the search again so soon after all the downtime we had just suffered would destroy everyone's morale. We were still covering quite a bit of the seabed, just not the amount I had planned or that we were counting on. There was also the practical issue that Carter had just spent a very long stretch working on the sonar and needed some rest. In terms of my own performance I was very aware that I would be called on to make a number of important decisions at critical junctures during the project and that the success or failure of the project could ride on whether I got these decisions right.

Above: Working on the search box.

I wasn't sure if this was one of those times or not, but I believed the right decision was to keep the search going.

At our daily meeting on 9 March, attended by Blair, Art, John and Robert, I reviewed the situation and having seen no improvement decided to recover the sonar when trackline No. 6 was complete. In my opinion the image quality was still poor and the swathe coverage was reduced by an unacceptable amount. The ground fault light had also come back on, indicating that the original short circuit problem was still with us. When the towfish was back on deck in the early afternoon the cause of the ground fault was finally isolated to a bad electrical termination of the steel tow cable. As a precaution Art also decided to change the 50-metre umbilical cable connecting the towfish to the depressor. For the third time running, Carter had to bring the two racks of towfish electronics down into the survey lab in his own personal hunt for the elusive faults.

Morale on the ship was clearly suffering. For those not involved in fixing the problems it was deeply frustrating to have to stand by and wait without knowing when the search might resume. John sensed that people were beginning to doubt whether we would find anything in light of all the problems. I hadn't seen Glenys for a few days during the rough weather but I gathered she was

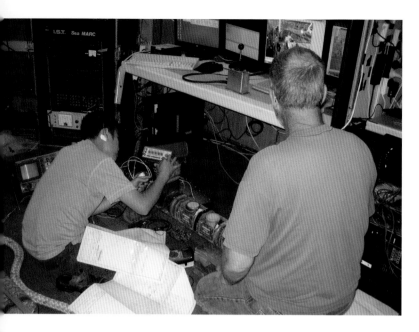

Above: Carter and Brian testing the SM-30 towfish electronics, and (bottom) relaunching the repaired towfish.

becoming a bit despondent about our situation. I spent more time talking directly with Carter to understand his approach to troubleshooting and fixing the faults. Although I didn't have a background in electronics I had been in this same situation many times before during my years with Eastport International and had worked side by side with engineers just like Carter. It was very important to me that Carter was open about the

situation and that he wasn't taking short cuts to get the sonar back in the water again only for it to fail. We were beginning to communicate better and I was pleased to see that the client/subcontractor barrier between us was breaking down.

The one bright spot in our collective misery was the terrific food that was being served up at every meal by *Geosounder*'s head cook, Peter Morgan. The quality and variety of his cooking was outstanding and it didn't drop even during the roughest weather when his cramped galley was without question the most uncomfortable and hazardous space on the ship. Good food is arguably the most important ingredient in maintaining morale at sea and we all owed a lot to Peter and his assistant, Joseph Larsen, for keeping everyone's spirits buoyed.

The towfish was launched just before midnight at the southern end of trackline No. 8 where the water depth was deepest. One look at the sonar display when I arrived in the survey lab the next morning at 0600 hours was all I needed to see that the problems hadn't been solved. The imagery on the port channel was okay but a combination of extreme noise and dropouts on the starboard channel rendered this half of the sonar's detection capability virtually useless. The obliteration of the starboard side imagery meant it would be like searching with one eye closed. This was simply unacceptable to me so I asked for the sonar to be immediately recovered. Art Wright didn't disagree with my assessment about the sonar imagery but he still preferred to keep searching, mainly for Carter to get some sleep, as he had just gotten to bed after another marathon day and night session. I had no choice but to overrule Art on the basis that it would be six hours before the towfish was back on deck and the electronics ready for Carter, during which time he could continue to rest.

This situation was now becoming critical and I felt the project was in real jeopardy. This was our eighth day at sea and we had hardly made a dent on the search box. I could see that Art and his team were working as hard as they possibly could to get the sonar working at full performance but the reality was that the situation was regressing. The worry for us now was that virtually everything hung on the shoulders of one man and he was clearly becoming exhausted. To his enormous credit Carter didn't want to rest until the sonar was completely fixed, despite Art's attempts to enforce a break on him.

I was keeping Patrick Flynn up to date with our situation and he was liaising with Williamson's office in Seattle to possibly get additional spare equipment and another engineer lined up to fly out on an emergency basis to support Carter. Carter must have heard about these discussions because he approached me later in the day when he woke and made it clear he was more than up to the job and didn't want the emergency relief. I couldn't help but be impressed by Carter. A lot of people would have wilted under the prolonged pressure he was under, but he remained focused and determined to solve the problems himself.

Nine more hours of intensive work by Carter and Bill on the sonar's electronics followed before the racks were ready to be stuffed into the twin pressure housing hanging from either side of the towfish. At the same time Phil Colvin, Williamson's mechanical technician, was making another termination of the steel tow cable as the one made the previous day was questionable and was undoubtedly the cause of the recurring ground fault. We had to wait four hours for the urethane resin of the electrical splice to cure and solidly bond to the cable before attempting another launch of the towfish. When the splice had cured I asked to inspect it myself and found a minute hole that under further examination opened up to a much bigger hole, which would have exposed the high-voltage wires directly to sea water. Needless to say the offending splice was promptly cut off and another splice was prepared.

We had to push the launch back another four hours, which was another unfortunate loss of time although it did give everyone a chance for a few hours of sleep. As I turned into my cabin after what had been a very long day I felt that the next launch could either make or break the project. If there wasn't a significant improvement in the sonar imagery there would be growing pressure from those watching on land to bring the *Geosounder* into port and take on additional engineers to help Carter. Art Wright was absolutely insistent that Carter was the best

person to get us out of this mess and from what I saw of Carter over the previous few days I had to agree. We had had such an incredible run of bad luck it seemed only fair that things would start to turn our way and that Carter be allowed to finish the job he started.

HSK *Kormoran* is found

At 0439 hours on 11 March the SM-30 towfish was launched at the southern end of the search box to re-examine trackline No. 8, which we had aborted on the previous day. Everyone was hoping for something positive to occur to convince us all that the search was truly back on track and to lift morale. Fortunately, we didn't have long to wait. In fact, we didn't even have to wait for the sonar to reach its correct towing depth or for it to enter the search box proper.

The 'something' was a sonar target located approximately six nautical miles south of the search box on the starboard side of the trackline at a depth of 3,600 metres. Even though the towfish was still being lowered to the seabed and had not yet reached its optimum position — it was too high, unstable and being towed too fast — the target did have the earmarks of possibly being a shipwreck. What I liked most about the target was that it was very straight, appeared to be quite hard and was roughly the right shape and size. Still, this was just my preliminary assessment and we would need much better sonar imagery before we could hazard a guess as to exactly what it was. I saw no urgency to collect this data immediately and instructed Art to continue with the search of trackline No. 8.

Nevertheless, this was our first moment of real excitement during the expedition and within minutes of the target popping up on the screen the survey lab began to fill up with people wanting to have a look. It was the same for the film team who were on board to document the search. They obviously wanted to catch every important moment of 'discovery' during the expedition, but until now the only shots they had were of the endless bad weather and the sick sonar towfish being tended to by tired,

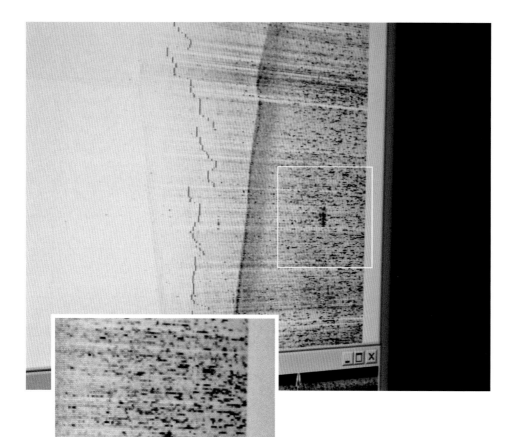

Above: The first sonar target.

frustrated technicians. As Matthew Kelley, the director of the documentary, filmed me assessing the sonar target I explained to him why it didn't discourage me that the suspect sonar target was found well outside my search box.

To begin with I had to be prepared for the possibility, although I believed it to be remote, that my search box was either a shade too small or not perfectly positioned over the right location. In a couple of my past searches we had actually found wrecks located outside my original search box so it was important to keep an open mind about targets that didn't fit my preconceived ideas. Most importantly, however, this sonar target did actually fit with

my thinking about *Sydney*. Specifically, that her wreck would be located south of *Kormoran*'s and that the hull would be found largely intact whereas I expected *Kormoran*'s hull to be destroyed by the explosion and possibly sheared in half. Part of my rationale for deciding on such a large search box was that it would also encompass the likely location where *Sydney* sank and thus there was a distinct chance we could get lucky and find *Sydney* first. We would know for sure in a couple of days when I planned for us to run the sonar back over the target when we were next down at the southern end of my search box.

In the meantime, the search continued to the north and everyone's eyes were glued to the four different computer screens that displayed the sonar imagery scrolling down with perfect metronomic regulatory. Coming across the sonar target lifted everyone's morale and heightened their senses to be on the lookout for further targets. The really good news, and a further boost to our confidence, was that the sonar imagery had definitely improved. Although we still had to contend with the annoying sea surface clutter at depths below 3,300 metres, the sonar was now working out to its maximum range and Carter was able to lessen the noise and dropout problems to a great extent. To my critical eye the imagery wasn't ideal but it was completely functional and I was satisfied the search could continue without any more delays. I called Patrick and advised that the contingencies he was putting in place for an emergency port call were no longer necessary.

After Cyclone Ophelia left the scene I was waiting for a favourable high pressure system located just to the west of us to move into her wake and grace us with a prolonged period of calm weather. Unfortunately, the path of the high was being blocked by a trough of low pressure that had been sitting over the coast of Western Australia for days. The 25-knot winds and 2.5-metre swells that buffeted the *Geosounder* were not enough to keep us from working but they certainly weren't helping the bridge officers with driving the ship or with producing the best quality sonar imagery. I learned from my new friends at the Bureau of Meteorology that the phenomenon was called the West Australian Summertime Heat Trough and that it was here to stay with us for a while. So much for the statistics that indicated March would be the optimum weather window.

Trackline No. 8 was finally completed at sunrise on 12 March. It was the third of fifteen tracklines in my revised search plan and the best to date in terms of sonar coverage and quality. Because the *Geosounder* was towing downwind with a following sea, it was also the quickest at just under nineteen hours. Other than the possible wreck-like target on the lead-in to this trackline there were no other significant targets to speak of, however. By my reckoning we had completed 20 per cent of the *Kormoran* search box but had consumed 40 per cent of the search budget in the process. There was no way to make up for the lost time without compromising my strict policy of maintaining 100 per cent search coverage, which I was not prepared to do under any circumstances. It was clear that for us to have a shot at finding *Sydney* we would have to find *Kormoran* sooner rather than later.

My plan from here on was very simple. I intended to search the east side of the search box in perfect geographic order before switching over to search the west side of the box the same way. This meant that trackline No. 9 was next up. That line was going to be run north to south and by the early afternoon the towfish had entered the search box and everyone was poised in front of their sonar screens. I had set up my own personal sonar imaging computer in a small space adjacent to the large open lab space occupied by the Williamson equipment and search team. This gave me a more private and quieter working space and it was also a better place for John and Glenys to observe what was happening. I had been teaching the fundamentals of sonar interpretation to John as a way of

passing the hours and hours of time we sat in this tiny two-square-metre space. I had no idea how quickly this training would actually come to use.

There was no warning for what was to happen next. The sonar screen showed a perfectly homogenous swathe of carnelian red, the colour I use to depict the soft sediments of the deep ocean seabed. Seconds later a dark navy blue shape appeared on the starboard channel that John was the first to notice. 'Hey what's that?' he exclaimed. The rectangular blocky shape of the target and the way the compact blue centre was fringed by dozens of pixels of greenish-yellow told me immediately that this was a man-made object and that it was quite big. I yelled down the hall to where the film team had their office that we had a good target and to get their cameras rolling. The time was 1730 hours on 12 March and the next 25 minutes were about to become one of the most satisfying highlights of my career.

As soon as I was able to I switched my computer to 'target mode' and took an approximate measurement of the object. It was roughly 35 metres long and there was the hint of an acoustic shadow behind it indicating that it was sitting quite high off the seabed. The intensity of the colours on my screen showed that the object was reflecting virtually 100 per cent of the sonar's acoustic energy — another very good characteristic. Within a minute or so a few other small sonar targets came into view, which to me was the first clear sign that a much larger debris field lay beyond them. Although they were out of my line of sight I could hear the animated voices of the Williamson team in the lab next to us. I'm sure they were making the same measurements that I was and their excitement was growing.

I explained to John and Glenys that I expected to see a large debris field come into view very soon. More and more sonar targets were being resolved as subsequent lines of imagery advanced in tune with the four-second round trip journey of each sonar ping. As the density of sonar targets increased in a pattern I had seen many times before there was no longer any question in my mind. This was the debris field of a shipwreck that had suffered a very violent sinking. Sure enough, the main oval-shaped

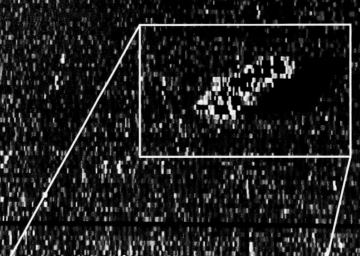

body of the debris field scrolled down my screen in a kaleidoscope of blue, green and yellow pixels. It was as impressive a debris field as I had seen for a wartime wreck and led me to comment, 'Whatever this is it's blown to bloody smithereens.' I wrote the only question left to answer in my logbook: 'Where is the rest of the hull?'

We finally had some good luck as the position and orientation of the trackline was absolutely perfect to image the entire field of wreckage. I knew we hadn't seen the remains of the major section of hull and that it was only a question of time. John was flabbergasted that I could predict what was coming next. As if on cue a hull-shaped form began to scroll down the screen. It had all the characteristics I wanted to see: size, shape and reflectivity as measured by colour intensity. However, it was the prominent acoustic shadow that pleased me most and removed any lingering doubts. As soon as I saw the first couple of lines of the shadow I knew that we had done it and confirmed with a single line in my log 'HSK *Kormoran* is found!'

I was bursting with happiness and judging by the wide grin on John's face he was feeling exactly the same as I was. Glenys slapped our backs and sank into the chair behind me. As John and I stared silently at the amazing scene of destruction we had just discovered, I could hear Glenys begin to sob. It all happened so fast and unexpectedly I don't think she was able to prepare for the flood of emotions that overcame her once she realised what we had done. Like many people, Glenys had spent a huge portion of her life researching the history of *Kormoran* and *Sydney*. I, too, had devoted more than five years of my life towards the achievement of this moment. It was a day I knew that neither of us would ever forget.

As terrific as it was to find *Kormoran*, the most exciting thing was that now we really had a chance to find *Sydney*. The search was working out as I had always said it would and had planned from the start: 'Find *Kormoran* first and this will dramatically increase our chances of finding *Sydney*.' I felt the project had been sensationally transformed by the quick location of *Kormoran*, which in the end only consumed 64 hours of actual search time for the simple reason that Detmers's position was remarkably accurate. The *Geosounder* was buzzing with excitement and there was a new air of confidence that completely replaced the gloom of the previous twelve days. Despite the considerable doubts that others had about the German accounts and Detmers's position, and the intense criticism of my search plans that continued to that very day, my belief never wavered. Belief, however, is not proof. It was up to me to prove that Detmers was telling the truth and now that I had, it was time to begin the hunt for *Sydney*.

CHAPTER SEVEN

...

Using *Kormoran* to find *Sydney*

With *Kormoran* found, I immediately shifted my thinking to a plan for finding *Sydney*. A new search box would have to be established; one that specifically covered the range of probable locations where *Sydney* might have sunk. The key to this new search box would be the precise seabed position of *Kormoran*'s wreckage, which was now an established fact beyond anyone's doubt. In a very real sense I was going to use the wreckage of *Kormoran*, along with the last German sightings of *Sydney*, to point me in the right direction to where we might find her wreckage.

The distance over which *Kormoran*'s wreckage was spread as a result of the simultaneous detonation of the 340 mines she was carrying was extraordinarily large. The largest piece of wreckage, which I tentatively identified as the forward half of *Kormoran*, was lying some 1,300 metres away from the second largest individual piece of wreckage that was too damaged to identify. In between these pieces sat the main oval-shaped debris field that measured nearly one kilometre across. I took the centre of this debris field at 26° 05'46" South and 111° 04' 33" East to be the position where *Kormoran* was drifting on the surface when the ship was scuttled. This position was critical to my reckoning because it was roughly where Detmers and the others last saw *Sydney* blazing away on the horizon before she disappeared. What none of them could be sure of, however, was whether *Sydney* sank then or whether she continued over the horizon and out of their sight.

This was the big unanswered question about *Sydney*'s loss that would largely determine whether we would find her wreckage, or not. If *Sydney* lost all power before she sank she would have been left, like *Kormoran*, drifting north with the current and wind such that the distance between the two ships would have stayed roughly the same. In this case, when Detmers last saw *Sydney* before he abandoned *Kormoran* this distance would have been about eight to nine nautical miles, which would make finding the wreck a fairly straightforward proposition. If, however, *Sydney*'s engines were still working and her crew

Left: Sydney *crewmen transferring ammunition on board.*

steamed her over the horizon there would be no way to know how long, and in what direction, they travelled before sinking. Every extra hour that *Sydney* stayed afloat could dramatically increase the expanse of ocean where she sank and thus reduce our chance of finding her. If this was the case the wreck could be literally anywhere.

Once again I would have to rely heavily on the accounts of Detmers and his fellow officers if we were to find *Sydney*. They were the last to see the cruiser on fire before she disappeared, and the range and bearing information they provided would be vital to my determination of a new search box. At least now we had proven that the Germans were telling the truth about where the action took place and that their testimony in this regard could be trusted. In fact, the Germans were more than just truthful; their positions were relatively accurate. For example, the nominal 26° South 111° East position that was most frequently reported in the German testimonies turned out to be less than seven nautical miles from where *Kormoran* sank even though it was obviously an abbreviated position in which the minutes of latitude and longitude were either forgotten or rounded up.[1]

With respect to Detmers's 26°34' South 111° East position and the vexing question whether it was the noon position or the action position, it was now possible to show to a fairly high degree of confidence that it was in fact the noon position of *Kormoran* on 19 November as first postulated by Wes Olson. There is no doubt that Detmers's memory wasn't perfect, otherwise he wouldn't have incorrectly associated this position with the site of the action. It is also obvious that neither Detmers nor the navigator Henry Meyer could fully remember the longitude component of the position and this is why they both abbreviated it to 111° East.[2]

Having established the position of *Kormoran*'s wreckage as the key reference point from where *Sydney* was last seen, the next challenge for me was to decide how far and in what direction she travelled before sinking. Fortunately, I had the three essential clues (her course, her speed and the time she was last sighted) I needed to fix her position relative to *Kormoran*. Of course I also needed the clues to be reasonably accurate, but there was nothing I could do

about this except pray that they were. Detmers's written accounts were once again the main source for these clues, as illustrated by his entry at 1825 (Zone 'G' time) when he ordered a halt to the shelling of *Sydney*.

> *Cease fire! Last range 9,000 metres. Last shot range 10,400 metres, last ship's bearing 225. Ammunition expenditure 500 Bdz 50 Cz. Decision: prepare to scuttle ship. All officers to the bridge. Order to XO: turn out all boats and life-saving equipment. Lensch and Noll inform impossible to get through to the engine-room. Check this myself. No 2 generator is still ready but useless. Mine-deck continually under watch. Outline of the enemy lost in twilight. At about 16,000 metres out of sight. Enemy course about 150 true. Large fire seen until about 22 hours.*

During the period covered by this entry in Detmers's account, *Kormoran* was dead in the water but *Sydney* was clearly still under way as her range increased from 9 kilometres to 16 kilometres. When last seen, Detmers estimated that *Sydney* was making a course of 150° true, which seemed to indicate that whoever was in command of the ship at that time had decided to head to Fremantle as the ship would have needed urgent repairs and immediate medical attention for the wounded. The actual course to Fremantle from this position would have been about 160° true, so Detmers's estimate was certainly in the realm of reasonable possibilities.

Although it was a smaller port, Geraldton was in fact much closer than Fremantle and given *Sydney*'s apparently extreme condition they might have been heading there instead. This possibility is supported by *Kormoran*'s gunnery officer, Fritz Skeries, who took the cruiser's last bearing as 225° relative to *Kormoran*'s bow.[3] As this bearing was taken at the time of *Kormoran*'s last shot it was undoubtedly made with instruments and as such should have been reasonably accurate. Taking into account the final movements of *Kormoran* I estimated this relative bearing would make *Sydney*'s course at the time to be 120° true, which was not far off from the actual course to Geraldton of 130° true. If *Sydney* continued on with this course it would indicate that their destination was actually Geraldton and not Fremantle. Either way, my search box for *Sydney* would have to cover both possibilities.

Wherever *Sydney* was heading, I was fairly certain that her speed was quite low. At 1800 (Zone 'G' time) when *Kormoran* fired her last torpedo at *Sydney*, Detmers estimated her speed to be 5 knots. By plotting all the gunnery information that was undoubtedly provided to Detmers by Skeries, it was possible to show that *Sydney*'s speed was decreasing further and by 1900 (Zone 'G' time) was down to as low as 3.5 knots. In his book Detmers described *Sydney* as 'drifting rather than sailing' after the last shots were fired by *Kormoran*. Although I felt it was likely that *Sydney*'s speed had dropped to 2 knots, or less, as her surviving crew dealt with battle damage control and their casualties, I still needed to be cautious in case they were able to recover their speed a bit before sinking.

With respect to the time *Sydney* was last seen there were a number of statements by German survivors that claimed she was on the horizon, burning fiercely in several locations up until 2200 (Zone 'G' time) and possibly as late as 2300 (Zone 'G' time), before her fires were seen to disappear. Detmers provides the best clue, however, saying in his interrogation on 7 January 1942 that 'before leaving I looked around and in the darkness, I could see *Sydney* still blazing fiercely. Then just before I abandoned ship I looked for *Sydney* and she was gone. All was blackness.' The importance of Detmers's statement is that we know he cast off his lifeboat from *Kormoran* at approximately midnight and as he was unable to see any glow of fire on the horizon from his elevated position on *Kormoran* it is possible that *Sydney* sank before this time.

When it came to plotting all these clues and using them to establish a new search box for *Sydney*, I knew it was impossible to take the same approach that I did with *Kormoran* and try to cover every imaginable possibility for her sinking position. If *Sydney* somehow miraculously recovered from her dire situation and continued over the horizon for a considerable time before sinking, then the chances of finding her during this expedition would be virtually nil. Taking everything into account, however, I didn't feel the evidence actually supported this. My view

Above: The need to find Sydney *began to affect every facet of our lives.*

was that it was much more likely *Sydney* sank anywhere from ten to fifteen nautical miles south-east of *Kormoran*, with the worst case being possibly twenty nautical miles. For safe measure, and because our search budget could afford it, I pushed this boundary out to 25 nautical miles and delineated a search box that measured approximately twenty nautical miles (north to south) by eighteen nautical miles (east to west) and encompassed 360 square nautical miles.

I wasn't at all surprised that my search box for *Sydney* was nearly five times smaller than the one for *Kormoran*, even though the conventional wisdom was that *Sydney* was the more difficult wreck to find of the two. Obviously, the chances of finding *Sydney* dramatically increased after finding *Kormoran* as this removed the cloud of doubt hanging over the German accounts. This is what I had predicted would happen when establishing the original concept for the search and the relative difference in the size of the search boxes reflected this prediction better than anything.

Not everyone shared my confidence, however, and there was some discontent leaking on to the *Geosounder* from researchers ashore. In particular, Jim Eagles, who took on the role of information officer for the Association of Family and Friends of HMAS *Sydney* II, wrote to Patrick

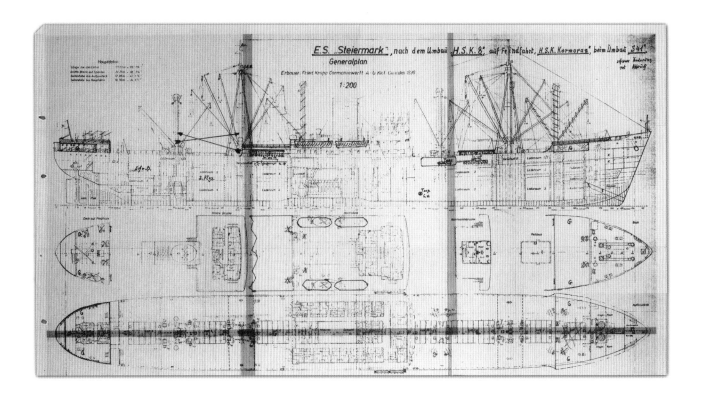

Above: The Kormoran's *distinctive hull shape would allow us to identify her wreck.*

Flynn to complain about various aspects of the project including where the search was being conducted:

> *While I expect that the search in Mr Mearns' position will use up all the tax-payer funds, I do not give them the slightest chance of being successful, even though I wish them the best of luck. Chances of finding the* Sydney? *None, where they are presently searching.*

What Eagles didn't know was that on the same day he sent Patrick this email we had already found *Kormoran* and were rapidly shifting our sights on to *Sydney*. Despite Eagles's cynical opinion of our search, I knew that the overwhelming majority of researchers would be delighted with our initial success and were behind us 100 per cent.

The search continues

In normal circumstances when a shipwreck is detected on the widest swathe of a low-frequency sonar such as the SM-30, the first thing to do would be to make a series of narrower swathe passes over the wreck to image it in progressively higher resolution, especially if there was any question about the identity of the wreck. I had no doubt that the wreck we found was *Kormoran* so this wasn't an issue for me personally. It did occur to me, however, that for the benefit of everyone else following the search the better quality images would make it easier for them to come to the same conclusion that we had. I had a decision to make. Do I turn the ship and sonar around straightaway and start the high-resolution imaging or do I continue on with the search for *Sydney*?

My decision was a compromise helped by the fact that we were already heading south. The plan was to continue searching trackline No. 9 beyond the southern end of the original search box where the first significant sonar target was detected on the lead-in to line No. 8. In light of locating *Kormoran*'s wreckage at the northern end of the search box I thought it was less likely that this target could be *Sydney* seeing that their positions were about 46 nautical miles apart. Nevertheless, the target needed to be ruled in, or out, and in the transit south we would still be in search mode covering a portion of the newly established *Sydney* search box.

The excitement of finding *Kormoran* was still very much in the air when more sonar targets started appearing on our screens. Within seconds everyone was back in front of their computers and the mini-celebration that was kicked off by *Kormoran*'s location was quickly curtailed. The targets were less than four nautical miles south of the *Kormoran* wreckage and had every appearance of being man-made objects, which formed a separate debris field. The hard-edged targets were widely scattered over a distance covering 1,700 metres and included one very large rectangular object that had a clear acoustic shadow. When I plotted the position of the targets in relation to *Kormoran*'s wreckage on my navigation chart they were very close to where I estimated the battle to have taken place. Were these targets more wreckage from one of the ships? Had we discovered the site of the actual battle?

If so, it was an amazing discovery that I never imagined was possible. The sonar targets certainly looked man-made and there was no sign of any other geological features they could be associated with. The thought immediately occurred to me that if this was wreckage it had to be from *Sydney* as we knew that *Kormoran* left the battle intact and had drifted north with the current and winds. *Sydney*, on the other hand, had been gravely damaged by a torpedo hit and was so heavily shelled by *Kormoran* that parts of the ship were seen to have been lost overboard as was vividly described by the German eyewitnesses. It also seemed a likely possibility because the north-north-east to south-south-west trendline of the targets mirrored the approximate movement of *Sydney* during the period of the battle when she altered course behind *Kormoran*'s stern.

As the search continued down trackline No. 9 to the south I was able to break away to call Patrick Flynn and tell him the good news about finding *Kormoran*. Our discovery constituted a major news event in Australia and had to be handled very carefully and sensitively. In anticipation of this moment the Finding Sydney Foundation[4] had agreed to a strict protocol with the RAN and the government about how such an official announcement would be made when either of the wrecks was found. In short, the announcement would be made by the government with representatives from both the RAN and the foundation in attendance as soon as practicably possible after the

Above: The main survey lab inside the Geosounder.

discovery. I was to inform Patrick immediately by phone, with technical details and imagery to follow by email, and he would in turn relay the news without delay to Fiona McNaught at RAN Headquarters. Communication from the ship to the outside world was thereafter restricted and I convened an all-hands meeting on board to reinforce the need for confidentiality. With this business swiftly out of the way we could all get back to concentrating on the hunt for *Sydney*.

It was mid-morning on 13 March by the time we reached the suspect target area south of the search box. John and Glenys were again at my side while the video cameras stood ready to possibly record history for a second time. Sure enough, a steady stream of sonar targets began scrolling down my screen. Initially the targets appeared man-made and in the bubble of the moment I convinced myself this must be the remains of *Sydney*, which appeared to have been ripped apart by a tremendous explosion. It was an awful scene to contemplate and it struck us all quite hard, particularly Glenys, who had the feelings of the relatives foremost in her mind.

As the targets continued to roll by for an unusually long time the sum total of the wreckage — if it was wreckage

— began to seem to be too much for a ship the size of *Sydney*. The area over which the targets were spread was too large to be explained by coming from a shipwreck. This was clearly an area of geology, but was it possible that some of the larger targets were wreckage intermingled with the outcroppings of rocks? I was beginning to change my mind about my initial interpretation and wanted to spend more time reviewing the sonar images with the Williamson sonar analysts who had come to their own conclusion that the targets were probably all geology and there was no wreckage. Everything was lining up against this being the site of *Sydney's* demise, but I wanted to be certain before we shifted our focus back to the search box so I ordered another higher resolution line to be run past the area as the *Geosounder* moved north.

The second run over the target area with the SM-30 sonar set on the three-kilometre swathe yielded excellent imagery that indicated the targets were all geological in nature and had nothing to do with *Sydney*. I was satisfied this ruled out the site and directed that the search resume along trackline No. 10 running south to north. The experience was a perfect illustration of how easy it was for the seabed conditions to make the search more difficult than it already was. It confirmed to me the need for taking an extra-cautious approach and to use all the resources and time I had at my disposal to be certain of our findings. It may sound odd but I think everyone was quietly relieved this wasn't *Sydney*. If it was upsetting for us to have thought we found her wreck in such an obliterated condition I could only imagine how painful it would have been for the relatives.

Telling Australia the good news

The second part of my compromise plan was to break off the search three-quarters of the way up trackline No. 10 to make a series of narrower swathe runs over *Kormoran's* wreckage and the possible battle site. As much as I wanted to keep searching for *Sydney* it was equally important that

Above: Mike Kelly and Brian Bunge analysing the sonar data.

we had the best possible imagery of *Kormoran*. If we were going to identify the wreck as *Kormoran* on the basis of sonar imagery alone then I wanted to have unmistakable evidence that supported my interpretation. The organisation of the official announcement was under way and the word from Patrick was that Prime Minister Rudd (who had replaced John Howard) was going to make it himself, with the Chief of Defence Force, the Chief of Navy, Minister for Defence Science and Personnel, and Ted Graham all in attendance. The significance of the announcement and the fact that the government was placing the highest level of importance on it compelled me to ensure I had done everything within my power to confirm our discovery.

In order to have the best imagery of *Kormoran* in time for the announcement I decided to take a small gamble and narrow the swathe straight away to 1.5 kilometres. Our first image on the six-kilometre swathe was so good I didn't feel that we would learn that much from a three-kilometre pass, although this would have been the safer option. The risk with a narrower swathe was that we could totally miss the wreck if the sonar was out of alignment with the ship's track by just a few degrees. The SM-30 was working extremely well now and I expected the imagery to be even better at the narrower swathe settings. Carter had performed his magic and was rightly proud that *Kormoran* was found on the troublesome starboard channel that he had worked so hard to correct. Carter was such a genuine person that all of us were pleased on his behalf.

Using the first image of the wreckage field as a guide, I showed Mike Kelly, the Williamson sonar analyst, and Nigel Meikle, the DOF surveyor, exactly where I wanted the next trackline to run. My wish was to place the hull and the other large piece of wreckage in the 'sweet spot' of the sonar's port beams where I knew it would provide the optimum resolution and spatial representation of the wreckage. If the sonar hit the line perfectly I believed we'd be able to get a good measurement of the hull's beam, which would be a strong indicator of the wreck's identity. At 20.2 metres *Kormoran* was a beamier ship than the 17.3-metre-wide *Sydney*, so this was an obvious means to distinguish between them.

Mike and Nigel got on with the job programming the trackline as the *Geosounder* slowly inched its way up trackline No. 10 with the SM-30 in tow. As no targets of any consequence were seen I gave the okay for the ship to break off line and start a series of small course changes that would hopefully guide the towfish past the wreckage field along the angled trackline I requested. If Mike and Nigel got their sums right I expected to see *Kormoran*'s hull first at a range of about 225 metres. Sure enough, after a handful of very small pieces of debris announced its arrival, the forward half of *Kormoran*'s hull came into view. The image was excellent. It revealed a prominent bow shape, towering acoustic shadow and a clean break across the after end where the explosion fractured *Kormoran*'s back. Generally it takes one or two attempts to achieve this level of precision but Mike, Nigel and *Geosounder*'s watch officers were spot-on the very first time.

As the sonar continued down the line, skirting the main debris field and perfectly imaging the other large piece of wreckage from an altitude of just 50 metres, I started measuring the hull. To be sure I took the measurements from a number of different points but they all returned the same dimensions; 20 metres breadth, 13 metres height and a length of 106 metres. The numbers fitted *Kormoran* like a glove and indicated that the break occurred at the forward end of the ship's original cargo

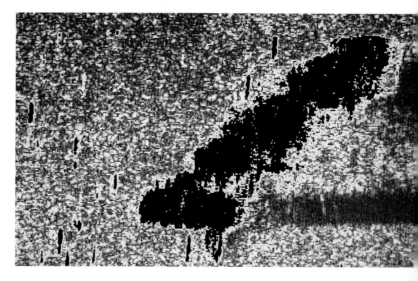

Above: The sonar image of Kormoran, *which I was able to identify by its distinctive acoustic shadow, (below).*

hold No. 4 that was converted into the mine storage room. I now had some qualitative evidence to back up my interpretations but I wanted one more sonar image to provide the conclusive, unquestionable proof that I knew the media and the public would demand after all the previous false alarms.

Unlike *Sydney* whose forward deck was flat, *Kormoran* had a flared bow with a raised forecastle deck above the well deck. If we could get the sonar in the right position and at the right height I knew it would produce an acoustic shadow to accentuate this structural detail that was particular to *Kormoran* alone. We would need to reset the SM-30 to its narrowest swathe of 750 metres and it

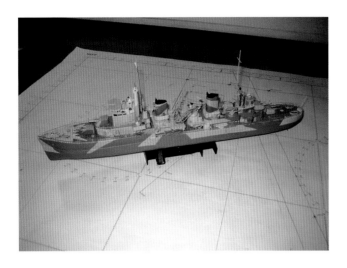

Above: Sydney's *shape was quite different to* Kormoran's.

would take another perfect performance from Mike and Nigel. I knew I was asking a lot of them — like threading a needle 2,500 metres below with a string 8,000 metres long — but the pair were developing a real chemistry and zest for each challenge I gave them.

It was another eight hours before the sonar was back in the wreckage field but the wait was well worth it. I have seen countless sonar images of wrecks in deep water but by any comparison this was a stunning image. The shape of a flared bow was unmistakable as was the acoustic shadow behind it, which could only have been made by a forecastle deck raised above the main deck. In acoustic terms the shadow was a veritable fingerprint identifying the wreck as *Kormoran*. There was also a shadow being thrown off whatever structure remained of *Kormoran*'s mid-ship superstructure. I compared the images to the drawings I found at the Peter Tamm Institute in Hamburg of both the original *Steiermark* and the converted *Kormoran* and the match was perfect. The team had done a brilliant job of producing the images I asked for and I felt we now had the proof to allow the Prime Minister's announcement to go ahead.

Following a short high-resolution run past the main sonar targets that comprised the possible battle site, we resumed the search by completing trackline No. 10 and then making a slow turn to starboard to start line No. 11 running north to south. It was 15 March and we had to decide, in advance, whether or not to take up the next

seven-day option period for the hire of the *Geosounder*. The decision was straightforward but it still required Patrick and me to talk through all the issues before mutually agreeing to trigger the option that would keep us at sea to at least 29 March. We still had to find *Sydney*, and it was likely we'd take the opportunity to film *Kormoran*'s wreckage as her depth of less than 2,600 metres was well within the 3,000-metre rating of the DOF ROV on board the *Geosounder*, so it seemed certain we would need every day of the next fortnight to complete the project. Patrick also confirmed that a cray boat out of Carnarvon was en route to transfer stores and fresh provisions.

In order to increase the duration of the *Geosounder* we needed some filters for the ship's reverse osmosis water plant, which the cray boat was bringing out to us along with more video tape stock for the film team. A lot of us came up on deck to watch the transfer as it was our first direct contact with the outside world since our departure from Geraldton. Earlier I had been on the bridge with Captain Cliffe when he discussed over the radio with the other captain how he wanted him to bring his boat parallel along *Geosounder*'s port side. I was surprised then to see the twenty-metre aluminium boat approach quite quickly at a right angle. The two young lads on the bow did well to off-load a few boxes as they heaved up and down with the two-metre swells, but then everything went suddenly wrong. The boat lost steering control leaving her captain powerless as they slid down *Geosounder*'s port side before banging heavily against the transom. Watching the cray boat struggle with the sea conditions brought home exactly how unlucky we had been with the weather. It was one of the nicest days in weeks but the winds were still blowing a steady 22 knots. Eventually all the packages were transferred but the fishing boat suffered a nasty gash on its starboard gunwhale for its efforts.

The search of trackline No. 11 was completed in the early hours of Sunday, 16 March with no significant targets detected. The announcement of *Kormoran*'s discovery was going to be made in Canberra sometime during the morning our time. Having bottled up the news on board *Geosounder* for more than three days I was keen to see the announcement made as soon as possible so everyone could relax again. John and I worked late to pull together the sonar images that would accompany the news release and our own Search Diary, which we were posting on a regular basis onto the Finding Sydney Foundation's website. It was another very long day but with the sonar being turned around to the start of the next line it was a good time to get some sleep before my shift formally started at 0600 hours.

The sequence of tracklines I planned for the *Sydney* search box meant that the water depth was getting shallower as we moved progressively eastwards. The next line, No. 12, was going to be run from south to north and it went directly through the heart of where I thought was the most probable area for *Sydney* to have sunk. The northern half of this line was the estimated distance away from *Kormoran*'s location in terms of *Sydney* going down not long after Detmers saw her for the last time. I believed that we would find the wreck on this trackline, but if we didn't, the search would go on for another ten days because this meant that *Sydney* stayed afloat for longer than I expected, making her sinking position far more unpredictable. I had such a strong feeling about this line that I joked to John how I wouldn't be surprised if we actually found *Sydney* at the same time the Prime Minister was making his announcement about *Kormoran*.

It didn't take long for us to find out when Australia heard the good news about *Kormoran* because the congratulatory emails started arriving soon after. I was greatly relieved there hadn't been a leak and I watched with pride as the news spread rapidly around the world via the internet. Not surprisingly, the main thrust of the stories was about how the discovery of *Kormoran* had raised hopes in Australia that *Sydney* would be found, although the Navy Chief, Vice Admiral Shalders, cautioned that 'it will be a long, hard and difficult search from this point onwards'. Prime Minister Rudd captured the renewed hope best in his statement that 'we are one step closer as a nation to finding *Sydney*.' As all of Australia rejoiced in our discovery they had no idea how close we actually

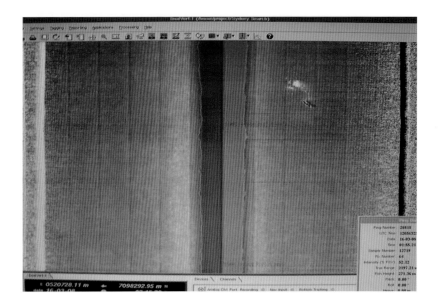

Above: 'Oi! What's that!'

were to giving them the ultimate news they had waited 66 long and painful years to hear.

HMAS *Sydney* is found!

The buzz on board the *Geosounder* had yet to die down as the search continued up trackline No. 12. John was monitoring how the news was being reported on the internet while I was back at the chart table concentrating on my navigation chart. I was moving around a new transparent chart I had drawn with all the *Sydney* sinking clues to help me decide where to place the next line when I heard John shout: 'Oi! What's that!' I turned to see him leap out of his seat in such a way that I knew this must be good. By the time I walked the couple of steps over to the sonar screen it was clear what John was so animated about. It was my turn to get excited: 'That's it, we've found her!' I yelled. The distinctive image of a hard black target complete with an acoustic shadow was just emerging from the top of the screen. The image was only seconds old but the unmistakable shape of a shipwreck was already forming. The time was 1103 (West Australian Standard Time) and the hunt for HMAS *Sydney* was over.

Above: The image we'd waited so long to see.

There was no restraining our feelings about this discovery. We jumped around like little kids and our euphoric shouts of joy must have reverberated through the entire ship because the survey rooms started to fill up as everyone came together to witness the historic event. It was hard to control my excitement as I screamed for Matthew Kelley to get his cameras rolling. The hull of *Sydney* was still scrolling down the screen as the SM-30 passed just 260 metres over the top of her position. For the second time it was the sonar's starboard channel which took the honours and made Carter beam with pride. My first instinct was to run next door to ask Bill Heather, the Williamson sonar operator who spotted the wreck the same time as John, what the water depth was. 'Two thousand, four hundred and sixty-eight metres,' he replied. I clapped my hands knowing this meant that the DOF ROV could easily reach and film both shipwrecks.

John and I sat down at the screen to begin analysing the sonar imagery as a small, compact debris field started to come into view. Shortly afterwards Glenys arrived and I said to her, 'We got it. That's it. That's HMAS *Sydney*!' Glenys took one look at the wonderful image of *Sydney*'s largely intact and upright hull and said, 'That will give people closure.'

I looked at my watch and couldn't believe our timing. A couple of hours earlier and we would have had to interrupt the Prime Minister's announcement with the news flash that we had just found *Sydney*. I wasted no time and immediately called Patrick to tell him the news so he could advise the RAN. Although the correct protocol was for Patrick to call Ted, I asked to have the privilege of breaking the news to him myself, which Patrick graciously permitted. I rang Ted on his mobile and caught him walking to meet a friend after leaving the Prime Minister's office. I asked him if it was possible to get the Prime Minister and everyone else back to reconvene

29 MARCH.

Next line (Line #12) will be 4300m to the east of Line #11.

0500	Complete turn and towfish at survey depth of 450m. Start Logging on CODA. (0542 Nav) S/o 6200m	
0559	Vessel enters survey area S/o 7166m Depth=246m	
0705	Towfish enters survey area S/o 7367	
1003	**HMAS SYDNEY II FOUND!**	

Above: The log speaks for itself.

the press conference. When he asked me why I said, 'We just found *Sydney*. We've got it. It's absolutely crystal clear. Exactly where we want [*sic*]. She's sitting upright in a small debris field. There's no doubt about it. You can take it to the bank. The Prime Minister or anybody else can announce it. We have found HMAS *Sydney*.'

Ted was so choked with emotion he couldn't say much more than 'Thank you, David.' I knew all about the years of effort Ted had put in to seeing this day come true but I only realised how much the finding of *Sydney* truly meant to him as I listened to him weep with happiness. I passed the phone to Glenys, who shared a wonderfully poignant moment with Ted as they both congratulated each other on this enormous success for the Finding Sydney Foundation and discussed how our discovery would help the relatives. After years of working separately to find *Sydney* their paths had finally converged and now they were sharing a dream come true and a bit of history in the making. Ted must have been in shock

because when John took the phone to congratulate him he had to assure Ted that it wasn't a dream and that we had really found *Sydney*.

Not long after we had joined the *Geosounder* together in Geraldton John told me quite seriously that I should start thinking about an appropriate and memorable way to inform the RAN that *Sydney* had been found. John's point was that such a historically significant event should be marked by an equally significant statement to go down in history alongside the discovery. To be honest, I had trouble thinking this far ahead about something that was still only a dream for all of us. Over the next fortnight I witnessed John's passion for the history and tradition of the RAN — a passion which I found inspiring. Through John I was able to appreciate more than ever what finding the wreck would mean to the navy rank and file who never forgot the sacrifice that *Sydney*'s crew gave in their service to Australia. In view of this I felt it was only right that John, as a former RAN signalman, be the one to send the following signal to the Chief of Navy:[5]

> *P 160003Z MAR 08*
> *FM SV GEOSOUNDER*
> *TO CN AUSTRALIA*
> *BT*
> *R E S T R I C T E D*
> *SIC ABA*
> *SUBJ: DISCOVERY OF THE WRECK*
> *OF HMAS SYDNEY (II)*
> *1. HMAS SYDNEY (II) LOCATED IN POSITION*
> *26 14 31S 111 12 48E AT 160003Z MAR 08 IN 2468*
> *METRES OF WATER*
> *2. BRAVO HOTEL TACK ALPHA DELTA TWO EIGHT*
> *3. LEUT D.J. PERRYMAN, RANR, SENDS*

Confirmation and commemoration

Although the search for *Sydney* was over there was still a lot more work I wanted to do on the wrecks before we came in to port to off-load the Williamson sonar equipment and mobilise the DOF ROV for the upcoming video investigation phase of the project. Owing to the equally quick location of *Sydney* — only 67 hours of active searching was required — we now had more than enough time and money to properly film both wrecks. It was hard to balance how we went from suffering such a horrendous start to the project to the stunning success of those last five days. Saying the search was a journey of highs and lows would be one of the all-time understatements. As little as six days earlier serious consideration was being given to suspending the search but we were soon in the position in which both wrecks were found, identified and within reach to be photographed. All I wanted to do was keep the momentum and positive results flowing.

My basic plan was to make a series of narrower swathe runs over *Sydney*'s wreckage with the SM-30 sonar before switching to the higher frequency AMS-60 sonar for one last run over both wrecks at the highest possible resolution. The first was a three-kilometre swathe run on a reciprocal (north to south) heading that would help Mike and Nigel pin down the precise seabed position of the wreck for the subsequent runs and give me a better image of the hull for taking measurements. The resulting image wasn't brilliant but it did the job I needed it to do. The one thing it showed was that the wrecked hull was shorter than *Sydney*'s full length. There was also a fairly large, square target with its own acoustic shadow situated in the debris field at the opposite end to the hull. My immediate suspicion was that this was *Sydney*'s bow that snapped off at some point in the final sinking sequence.

For the next run on the 1.5-kilometre swathe setting I asked Nigel to give me a trackline that would put the wreckage on the port channel, as all the others were on the starboard channel, and produce the most revealing acoustic shadow of the hull. Phil Colvin, operating the winch, had obviously responded to my request for faster turn times because he reduced this one to 4.5 hours whereas previously the average was 6.5 hours. I suspect his shift was also keen to see the wreck one more time as they had the sonar in position just before the midnight shift change. This yielded a superb image and another terrific job by Nigel and the team. A close look at the hull and acoustic shadow left me in no doubt that *Sydney*'s bow was gone. Using the position of the shadow being thrown from what remained of *Sydney*'s bridge superstructure for orientation, it was clear that it was the bow missing and not the stern. This interpretation also fitted with what was known about where the torpedo from *Kormoran* had hit *Sydney*: on her port bow somewhere in the vicinity of her forward gun turrets.

Knowing that Prime Minister Rudd would be announcing the discovery of *Sydney* the very next morning — his second announcement in two days — John and I thought it was very important that we gave the RAN an accurate sense of the damage suffered by *Sydney*. I wanted one last run of the SM-30 sonar on the 750-metre swathe focused just on *Sydney*'s hull, but was grateful for the five-hour break imposed by the turning around of the sonar. At 0521 hours on 17 March we were all back in position to watch the live high-resolution sonar imagery as the line began. Six minutes later the most stunningly vivid sonar image of a deep-water shipwreck I had ever seen was on the screen in front of us. The detail in the acoustic shadow was remarkable. It was as if someone had shone the biggest light in the world on a modified *Leander* class cruiser and snapped a picture. In terms of confirming that the wreck was HMAS *Sydney* this image was much better than the one we had for *Kormoran* and as conclusive as it possibly gets. This was a heavily damaged warship with a nasty fracture in place of where its bow once was and with a lot of her upper structure missing. I wasted no time and immediately transferred the images ashore to Patrick along with the note that I believed the loss of the bow was the final event that sent *Sydney* plunging to the seabed.

Over the course of the next day and a half we recovered the SM-30 towfish and conducted two runs using the AMS-60 sonar over *Kormoran*'s and *Sydney*'s hulls. It was an eventful period marked by one aborted dive of the AMS-60 sonar, winds of 25 knots gusting to 30 knots and a problem with *Geosounder*'s main engine (specifically, the head gasket) that threatened to seriously curtail the remaining tasks in my operational plan. The final high-resolution image of *Kormoran* added nothing to our existing knowledge, but that was primarily because the previous sonar image was exceptional. To a lesser extent the same was also true of the final high-resolution image of *Sydney*, although this did provide a very good basis for determining the damage around the fractured end. Another set of measurements indicated that the bow broke off just forward of gun turret 'A'. It was also becoming increasingly clear that the largest target in the debris field was the separated bow.

As the time ticked down on this phase of the project our thoughts turned to how we should pay our respects to the men who lost their lives on 19 November 1941. Previously we had been totally focused on finding the wrecks and documenting their condition on the seabed,

Above: The Church Pennant flying high from Geosounder's *mast.*

but now it was time to reflect on the tragic loss of life and the scenes of destruction 2,500 metres below us. We opted for simple but solemn ceremonies, with the only formality being that John changed into his white naval uniform to lead the services. For geographical and timing reasons we conducted the first commemorative service over the site of HSK *Kormoran*.

I asked John to create the order of service and to read the brief opening history of 19 November 1941 that concluded with us paying our respects to the approximately 80 members of *Kormoran*'s crew who died as a result of the action with *Sydney*. For the traditional 'Naval Ode', I decided to ask Ullrich (Ulle) Krafzik, the German-born cameraman in the film documentary team, if he would like to read this for the simple reason that it seemed right for the ode to be read in German. Although Ulle was visibly moved when I asked him to read the ode it wasn't an easy responsibility for him to accept. First, there was the issue of him stepping out from behind the camera to become part of the story, which is rarely ever done in documentary films. The bigger issue, I suspect, was that as a postwar baby Ulle was raised as a pacifist and he was concerned that by taking a central role in the service he might be seen to be giving honour to *Kormoran*'s act of war when in truth he was totally

against war for any purpose. I explained to Ulle that we were not commemorating *Kormoran* or the Kriegsmarine, and that there were no words in the ode related to war. This was simply a commemoration of the men as sailors who went to sea and died. I was very pleased when Ulle agreed to read the ode and the service was so much better for it. I had the honour of laying the wreath off *Geosounder's* fantail.

At 1600 hours on 18 March our last act before heading in to Geraldton was to conduct the service over *Sydney's* final resting place. John again created the order of service and read the opening which ended with our solemn respects to the 645 men who died in *Sydney*, which included six members of the Royal Australian Air Force, nine members of the Royal Navy and four civilian canteen staff. John also brought a Church Pennant to fly from *Geosounder's* yardarm to show that we were at Divine Service. He felt that the *Sydney* boys would have liked knowing we followed this important naval tradition. Glenys recited a poignant prayer written by H.B. Shipstone, a petty officer in *Sydney* who now lay with his fellow shipmates in the watery tomb beneath us. Because he was a former Royal Navy officer, I asked *Geosounder's* master, Blair Cliffe, to read the 'Naval Ode'. Then it was John's turn to lay the wreath before standing erect and saluting as the 'Last Post' was played followed by the observance of a one-minute silence.

As the *Geosounder's* crippled engine coughed back into life for the slow transit home the normally empty back deck was awash with everyone on board who was able to attend the service. To a person we were all rightly proud of what we had accomplished and at the same time, there was a strong sense of privilege to be part of the team that discovered *Kormoran* and *Sydney*. There was a lot of work ahead of us in the next phase of the project, and, I suspected, more highs and lows. Nevertheless, for a few hours at least we could relax and reflect on our incredible experience. As I watched John's Church Pennant flutter in the wind my mind was drawn back to Shipstone's poem. For 66 years there was no grave where the epitaph he penned could be read. *Sydney* might be out of sight of land and below thousands of metres of the Indian Ocean but she is lost no longer.

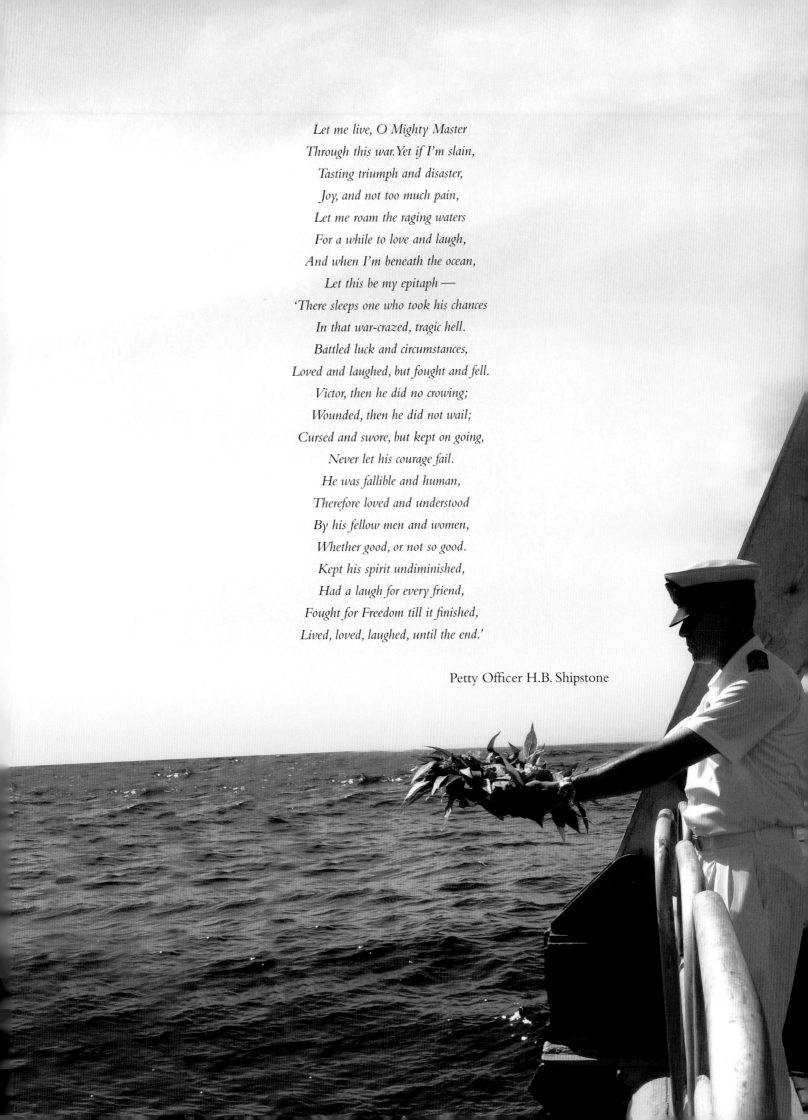

Let me live, O Mighty Master
Through this war. Yet if I'm slain,
Tasting triumph and disaster,
Joy, and not too much pain,
Let me roam the raging waters
For a while to love and laugh,
And when I'm beneath the ocean,
Let this be my epitaph —
'There sleeps one who took his chances
In that war-crazed, tragic hell.
Battled luck and circumstances,
Loved and laughed, but fought and fell.
Victor, then he did no crowing;
Wounded, then he did not wail;
Cursed and swore, but kept on going,
Never let his courage fail.
He was fallible and human,
Therefore loved and understood
By his fellow men and women,
Whether good, or not so good.
Kept his spirit undiminished,
Had a laugh for every friend,
Fought for Freedom till it finished,
Lived, loved, laughed, until the end.'

Petty Officer H.B. Shipstone

CHAPTER EIGHT

...

A warm reception

Our arrival in Geraldton at midday on 20 March was met by a small welcoming party that included the other Finding Sydney Foundation directors and their wives, Mayor Ian Carpenter, Glenys's son David and a couple of press photographers who were being marshalled by Gary Booth from Defence Public Relations. As *Geosounder's* thrusters gently pushed us the final few metres against the quayside I could hear the distinctive sound of a bagpiper playing in the distance. Ted Graham, Bob Trotter, Keith Rowe and Don Pridmore all reached across the ship's railings to shake my hand before we were tied up fast. Before anybody could get on or off the vessel it had to go through its normal clearance procedures, which Patrick Flynn was on hand to oversee. As we waited I gave a double thumbs-up salute for the cameras, which was my way of signalling our success in finding both *Kormoran* and *Sydney*. John and Glenys followed my lead and flashed their own thumbs-up, but it was our broad smiles that said it all. We were delighted to be back, nearly on land, and to be met by the others who had worked so hard to see this day come true.

Although port security necessitated that our arrival in Geraldton was a low-key affair, we had been made well aware of the overwhelming public reaction to our success. Our primary connection with the outside world during the search was via the internet and the Search Diary we were writing to be posted on the foundation's website <www.findingsydney.com>. Regardless of the outcome of the search, it was an important objective for us that the search was as transparent as possible and that the public had the same unfiltered access to how we were getting on in our quest to find the wrecks as the media were. It added a lot of extra work and pressure on myself, John and Glenys but I had no doubt it was worth it and the right thing to do. Fortunately, Richard Sojka had the foresight to have the foundation's website hosted by the highest capacity internet server in the world based in America in case the traffic to the website suddenly exploded. He felt this was necessary if the number of hits reached the top end of his maximum estimate of one million. This is why we were all blown away when he reported that there

Left: Launching the ROV over the wreck site of HMAS Sydney.

Above: A bagpiper greeted us on our return to Geraldton.

were already several million hits on the website and the total was climbing rapidly.

The media interest was also enormous. Patrick was single-handedly fielding all the press, TV and radio inquiries from outlets in Australia and around the world. His mobile phone hadn't stopped ringing since the announcement of *Kormoran*'s discovery and he and Richard were working virtually around the clock to satisfy the media's demands for interviews and information. Although in recent years the media had become a bit jaded with the *Sydney* story, what with all the unending controversy and false alarms about the wreck being found, we had all felt that this would change once the wrecks were truly found. However, even we were surprised by the incredible level of interest. The profile of the project was certainly raised when the Prime Minister decided to take a personal interest and announce the discoveries himself. Another factor that may have excited people's imaginations was the apparent speed with which we found the wrecks. Although the discoveries were actually separated by four days, the timing of the announcements on Sunday and Monday made it seem as though it took us just one day to find *Sydney* after the initial discovery of *Kormoran*. As *Sydney* was supposedly impossible to find, it was understandable that people were curious to learn how we located the wreck so quickly.

Without question, however, the most satisfying feedback we received was from relatives of the men lost in *Sydney*. Glenys, in particular, because of her close association with many relatives, received numerous emails while we were still at sea expressing congratulations and deep appreciation. For Glenys this was a personal vindication of her decision to support the search in the face of some withering and uncalled-for criticism. I received a handful of emails from some resourceful relatives who tracked down my details to write and say how much the discovery meant to them and their families. This email from Lieutenant Colonel Jackson Harding, received on 17 March, typifies the messages we were being sent.

Dear David,
On behalf of my family and I, I wish to offer you our most heartfelt congratulations on the finding of the wreck of HMAS Sydney *(II) and the resting place of her crew, as well as that of HSK* Kormoran. *My grandfather, AB Jackson Nesbitt, was one of* Sydney's *complement lost following her action with* Kormoran. *At the dedication of the memorial in Geraldton we met one of his former shipmates who had left the ship immediately prior to her sailing from Fremantle on her last voyage, from him we understand my grandfather was one of the gunners in either the A or B turret. I have had a long conversation with my mother since the news of your discovery was released in the media this morning, she is overwhelmed with relief that after 67 years she now knows exactly where her father lays. Recently she expressed to my father her fervent wish that the wreck would be found before she dies, thanks to your outstanding efforts this has now come to pass. Once again on behalf of my family thank you so much for helping illuminate this enduring Australian naval mystery, like many other relatives of* Sydney's *crew I share an enormous, almost overwhelming, sense of relief. I understand from the* Sydney Search *website that as the next stage of your effort you are planning on using an ROV to provide images of both wrecks. I look forward to seeing these images with great interest and anticipation.*

Warmest regards, LTCOL Jackson Harding

That night the Finding Sydney Foundation hosted a celebration dinner for the entire search team and marine crew of the *Geosounder* at the African Reef Hotel close to the motel where many of us were staying. The dinner was a way of saying thank you and acknowledging the efforts of so many dedicated and talented people who were leaving the ship. The majority of the Williamson sonar team were heading back to America and all but three of the *Geosounder* marine crew were due to be rotated for a new crew that was arriving the following day. It was also a chance for everyone to have a drink together after being on a dry ship for nearly three weeks. There were plenty of speeches and awards and everyone went home with a handsome Letter of Appreciation signed by the foundation's directors, Patrick, John, myself and Commodore Rick Shalders, RAN, who was the senior naval officer based in Western Australia and was at the dinner along with Gary Booth.

When my turn came to speak I decided to keep my thank yous short and instead use the opportunity to mention someone very special at the back of the room whom I invited to the dinner earlier in the day. His name was Garry Baverstock and his uncle, Able Seaman Ernest Baverstock, served in *Sydney* and was lost with her when she sank. Incredibly, Garry's father, Frederick Baverstock, also served in the RAN and as a family-related serviceman he was invited to join the crew of the *Yandra* during the search for *Sydney*'s survivors in the hopes of finding his brother alive. Garry was in contact with me by email during the search and when he realised we were coming into port he decided to extend his stay in Geraldton to meet me and shake my hand for finding his uncle's ship. The dinner was a great celebration but I felt having Garry there, with his wife Julia, gave a tangible meaning to the cause we were celebrating. I ended my short speech by encouraging everyone to take a few minutes to talk with Garry, as I knew from my own experiences that in years to come the moment they would truly cherish would be meeting a relative such as Garry and receiving his deep appreciation.

As the party continued into the night I left early to prepare for the next morning's official media conference at the Geraldton-Greenough Chambers, just a short drive outside the centre of town. Trevor Beaver, a friend of Glenys's who was a diver and assisted with some of her previous investigations of shallow-water anomalies suspected to be connected with *Sydney*, kindly lent me his wife's car so I could make it to the conference in my own time. When I arrived the chambers were heaving with a mixture of local well-wishers, journalists, photographers and TV cameramen. Keith Rowe introduced the speakers, including Ted Graham, Commodore Rick Shalders and Alan Carpenter, the Premier of Western Australia who had given up part of his Easter weekend to fly to Geraldton especially to attend the conference. I was to give a presentation recounting the search and a broad outline of our plans for the ROV investigation of the wrecks.

After Commodore Shalders spoke eloquently of the navy's delight in seeing one of their most famous and loved ships discovered, it was my turn to explain how we did it. The first part of my presentation focused on how I based my search box on just a handful of the German positions and then used the drift analysis of the *Aquitania* life raft to help me prioritise where to search first. Although the underlying science of my methodology was quite technical I sensed that the audience understood the summary I presented because the principles of my approach, when boiled down, are based on plain common sense. For the second part I showed the best sonar images we collected of the wrecks to help everyone appreciate how we were able to identify them based on this imagery alone. I also began to prepare people for the fact that when we got back down to the wreck with the ROV for filming we expected to find *Sydney* in a much damaged condition.

To finish the talk I chose to show two wireless messages between the Commander-in-Chief of the Mediterranean fleet and the Naval Board that John had found in his research of the signals logs for the period immediately after *Sydney*'s loss. The first message spoke of the Mediterranean fleet's regret in hearing of the loss of *Sydney* and how 'this fighting ship was an inspiration to our own forces and a standing menace to our enemies.'

The heartfelt reply from the Naval Board simply said, 'Sydney counted it an honour to serve under your command. She will rise again.' After reading the messages out to the audience I told them that in a sense Sydney had risen again. Our discovery of her wreck had led to an unprecedented outpouring of public feeling about the sacrifice of her crew and a renewed interest in the history of the exploits of this remarkable ship that was once known as the Grey Gladiator. This seemed to catch the mood in the chambers because as I showed my last slide of the wreath floating on the water above Sydney the audience broke into a resounding applause that seemed to never stop. I was glad my talk was finished because I was so choked up I wouldn't have been able to say another word.

Premier Alan Carpenter took the stage next and expressed his gratitude, on behalf of the people of not only Western Australia, but Australia as a whole. 'This is an historic moment for Western Australia and indeed, for the nation. The discovery of HMAS Sydney's final resting place will hopefully end years of speculation on what actually happened that fateful November day and provide answers as to why none of the 645 Australians on board survived the battle.' He also admitted that while his state made a significant donation to the search, he like a lot of people thought Sydney would never be found and that her location would forever remain a mystery.

After a few hours conducting television interviews and being photographed with Alan Carpenter up at the Sydney memorial on top of Mount Scott we were finally able to sit down and discuss the objectives of the upcoming ROV video investigation. The ROV mobilisation was scheduled to take about two days, which would allow the Geosounder to get away either on Sunday or Monday at the latest so a detailed plan was needed as soon as possible. While the Finding Sydney Foundation's mandate only went so far as visually identifying the wrecks there were also calls from other quarters to conduct a more forensic-style investigation with a view to conclusively determining what happened during the battle and what caused Sydney to sink. This was a very tricky call to make and, to be fair to those who had to decide what approach we were

to take in the next phase of the project, I honestly don't think they imagined we'd be in this favourable position with both wrecks found so soon. Whatever was decided we also had to stay within the strict limits laid down by both the Australian and German governments that there was to be no disturbance of the wrecks or internal penetrations by the ROV.

Planning the ROV investigation phase

Crammed into a tiny room on the side of the Chambers the foundation's directors (minus Ted and Glenys), Commodore Shalders, Patrick Flynn and Gary Booth sat down to listen to John's and my recommendations. In short, there were three options to consider. At one extreme, a very short ROV dive of approximately 30 minutes to each wreck could be conducted simply to visually confirm the identity of the wrecks and nothing more. While this would satisfy the narrowest reading of the foundation's mandate, everyone realised it would satisfy no one's questions and would be highly unpopular. On the other extreme there were the calls to conduct a detailed forensic investigation of both wrecks, which in theory at least would set out to answer every imaginable question about the battle and sinkings to a standard acceptable in a court of law. As the only one in the room with any experience of what it takes for such an investigation I explained that in practical terms it was beyond our means in terms of time, money, equipment and expertise. John also articulated his concerns about the next phase falling into the trap of 'mission creep'.

There was, however, a reasonable and practical middle option that was within our budget and capabilities and this was the plan that we recommended and which was approved by the foundation. Ours was a two-pronged plan that started with a baseline video/photographic survey of both wrecks and their associated debris fields. Such a survey was fundamentally important in order to map out the relative seabed position of all the wreckage and to document the damage inflicted on both ships during the battle and sinking. Should the government ever want to return and make a fuller investigation of the wrecks then this baseline survey would be an absolute requirement for planning purposes and more. The second prong of the plan was to specifically film and photograph parts of the wrecks to either support or discount the main aspects of the existing historical account of the battle. For example, the German accounts state that it was their shelling of *Sydney*'s upper bridge and forward gun turrets in the opening seconds of the battle that was instrumental in them gaining a decisive advantage. Over and above the baseline survey, we proposed to film this area of the wreck in somewhat more detail than other areas so historians and other interested parties could compare the physical evidence against the German accounts. John and I would develop the details of the plan in advance of the ROV dives and ensure it was executed within the allotted budget.

There was a large amount of work to be done in a short period of time if we were going to get back out to sea in the next couple of days. I met the incoming ROV team, which was made up of six DOF technicians and one specialist engineer from the manufacturer of the ROV named Comanche. The team had recently completed two demanding survey projects in deep water with the Comanche ROV and appeared confident in its ability to handle our requirements. The one unexpected knock-on effect of the success we had in the search phase was that it greatly raised expectations across the country in the next phase of the project. Everyone was keen to see the first photographs of *Sydney* as soon as possible and I was absolutely intent on ensuring they were of the highest quality. To that end, I even brought along my company's state-of-the-art HMI lights and some extra video cameras to improve the ROV's filming capabilities. Although the pressure was already mounting about the next phase, I knew in fact that what we were planning to do was fairly routine in terms of ROV work and so long as the vehicle operated reliably we would do just fine.

With Rob Bruinsma looking after the ROV mobilisation and integration of my HMI lights on the vehicle, I was able to concentrate on preparations for the wreck survey and investigation. The Mayor of Geraldton, Ian Carpenter, kindly gave me the use of the printing facilities at the town hall so I could print two sets of large-format drawings of the builders' plans of both *Sydney* and *Kormoran*. My plan was to use these drawings, in conjunction with the dozens of historical photographs compiled from all our collections, to help in identifying the different parts of the ships and to guide us in directing the ROV pilots around the hulls. A damaged wreck that has been sitting at the bottom of the ocean for 66 years looks a lot different than when it was afloat and we would need every piece of information we had to hand to keep track of the survey in progress.

In addition to the hundred other things he was looking after, Patrick Flynn was working on getting us a very important piece of paperwork. It was a permit granted by the Department of the Environment, Water, Heritage and the Arts, under Section 15 of the Commonwealth *Historic Shipwrecks Act* of 1976, which officially authorised HMA3S 'To conduct searches using the SV Geosounder equipment to confirm the identity of the historic shipwrecks of HMAS *Sydney* II and HSK *Kormoran*.' Now that the wrecks were found their sites were legally protected by the government from unauthorised disturbances with the penalty for breaching the Act being a fine of up to $10,000 or imprisonment for a period of up to five years. As firm proof that this protection was actually in place Patrick had to apply for the permit, and it had to be granted, before we were allowed to dive on the wrecks with the ROV. The conditions of the permit that was granted on 23 March prohibited all contact with the wrecks and associated relics, and undue disturbance of the same.

In 1976, when the newly promulgated Commonwealth *Historic Shipwrecks Act* went into force, the Director of the Western Australian Museum, and ultimately the Department of Maritime Archaeology of the Western Australian Maritime Museum, became responsible on behalf of the Federal Government for all the historic wrecks off the coast of Western Australia including *Sydney* and *Kormoran*. It was entirely appropriate,

Above: The phase-two team.

therefore, that an observer from the maritime museum joined the next phase of the project. There was only one logical person who that observer should be: Dr Michael 'Mack' McCarthy, the curator of Maritime Archaeology. In addition to a long history with the subject dating back to the early 1980s, Mack was an expert maritime archaeologist and had worked on shipwrecks for his entire professional career, albeit in much shallower waters. While having to maintain impartiality towards competing search groups over the years Mack still found a way to encourage genuine research and was one of the earliest proponents of the concept that the way to find *Sydney* was to first find *Kormoran*. He was also a real character and would bring tremendous enthusiasm to the role. We were all delighted to have him join the team.

Will this ROV ever work?

The first indication I got that there was a serious problem with the Comanche ROV was on Easter Monday, 24 March, when Rob Bruinsma called me while I was in town having dinner with Patrick, John and Matthew

Kelley. The ROV mobilisation hadn't gone particularly smoothly, causing a delay to our departure, but up until then the problems were all relatively minor and the DOF team were still confident of having the vehicle ready the next morning. Rob's call broke the mood of the evening and definitely changed our expectations for getting back out to sea. During a wet test of the ROV in Geraldton harbour my HMI lighting system, which consisted of two 400-watt HMI light heads and a dual-ballast, had failed and the lights were destroyed.[1] I had used these lights for more than ten years and they had never failed this way. Moreover, they had just been returned from the manufacturer after a complete overhaul and thorough testing.

When I got back to the boat later that evening the light heads were disassembled and waiting on the work bench for my inspection. Rob wasn't kidding about the lights being destroyed. The top half of the igniter assembly from both lights had disintegrated and showed signs of having been on fire. No one knew what caused the damage, although my guess was that somehow the lights were exposed to a high-voltage pulse with lots of energy content. As I struggled to understand what could have gone so disastrously wrong with the test I was forced to accept that my plans for filming the wrecks using the best quality lights available had been dashed. There was no way we could get the lights sent back to America for repair without incurring at least a week's delay and I wasn't about to hire in a replacement set until we understood the root cause of the failure. Our only practical option was to use a different set of lights being shipped in on an emergency basis from Singapore; they were good quality but hardly the best available.

The bad luck we experienced during the search phase, which we had all prayed was gone for good, was unfortunately back with a vengeance. My HMI lights were the first spectacular casualty but not the last. Over the next five days the *Geosounder* was stuck in Geraldton port as the ROV system suffered one failure after another. The catalogue of components that broke and had to be repaired or replaced was staggering. It included the camera pan and tilt mechanism, countless thruster motors, the starboard 7-function manipulator, the sound velocity profiler, the scanning sonar, the bathymetric survey system, a multi-pin bulkhead connector, a drive motor for the tether management system, a gyro power supply board and both the primary and spare rotary slip ring units without which the ROV would not work.

It was this last failure of the two rotary slip ring units that placed the project in jeopardy again. The slip rings operate inside the winch drum that holds the thousands of metres of ROV cable and they act to keep a constant flow of high-voltage electricity, control signals and data (primarily video) being sent to and from the ROV as the winch drum is rotated. Like my HMI lights, these units had suffered a high-voltage electrical failure and could only be repaired by a manufacturer-trained technician. Fortunately, a technician in Perth was found who was willing to work virtually round the clock to repair both units. The root cause of all these electrical failures was still a mystery and this is what troubled me most. The ROV team was working incredibly hard to solve the myriad problems and I couldn't help but feel sorry for them as they began each twelve-hour shift with the prospect of trying to fix a seriously sick ROV.

The cost of the delay to the project in terms of our remaining budget and schedule was now a major

Above: My HMI light, well and truly destroyed.

problem. The tension and pressure on the *Geosounder* was understandably high and at least for one technician was too much to bear, causing him to walk off the job. We knew that people all across the country were desperate to see the first photographs of *Sydney*. However, in Geraldton the situation was at a critical juncture and there was a risk the ROV phase would have to be aborted unless DOF were able to turn things around. To their considerable credit the DOF management seized the initiative and diverted one of their larger offshore vessels past Geraldton to disembark three of their most senior ROV crew to assist with the repairs along with vital spare equipment.

As soon as the refurbished slip rings arrived in Geraldton by truck the expanded ROV team worked round the clock to install them and prepare the ROV for a rigorous early morning wet test. After more than three hours immersed in the murky waters of Geraldton harbour without any failures the ROV was finally passed fit for service. It was Saturday morning, 29 March, and we were finally in a position to set a sailing time. There

Above: The ROV secure in its garage.

was, however, one last problem to deal with and its name was Pancho.

Cyclone Pancho, which had reached Category 4 intensity two days earlier, was tracking south-east directly towards the wreck site. Although Pancho was beginning to weaken in intensity he was still a dangerous storm and was blocking our path. There was no point in us leaving port to face yet more weather downtime until we knew in which direction Pancho was going to turn next. While we were waiting for the next cyclone update from the Bureau of Meteorology the new captain of *Geosounder*, Deland Van Wieringen, was advised by the port supervisor that they were expecting 1.5 metre swells *inside* the harbour because of Pancho's approach. The dilemma for Deland was either to stay in port and have *Geosounder* bashing against the quay wall fenders or to brave a rough ride out in the open sea. Deland wasted no time and ordered a quick departure at 1500 hours.

Once at sea it was clear the conditions for diving the ROV were marginal. We had planned to return to the test site west of the Abrolhos Islands and attempt to make a trouble-free dive of the ROV to about 500 metres before making the long transit north. Pancho was still far away but his reach was long enough to leave us battling 30-knot winds with gusts to 40 knots and seas of three to four metres. The *Geosounder's* dynamic positioning system was holding the ship stationary but we were still taking large swells that prevented us from launching the ROV. There was nothing else we could do but go fishing.

After watching morale on the ship slide during the search phase because of all the downtime we experienced, I decided to buy some fishing gear in Geraldton and break it out in case we were faced with a similar situation. If we couldn't work, at least the fishing would provide the crew with fun for a few hours and lift everyone's spirits. Our quarry was the handful of dolphin fish that were always lurking about the port side of *Geosounder* looking to make a quick meal of the flying fish and squid that were attracted by the ship's lights. Our gear was fairly primitive but once we mastered the art of placing our lines on to the nose of the dolphin fish we found they were keen to hit the bait. Landing the five to seven kilogram fish was another matter made more difficult by having to haul them up the ship's four-metre freeboard. After hooking up four fish we finally landed one and it was a wild scene as I tried to quickly dispatch the powerful fish. The fishing only lasted a couple of hours but it was great fun and definitely proved to be a popular diversion.

After another aborted attempt at a test dive of the ROV because of rough seas, Deland and I reviewed our options. I wanted to start our journey to the wreck site even though we hadn't yet passed the 500-metre depth ROV test dive that DOF required before we would be allowed to take the vehicle down to the full depth to *Sydney*. The risk, which I was happy to accept, was that we'd have a long transit back to Geraldton if the ROV failed the test dive and a return to port was necessary to get it working again. Deland, who knew what it was like to take the *Geosounder* through a cyclone with 100-knot winds, having done so in 2007, was happy to go with my plan but cautioned that the ride north would be uncomfortable and that we would need to monitor Cyclone Pancho very carefully for any sudden changes of direction or intensification.

As Deland predicted, the transit was a bit bumpy at times but at least we were doing something positive. The worst period came in the early hours of 31 March when the winds veered to the south and a squall with 50-knot

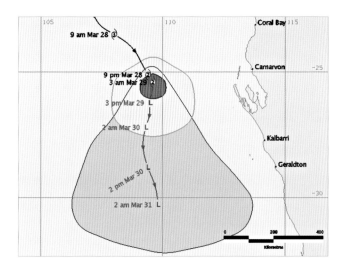

Above: Cyclone Pancho, right where we didn't need it to be.

winds whipped up the seas, forcing the ship to hove to for a couple of hours. Later in the morning we also took some bad rolls that sent everything not tied down in the survey labs crashing to the floor and making a huge mess. Nevertheless, the *Geosounder* continued to make slow progress and we eventually arrived on site at 0200 hours on 1 April with the weather easing and favourable conditions for a launch.

This time the ROV only made it to 40 metres before suffering multiple system failures. Robert Bruinsma woke me to break the news and all I can remember is having the most awful feelings of frustration. As bad as I felt, I knew it was worse for the two ROV supervisors, Simon Hall and Dave Norton, who were very likeable and conscientious guys and didn't deserve the bad breaks they were getting. Dave, in particular, seemed to take the problems personally. He was obviously very proud of his work and his team, which made it worse for him having to continually report nothing but bad news to me.

The next two days were without doubt the lowest ebb of the expedition. It seemed that the ROV and the weather were taking turns to foil the project and add to our growing frustration. There was nothing we could do but be patient and wait for the weather to moderate and pray that the latest repairs to the ROV would eliminate the last of the electrical problems plaguing us. Our only relief was the nightly fishing forays that managed to bring

some lightness to what was generally a very depressing period. HMAS *Sydney* never seemed so close while at the same time so very far away.

We're on it! That's it!

The morning of 3 April finally brought promise that a dive might be possible. The weather had abated and the ROV crews had spent the previous two days conducting every possible test on deck that they could and replacing any component deemed to be questionable. By 0755 hours *Geosounder* was back in position over the wreck holding steady on dynamic positioning. Dave Norton and his crew conducted one last pre-dive check of the ROV. Unbelievably, the main pan/tilt unit that allows our cameras to be moved in virtually any position lost its pan function. This was another blow to my filming objectives but it wasn't a show-stopper in terms of the launch, so I gave the okay to proceed.

At 1132 the ROV, nestled inside its protective garage, was launched off *Geosounder*'s port side and plunged into the water on her way down to the test depth of 500 metres. Because of all the delays we experienced, DOF had agreed to my request that if the ROV passed its 500-metre test we would be allowed to continue down to the seabed rather than having to recover the vehicle back on deck to double-check that it was ready for a dive to the full 2,500-metre depth.

At 1138 the ROV was at 100 metres depth and the first set of function tests had just begun when one of the technicians operating the winch noticed that the level-wind device, which neatly spools the lift cable on and off the winch drum, had stopped working. As soon as I came out on deck to see the problem my heart sank because this *was* a potential show stopper. Without some mechanism to level-wind the 2,500 metres of cable on to the winch drum, we could irreparably damage the main lift cable and that would effectively end the project there and then.

As the ROV dangled beneath us the activity to find the problem was frenetic. Because the failure occurred at shift change time, both ROV crews were involved as well as a couple of the ship's integrated ratings. Within minutes the problem was found to be a rusty chain drive for the level-winding gear that simply snapped because it was corroded. With no spare chain or links on board the solution was to jury-rig a chain hoist to physically pull the level-wind roller into the correct position as the cable was paid out or hauled in. It wasn't an ideal situation but the fix would work and that's all anybody cared about. Thankfully, the dive continued.

At 1308 hours the ROV had reached the 500-metre test depth. The plan was for the vehicle to swim out of its protective garage into open water whereupon a long checklist of functions would be tested. However, as the chief pilot Bruce Burman pushed his joystick forward to propel the ROV out of its garage, nothing happened. There was no movement: nothing at all. Like an eager racehorse trapped inside a starting gate that refused to open, the vehicle was imprisoned within its surrounding garage and denied all freedom of movement. This time both my stomach and heart sank.

I had always felt that the success or failure of the project might ride on just a few key decisions. A couple had been made already and this was probably the moment for one more. In my mind it came down to a simple choice. We could either recover the ROV and start the morale-sapping cycle of equipment downtime followed by weather downtime all over again or we could just go for it. Having listened to everyone's input during a meeting on *Geosounder*'s bridge I decided to continue the dive to the wreck even though having the ROV locked inside its garage would severely restrict our filming ability. My thinking was that we only needed a single decent picture of *Sydney* to satisfy the immediate needs of the public and there was a reasonable chance we could position the garage close enough to the wreck to get it. It would all depend on the quality of Mike and Nigel's navigation in pinpointing the seabed position of the wreck. If they were on target, we would probably find the wreck straightway. But if they weren't, we could spend hours hopelessly searching the wrong location and not knowing where to turn next. There was no time to waste. At 1345 the ROV

was once again descending in to the abyss of the Indian Ocean.

I explained to Nigel that I wanted us to come down off the stern port quarter of the wreck where there would be less damage and jagged steel to contend with compared to *Sydney*'s fractured bow. Nigel was quietly confident that his positioning was good and as he had already proven himself during the search phase I allowed myself a brief moment of optimism. At 1500 hours the ROV was at a depth of 2,300 metres and I decided to head up to the ROV pilot's control van on the boat deck where I could sit with pilots Bruce Burman and Simon Hall and monitor all the incoming camera and sonar feeds. I asked John to join me in the small cabin while Glenys, Mack and everyone else crowded into the main survey lab to watch on the large wide-screen monitor.

We descended the last 100 metres to the seabed very, very slowly. The ROV's cameras were tilted down to pick up the seabed as soon as it came into sight. I was waiting for the vehicle's lights to begin reflecting off the featureless seabed when I began to see a faint shape emerge from the blackness that clearly wasn't the seabed. We all craned our necks forward in unison to get a better look at the object coming into view and in the shortest of split seconds I realised we had come down directly on one of *Sydney*'s 6-inch gun turrets. 'We're on it — it's a gun — that's it!' I exclaimed. Of all the places for the ROV to touch down first I never, ever expected we would be so unbelievably lucky to come down within sight of 'X' turret. The picture Australia had waited decades to see was suddenly and unexpectedly in front of our faces. John perfectly summed up the significance of this wonderful picture: 'My God, there is no doubt about that at all!' Indeed, there was no doubt about it. HMAS *Sydney* was well and truly found, and having located her position we could start unravelling the mystery surrounding her demise.

Right: Our first view of HMAS Sydney *— 'X' turret pointing straight at us.*

CHAPTER NINE

...

The first pictures of *Sydney*

Taking advantage of our good fortune in landing so close to *Sydney* I decided we should stay in that position, on the port side, and film as much of the wreck as possible before moving the ship and the ROV to the stern where I wanted to start the survey. The ROV was still locked inside its garage, and with the pair moving up and down in concert with the rolling and pitching of *Geosounder* in the 2.5-metre seas, it was incredibly difficult to focus our eyes on the wreck. The only control Bruce Burman had to try and increase our field of vision was to slowly rotate the garage and ROV left and right using the vehicle's thrusters. I knew the constant yo-yoing of the ROV would blur the digital still pictures we wanted to take while we were doing the video filming; nevertheless, I left instructions with the new survey technician, Johannes Van Rooyen, in the survey lab below, to shoot as many pictures as he could, hoping that a few would be usable. The difficult conditions meant we would have to be satisfied with this dive being a reconnaissance survey. Although the situation wasn't ideal we were all very excited to be seeing the first pictures of *Sydney*.

What was immediately apparent in the first few minutes was that the twin gun barrels of *Sydney*'s 'X' and 'Y' turrets were both trained to port and as far forward as possible, presumably in the same position as when they fired their last shots at *Kormoran*. Unsurprisingly the gun barrels were all fixed at low elevation angles, reflecting the extremely short range of the battle. We know from the German accounts that *Sydney*'s first salvo went over, so a reduction in gun elevation would have been needed to score hits. In particular, 'X' turret's barrels were actually depressed and seemed to be resting on the safety depression gears below each barrel.[1] As the ROV moved closer to 'X' turret we could also see that the lower sighting ports, through which the men responsible for aiming the guns would sight the enemy, were cranked wide open. The sighting ports of 'Y' turret were in the same open position.

Left: 'B' turret's roof is blown away, verifying Lieutenant Bunjes's testimony.
Previous page: Sydney's bakery, which took a direct hit from a 15-cm shell.

Above: Sydney's stern crumpled by its heavy impact with the seabed. *Inset: A dislocated propeller.*

It didn't take long for us to find compelling evidence of the courage of *Sydney*'s gunners. Seeing the guns this way left us in no doubt that the men closed up in these turrets had fought to the bitter end, despite the sickening knowledge that their ship had been heavily hit and many of their shipmates were undoubtedly killed or wounded. These men fought bravely and they fought well. Having lost central firing control at the outset of the battle, they would have had to switch to local control and quickly readjust the aim of their guns while taking heavy fire from one or more of *Kormoran*'s 15-cm guns in return. It is impossible to know how long these guns continued firing before they took the direct hits that silenced them.

A number of Germans credit 'X' turret with scoring the fatal hits on *Kormoran*, and Detmers stated that this turret fired with 'considerable accuracy'.

Having had a good look at the aft turrets I asked for *Geosounder* to shift its position in order to bring the garage over the stern. Our primary interest in the stern was to see whether *Sydney*'s brass nameplate was still there. It would have been terrific to find her name but sadly it wasn't there. As John suspected, the letters had been removed, most likely when the ship was painted over with the camouflage pattern she wore throughout

Above: The fire-ravaged officers' WC compartment, which was located in the aft superstructure.

the war. Nevertheless, the condition of the stern was very interesting to me and told its own story about the damage caused when *Sydney* hit the seabed. We found the stern badly crumpled and the quarterdeck collapsed, leaving the capstan in the centre of the deck oddly suspended on its spindle above the sunken timber deck. The side of the ship also had a large Z-shaped fold that I recognised as impact damage I had seen in many other deep-water shipwrecks. This characteristic damage was a sure sign to me that *Sydney* hit the seabed stern first.

Very slowly we began to move forward along *Sydney's* port side, stopping here and there to inspect signs of damage and interesting features. At the bottom of our screens we

could just about make out one of *Sydney's* three propellers sticking out from the hull at a strange angle. Just forward of that, a second partially buried propeller was spotted at the end of a bent and dislocated propeller shaft. Rising back up to the quarterdeck we had a quick look for the ship's bell in case it was hanging in its normal peacetime location outside the senior officers' bathroom. Although the original construction drawings for *Sydney* placed this bell in the lobby below the 4-inch gun deck just aft of the funnel, we had information (including a photograph of *Sydney's* sister ship HMAS *Perth* with her bell in this location) that when not at war the bell was mounted in the quarterdeck location. As we would never have been able to reach under the 4-inch gun deck with the ROV, our only chance of sighting *Sydney's* bell was if, for some reason, it was on the quarterdeck. Sadly it was not.

Despite the frustration of not having a free-flying ROV, we were still seeing quite a bit of the ship, which helped identify potential snagging hazards for the ROV which the pilots would want to avoid during future dives. I was relieved that the underwater visibility was quite good and that the amount of siltation, corrosion and encrustation by organisms wasn't too bad for a wreck that had lain at the bottom of the ocean for more than 66 years. Importantly, *Sydney*'s paintwork was also in generally good order, which would help us in spotting the hits of both large and small calibre shells and in identifying places that suffered serious fire damage. In the case of the former, paint is blasted away by flying shrapnel and leaves a distinctive shell-burst pattern, whereas for the latter the paintwork is simply burnt away leaving the bare surface to corrode with time by a combination of normal iron oxidation and microbial corrosion. One such place we found was the senior officers' galleys, located just forward of 'X' turret. Based on the complete absence of paintwork and the rivers of orange-brown rust which now clung to its exterior walls, this section of *Sydney* had obviously been subject to one of the several fires that raged through the night and could be seen by the Germans miles away.

By moving the ship in ten- and fifteen-metre jumps we continued to work our way forward, keeping the garage and ROV just outboard of *Sydney*'s port side. Next in line was the aft 4-inch high-angle gun (designated P2), which was still pointing skywards at an extreme angle ready to defend *Sydney* against the threat of enemy aircraft, as it was designed to. Clearly this gun didn't factor in the action at all. The forward gun (designated P1) might have, however. Its barrel was at a suspiciously low angle, roughly estimated to be 10 degrees, indicating that a gun crew did attempt to put this gun into action after they had stopped taking direct fire from the German 2-cm anti-aircraft machine guns. Unfortunately, *Sydney*'s turn behind *Kormoran* at the same time would have made it impossible for the P1 gun crew to train its barrel on the enemy. Seeing these guns standing naked on the raised gun deck, with only ⅜-inch thick steel plates around the guard rails for protection, we realised just how horribly exposed the gun crews would have been in a close range naval engagement with

Above: Port-side forward (P1) 4-inch gun ...

Kormoran, where her fully automatic guns were able to direct their rapid fire with impunity.

Directly below the 4-inch gun deck we expected to find one of *Sydney*'s 21-inch Mark VII quadruple torpedo tubes. Instead, what we found was just the bare mount complete with the ring gear that facilitated training of the tubes. The tubes and the torpedoes themselves were missing and had obviously been dislodged from the mount when *Sydney* sank to the seabed. Although the four torpedoes and tubes would have weighed in the order of 10 tons, they were held in place by gravity alone and were probably dislodged from the low-profile mount by the enormous hydrodynamic forces created during the sinking. This finding didn't bode well for our investigation of the starboard torpedo tubes, the purpose of which was to determine whether their torpedoes were fired by *Sydney* as the Germans claimed.

Like every other deep-water shipwreck I ever investigated, *Sydney* had lost a lot of her superstructure and deck fittings during the sinking, which in itself can be a very violent event, especially when it occurs rapidly. Both funnels and masts were missing as well as all the wooden boats on the port side, the aircraft catapult and the aft searchlight platform. I expected that virtually all the missing items would be found in the debris field a relatively short distance north-east of the wreck. For

... and how it looks now (l) and P2 (r).

some pieces of the ship it would be easy to tell whether the damage was caused in the battle or in the sinking, whereas for other pieces it would be very hard to know for sure. All we could do was film and photograph every piece from multiple angles and hope that this would be enough for the naval architects, historians and the public who would undoubtedly study what we collected for years to come.

We had traversed beyond the mid-point of the ship but hadn't seen any real evidence of shell fire until we reached the bakery upon whose roof the aircraft crane was mounted. A very large hole had been ripped through the bakery's wall and about a dozen smaller shrapnel holes were dotted around it. It was hard to tell, what with the ROV badly jerking up and down, but the holes appeared to be the result of exit rather than entrance damage. To the side of the bakery was a large section of open deck that gave us the best view of the timber decking, which Wes Olson reliably informed me was made of Borneo whitewood and not teak as most people assumed. The timber had mostly rotted away, however, and all that remained were the lines of pitch between the missing planks and the studs that had once held them in place.

Another fifteen-metre jump forward by *Geosounder* put us level with what remained of *Sydney*'s bridge superstructure. Here we got our first real taste of the

extraordinary damage that was inflicted on *Sydney* and her crew. It was far worse than anyone had dared to imagine. To begin with, the compass platform where Captain Burnett and his officers directed the pursuit of *Kormoran* was utterly devastated. The bulletproof roof that covered the upper bridge area was gone, as was the director control tower and the high-angle control station. At first sight we had no way of knowing whether they were shot away by *Kormoran*'s guns or swept away in the sinking, although two large 15-cm shell holes straight through the base of the director control tower was firm proof of the punishing fire the Germans directed at this strategically important area of *Sydney*. The only things left standing were the bases of the twin twelve-foot rangefinders fixed at opposite sides of the bridge. Everything else, including the entire front section of the upper bridge where the revolving chart table, compass and pelorus once stood, was simply gone. The most vital part of *Sydney*, described by Heinz Messerschmidt as being full of officers and a hive of activity in the minutes before the shooting began, had been reduced to a giant crater that opened up to the wheelhouse below, and into which the forward screen of the superstructure had collapsed. It was a sobering sight that left us feeling cold for the fate of the men stationed there.

Judging by the extensive corrosion that covered every inch of *Sydney*'s bridge, we came to the conclusion that the fire that was started there by hits from *Kormoran*'s

Above: The shocking state of 'A' turret.

opening salvos was incredibly intense and probably raged out of control right up until the moment *Sydney* sank. There was also considerable fire damage along the side of *Sydney*'s hull adjacent to the bridge, where there were a number of holes caused by strikes from both 15-cm and 3.7-cm shells. It was yet more evidence that *Kormoran*'s gunners specifically targeted the cruiser's bridge. Not all of *Kormoran*'s shells penetrated, but even those that didn't would have caused a great deal of damage inside the ship by the release of kinetic energy alone. On the basis of what we had seen so far there would have been few places on *Sydney*'s upper decks that would have provided safe refuge from *Kormoran*'s withering fire.

We had been filming *Sydney*'s port side for nearly two hours before we finally reached her forward section. One of the biggest questions about the battle was: where did *Kormoran*'s torpedo hit? I knew the answer could be found by inspecting the break at the bow, and not wanting

Previous pages: The complete damage to Sydney's *critical nerve centre can be seen in these images of her devastated bridge and compass platform.*

to wait any longer I asked Bruce to rotate the cage to the left towards this area. We had already seen that 'B' turret was in place and now the ROV's lights began to illuminate the shape of a second turret, but nothing beyond that. I asked for one last five-metre shift of *Geosounder* to put us in the perfect position to film the break, as well as 'A' turret, which from a distance looked to be badly damaged. On the way over to the break we spotted a few more nasty-looking holes that were punched clean through *Sydney*'s side, as well as two direct hits to the front of 'B' turret, whose roof was half blown off from the resulting explosion. As with 'X' and 'Y' turrets, the lower sighting port of 'B' turret was cranked wide open.

In contrast with the aft turrets, which were both pointing as far forward as possible, the gun barrels of 'A' and 'B' turrets were trained directly to port, as would be expected for the start of a broadside battle fought at close range. Their position, frozen in time, was a telling indication of the short period they were in action during the battle. The shocking state of 'A' turret seemed to answer the question why that was the case. Its entire roof, back and starboard sidewalls were gone, exposing only the heaviest components of the twin 6-inch guns not blown away by the terrible blast that tore this turret apart.

The port sidewall was still hanging on, although its rear half was bent outwards in the same way the floor of the turret was lifted upwards at the back. I had seen damage virtually identical to this with *Bismarck*'s 5.9-inch gun turrets, which had been destroyed by the British Home Fleet when they finally caught the fleeing battleship and meted out Winston Churchill's call for revenge at the sinking of *Hood*, and knew that it could only be caused by a direct hit from a high-explosive shell. As we looked, unsuccessfully, for the evidence of that direct hit we were surprised to find that unlike the other three turrets the sighting ports on 'A' were shut tight.

The break across *Sydney*'s bow spoke volumes about the destructive power of a well-placed torpedo and the resulting carnage that occurs when structural failure of the hull follows. With our cameras pointed downwards we had a bird's-eye view of the break from port to starboard and from the forecastle deck straight down to the seabed. Viewed from a height, the break looked relatively clean, but as we dropped the garage a little lower and pushed in with our zoom camera, the bent and torn plates of steel

began to reveal the catastrophic hull failure that led to *Sydney*'s demise. Immediately forward of 'A' turret there was no intact hull structure remaining. All that was left were disconnected sheets of deck plating, flopped down over the front of the break like half-cooked layers of lasagne. While the forecastle deck plates were helpful with identification and orientation, as they included the odd recognisable fitting, such as a fairlead or a mushroom vent, they weren't much use in helping us pinpoint the position of the torpedo strike which happened several decks below. To answer that question conclusively, we would have to come back when the ROV could film the entire scene in free-flying mode and also inspect *Sydney*'s bow, which I had no doubt we would find in the debris field.

Having completed our reconnaissance survey of *Sydney*'s port side, I decided to suspend the dive to give the ROV pilots a break and to give John, Glenys and Mack time to write up their thoughts on what they had just observed for a search report I wanted to send Patrick for immediate uploading onto the FSF website. Our last brief report was made on 22 March, and since that time the public had no knowledge of the myriad problems we suffered in getting the first pictures of *Sydney*. I felt no reason to bore them with our trials and tribulations when

Above: The aircraft catapult found in the debris field.

all they wanted was to see the pictures. So when I was told that a low oil level alarm had gone off on the ROV I wasted no time in instructing Simon to recover it, which would allow us to retrieve the photographs stored on the digital still camera's memory card and include them in our report.

Although the photographs were blurred by the constant movement of the ROV stuck inside its garage, I had to accept that these were the best we could give to the public under the circumstances. As I viewed the photographs and a playback of the video footage to pick out the most representative of *Sydney*, I noticed something that didn't occur to me during the live survey. Virtually every single watertight door that we could see along the full length of *Sydney*'s port side was wide open. This was no coincidence I thought, especially as each of those doors would have been shut and securely fastened during the battle. I couldn't help but wonder whether those images of the open doors told their own story of the tragic last moments of *Sydney*'s crew as they tried to save their beloved ship, their own lives and those of their shipmates.

Verifying the German accounts

Our photographs were sensationally received by the media, leading television news reports and dominating front pages of newspapers all across the country, although in our cocooned state on *Geosounder* we were virtually oblivious to the enormous public reaction the photos were generating. The only real indication we had to go on of our newsworthiness was the intrepid airplane that flew hundreds of miles to visit us and buzz the ship with a series of low-altitude passes. It seemed that everyone was delighted and grateful to see the Grey Gladiator again. The robustness of Richard Sojka's website structure was being sorely tested, as he reported 60,000 visits to the press room to download the pictures, and millions more hits to the general site by the public. It certainly felt better to finally start delivering on the promises we had made weeks previously about filming the wrecks, but I wouldn't be fully satisfied with our efforts until the ROV system was repaired and we were able to take pictures of a quality I knew was possible and which I would demand from the team, starting with myself.

During the long period of downtime I asked John to take the lead in outlining our objectives in terms of what areas of the ships we should examine for both the general baseline survey and for verifying specific aspects of the German accounts. A balance had to be struck in how much we could achieve in the time we had remaining according to our budget, but the unanimous feeling was that we should use some of this time to see whether we could prove, or disprove, a number of the key claims made by the Germans, which in the absence of any other eyewitnesses have become accepted as part of the official historical account of the battle. John worked diligently during the enforced downtime breaks to put together two excellent documents, complete with photographs, which the ROV pilots could use as a guide during the filming.

Although John and I sat with the ROV pilots in their hut during the first dive to help them get to know their way around the ship, my plan was always for all the observers and me to work in the main survey lab, which was now empty following the departure of the Williamson search team. There was a long table in the centre of the room where John, Glenys and Mack could sit together and work around the large-format drawings I

had specially printed in Geraldton. On the wall opposite we had mounted a 54-inch-wide video screen to show the live feed from the main ROV camera. I had my own video monitor, which allowed me to frame and focus the still photographs I was shooting and a two-way voice intercom link with the ROV pilots to direct them during the dives. The lab was also equipped with a remote monitor of the ROV's scanning sonar so I could make decisions about which sonar targets to investigate. I asked Mike Kelly and Brian Bunge of W&A to stay on for the ROV phase, as I needed them to provide instantaneous information about the large database of sonar targets found during the search that would serve as a roadmap for navigating the ROV, especially in and around the debris fields. As with the search phase, all the critical expedition data (video, still photographs, navigation) were digitally recorded to become part of a permanent archive of the expedition, which would also include the unedited logbooks kept by the various team leaders.

Over the next four days we made five more dives, including three to film Sydney's wreckage, during which approximately 38 hours of high-quality video footage and more than 1,400 still photographs were taken. This impressive level of productivity was only possible because

Above: 'B' turret destroyed by two 15-cm shell hits.

the DOF ROV crew persevered in overcoming the mysterious electrical problems that initially plagued the Comanche ROV system. Amazingly, even the weather, which had been uncooperative the entire time we were at sea, began to moderate and allowed us to work without the threat of downtime. We worked pretty much full on, with only a couple of hours of sleep grabbed here and there each day, but nobody was complaining in light of the terrific results we were getting.

On our second dive we returned to *Sydney*'s hull and with enormous relief cheered as the ROV successfully flew out of its garage and scampered over to the wreck. The difference between having the vehicle jerked about uncontrollably and being able to fly freely around the wreck was like night and day. This time we started the survey at the break of the bow and made a full circle of the wreck, moving from the port side around to the stern and over to the starboard side before finishing back

at the break again. Our survey of the break confirmed that it occurred approximately in line with the forward end of 'A' turret, although there was undoubtedly some internal damage and weakening of the hull structure abaft this position. Peering through a jumble of wreckage below the overhanging deck plates, it was possible to see what appeared to be a transverse watertight bulkhead (WTB). The excellent construction drawings we had of *Sydney* indicated that this was the WTB at frame 35 that separated the 6-inch magazine room from 'A' turret's 6-inch shell room, although the manner in which we found the port and starboard side plates bent outwards from the hull in this area surely meant that this WTB had been breached.[2]

Kormoran's torpedo obviously struck forward of the break but we would need to examine the other half of *Sydney*'s fractured bow in the debris field to estimate the position of the strike more precisely. Nevertheless, the damage we did find correlated well with the testimony of the handful of Germans who placed the strike in the

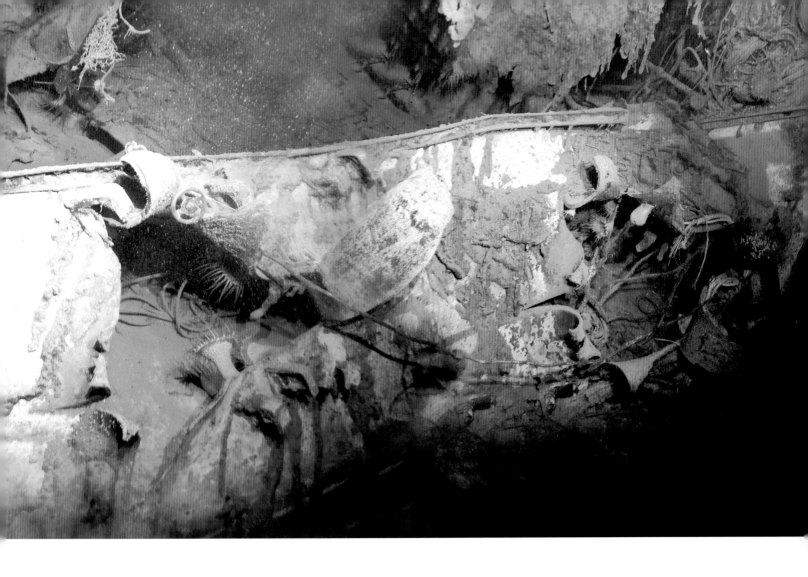

Above: The sidewall of 'A' turret, devastated by two nose-fused 15-cm shells, lies on the seabed close to the wreck of Sydney.

region of the forward turrets, based upon where they saw the enormous column of water kick up along *Sydney*'s side when the 280-kg charge of *Kormoran*'s G7a torpedo exploded. As usual, Captain Detmers's description of the torpedo strike was the most precise: 'Raider fired two torpedoes, one of which missed, and one hit, about 20 metres from the bow.' Lieutenant Willy Bunjes, who was also proving to be a very reliable eyewitness to the battle, showed in his diagram of the action that he too felt the torpedo struck just forward of 'A' turret.

There was one important historical point that pertained to the firing of *Kormoran*'s torpedoes that we were able to clear up straightaway. Despite the Germans' steadfast testimony that they fired these torpedoes from their twin above-water tubes mounted on *Kormoran*'s main deck, a number of Australian researchers doubted them on this point and have controversially claimed that they used the hidden underwater tubes instead to gain an unfair, and possibly illegal, advantage over *Sydney*.[3] Neverending questions about *Kormoran*'s use of its torpedoes in the battle have been a sticking point for many people and have influenced them with respect to the credibility of the German version of the battle.

We found the truth to this question in the frozen position of *Sydney*'s forward guns trained directly to port and the hole from a single 15-cm armour-piercing (base-fused) shell punched straight through the front of 'B' turret. These images bear witness to the fact that at the time *Sydney*'s forward guns were taken out of action, she was fighting a broadside battle against *Kormoran* with both ships travelling virtually parallel and at the same speed. A hit on *Sydney*'s bow by an underwater torpedo at this point in the action would have been impossible because *Kormoran*'s underwater tubes were fixed at a 125° angle relative to her bow, meaning that she could only fire on ships that were quite a way astern, *not* abreast of her as *Sydney* evidently was at the time.

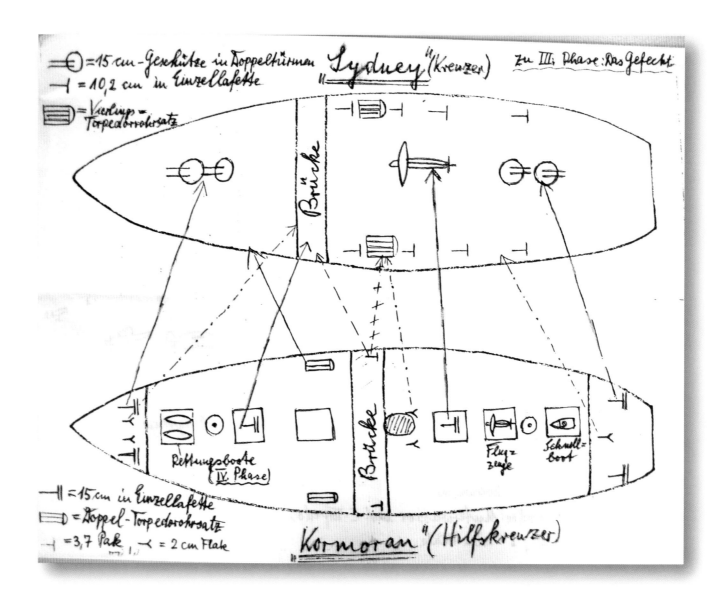

Above: Lieutenant Heinfried Ahl's diagram showing
Kormoran's battle strategy.

For *Kormoran* to have hit *Sydney* with its underwater torpedo, given the distance of at least 900 metres between the two ships, the cruiser would have had to have been about six boat lengths (more than half a nautical mile) astern of the raider.[4] If this was the case, then why weren't *Sydney*'s 'A' and 'B' turrets aimed forward rather than to port as we found them? Also, how would it have been possible for *Kormoran*'s forward (No. 2) 15-cm gun to have scored the devastating blow to the front of *Sydney*'s 'B' turret that had obviously been hit on a perfectly straight trajectory?[5] Had *Sydney* been three to four boat lengths behind, in keeping with the controversial claim about it being an underwater torpedo, then this gun would have had to have been fired at an acute angle of about 35° and the resulting entrance wound would have looked very different from what we found it to be. The other impossibility connected with this unsupported allegation is the fact that *Kormoran* was unable to fire its underwater torpedoes while steaming at 14 knots because the force of water moving past the hull would have jammed the torpedo as it exited the tube and skewed it wildly off course.[6]

As we continued our survey around the base of the break we unexpectedly found the answer to what caused the total destruction of 'A' turret. Previously, we had examined what remained of the turret housing for shell holes, but all we could find was the hint of a hit on the front of the turret below the closed sighting ports in the form of the telltale sign of blasted paintwork. Unfortunately, our vision of whatever damage this shell hit might have caused was obstructed by a section of forecastle deck plating draped curiously over both gun barrels. What we did find, however, was the starboard sidewall of the turret housing, which had two massive holes undoubtedly caused by individual 15-cm nose-fused shells fired by *Kormoran* which exploded on contact. The turret sidewall was upside down, thus revealing the inner surface of the 1-inch plate distinctively peeled back in a manner that appeared to show the trajectory of the shells as they struck the sidewall before violently exploding and blowing out the entire back wall and roof structure of the turret housing.

Unlike 'A' turret, there was no need to hunt for the cause of 'B' turret's destruction, as it was staring straight at us. It had been struck by a 15-cm shell at its base as well as the aforementioned 15-cm base-fused shell at its front, the effect of which was to blow off the left-hand side of the turret's roof and rear hatch with such force that the three dogs (fasteners) keeping the hatch firmly shut were shattered in half. Once again, it was Lieutenant Bunjes who proved to be an accurate eyewitness to the incident, as he wrote of seeing 'the armour cover of its second gun [flying] into the air'. Although we have no way of knowing for sure exactly when *Sydney* took these hits, they do fit with the German accounts that *Sydney*'s forward guns were hit several times at the outset of the action and thereafter never fired again.[7]

One thing that was certain was that the light steel plate protecting *Sydney*'s crew in vital areas of the ship was no match for either *Kormoran*'s 15-cm or 3.7-cm guns at such close range. Of course the same was also true for *Kormoran*, as she had essentially no protection and her men were much more exposed than *Sydney*'s. However, the annihilation of *Sydney*'s forward gun turrets was stark proof of how lethal a German raider such as *Kormoran* actually was in a battle at close quarters. The assumption that *Kormoran* was lightly armed compared with *Sydney* is a fallacy and one has to look no further than *Sydney*'s forward gun turrets for the disturbing evidence of this. When just a few well-placed shells could destroy half of the enemy's firepower, the key to this battle was surprise, not might. This was the naval equivalent of a street fight and whichever of the two ships landed the first telling blows was bound to be the victor.

During my last research trip to Germany in late 2007 I found a document in Peter Tamm's collection of archives (recently moved from his mansion on the banks of the Elbe to an immaculately refurbished ten-storey building in the Port of Hamburg, soon to become the new International Maritime Museum Hamburg) that revealed Detmers and Skeries's battle strategy. The document was a drawing made by Lieutenant Heinfried Ahl, *Kormoran*'s aviation officer, apparently just after he was imprisoned at the officers' camp in Dhurringile, which depicted the two vessels abreast of one another and showed how each of *Kormoran*'s weapons were aimed at specific targets on *Sydney* to either destroy or neutralise them. Ahl's drawing matched both Detmers's account of the battle and the damage we were able to document in our investigation of *Sydney*'s shell-riddled hull. Importantly, it also showed how *Kormoran*'s gunnery was at least equal, and in some respects superior, to *Sydney*'s.

Despite *Sydney*'s assumed superiority, especially at long range, it was actually *Kormoran* which arguably had the most effective weaponry for a close quarters fight. In addition to his main 15-cm guns, which were strategically directed at *Sydney*'s 6-inch gun turrets, bridge and airplane, Detmers was also able to make effective use of *all* his secondary armament during the crucial first minutes of the battle. When I showed Ahl's diagram to Heinz Messerschmidt he confirmed it was correct and stated that 'the aims [targets] were given during the time we were at action stations [before the shooting began]'. Detmers's premeditated targeting meant that *Kormoran*'s gunners all knew where they were to aim and could find their targets straightaway, as soon as their respective guns were de-camouflaged. In order to have any chance against *Sydney*, Detmers knew that he would have to make the most of the advantage he had in knowing his enemy better than the enemy knew him by scoring hits immediately. In the final analysis, the success of *Kormoran*'s attack boiled down to a combination of surprise and speed.

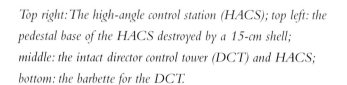

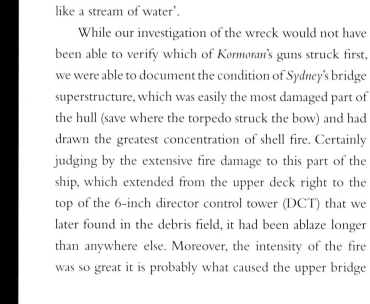

Top right: The high-angle control station (HACS); top left: the pedestal base of the HACS destroyed by a 15-cm shell; middle: the intact director control tower (DCT) and HACS; bottom: the barbette for the DCT.

Clearly, a key weapon in Detmers's mind was his starboard 3.7-cm anti-tank gun, which led him to single out its gunner, Jakob Fend, for special commendation with the award of an Iron Cross First Class. Because this gun was hidden by a light cover that could be quickly removed, it should have been the first to fire and strike its key target: *Sydney*'s bridge. In the five minutes or so that *Sydney* was to starboard of *Kormoran*, before dropping astern and turning sharply to port, Fend's 3.7-cm gun could have fired as many as 65 shells at the bridge superstructure with nearly every one hitting. In the eyes of Heinz Messerschmidt this relatively fast-firing anti-tank gun was pouring shells into 'the bridge of *Sydney* like a stream of water'.

While our investigation of the wreck would not have been able to verify which of *Kormoran*'s guns struck first, we were able to document the condition of *Sydney*'s bridge superstructure, which was easily the most damaged part of the hull (save where the torpedo struck the bow) and had drawn the greatest concentration of shell fire. Certainly judging by the extensive fire damage to this part of the ship, which extended from the upper deck right to the top of the 6-inch director control tower (DCT) that we later found in the debris field, it had been ablaze longer than anywhere else. Moreover, the intensity of the fire was so great it is probably what caused the upper bridge

Above: The starboard-side torpedo mount. Inset: The missing torpedo lying by itself on the ocean floor

and compass platform to collapse in on itself, either at the time of the sinking or later while on the seabed because of the accelerated corrosion that would have taken place in this weakened area devoid of all its protective paint.

Both the director control tower and the high-angle control station (HACS) for fire control of *Sydney*'s 4-inch guns were swept away from the ship when she sank and were found in the debris field. Although the DCT was badly burnt, it was found basically intact without obvious shell damage. Despite the fact that there is no physical connection between them, the deckhead (roof) of the former bridge compass platform, also exhibiting fire damage, was found leaning against the front of the DCT. The HACS was found in two pieces on the seabed; or rather the control station and what remained of its support

base were lying about 75 metres away from each other. As further evidence of *Kormoran*'s targeting of *Sydney*'s bridge superstructure, the HACS support base was very close to being completely severed by another well-aimed 15-cm shell. Similarly, we also found *Sydney*'s Walrus aircraft in the debris field, although identifying it from the pile of twisted and bent frames was initially a struggle, as it too was completely destroyed by another direct hit from a 15-cm shell, which Skeries called a 'lucky shot'.

According to the German accounts, another key to its defeat of the Australian cruiser was putting *Sydney*'s forward gun turrets out of action very early in the fight. Skeries's testimony indicates this happened after *Kormoran*'s third 15-cm gun salvo hit the 'forward tower', or DCT, which was the central gunnery control system for *Sydney*'s four 6-inch gun turrets. The open sighting ports we found on three of *Sydney*'s four turrets indicate that the gun crews inside were forced to switch to local

control as soon as it was apparent that central control had been lost. We also found two 15-cm shell holes at the base structure of the DCT, one clearly entering from the starboard side and a larger hole from the port side. The explosive force of either shell would have been enough to destroy the functionality of the DCT, although it was undoubtedly the strike to the port side of the base, fired by *Kormoran*'s No. 3 gun, which did the critical damage at the critical time. With the loss of director control, the gun crews would have scrambled to get into local control, to open their sighting ports if not already opened and to re-aim and resume firing as soon as possible. Turrets 'X' and 'Y' appear to have been able to make this switch by the time *Kormoran* had fired eight to ten times, meaning that *Sydney*'s guns were silenced for anywhere from 30 to 40 seconds during this all-important phase of the battle. Turrets 'A' and 'B' never resumed firing, however, as they were either destroyed by the shell hits we documented previously or by *Kormoran*'s torpedo, which would have struck at about the same time as their eighth or ninth salvo, according to Detmers.[8] Whatever the case, the position of these forward guns — trained to port at a 90° angle as they would have been at the very start of the action — does substantiate Detmers's and Skeries's accounts about the timing of their elimination.

For anyone still in doubt about whether Detmers or Skeries told the truth about how close the two ships were when the action began (900 to 1,500 metres) the effect *Kormoran*'s 2-cm C/30 anti-aircraft machine guns had in the battle should settle that question. These were the shortest range guns in *Kormoran*'s arsenal and would not have been able to reach their targets unless *Sydney* was as close as reported. As Ahl's drawing shows, the Germans were able to use three of these fully automatic guns in targeting the various crews assembled along *Sydney*'s port side, thus preventing them from manning their own weapons and possibly changing the course of the battle in their favour. *Kormoran* was equally vulnerable to being hit by one, or more, of the cruiser's four torpedoes or a volley of shells from her 4-inch guns. Yet these weapons appear never to have been used. Our initial inspection of *Sydney*'s port side had already revealed that the 4-inch guns played no role in the crucial first phase of the battle, but what of the torpedoes? The answer to that question was found in the debris field when what was later determined to be the port-side

Above: Sydney's *distinct cruiser bow; right: the upturned bow with both anchors in place.*

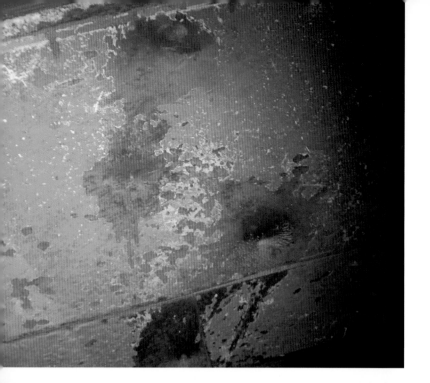

torpedo mount was located lying upside down with just two of its four torpedoes still loaded. While the two empty tubes indicated that *Sydney* did fire a pair of torpedoes at *Kormoran*, as Detmers originally testified, there can be little doubt that these were fired later in battle and at long range by *Sydney,* as depicted in Lieutenant Bunjes's drawing (see page 85, panel 4). The final proof may lie in the small strikes we found on *Sydney's* unarmoured side plating, which could very well be hits from the 2-cm guns.

Although we didn't attempt to find or count every shell strike or hole in *Sydney's* riddled hull we did try to film and photograph as much of the exterior of the wreck as we possibly could in case others wanted to make such an analysis in the future. What we did find, however, was that in general the German claims about their rate of hitting *Sydney*, which was the subject of serious doubt among many researchers, were in fact reasonably accurate. Certainly, the areas on *Sydney* that were targeted by *Kormoran's* guns (i.e. the gun turrets, the bridge superstructure, the gunnery control towers, the hull near the water line) were all hit repeatedly and suffered heavy damage. We fully expected *Sydney's* port side to have borne the brunt of the onslaught, especially when it was clear that her gun turrets never had the chance to swing round to starboard and become targeted from that side. This is why we were all shocked to witness how damaged the starboard side actually was once we were able to move the ROV across after completing our filming of the port side. The concentration of 15-cm and 3.7-cm shells that slammed against *Sydney's* starboard mid-section was alarming. A remarkably tight cluster of four 15-cm shell strikes just forward of the starboard torpedo mount revealed the stark truth behind the statement by some of *Kormoran's* gunners that once they found the range, they were hitting the cruiser with virtually every shot. Although these four (apparently nose-fused) shells failed to penetrate *Sydney's* combined 3-inch armour belt and 1-inch hull plate, they would have caused enormous damage inside the ship. In particular, the lowest of the

Above: Port-side torpedo tubes with two torpedoes still intact.

four strikes just slightly above the boot topping could well have had a disastrous effect on the ship's ring-main electrical system which was run behind the armour belt in this area level with the platform deck.

Numerous other shells did penetrate *Sydney*'s starboard side, even punching through its protective armour belt. Many of these were apparently base-fused shells that would have exploded inside the ship after piercing the hull and would have thus had the double effect of causing extreme internal damage in addition to making an opening through which the ship would eventually flood if the hole was near enough to the water line. As *Sydney* turned behind the raider and slowly limped away following the opening exchange of shells, *Kormoran*'s gun crews were then directed to target the water line of the ship in a clear attempt to sink her. We found several such shell holes along the starboard side just above *Sydney*'s boot topping that would surely have had a telling effect later on as the seas worsened and the ship began to settle by the bow because of the enormous torpedo damage forward.

Following our investigation of the hull I knew that the only other part of the ship which could tell us more about *Sydney*'s final moments afloat was the bow. So when we were ready to investigate the wreckage that comprised the debris field, I had the ROV dive directly on the large sonar target, which I fully expected was *Sydney*'s missing bow. I was not disappointed when we quickly located it lying inverted on the seabed at the far north-west end of the debris field. As the ROV approached the knife-edge stem of the bow, the first thing that we could see, other than that it was upside down, was its two anchors stowed firmly in place. I asked the pilots to fly down the port side of the bow along the line of portholes, which we were counting to stay oriented, in order to document the damage caused by the strike of *Kormoran*'s G7a torpedo. Fortunately, the bow was listing slightly over to starboard, which meant that the portholes and line of the forecastle deck on the port side were well exposed for filming. Shortly after reaching the seventh porthole (counting back from the stem) the break came into view. As the ROV rose upwards towards the keel we could see that the break was very irregular and there were large sections

Above: A mosaic showing one of HMAS Sydney's *wooden boats. The ship's badge can be made out quite clearly.*

of hull plating bent and torn in a multitude of directions. It was easy to imagine the impact point of the torpedo between *Sydney*'s normal water line and the keel, although in reality the plating against which the warhead detonated was surely obliterated in the resulting explosion.

Seeing *Sydney*'s bow in this condition reminded me very much of HMS *Hood*'s bow, although we found that one resting on its side rather than upside down. Both bows were like eggs that had been cracked open and emptied of their contents. All their internal structures, such as decks and bulkheads, had fallen out, along with any equipment that once resided there. The only remaining item (as with *Hood*) was the anchor cable (chain) that was hanging down from above like the strands of a chain necklace, with one seemingly endless length snaking its way out of the bow and into a looping heap on the seabed nearby. Lying no more than fifteen metres away we found the aviation spirit tank near the aft control station which served as the platform for one of *Sydney*'s 0.5-inch machine guns. The undamaged condition of the tank was a clear pointer

for the torpedo striking aft of the tank's position in the compartment between the watertight bulkheads at frames fourteen and nineteen.

In all, we spent roughly 22 hours combing through *Sydney*'s wreckage during the two dives we made in the debris field. Using the highest resolution AMS-60 side-scan sonar image from the search as a roadmap, in combination with the ROV's scanning sonar, we navigated around the debris field with the simple objective of locating and identifying every large or distinct sonar target on the map. *Sydney*'s debris field, in comparison with others I have investigated, was relatively easy to work in. This was primarily because the majority of objects were known parts of *Sydney*'s upper structure that were easy to identify. Also, the main debris field was relatively compact and there were a good number of large objects to use as reference points for navigating the ROV. Having already investigated *Sydney*'s hull we knew which pieces were missing and checked them off as they were located in the debris field. In the end we able to find virtually every missing part of the ship with the exception of some of *Sydney*'s wooden boats. Finding the five boats we did was without doubt

the most exciting aspect of this phase of the project for everyone on board *Geosounder*, probably because finding them was so unexpected and because each one still had *Sydney*'s official badge mounted on its bow.

A final mystery that was solved by our investigations in the debris field revolved around the last aggressive act performed by *Sydney*'s crew when they fired their port torpedo battery at the raider about fifteen minutes into the battle. Questions about how many torpedoes, if any, the cruiser fired at *Kormoran* have persisted among the raider's crew until the present day. The reports varied from two torpedoes to four torpedoes, while some of the Germans, including Heinz Messerschmidt, never saw the characteristic trail of bubbles, and privately doubted whether any were fired at all. The answer was plain to see when we located *Sydney*'s port quadruple torpedo tubes with only *two* torpedoes still loaded.

Even though *Sydney* had taken a terrible pounding and the number of killed and injured aboard her would have been very high, the crew manning the port torpedoes showed that *Sydney* was not yet finished as a fighting force. At more than 5,000 metres a strike on *Kormoran* under the conditions would have been a

very good shot and given *Sydney*'s crew something to cheer about. The good fortune in this instance, as it was throughout the battle, favoured *Kormoran* and the two torpedoes missed.

What caused *Sydney* to sink?

Before any discussion can be had about *Sydney*'s final moments it must be said that there were no witnesses, including the Germans, who actually saw the ship go down. Similarly, the German accounts are vague with regards to time so we also don't know with absolute certainty the precise moment that *Sydney* sank. This complete lack of information has frustrated researchers for decades and made it virtually impossible for anyone to reconstruct *Sydney*'s sinking. Finding the wrecks has obviously changed all that.

Two of the most commonly asked questions about the loss of *Sydney* are what caused *Sydney* to sink and why were there no survivors. Prior to our location of the

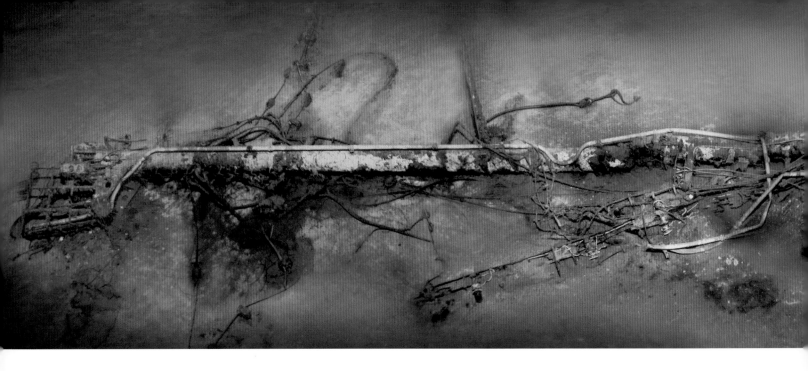

Above: The foremast and crow's-nest on the ocean floor.

wrecks these questions fell squarely in the category of the 'unknown and the unknowable'. What the expedition has provided, however, is the first real factual information on which a reasoned analysis can be made about the damage suffered by *Sydney*. Whereas previously researchers and historians could only speculate about the answers to such questions, they now have available a new archive of physical and visual information to study and use in drawing their own conclusions about what ultimately happened to *Sydney* and her crew.

In my own analysis, the first question I wanted to look at was whether *Sydney* sank before or after *Kormoran* was scuttled at just before midnight WA time on 19 November. I thought it was a fundamentally important question, mostly for the sake of the relatives, to know whether *Sydney* was lost on the 19th or the 20th, as the latter was a distinct possibility. The answer to this question hinged on whether Captain Detmers, having left *Kormoran* last and being able to see the furthest from his position on deck, was correct in his memory that he was still on board at the time the blazing *Sydney* suddenly disappeared from his view. The new piece of physical information the expedition provided was that the distance between the two ships' sinking positions was approximately 11.4 nautical miles. Even though the outline of *Sydney* couldn't be made out at this distance in the darkness, the severity

Previous page: The torpedo hole and portside-hull break.

of the fires on board were such that the flames could be. Therefore, if Detmers was on board when the flames were last seen, it can be reasonably concluded that *Sydney* sank before *Kormoran* on 19 November. Detmers's dictionary account also supports this conclusion, as his last mention of the fires on *Sydney* was at 2200 (G) or 2300 hours WA time: 'Outline of the enemy lost in twilight. At about 16000 metres out of sight. Enemy course about 150 true. Large fire seen until about 22 hours.'

It is also clear from Detmers's account that, during the time *Kormoran* was dead in the water, *Sydney* was still moving away from her, albeit at very slow speed. In the end the distance between the ships reached 11.4 nautical miles, or 21.1 kilometres, which would have been impossible if both ships were dead in the water and subject to the same wind and current conditions. Had *Sydney* stopped moving at any time then she would have drifted at roughly the same speed and in the same direction as *Kormoran*, and the distance between the ships would not have continued to increase as it evidently did. There is no question that *Sydney*'s speed continued to decrease after the battle; however, my conclusion based on a plot of her final course is that she was able to maintain a final speed of about 1.5 knots and make headway on a course of between 130° and 140° true.

Sydney's hull, minus about 28 metres of the bow, lies upright on the seabed oriented on a heading of 140° true. The wreck landed stern first and after the initial impact there was essentially no further movement of the hull. Although the hull clearly glided to the seabed on

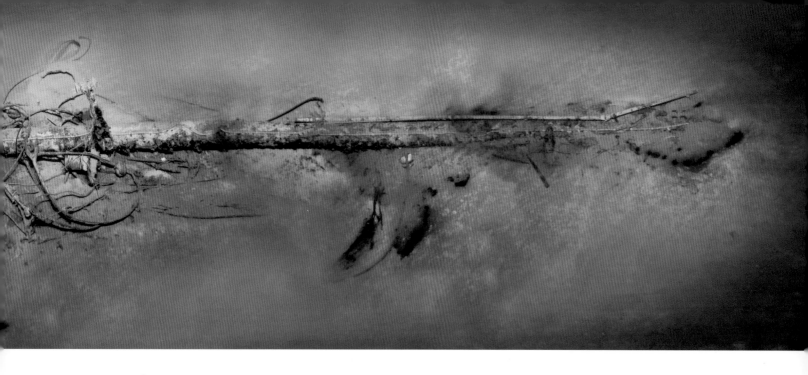

an angle, there are no signs that its orientation changed during the descent or that the hull rolled over at any time. In short, I believe that on its downward trajectory to the seabed, the hull more or less kept the same heading it had on the surface before sinking. The significance of this conclusion is that, when taken in consideration with the relative position of the bow in the debris field, it leads me to believe that *Sydney* was under way right up to the last few minutes before she sank and that the sinking was triggered by the sudden and catastrophic loss of her bow.

The key finding behind my conclusion was the position where the bow was found, approximately 480 metres away from the hull at the far north-west end of the debris field. Unlike the hull, the bow had turned turtle and rather than gliding to the seabed it had plummeted straight down almost directly below the position where it snapped off from the ship. The cause of the bow's direct descent to the seabed was a combination of factors, which included its extreme weight due to the heaviness of its anchors, anchor cable and the water it was carrying, along with the fact that it had lost any semblance of having a hydrodynamic shape that would allow it to glide to the seabed. Other than some relatively light and bulky pieces, like the foremast and forward funnel, which would be the first to be torn off and carried away from the hull as it sank, all the other pieces of wreckage lie south-east of the bow and between it and the hull. This orientation and distribution of the debris, in relation to the position of the bow and hull on the seabed, confirms to me that the bow broke off at the surface.

Sydney's condition when she broke away from the action with *Kormoran* was undoubtedly grave. The ship had been hit an unprecedented number of times by 15-cm and 3.7-cm shells, many of which penetrated her plating and exploded, causing internal damage which was unseen by our cameras but which would have been nonetheless devastating to personnel and the fabric of the ship. This onslaught by *Kormoran* had started serious fires throughout *Sydney* which were able to rage uncontrollably, as the shelling also appears to have crippled the ship's fire-fighting capability. Tons of seawater was pouring into the ship through shell holes at or near the water line. The system of transverse watertight bulkheads designed to keep the ship afloat was rendered ineffective. The catalogue of damage suffered by *Sydney* was horrific, but with respect to the basic seaworthiness of the ship the major concern for those thrust into command would have been the damage *Kormoran*'s torpedo caused to the bow. Unfortunately, what they were probably unaware of — because of an inability to get forward and make an accurate damage assessment due to the extensive flooding and fires — was that the torpedo had struck very near to the ASDIC compartment, which was the weakest part of the *Sydney*'s hull structure, owing to the need for this anti-submarine sonar to be lowered through the hull. Needless to say, their situation was extremely precarious, which is reflected in the fact that the best speed *Sydney* could manage just before she sank was less than a couple of knots. If they could have gone any faster, they most certainly would have.

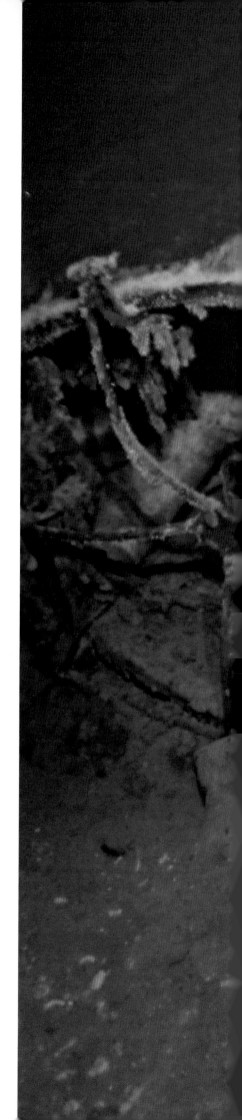

We can only guess how *Sydney*'s surviving crew responded in the face of their impossibly dire situation. Perhaps those that had served in the Mediterranean were aware of the Royal Navy light cruisers HMS *Coventry* and HMS *Glasgow*, which were both hit in the bow by torpedoes ten days apart in December 1940 but were able to make it back to Alexandria for repairs. Did this encourage them to think that they could get to a safe port, or prompt them to try *Coventry*'s trick of steaming stern first to protect their weakened bow? In later years a number of other light cruisers were hit by torpedoes in their bows; however, none of these ships sank and only one lost its bow while being towed to safety. One was even able to continue its transit to port at the remarkably swift speed of 20 knots. A number of others were clearly in a bad way and could very well have been lost if other ships weren't immediately on hand to provide crucial assistance. *Sydney*, by comparison, had suffered far more damage than just a single well-placed torpedo strike. Her surviving crew would have been devastated by witnessing the heavy casualties they took and knowing that Captain Burnett and so many senior officers were included in that number. Last, but not least, they were all alone and as far as the Australian Navy and the rest of Australia was concerned were in no danger at all.

The end, when it finally came sometime before midnight on 19 November 1941, was apparently quick and cruelly unexpected. Despite the miraculous efforts and evident seamanship of the surviving crew to keep *Sydney* afloat and heading to safety, her weakened keel ultimately succumbed to the damage inflicted by *Kormoran*'s torpedo and the worsening sea conditions.

There was really no other option for the crew but to maintain the course they set for Geraldton and to keep *Sydney* moving just fast enough in the opposite direction from the enemy, but without adding to the strains they could already feel and hear shuddering through the hull. Unfortunately, luck was not with them that night, as the wind freshened from nearly the opposite direction, fanning the flames of their fires and steepening the seas that crashed against *Sydney*'s fragile bow while pouring yet more water into her gaping wounds. At that point it would only have taken one slightly larger swell to wash across *Sydney*'s forecastle deck and force it fractionally lower, until instead of rising, the bow simply snapped off as the keel fractured in the area of the ASDIC compartment under the additional weight of water. As the bow fell away, tearing deck plates in the process, more bulkheads in the hull would have been breached, thereby destining it to a watery grave. Suddenly, within seconds, the

Right: The aft funnel, and (above) as it was, intact.

surviving crew that had fought so bravely and unselfishly to save their ship and the lives of their shipmates would know that their last remaining hope was gone.

Why no survivors?

Why there were no survivors from *Sydney* is undoubtedly the most painful and heart-breaking question that the nation was left to dwell upon in the immediate aftermath of the battle, with only a couple of empty lifebelts and a shrapnel-riddled Carley float left as clues. As Barbara Winter has rightly pointed out, *Sydney* is not unique in this regard, as a number of larger warships have sunk with total and greater loss of life.[9] Nevertheless, this question goes to the heart of the mystery about the loss of *Sydney* which many people, especially relatives, have never been able to accept or understand. Michael Montgomery, whose 1981 book can be credited with causing the first ripples that led to the unstoppable wave of interest to actually find *Sydney's* wreck, devoted a chapter to this question and it has become his life's quest to find an answer that he, and others, can fully accept. I harbour no illusions that I can offer Michael an explanation that will resolve his long-held suspicions or put his mind at ease after all these years. Nevertheless, I will try to answer this question based on an honest assessment of the factual information our expedition produced and with a deep respect for the memory of the 645 men lost with *Sydney*.

The starting point in answering this question has to be the grim realisation that scores of men on board *Sydney* would have been killed outright by the shell and torpedo fire during the battle, with many others so critically wounded they would have been beyond medical help. For instance, it is conceivable, based on the shell hits and fire damage we witnessed to all four of *Sydney's* gun turrets (twenty men per turret), the bridge compass platform (twelve men), the DCT (eight men), the HACS (five men) and the Walrus aircraft, that virtually all the men closed up in these locations would have been killed or very seriously injured. It is more difficult to estimate how many men would have been lost as a direct consequence

of the torpedo strike. When HMS *Arethusa*, another light cruiser, was also hit on the port bow (further aft under 'B' turret) by a German torpedo on 18 November 1942, there was a total of 156 men killed. However, *Arethusa* was not at action stations at the time — it is likely there would have been more deaths had the entire ship's company been closed up as was the case with *Sydney*. Still, it is probable that in the order of 100 to 150 of *Sydney's* crew, including Burnett and other senior officers, were lost in these locations alone in the first two minutes of the battle.

Every additional shell that *Kormoran* continued to pour into *Sydney* from her 15-cm, 3.7-cm and 2-cm guns potentially had a lethal effect on the men above and below decks. At the close range of the battle, *Kormoran's* shells — in particular the nose-fused (armour-piercing) 15-cm shells — would have had a devastating effect as they exploded, creating fires and a blast of splinters that would have torn through any person in their path. Naval architects at Australia's Defence Science and Technology Organisation have counted at least 85 separate shell hits on *Sydney's* hull and bridge superstructure (excluding hits on the gun turrets), of which more than 80 per cent penetrated the ship's shell or structure.[10] It is impossible to estimate the death toll caused by the repeated shelling *Sydney* suffered with any sort of accuracy. However, there can be little doubt that the toll would have been shockingly high.

For those who were not directly killed by the shell fire or torpedo strike, the next hazard they had to survive was the series of fires that erupted along *Sydney's* length. Detmers described the fire as 'blazing fiercely' right up to the time the ship disappeared from his view, whereas an unidentified German, when interviewed at Murchison POW camp, was more specific, saying that the cruiser was 'illuminated by three fires burning aboard her'. These descriptions have been substantiated by our investigation of the wreck, which documented extensive fire damage to *Sydney's* bow, the bridge superstructure and officers' accommodation aft. The fact that these fires blazed up to the time of sinking indicates that the surviving crew on board were unable to get the fires under control,

Above: Another of the ship's boats with emblem clearly visible, and (below) the empty boat-davit sockets on the starboard side.

either because they were overwhelmed by the extent and intensity of the fires and/or *Sydney* suffered the same fate as *Kormoran* and had its fire-fighting systems destroyed during the battle.

In *Sydney*'s case the loss of fire-fighting capability could have been directly caused by the fire-mains being destroyed and/or a loss of electrical supply to the pumps. When *Arethusa* was torpedoed, a loss of power caused all but one fire-main pump to be thrown off. The pumps, except for those in the damaged section, were put back on line when the electrical supply was restored.[11] Like *Arethusa*, *Sydney* would have undoubtedly suffered some

loss of power, at least temporarily, when the torpedo struck.[12] Although *Arethusa* was eventually able to restore most of its electrical supply after 30 minutes, in part by the running of emergency leads, it has to be remembered that *Sydney*'s situation was far worse, as she continued to take heavy shell fire from the enemy. Each of *Kormoran*'s 15-cm nose-fused shells weighed 45.3 kg and carried a bursting charge of 4.09 kg; meaning that in the space of less than one hour *Sydney* was hit with something in the order of four tonnes of shells which contained explosive charges weighing about 360 kg. While *Sydney* was built with a fair amount of redundancy to prevent the ship from being lost to a single cause, the infrastructure of the ship would not have been able to cope with this extraordinary level of destruction. Given the cumulative

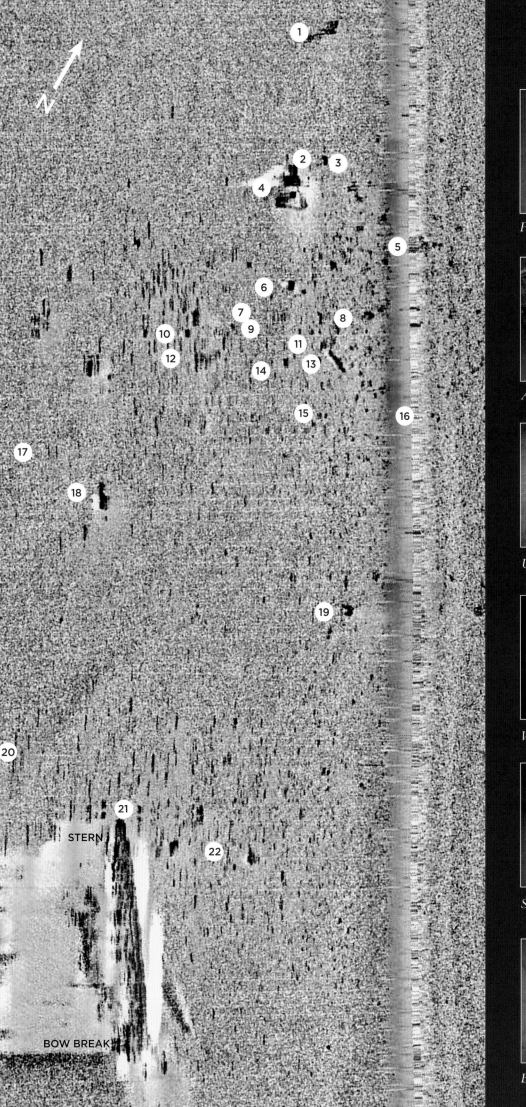

N

1

2 3

4

5

6

7

8

9

10

11

12

13

14

15 16

17

18

19

20

21

STERN

22

BOW BREAK

Foremast and crow's-nest

Aft funnel

Upturned depth-charge rack

Walrus catapult

Single torpedo

Boat crutches

Aviation spirit tank

Aft searchlight platform

Port anchor on bow

Director control tower (DCT)

Port 12-foot range finder

Upturned 4-inch gun, starboard (S1)

High-angle control station (HACS)

Ship's boat with badge

Ship's boat

HACS base

Wrecked Walrus aircraft

Starboard torpedo tubes

Two of Sydney's boats

Port torpedo tubes

Ship's boat

Section of hull plate

The distribution of items in the debris field told me a lot about how Sydney broke up and sank. When the flooded bow snapped off it fell straight to the seabed, while the rest of the hull glided for another 480 metres. As the hull sank with increasing speed, the force of water would have ripped everything pictured here away. Excluding the foremast, which clearly glided in an opposite direction to the hull, no other large items were found north of the bow. From this I concluded that the bow snapped off at the surface and was the trigger for Sydney's sinking.

211

Above: A gas mask on the ocean floor.

effect of explosions inside *Sydney*, it is quite probable that the ship experienced a complete loss of electrical supply and fire-fighting capability, leaving her crew unable to conduct any sort of meaningful damage control. The one example we were able to document during our investigation of the wreck was that the crew of *Sydney* did not jettison her anchors and cable the same way that *Arethusa* did the following year in order to lessen the load on her weakened bow. The difference was that *Arethusa*'s crew was able to extinguish the fire on their bow and get forward to release the anchors, whereas *Sydney*'s crew were not.

In the face of the hellish scene of death, destruction and fire that surrounded them, the surviving men on board *Sydney* were able, miraculously, to keep their ship steaming, albeit very slowly, away from the enemy and towards a safe harbour. There is no other explanation for how far we found *Sydney* away from the stationary *Kormoran* (more than five kilometres further than Detmers's highest estimate of sixteen kilometres) other than the simple fact that *Sydney* continued to steam away under her own power well into the night. By my reckoning *Sydney* was under way for three and a half to four hours after the last shot was fired. The survivors were making a heroic effort to save *Sydney* and all the evidence

points to it being most likely that the ship was under way right up to the moment the keel snapped and she sank.

During those last unimaginably horrific hours the senior crew in command of *Sydney* appear to have decided that the ship was seaworthy and could be saved (along with their lives and those of their shipmates), or at least that their chance of survival was greater staying with the ship rather than abandoning her. A factor in this decision must have been the state of *Sydney*'s nine wooden boats as well as the prospect of being able to launch them safely. Finding the five boats (the two 27-foot whalers, the 36-foot motor pinnace, one of the 35-foot motor boats, and one unidentified boat that is possibly the 30-foot gig) in the debris field told us only two things: that they sank with the ship and that they obviously weren't used. Unfortunately, the wooden hulls of the boats were all badly eroded so there was no way of knowing what condition they were in when they originally sank with *Sydney*. Looking at the concentration of shell hits amidship where the boats were stowed, however, it would have been virtually impossible for any of them to have avoided being hit directly by the raider's gunfire and/or damaged by splinters from exploding shells. The boats nearest to the worst shelling were the two 32-foot cutters stowed on opposite sides of the forecastle deck, which weren't found. The cutters were the only boats that could be launched by davits; however, when we looked for the davits, all four were gone and next to each pair of empty brackets were ominous looking shell holes. The other boats were normally launched using the ship's crane, which in itself would have been impossible if the crane had either been damaged in the shelling or couldn't be operated if the electrical supply had been lost.

Whatever was or was not possible with regards to the use of *Sydney*'s boats, the fact that the two 27-foot whalers were found in the debris field is probably the best proof of all that an orderly attempt to abandon ship was never made. Of *Sydney*'s nine boats, the whalers were the furthest from the worst of the shelling and resulting fires; the nearest to the waterline; and the lightest in case they had to be manhandled to be launched. In short, on the basis that these two boats weren't launched, it is reasonable to assume that none of the other boats was launched, and therefore that *Sydney*'s surviving crew had decided to stay with their ship and nurse her home to safety as best they could.

Sadly, *Sydney* and her crew never made it home and we now know that the sudden loss of the bow was probably the trigger that finally caused her to sink. How long the rest of the hull stayed afloat while the bow plummeted to the seabed is anyone's guess, but based on the relatively short distance between their final positions I believe it would have been no more than a minute or two. The realisation that the ship was going down would have sent the remaining crew rushing to the upper decks to escape an immediate watery death. A formal order to abandon ship was not necessary, nor was there time for it to be given. The sight of all the ship's watertight doors flung wide open bears witness to the fact that an evacuation was under way. Such was the loyalty to the wounded shipmates they were tending, some men might have resisted the natural urge to flee and have remained by their mates' sides. Even though we will never hear them I have no doubt that there were many stories of valour and self-sacrifice during *Sydney*'s last moments.

For the men who were able to get away from *Sydney*'s sinking hull, their prospects for survival were not good, even if they were able to scramble into a surviving Carley float as at least one man did. To survive beyond a few days a supply of fresh water was essential, but the main problem wasn't food or water or shelter from the burning sun and chilling sea. The problem was the fact that nobody in the RAN or Australia knew that *Sydney* had been in a fierce battle and had been sunk until more than four and a half days had passed. An air search of the probable battle position wasn't organised until the following day after that. That morning one of the German lifeboats had reached the beach north of Carnarvon, while a second was spotted just off the coast where it was about to land. The men in those boats did well to reach the safety of land, yet even though they had water, food and shelter — everything the men from *Sydney* apparently did not have — they honestly didn't think they could have lasted a day or two longer without casualties. The desperately sad reality of the situation was that by the time there was even the slightest chance of a plane or boat being in the right place to spot a single Carley float from *Sydney*, anyone within the raft would have probably died from a combination of exposure and dehydration, if injury or shock hadn't taken his life sooner.

One of the highlights of my professional life was the day I was able to take Ted Briggs with me to the Denmark Strait off Greenland so he could personally lay a plaque on the wreck site of HMS *Hood* where 1,415 of his former shipmates died. There were only two other survivors from *Hood*, and Ted had outlived them both. The thought that ran through my mind that day was how lucky we were to have Ted with us, and how lucky Ted was to have survived the magazine explosions that literally obliterated his ship. The question our expedition set out to answer was why so few survived from the loss of *Hood*. Yet after we documented the condition of her wreckage that question was replaced by a different one: how was it possible that *anyone* survived what happened to the *Hood*? Having witnessed the tragic destruction of another of the world's famous warships sunk in an equally remote location, I feel that the relevant question about *Sydney* should also change. It should be: how did *anyone* manage to get off the *Sydney* alive?

CHAPTER TEN

▪▪▪

Discounting the battle site

Having completed our ROV filming of *Sydney*'s wreckage in the early hours of 6 April, it was time to turn our attention to the wreck of *Kormoran*. The expedition was now into its fortieth day and the end was clearly in sight. The *Geosounder* was still buzzing with excitement and the extra adrenaline was helping me get through the daily workload that now only afforded a couple of hours of sleep at most. After all the initial problems with the Comanche ROV I was delighted with the video footage it was producing and the quality of the still photographs I was able to shoot. We had uploaded two additional sets of photographs onto the Finding Sydney Foundation website from the previous dives to the wreck of *Sydney* and the feedback we were getting from the relatives was tremendously positive. The DOF ROV crews, led by Simon Hall and Dave Norton, were enjoying their days a lot more now that the ROV was working and spending most of its time submerged. Bruce Burman, in particular, was revealing himself to be a very skilful pilot who relished the challenge of flying the ROV around the wrecks in accordance with my instructions, no matter how difficult the manoeuvre. Without his deft touch the excellent photographic record I was creating of the wrecks would not have been possible.

Before moving over to the site of *Kormoran*, I wanted to investigate the large cluster of sonar targets we found just to the south that I named the 'battle site' because its location was very close to the projected line of the battle. The sonar targets had all the right characteristics to be wreckage from *Sydney* and they were in an area devoid of geology. However, one thing didn't fit after we had finished our investigation of *Sydney*'s hull and the wreckage in the debris field.

Initially, the number and size of the sonar targets led me to believe that collectively they represented a significant amount of structure (either hull or superstructure) that had been blown away from *Sydney* as a result of the shelling and torpedo explosion. This belief actually influenced my thinking when I was devising the search box for *Sydney* because I couldn't imagine that the ship would have been able to travel very far, given the apparently severe damage it had experienced. As a result I opted for a relatively compact search box

Left: The haunting image of shoes found on the ocean floor.

Above: One of the angular volcanic rocks which fooled us.

when others were advising I should make it much larger.

We were forced to re-evaluate this scenario because in the time we spent filming *Sydney*'s wreckage we were able to account for virtually all the major pieces of the hull, superstructure and deck equipment such that it was becoming increasingly hard to understand what sections of *Sydney* might be found at the battle site. The only big parts of *Sydney* that were still unaccounted for were sections of 'A' turret's housing and half of the top of 'B' turret. These large steel pieces would have made excellent sonar targets but they did not equate to the dozens of targets we found scattered over an area covering 1,700 metres nor was either of them large enough to match the one target we provisionally measured to be 33 metres long and 13 metres high. So as Matthew Kelley, the documentary film director, was getting his cameras ready to film our reactions as we were supposed to see more *Sydney* wreckage for the first time, I forewarned to him 'be prepared for a surprise'.

It took nearly three hours before we found the first target but just a fraction of a second to realise that what we had found was not the wreckage of a ship, but a large angular rock. As soon as the rock face came into view I knew immediately that this wasn't going to be just one isolated rock among a field of *Sydney*'s wreckage. Instead, all the sonar targets were going to be revealed as rocks and our original interpretation was wrong. To confirm this we moved on to another nearby target and sure enough it was a long outcrop made from a type of volcanic rock called a pillow basalt. For a few minutes I allowed myself to be fascinated by the geology of the rocks and the biological organisms that were using the hard rock surface as an anchor point from which to live and filter the passing sea water for food. I took just enough time to take a series of photographs to document the site and then asked for the ROV to be recovered.

There was no point in being disappointed by mistaking the field of rocks for wreckage. On the contrary, I was pleasantly relieved to discount the large battle site scenario as I believed it meant there was a simpler explanation for *Sydney*'s loss and that the relatives would be happier to know that parts of the ship are not strewn over such a large area. Also, the time we saved not having to document another large and scattered debris field would be better spent filming our final objective: the wreck of *Kormoran*.

Investigating the enemy: *Kormoran*

From the side-scan sonar images alone it was clear that *Kormoran* had suffered a far more violent end than *Sydney*. *Kormoran*'s wreckage was spread over a larger distance than *Sydney*'s (1.2 kilometres versus 600 metres) although the main debris field marking the exact spot where the ship was scuttled was itself incredibly concentrated. As vividly described by Captain Detmers, and those who left the ship in the last lifeboat with him, the simultaneous detonation of the raider's cache of 340 mines (300 EMC moored contact mines and 40 TMB magnetic ground mines)[1] resulted in an almighty explosion that ripped the

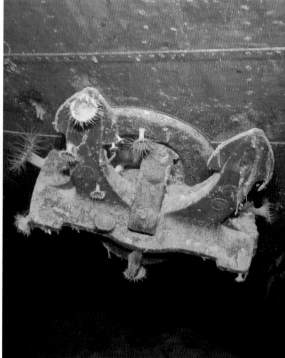

Above: Kormoran's *bow and (right) the port anchor still secure in its hawse pipe.*

ship apart and propelled large pieces of wreckage over an area covering hundreds of metres. Miraculously, Detmers's boat somehow missed being hit by the wreckage that rained down all around them and the men were able to row to safety.

I had worked in debris fields like this before (*Derbyshire*'s immediately sprang to mind) and I knew that it was going to be extremely difficult to identify individual pieces of wreckage. I cautioned John, Glenys and Mack of this as I wanted them to be prepared for what they were about to see and for them to avoid getting frustrated by not being able to make head or tail out of what was surely going to be a confusing jumble of wreckage.

The dive down 2,560 metres to the wreck started well but once we reached the seabed it was clear that there was a problem as the ROV was unable to fly out of its garage. The pilots suspected that one of the vehicle's manipulator arms had jammed itself inside the garage, effectively blocking the ROV from exiting. It was a minor

problem that could be easily solved but it would require a recovery of the ROV back to the surface. As the vehicle was otherwise perfectly operational I decided we should stay on the seabed and conduct a reconnaissance dive of the wreck as we had done with *Sydney*. With the ROV stuck inside the constantly heaving garage the video footage would be less than ideal and still photographs were out of the question altogether. However, despite these handicaps the reconnaissance dive would be beneficial to get a general idea of the wreck's condition and to spot any potential snagging hazards that we would want to avoid later on.

The garage landed off the starboard side of what remained of *Kormoran*'s hull, which we were calling the bow only because it included the bow, but in fact the piece was much bigger and accounted for very close to half the ship. As we inched our way over to the wreck the magnitude of the explosion that sent *Kormoran* to the seabed became apparent straightaway. The hull was violently torn in half, as expected, but in addition virtually the entire bridge superstructure was missing, which was not expected. All that remained of the bridge was one level of the front screen, complete with its rectangular

Above: The high rate of fire caused the paint to blister on the barrel of Kormoran's *No. 3 15-cm gun.*

windows, flopped forward against the aft coaming of hatch No. 3. As we landed aft, my plan was to move the garage and ROV very slowly towards the bow while we observed the general condition of the wreck.

The dive only lasted 75 minutes but in that short period we saw for the first time the weapons and camouflage screens that made *Kormoran* such a dangerous ship, which before now we were only able to read about. There was the No. 3 15-cm gun mounted in the centre of cargo hold two; the false hatch coaming that screened this gun position; the flap that hid the above-water torpedoes; the fold-down railings; the port and starboard 15-cm guns

set back in their cut-out positions beneath the forecastle deck; and the 2-cm anti-aircraft machine guns perched on their hydraulically raised mounts. Other than the *Komet* (HSK-7), which was found in shallow waters in the English Channel and as a result is very heavily encrusted with marine growth,[2] no other *Kriegsmarine* auxiliary cruiser from World War II has been filmed this way. In terms of documenting the weaponry of a German raider this was a unique opportunity and as much an historical milestone as our first dive on *Sydney*. I could hardly wait to get the ROV back on deck and repaired in order to photograph the wreck properly.

Four hours later we were back at the point of *Kormoran*'s bow ready to begin the investigation in earnest. In contrast to the scene of total destruction we

*Above: The missing camouflage steel cover left the No. 1
15-cm gun clearly visible.*

found at the other end of the hull, the bow was relatively
undamaged; its peaceful state belying the violent event
that delivered her to this final resting place. The hull was
being colonised by a scattering of large sea anemones and
sponges that softened the lines of the ship, but luckily
there weren't too many of them to detract us from what
we came to see. There were also signs that the bow's
impact with the seabed was a heavy one. We found folds
and buckling along the ship's side and decks jolted out of
place. Luckily for us, however, the ship's paintwork was in
remarkably good order.

To take on the guise of the neutral Dutch steamer
Straat Malakka, Detmers had *Kormoran*'s hull painted
black, her superstructure brown and a yellow ring around
the funnel. The repainting was done quickly while at
sea before entering the Indian Ocean. Although not up
to the standards of a proper shipyard job, the repainting
was good enough to reinforce the illusion (especially at
long distance) that the deadly raider was an innocent
merchantman. Detmers wrote in his *Kriegstagebuch* (war
diary) for 23 April 1941:[3]

> *Stopped. Outboard painted. The painting must take
> place because the colour had suffered in such a way that
> the camouflage of the weapons endangered warning. I
> have now decided to paint the hull black in order to*

*be able to recamouflage quickly in the Indian Ocean as
Japanese. Thus, the grey of the central superstructure also
comes down because more than two colours on the ship
appears conspicuous. Central superstructure and boats
will become brown, the red chimney ring somewhat more
yellowish and then we sail as Straat Malakka from Rio
to Batavia.*

So as the lights of the Comanche ROV began to
illuminate the paintwork on the bow of the wreck it was
reassuring to see that the black hull matched Detmers's
description. Strangely, however, the starboard anchor
was missing. I couldn't recall ever seeing a wreck which
had lost an anchor when sinking and this was doubly
surprising given that the bow was the part of the ship
least damaged by the action and scuttling.

Next in line was the forward 15-cm gun designated
No. 1 that was a key weapon firing at *Sydney*'s forward
gun turrets. The large cantilevered and hinged cover that
the gun hid behind was missing, having been torn away
by the force of water rushing past the hull as it sped to the
seabed below. While not being able to see the cover was
disappointing, it did mean that the gun was fully exposed
and a close inspection would be possible. We expected
this gun to be pointed aft, where it would have been last
aimed at *Sydney* just before the cruiser turned to port
behind *Kormoran*. But as explained by Fritz Englemann,
who helped with the loading of ammunition for both the
forward 15-cm guns, they were ordered to 'Put everything

Above: The encircled area beneath the fallen foremast of Kormoran *appears to be damage inflicted by* Sydney's *'X' turret gun crew.*

back to zero'; or in other words, swing the guns back and lower the covers.[4]

Kormoran's six 15-cm guns, which dated back to World War I, might have been old disused relics but they were certainly not primitive. With the No. 1 gun pointed forward we had a full-length view of its right-hand where the gun trainer would sit directly behind a shield of reinforced steel protecting him from incoming fire. From this position the trainer would control the aiming (left/right) of the gun by turning the two wheels in accordance with voice instructions he was getting from the gunnery director through his headphones and by looking at the cross-hairs in his sight. While none of us was an artillery expert capable of naming each piece of the gun, we could plainly see various switches, electrical connections and cabling that indicated the gun was a fairly sophisticated weapon for its time, and engineered to fire quickly and reliably. The gun barrel was a recoiling type and the breech apparently had some form of semi-automatic closing mechanism.

As for the missing camouflage cover, the only physical clues we had about how it operated were the two central and corner brackets that would have been the hinge points for the cover as it pivoted upwards. Unfortunately, there was no sign of the counterweight system that was used to lift the cover as any part of it that was connected to the cover is now missing along with the cover itself. On the forecastle deck above the gun there were two small hatch openings which, because of their location behind the cover, may have been connected with the counterweight system, but we were unable to confirm this. The camouflage system on the No. 1 gun certainly seemed simple, as it should have relied only on the release of clips that retained the cover in its closed position before the counterweights swung into action and lifted it open.

As simple as this counterweight system appeared to be, however, the mechanism for uncovering *Kormoran's* No. 3 15-cm gun was even simpler. Because this gun was positioned in the centre of a false cargo hold, the ingenious solution of the German engineers was to use the elevated hatch coamings to hide the gun as this would mean that anyone looking at the ship from sea level would think it was a perfectly normal cargo hold. However, at the push of a single button the port and starboard coamings would be hydraulically lowered to reveal the gun and allow it to train and shoot to either side of the ship. Because the width of the cargo hold was so great it was even possible

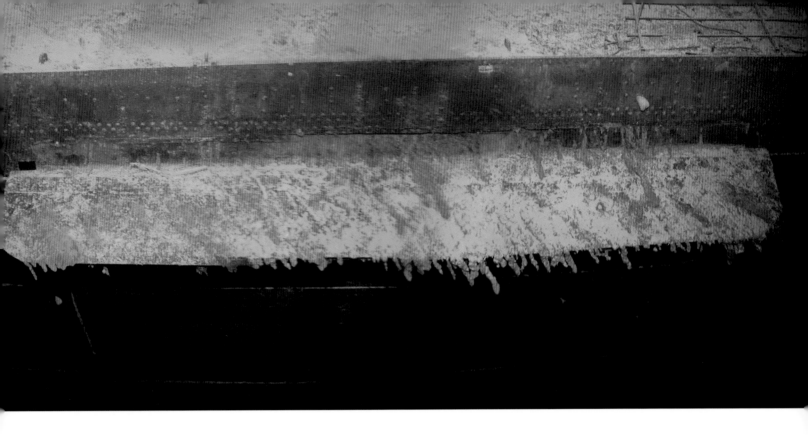

Above: The flaps which hid Kormoran's *above-water torpedo tubes.*

to train the gun with the coamings in the raised position, and as such the gun trainer was able to aim his gun before the order to de-camouflage was given and find his target almost immediately.

The hydraulic hatch coamings were one of the first things I wanted to photograph when the ROV reached the No. 3 gun position, and sure enough both the port and starboard coamings were lowered as far as they possibly could be. As best I could estimate the gun itself was pointed about 30° aft of the beam, and true to the German testimonies the paint on the barrel had been burnt off by the intense heat generated with the rapid firing of shells. As a result of either the mines exploding or the sinking, Kormoran's foremast had collapsed in a heap at the forward end of the cargo hold, strewing heavy rigging everywhere. Months later, when studying the photographs I shot of the cross-trees of the foremast, I noticed some damage to the starboard coaming that we did not spot during the expedition. The damage to the coaming is possibly the result of a 6-inch shell from Sydney that we know hit somewhere around this gun position, because it killed one man and injured another. If this damage was due to a shell strike, as it appears, it is the only direct evidence we saw of Sydney's 6-inch guns hitting Kormoran.

Kormoran's torpedoes, and how they were used against Sydney, have been the subject of considerable controversy and debate from virtually the moment it was learned that the raider was fitted with an underwater tube that could surreptitiously fire a torpedo. For this reason we were especially keen to investigate the underwater and deck-mounted (above-water) tubes on the starboard side to see whether we could shed any new light on how these weapons were used during the action. Detmers's and torpedo officer Greter's accounts were unequivocal that the two torpedo fan fired at the cruiser in the early phase of the battle came from the starboard above-water tubes, which I hoped we would be able to get a glimpse of when we saw that the flap used to hide the tubes was still in the raised position. Greter's written account included the additional detail that all the information needed to 'set' the torpedo had been previously ordered:

At the same time the commander turned with the vessel towards Sydney *in order to be able to release the two-torpedo fan. All settings on the targeting device and the torpedo tubes had been ordered previously. Now all that mattered was to let the enemy move into the cross-hair of the target device and to release the torpedo fan.*[5]

Above: One of Kormoran*'s two underwater torpedo tube openings.*

The flap itself couldn't have looked simpler. It was constructed of a single sheet of steel that was hinged along its entire upper length to Kormoran's side. As with the covers that concealed the bow and stern 15-cm gun positions, the flap was lifted by a counterweight system following the release of whatever mechanism secured the flap when closed. Beneath the accumulations of rust at the edge of the flap we did see a couple of small tabs with holes in the centre that were probably part of this securing mechanism. Unfortunately we were unable to see either the tubes themselves or the targeting device because the flap was at a slightly depressed angle and this made it impossible for our cameras to look underneath it.

I hoped to have better luck with the underwater tube and asked the pilot to send the ROV a bit deeper in search of the relatively small opening. I had a good idea

of the tube's position from the shipyard drawings I found of Kormoran (as converted from the Steiermark) in Peter Tamm's collection and from a plan of the ship's weapons found in the official military archive in Freiburg, Germany.[6] The drawings led us to the correct location straight away, but frustratingly we found the opening partially covered with thick rivers of rust cascading down from above. Although I knew that the torpedo loaded in this tube had been fired by Greter after the battle (as requested by Detmers to prevent it from exploding while the crew were still working to free the last lifeboats)[7] and thus would be empty, I felt it was important to document the shape of the opening to help confirm the angle of the tube.

Because the tube's angle was fixed at 125° (relative to the bow) the opening in the hull would have to be elliptical in shape, as opposed to round, for the torpedo to exit at this angle. The problem with the rust was that it was obscuring the full shape of the opening and as per my agreement with the German Government we were not permitted to disturb the wreck in any way, even if it was simply to sweep some rust away. Just as I was about to give up hope of getting the image I wanted, the pilot shifted the ROV's position fractionally and all of a sudden we could see through a sliver of space behind the rust. The opening was definitely elliptical and any torpedo fired from this tube would have to be at a target located well behind *Kormoran*, not directly on her beam where *Sydney* was positioned.

With our investigation of *Kormoran*'s starboard side complete we moved aft to the major break in the hull. At first it was difficult to know exactly where the break occurred, given the extreme damage caused by the explosion and lack of recognisable structure amid the twisted and torn steel that filled our screens. Finally, an opening was found through which we were able to see some large pipework and a wheel for a control valve that indicated a pump room. Then a forest of even bigger pipes and a small tank came into view, which confirmed that we were looking at an area just forward of the engine room where all of the ship's oil tanks were situated. Could this mean that the explosion literally blew away half of the ship, including the engine room — far more than was indicated by the side-scan sonar images? Beforehand, it was impossible to imagine what the detonation of 340 mines containing more than 100 tonnes of TNT could do to a single ship, given that the explosive force of just one mine could sink a ship by itself. These first images of *Kormoran*'s shattered hull left us with no doubts about the enormity of the explosion that occurred and put the incredible destruction and spread of wreckage first revealed in the sonar images into its full context. The explosion was so extraordinarily massive it obliterated half the length of Germany's largest raider and lifted its entire bridge superstructure off the hull.[8] No wonder Detmers decided to abandon his ship as soon as he realised he could not prevent the fire spreading to the mine deck. The only question now was how far away from the hull we would find the engine room and the bridge.

Right: The break in Kormoran's *hull at the aft end of her well deck.*

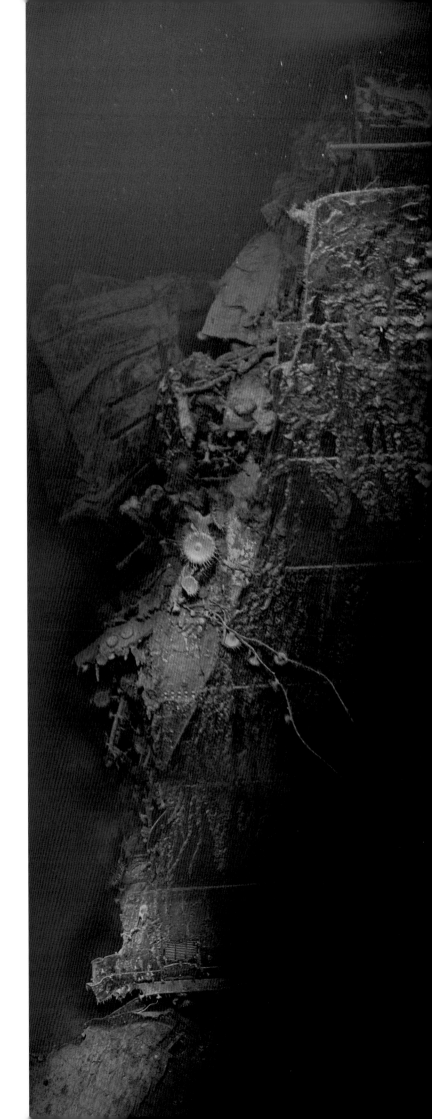

Above: (l) Kormoran's No. 2 15-cm gun and (r) starboard 2-cm anti-aircraft gun mount.

The investigation of *Kormoran*'s port side was pretty much a mirror image of the starboard side. The flap concealing the above-water torpedo tubes was raised but again not enough to permit a peak underneath. As for the underwater tube, an even heavier accumulation of rust choked the opening although its oval shape was still partially visible. The torpedo from this tube had also been fired, but this time directly at the cruiser near the end of the action as Detmers's account recorded: 'About 1800. Own torpedo shot on 70 hm, inclination 80, enemy speed 5 knots. Miss astern'. Detmers would have known this was a futile attempt as he had virtually no hope of hitting *Sydney* once he lost his engines and ability to aim the torpedo by altering *Kormoran*'s heading.

Our steady progress towards the bow was interrupted when the ROV encountered *Kormoran*'s downed Samson posts and foremast. The heavy rigging that had crashed to the deck also hung off the ship's port side and was a dangerous obstacle that the pilots had to work around. The last thing we needed now was for the yellow tether trailing

behind the ROV to get entangled. After the hazardous rigging was safely cleared the pilots flew the vehicle back in so we could see *Kormoran*'s most forward cargo hold where the two steel lifeboats that were the last to be literally launched off *Kormoran* were once stowed. True to the German accounts we found the hold completely empty, save for a couple of crutches that once held the boats in place. They were the last trace of the crew's frantic efforts to get the one-tonne boats lifted out of the hold using traditional block and tackle and the force of dozens of men who must have known this was their only chance of survival and that the clock was rapidly ticking down. Also gone were the side railings, which had to be removed for the boats to be manhandled over the side with one great push and a prayer that they would stay afloat.

Like its starboard twin, *Kormoran*'s 15-cm port gun was swung forward and plainly visible as its concealing cover had been ripped away as well. Conveniently, I now had a chance to completely document this gun by photographing the gun layer's position. Other than some rust spots and cracking paint, the gun itself looked in perfect condition even though its pedestal base had been thrust upwards as the bow slammed into the seabed, with

Above: One of Kormoran's *four engines.*

the effect of driving the top of the gun shield into the heavy beam above. This gun might have had to wait until *Sydney* came clear on the port side before joining the action but judging by the paint burnt off the barrel it fired its fair share of shells at the retreating cruiser.

The last of *Kormoran*'s weapons on the bow we could document were the twin 2-cm machine guns that were on mounts standing proud of the forecastle deck. Although we found the mounts intact, hardly anything remained of the port gun while the starboard gun, although far more complete, also had parts missing. Nevertheless, the most interesting aspect of these weapons was how they were concealed and placed into action once the order to de-camouflage was given. Apparently, these guns and

their mounts were on pneumatic lifts and at the push of a button were revealed and raised into position in about six to seven seconds.[9] Although we couldn't see the inner workings of the lifts, the platform to which the mount was attached and raised and the light-weight hatch cover that concealed the gun position were entirely consistent with the descriptions provided by the Germans.

The dive had gone so well we finished our inspection of the remains of *Kormoran*'s hull and weapons in about three hours of bottom time and were ready to shift our attention to the wreckage in the debris fields further north. Before leaving the hull, however, I asked the pilot to fly over towards the bitter end of the starboard anchor chain to see if we could shed any light on what happened to the missing anchor. Because *Kormoran*'s port anchor was still firmly in place the whereabouts of the starboard anchor was now an even greater mystery. The ROV picked up the thick stud chain coming off the windlass and followed it past the 2-cm machine gun hatch cover and around a pair of bollards before finding it still shackled to the eye at the top of the shank of the anchor. However, the bottom part of the anchor, including the flukes, was gone. As we didn't find anything in the mud just beneath where the anchor was supposed to be, it was a safe bet that it didn't fracture upon impact with the seabed. This could only mean that it must have happened as a result of the explosion, and in that case the rest of the anchor will probably never be found.

The hour and a half it took *Geosounder* and the ROV to transit the 590-metre distance from the hull over to the centre of the main debris field gave everyone a chance to take a much needed break. Flying around a virgin shipwreck site with hazards around every corner requires enormous concentration and we'd been going at it pretty much full tilt for the past four days. When the ROV touched down on the seabed again the complete and utter destruction of the wreckage we found in every direction was quite shocking. The individual pieces of debris were just so ripped apart and mangled that it was impossible to say with any confidence what the pieces were and what part of the ship they came from. About the best we could manage was to say whether we were looking at a part of the exterior of the ship or of something from inside the hull. I had worked in debris fields like this before and knew that our best chance of safely identifying anything was to find the biggest piece of wreckage.

Fifteen minutes later the pilots had manoeuvred the ROV over to one of the largest targets on their sonar, which turned out to be a huge box-like structure we later measured to be twelve metres high. The structure was damaged, heavily corroded and obscured by various pieces of debris that had fallen on top of it, including an equally large rectangular section of plate. I asked the pilots to circle around the piece as we examined it from every angle to get a clue as to its identity. Finally, we found a clear view of one of its corners that had a distinctive rounded shape and we could also see large openings at its front and side. The piece could only be one thing: *Kormoran*'s

bridge superstructure. As we compared the image in front of us with the archive photos I had collected of the ship, both as *Kormoran* and *Steiermark*, it also became apparent that the bridge had landed upside down on the seabed. I was convinced that this location must have represented the position where *Kormoran* finally exploded and sank.

Seeing that it took us 40 minutes to make this single identification, and that there were literally hundreds of pieces of wreckage in far worse condition scattered all around, I decided that spending hours in the *Kormoran*'s debris field would not be a very productive use of our remaining time. It would take days for us to film and photograph all the wreckage; days that we did not have in our budget. In fact this would be our last day of diving and I wanted to use the time we had left for one more dive in *Sydney*'s debris field to make absolutely sure we found and filmed every significant piece of her wreckage. Our documentation of *Kormoran* was very important, but the priority was still *Sydney*.

My plan was to leave the main debris field and travel the 850 metres over to the most northern piece of *Kormoran*'s wreckage to attempt to identify it before recovering the ROV and making the two-hour trip back to *Sydney*'s location. The northern piece happened to be the first target we saw on the side-scan sonar when discovering the wreck and it was a very large piece (measuring 31 metres by 25 metres and 12.7 metres high) definitely worth inspecting. When the ROV touched down on the seabed it was immediately clear that while this was a substantial piece of wreckage, it was not *Kormoran*'s stern as I had initially expected. The first good clue as to its identity was the bilge keel jutting out prominently from a very large section of bottom plating from the midships area. As the ROV traversed the length of the bilge keel I spotted what I thought was white writing that stood out against the dull red paint on the ship's bottom and requested that we stop to investigate.

As the ROV approached closer, and I pushed in with the zoom of my still camera, there was no doubt that something was painted on the bottom of the hull. It took a minute or so to get the best lighting but when we did it was hard to believe what we had found. There, in quite neat

Above: Proof that we had found Kormoran.

and reasonably clear writing was *08 KO* and what looked like a *3* written above that. It didn't take long for us to jump to the obvious conclusion that the writing was some sort of abbreviation for *Kormoran*, as the eighth *Hilfskreuzer* converted by the *Kriegsmarine* during the war. Perhaps this conclusion was a bit too convenient but nobody could come up with a better explanation for this unusual writing found in the most unusual of places. Whatever the case, it was an absolutely remarkable discovery, as finding identifying writing of any sort on the hull of an old shipwreck, in my experience, is exceedingly rare.

Further along this same section of hull plating we began to see some exposed framing that I thought might tell us more about what part of the ship this piece was

from. As the ROV's lights peered through the web of frames they lit a dark piece of machinery that could only be one of the raider's four diesel-electric engines. It was difficult to make out any detail on the engine as it was set back from the edge of the wreckage and its weight had caused it to bury into the sediment. What this indicated was that the explosion blew the bottom of the ship away along with its entire engine room, as I was pretty sure the other three engines, if we could see them, were sitting next to the one we found.

With this major piece identified it was time to think about ending the dive. I wanted a few more photographs of the *08 KO* writing, which I duly took, and then a final look at an object we noticed earlier sitting smack in the middle of the ship's bottom plating. As the ROV drew near and the unusual shape became clear everyone

Left: The starboard anchor, found 1,300 metres away from the Kormoran's bow embedded in steel plate.

was stunned to find that it was the missing lower half of the starboard anchor! The shank was cleanly fractured, as was one of the flukes, and the crown of the anchor was embedded into the plating, having created a massive gash in the process. At first it was hard to understand how this broken half of the anchor could be found more than 1,300 metres away from the its rightful location on the bow. The only possible explanation was that the force of the explosion and violent shock reaction of the hull sheared the stock and fluke and sent the bottom half of the anchor cartwheeling through the night sky before it splashed down and ultimately crashed into the large hull section, which beat it to the seabed. If any one image was tangible proof of the enormous explosion that obliterated *Kormoran,* this had to be it.

Assessing the German accounts

We were able to make one last dive in *Sydney's* debris field, and find a lot of smaller items that we hadn't seen in previous dives, before I officially declared the expedition over and successfully completed at eighteen minutes before midnight on 7 April. I hadn't slept more than a couple of hours at any time in the past five days so it wasn't the best time for reflection. That came later during the transit to Geraldton, and in the days and weeks following.

I had started this quest hoping to prove that Captain Detmers was completely truthful about the location of the battle. I knew that if he was not, there could never be a search for the wrecks because no one could possibly know where to look for them. As a shipwreck hunter keen to take on the challenge of finding *Sydney*, I also had an obvious self-interest in Detmers's veracity. Excluding the specific question of navigation, however, I had absolutely no vested interest in the outcome about whether or not the Germans accurately or honestly portrayed the action in their written accounts and testimonies. My only agenda was to go out and find the wrecks and then let the chips fall where they may.

Others will no doubt have their own opinions, and the debates that have raged for decades among a small minority of people may well continue. My own opinion, based on the whole of my experience over the past six years spent in archives, in interviews with *Kormoran* survivors and at sea over the top of the wrecks, is that the German accounts have proven to be entirely and remarkably accurate. The list of the main German claims that I believe were satisfactorily proved during the course of the expedition is long and covers the entire action from the ships' mutual sighting to their sinking. It includes the location of the action; the location where *Sydney* was last seen; the proximity of the action; the location of the torpedo strike on *Sydney's* bow; the number of shell hits on *Sydney's* port and starboard sides; the use of and specific targeting by all of *Kormoran's* guns; the destruction of *Sydney's* bridge and aircraft; the fire damage suffered by *Sydney;* the methods of concealing *Kormoran's* weapons; the damage inflicted on *Kormoran* by *Sydney* and by

Right: Chart of the final wreck positions and Kormoran's *corrected navigation.*

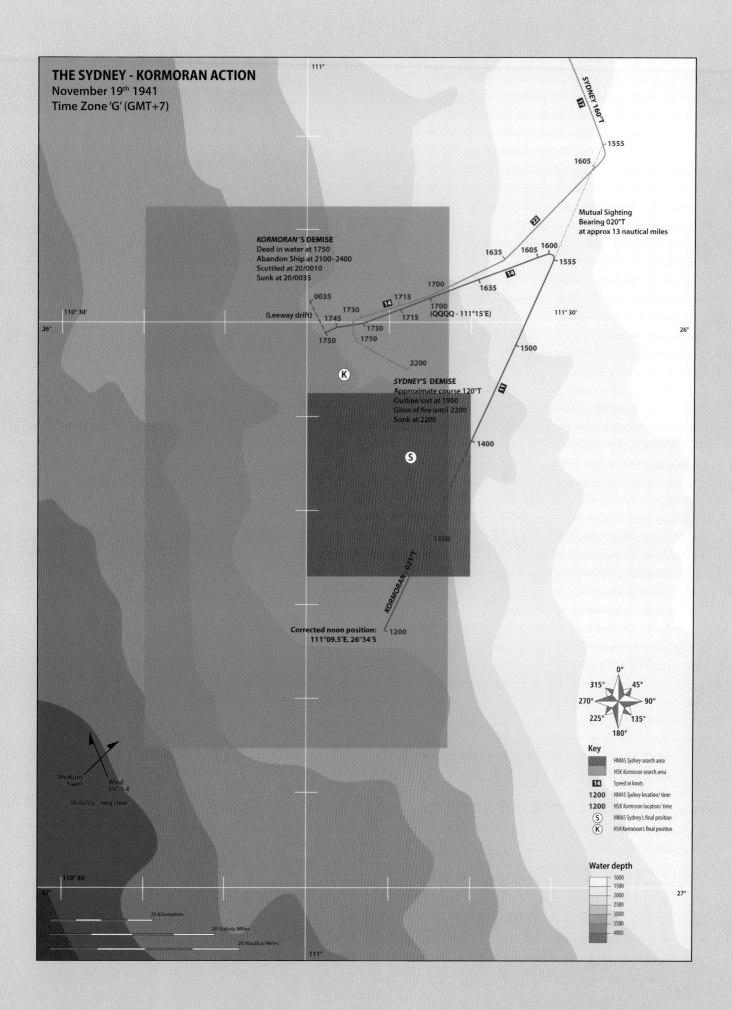

THE SYDNEY - KORMORAN ACTION
November 19th 1941
Time Zone 'G' (GMT+7)

SYDNEY 160°T

17

1555

1605

Mutual Sighting
Bearing 020°T
at approx 13 nautical miles

22

KORMORAN'S DEMISE
Dead in water at 1750
Abandon Ship at 2100–2400
Scuttled at 20/0010
Sunk at 20/0035

1600
1605
1635
1555

14

1635
1700

0035
1715
14
1700 (QQQQ - 111°15'E)
1730
1715

(Leeway drift)
1745
1730

1750
1750

2200

K

1500

SYDNEY'S DEMISE
Approximate course 120°T
Outline lost at 1900
Glow of fire until 2200
Sunk at 2200

11

1400

S

1300

KORMORAN - 025°T

Corrected noon position:
111°09.5'E, 26°34'S

1200

110° 30'
111°
111° 30'
26°
26°
27°
27°
110° 30'
111°

Medium
Swell
Wind
SSE 3-4

Visibility - very clear

0°
315° 45°
270° 90°
225° 135°
180°

Key

HMAS *Sydney* search area
HSK *Kormoran* search area
14 Speed in knots
1200 HMAS *Sydney* location/ time
1200 HSK *Kormoran* location/ time
S HMAS *Sydney*'s final position
K HSK *Kormoran*'s final position

Water depth

1000
1500
2000
2500
3000
3500
4000

20 Kilometres
20 Statute Miles
20 Nautical Miles

their own scuttling actions. I would be truly surprised if anyone who considered the evidence generated by our expedition objectively came to a different conclusion.

Of all the German claims, the one that interested me most and that my own personal expertise allowed me to forensically examine was the position (26°34' South 111° East) that Detmers repeatedly and consistently referred to in his testimony and written accounts. The fundamental problem with this position was that Detmers never made it absolutely clear at what time *Kormoran* was at this position. Wes Olson was the first to raise the possibility that Detmers was referring to the noontime position of his ship and it is undeniable now that Wes was right. Reverting to the standard format he followed for every daily report made in his official war diary, Detmers simply followed normal practice and headed the master account he kept hidden in the Cassel's dictionary with *Kormoran*'s noon position on 19 November 1941. There is also no doubt that Detmers (and Meyer) was unable to remember the minutes of longitude for the position so he truncated it to 111°. Fortunately, Geraldton radio's receipt of the full longitudinal coordinate *Kormoran* broadcast when sending out its 'QQQQ' signal at 1700 hours allowed me to compensate for Detmers's imperfect memory. The net effect was to shift the longitude east to 111°09.5' East.

It all becomes clear when comparing a chart of *Kormoran*'s dead-reckoning navigation against the known seabed position of the wrecks. Starting with Detmers's corrected noon position of 26°34' South 111°09.5' East, the dead-reckoning track of *Kormoran* places the sinking position (after factoring in six hours and 45 minutes of nor'-nor'-west leeway drift) approximately 8.4 nautical miles away from the actual seabed position of the wreck. This amount of error is about average for German ships on the high seas during the war, but considering *Kormoran* hadn't seen land for nearly a year it is remarkably good navigation. For all the other Germans such as Linke and Bunjes who gave 26° South 111° East as the action position in their testimony, this was not a bad approximation either. Indeed, it is somewhat ironic that the most imprecise and approximate position offered by the Germans when interrogated by their Australian captors has in fact turned out be closest to the wreck.

Back where it all started

The day after disembarking from the *Geosounder*, our home for the past 43 days, John, Glenys, Mack and I were all on the same early morning flight back to Perth for a final press conference scheduled to start at noon. The purpose of the conference was to present the results of the ROV investigation of the wrecks and to give our preliminary assessment about the damage they suffered, including what caused them to sink. The conference was being held in the main lecture auditorium of the Western Australian Maritime Museum in Fremantle, which in a way was closing the circle for me as it was in this same auditorium in 2004 on the date of the sixty-third anniversary of *Sydney*'s loss that I publicly made clear my intentions to search for and find the wrecks.

As with the previous press conferences in Geraldton, I was asked to give the main presentation using still photographs selected from the 1,435 that I shot during the expedition. My time that morning to put together such an important presentation was so incredibly short that I was still putting the final touches to it on my computer as Keith Rowe was making my introduction. The auditorium was packed with press and TV cameras, and many familiar faces that I wanted to stop and greet, although at the time I found it impossible to focus on anything except being ready to talk when I was called. I started by briefly reminding everyone about how the search was conducted using the historical information and analytical methods I relied on to find the wrecks. However, I knew the reason that everyone had come was to see previously unreleased pictures, so I did my best not to disappoint and selected 34 of the best images that I believed would explain why *Sydney* was defeated and lost with all hands.

Some of the photographs had already been posted on the FSF website but most were new and I suspect nearly all were revelations to the people sitting in the audience. The nation had waited decades to lay their eyes on *Sydney* and I was sensitive to the fact that it would be painful for people to see Australia's glory ship of World War II so badly damaged and defeated, especially for relatives of the crew who were invited guests. Based on the feedback we were getting on the ship I knew that there was a great deal of interest in the five ship's boats we found in the debris field. For this reason I included a photograph of each one, and explained that as the boats were found in the same location with the wreck (11.4 nautical miles distant from the wreck of *Kormoran*), this fact disproved one of the most contentious claims that the crew of *Kormoran* machine-gunned *Sydney's* survivors while in their boats.

Probably the two most telling pictures about *Sydney's* demise were of the torpedo strike against her port side and her inverted bow. While I thought it was appropriate for me to share my ideas about the loss of the bow being the trigger point that led to *Sydney* finally sinking, I also made it clear that this was a personal opinion and not one shared or sanctioned by the directors of the FSF. Other than Glenys, none of the other directors had seen the pictures so they were in no position to form a view of their own even if they had wanted to. For them, the expedition was solely about finding the wreck of *Sydney* and commemorating its missing crew and with their job done they were content to leave the technical analysis to others more qualified and experienced.

I gave a lot of thought to how I would present the next two photographs I had shot of leather shoes we found scattered in *Sydney's* debris field. As a group, the three observers and I unanimously agreed during the expedition not to include these images in the ones we posted on the FSF website because we knew how upsetting they would be to scores of people if shown that way. I did feel that the images of the shoes were important and needed to be shown to connect people with the human tragedy of *Sydney's* loss. However, it was equally important to be able to explain the context of the images: that the shoes had actually fallen from some kit lockers located where the bow snapped off from the hull and they were *not* being worn at the time they fell to the sea bed.

I was hoping my explanation would soften some of the emotion people might feel in seeing the shoes but suddenly the emotions I wanted to suppress in the audience welled up inside of me. Until that moment I had dealt with the pictures, and the entire expedition, in a professional manner which enabled me to avoid becoming too connected with the human aspect of the scenes we were witnessing. However, seeing a shot of a single shoe magnified on the giant screen behind me hit me in a personal way and my voice began to crack. I confessed that despite having seen this picture dozens of times it still had a very powerful impact on me, which perhaps I hadn't allowed myself to fully admit to until just then.

As the last slide of my presentation flashed up on the screen, of the wreath that John laid floating on the water above the wreck of *Sydney* along with the words *LEST WE FORGET*, I stepped back from the lectern and took a deep breath. The applause from the audience began to rise and continued for some time, but rather than feeling uplifted I was completely drained. I knew I was very tired but this was an altogether different feeling. My six-year journey was finally over and this realisation, in combination with my emotional reaction to the pictures, left me overwhelmed.

Our location of HMAS *Sydney* II was a stunning achievement that in Glenys's words would give people closure. We all hoped it would also bring an end to the questions, claims and controversy surrounding the battle, the conduct of Captain Detmers and his crew, and the loss of *Sydney* and her men. Our expedition had answered a lot of what had been previously unknown and gave historians some real facts to ponder the unknowable. Perhaps now, however, a line could finally be drawn under the events of 19 November 1941 and *Sydney* could be best remembered for the glorious and gallant ship that she most definitely was.

EPILOGUE

...

The Commission of Inquiry

Not long after *Sydney*'s wreck was discovered on 16 March 2008, we heard of news that the Australian Government, via the Chief of the Defence Force, Air Chief Marshal Angus Houston, AC, AFC, was considering opening a Commission of Inquiry into the loss of *Sydney*. This was a very surprising development as there had been no mention of any sort of inquiry at any time in the lead-up to the search. It was truly a bolt from the blue that gave me and others mixed feelings.

My concern, which was shared by John and Glenys, was that a major government inquiry would reopen the whole *Sydney* story just when we felt we were very close to providing the closure that the relatives, and indeed the nation, had for so long wanted. The findings of our expedition seemed to resolve a lot of the unknowns about the battle with respect to the main question of how *Sydney* was lost and why none of her crew survived. The expedition also provided a comprehensive body of evidence on both wrecks, which if analysed in a reasonable manner would surely lead a person to reject many of the most disturbing conspiracy theories. Would an inquiry give fresh oxygen, and a platform, to the conspiracy theorists in a process that would reopen wounds which were about to heal and prolong the genuine distress felt by relatives? The exhaustive 1997–99 Parliamentary Inquiry was indecisive and did not end the raging debates about the action between *Sydney* and *Kormoran*, but then that inquiry didn't have the benefit of knowing where the wrecks lie, and their condition, which a new inquiry would.

On the other hand, perhaps a formal official inquiry is exactly what was needed to put an end to the debate and controversy once and for all. After all, the fact that an official Board of Inquiry into *Sydney*'s loss wasn't conducted in the first place, as it should have been,[1] is one of the main reasons that so much speculation has filled the void left by the absence of solid factual information. In my own experience, this was certainly the case with the loss of the British bulk carrier *Derbyshire*. The families of the 44 people who died in *Derbyshire* campaigned for years for the British Government to open a formal investigation into her mysterious loss. They were finally rewarded for their persistence

Left: Sydney's *distinctive badge on one of her boats.*

when, twenty years after *Derbyshire*'s loss, the inquiry absolved the crew of any responsibility and concluded that deficiencies in the strength of the ship's hatch covers were a primary cause for the sinking.

We didn't sense that there was a groundswell of public opinion, or calls from the relatives of *Sydney*'s crew for a government inquiry. Even if there were, however, we might not have known about it as we were stuck on a survey ship in the Indian Ocean partially disconnected from the outside world. The *Geosounder* was a very insular environment and in our situation there was a danger we might be missing the broader perspective when we were looking at the issue with such an intense and rigid focus. If any inquiry was established a lot would depend on the terms of reference and how the inquiry was actually conducted.

As it turned out, the Commission of Inquiry (COI) was announced by the Acting Prime Minister, the Hon. Julia Gillard, and the Chief of the Defence Force, Angus Houston, days before we got our first pictures of *Sydney*. Mr Terence Cole, AO, RFD, QC, an expert in maritime law and a former Deputy Judge Advocate General of the Australian Defence Force, was selected to head up the commission as its president. The government was moving fast, but not fast enough to instruct or influence the ROV dives to film and photograph the wrecks that took place over the following week. Clearly the government was counting on our pictures to aid the commission with new film and photographic evidence; but in lieu of any direction from Mr Cole it would have to make do with the scope of the investigation that John and I established as being a sensible compromise, given the limited objectives and budget of the FSF expedition.

The commission was to have just a single term of reference: 'To inquire into and report upon circumstances associated with the loss of the HMAS *Sydney* II in November 1941 and consequent loss of life and related events subsequent thereto.' The scope was almost infinitely broad and the comments made by Air Chief Marshal Houston made it clear they were planning for a 'very complex and comprehensive and complete inquiry'.

I think it's absolutely fundamental that we must leave absolutely no doubt as to what happened. We have to establish the facts and we will use everything that is available to His Honour to enable to determine with reasonable certainty what happened to Sydney.

I think this is very, very important from the families' point of view; it's also important from our point of view because, strange as it may seem, no board of inquiry was conducted during World War II after the loss of Sydney. *So this is very much unfinished business and we think that this is the best way to go.*

Two months later, when President Cole held his first hearing of the COI in Sydney, he echoed many of the earlier comments made by Air Chief Marshal Houston regarding the reasons for the inquiry and its broad scope. He also made clear that barring national security issues, the inquiry would be open and that all material admitted into evidence and transcripts of hearings would be made public and placed on a website.

The finding of the Sydney II *and the* Kormoran, *their location and the obtaining of visual footage of their condition, allows, for the first time an analytical assessment of the damage suffered by* Sydney II; *a deduction based on empirical evidence and expert assessment of the immediate cause of the sinking of* Sydney II; *and a comparison of the accounts of the battle provided by the German survivors with the now observable damage suffered by both ships. This comparison may enable reasoned conclusions to be drawn regarding the veracity of their accounts. Importantly, it may also allow for a deduction to be made, based on such facts as can now be established, as to why there were no survivors from* Sydney II.

As I put the finishing touches to the last few pages of this book, some eight months after Mr Cole's first hearing and with the inquiry still in full swing, there can be no question that the COI has lived up to the initial promises made by Air Chief Marshal Houston and President

Cole. By any standard the COI has been extraordinarily comprehensive in the questions it has investigated and all manner of subjects it has accepted submissions on from the public. By the time the closing date of 31 October 2008 rolled around, 86 people had made submissions to the COI (most of those involving multiple submissions, which in one instance totalled 175 individual submissions of reports, photographs and other materials that could easily fill several volumes). The COI has travelled to Germany to interview at least a dozen of *Kormoran*'s surviving crew; heard the testimony of some fifteen former crew members that served in *Sydney* in the months and years before she was lost; and accepted into evidence over 150 exhibits, a number that will undoubtedly grow until the inquiry is complete. As to the openness of the COI, all of this information has been made publicly available on its website within a very timely manner.

The commission also instructed experts from the Defence Science and Technology Organisation (DSTO) and the Australian division of the Royal Institution of Naval Architects (RINA) to provide their expert advice and opinion on the extent and type of damage to both *Kormoran* and *Sydney*, based on the video footage and still photographs collected during our expedition. The result of the DSTO and RINA joint analysis was an impressive and authoritative 392-page report, written by twelve scientists, engineers and naval architects, which covered every imaginable technical aspect of the sinking of the two ships, including an explanation for the total loss of life of *Sydney*'s men.[2] As with any technically complex investigation of this magnitude, there will be those (including me) who will find the odd error in the report and question some of its conclusions. However, that should not detract from the excellent work done by the authors in providing a scientifically sound basis for understanding the events and aftermath of 19 November 1941. Thanks to this report many more of Tom Frame's unknowns are being revealed and answered.

Because the release of President Cole's final assessment and report will precede publication of this book, Australians will be able to hear his much anticipated judgment on the loss of *Sydney* before they read these

Above: Terence Cole (l) and Cole Commission solicitors interviewing Heinz Messerschmidt in Kiel.

words. A question on many people's minds will be how President Cole judges the decisions and actions of Captain Burnett and his senior officers in taking *Sydney* so close to an unidentified ship when the possibility of a raider being in Australian waters had been raised by Burnett himself.[3] Others will wonder whether it is even possible, or fair, to judge the thought processes of Burnett and those in command on the bridge of *Sydney* based on what we know today about the condition of the wrecks. Burnett and everyone else who was privy to his thinking and the tactics employed in dealing with what they saw as a poorly communicating Dutch merchant vessel were killed in the action, so how can anyone ever know with absolute certainty what was said or understood between a small number of men who are long dead? Is this the ultimate unknowable aspect regarding the loss of *Sydney*, or will President Cole be able to somehow piece together the answer from the mountainous jigsaw of evidence his commission has accumulated?

It is a question I have thought long and hard about, but have been unable to find a completely satisfactory answer. There are certainly some aspects that I am surer about than others and these do help build a better understanding of what went wrong for Burnett and *Sydney* on the day.

For example, I don't believe that Burnett would have been able to tell the difference between the hull shapes of the real *Straat Malakka* and *Kormoran* at long range (more than six nautical miles) when you take into account the disadvantage Detmers cleverly placed him under by heading directly into the shimmering late afternoon sun, along with *Sydney*'s approach from the starboard quarter. From this angle the counter stern of the *Straat Malakka* wouldn't look much different than *Kormoran*'s especially if Burnett was relying on a ship recognition drawing that was of a beam-on profile. Like others before and after him, Burnett probably had get closer in order to make a positive identification.

I am also reasonably sure that Burnett never suspected the ship to be a dangerous German raider. This statement might seem to fly in the face of logic given that in his testimony to the COI, Tom Fisher, an ordinary seaman who served in *Sydney* from 17 March 1940 to 26 October 1941, corroborated the well-worn anecdote that Captain Burnett had told his men at Sunday divisions on a return trip from the Sunda Strait that he was aware there was a raider out there (in the Indian Ocean), for the men to be on their toes and that he intended for *Sydney* to get the raider.[4] Despite this being the second instance in which Burnett mentioned the presence of a raider lurking off the west coast of Australia, it is almost inconceivable to imagine that he would have approached such a potentially dangerous ship the way he did and not have his guns, including his secondary armament of 4-inch guns, aimed and ready to fire at the slightest hint of any aggressive movement.

The latest tactical advice Burnett had about dealing with a raider came from RACAS in the form of a secret memorandum dated 21 September 1941 that was sent to the commanding officers of all Australian cruisers. It advised that if a raider 'decides to fight he may be expected to develop rapidly, an accurate fire up to 16,000 yards'.[5] The same memorandum advised against trying to salve a raider that decides to scuttle itself because it could be an old 'Q' ship trick to lure in a cruiser and attack it with its own guns and torpedoes. Set against this advice, the fact that *Sydney* steamed directly alongside the unknown ship at ranges approaching 900 metres for fifteen minutes, and

possibly longer, strongly indicates that Burnett and his senior advisors did not perceive they were facing anything close to this level of threat.

If Burnett was seriously suspicious that the unidentified ship was a raider, why didn't he use *Sydney*'s Walrus aircraft to investigate the ship from a safe distance when it had been readied for just this purpose? In fact, the decision to rotate the catapult back inboard and effectively stand down the pilot and aircraft whose engine was running indicates a completely different, almost relaxed, mindset. At least this is how this action was read by Detmers and everyone in *Kormoran* who were nervously watching the cruiser's every move. At this point Detmers seemed sure that *Sydney* had accepted their disguise as the *Straat Malakka* and was about to bid them a good voyage when the final question was asked to show their secret sign. In the seconds immediately after this, but before Detmers's order to de-camouflage and fire, it does appear that having not received the correct response from *Kormoran* Burnett signalled for the raider to stop. By then, however, it was too late. *Sydney* had somehow stumbled into a situation where she was facing a determined and equally powerful enemy who was coiled like a spring and more than ready to take full advantage of the element of surprise and speed in their attack.

One of the most vexing questions of all relates to the state of readiness that *Sydney* was in after altering course to chase *Kormoran*. Because of the nature of the encounter and the fact that she approached the raider with all her 6-inch guns and her port torpedo battery aimed, the presumption by many people was that *Sydney* was completely closed up in action stations, otherwise known as first degree of readiness. However, observations made by the Germans of men walking calmly on *Sydney*'s exposed decks and watching from the rail suggests otherwise.[6] It is also known that *Sydney*, with Burnett in command, did not always go into action stations when investigating unknown ships. In fact, in the month preceding the battle *Sydney* did not go to action stations on two of the five instances where they altered course to investigate other ships. This question about *Sydney*'s state of readiness is a hugely important one because it strikes right at the heart

Above: The directors of the Finding Sydney *Foundation, John Perryman, the former premier of WA, Alan Carpenter, and me.*

of what was in Burnett's mind in that it directly reflects his preparedness, or lack thereof, in taking on a suspicious ship. I am sure it is a question high on the agenda of President Cole and his commission.

Returning to Geraldton

Months after the expedition was over and the excitement of finding *Sydney* had all but died down, I received an invitation from Ian Carpenter, the mayor of Geraldton, to attend a sunset service to commemorate *Sydney* and her 645 men to be held on the sixty-seventh anniversary of the ship's loss. Having returned to Britain and thus missed the national memorial service held at St Andrew's Cathedral in Sydney the day before Anzac Day, I was pleased to accept Ian's kind invitation as I felt the service would be an ideal opportunity for me to meet some of the large community of relatives who would be attending. John Perryman had sent me a DVD of the deeply moving St Andrew's national service, which convinced me I shouldn't miss a second opportunity like it.

I had made firm friends with Garry and Julia Baverstock and arrangements were made for me and my wife, Sarah, who was joining me on her first trip to Australia, to stay with them when we arrived in Perth. Over the years I had exchanged emails with a dozen or so relatives but Garry was the first I got to know more personally and through our friendship I got the best insight to the powerful connection the relatives had to *Sydney* and why they strongly supported the wreck being found and every effort to reveal the truth about her loss and the fate of her men. Garry felt it was unfair for the relatives to have to carry the burden of not knowing the true story about *Sydney*'s loss for so many years and he, like many others, was desperate for the truth to be uncovered. His interest in the uncle he never met had grown, especially when after his father's passing the few artifacts that belonged to Able Seaman Ernest George Baverstock were handed down to him and his brother Sydney, who was named after the ship. Garry was inspired by his uncle's service to Australia, no more so than when he learned that Ernest was one of the brave crewmen in 'X' turret who had fought to the end and whose shells disabled *Kormoran*.

The return to Geraldton was like a reunion for everyone involved in the expedition. Ted Graham organised a dinner the evening we arrived to which everyone came: the FSF directors, John Perryman, Mack McCarthy, Patrick Flynn, Richard Sojka, and Penny Buchan, who along with Lee-Ann Evans did a terrific job in running the daily operations of the FSF office during the project. Wes Olson was also in the restaurant at a different table with his wife and friends, but in my eyes he was part of the team and its success.

John filled me in on the events planned for the week, which were to include a funeral service for the

Above: The HMAS Sydney *Memorial, Geraldton.*

unknown *Sydney* sailor who was going to be reburied at the Geraldton Cemetery mid-morning the next day. John was particularly proud to have been asked to speak at the service as the RAN's senior historical officer but also in recognition of his critical backing for the second attempt to recover the body from its unmarked grave on Christmas Island. The Australian Navy was still conducting DNA testing of related family members in the hope that the identity of the Christmas Island man, as he was commonly known, could be determined. It was a question on the minds of all the relatives, whether the Christmas Island man belonged to their family, so the funeral service and reburial were expected to give the day an emotional start.

Along with Mack McCarthy, I was asked to take part in a live radio broadcast that ABC Perth's *Morning Show* was making from the Maritime Museum in Geraldton in the morning before the funeral service. The museum was another central point for the commemoration week as it ran a program of lectures and exhibits that included a display on the search expedition and associated *Sydney* artifacts such as the striking of the *Bartolomeo Colleoni* medal, which was kindly donated by Garry Baverstock in memory of his uncle Ernie. After the interview I got a

chance to meet a handful of the relatives who were milling about the museum and answer some of the questions they had about the condition of the wrecks. One group of three men were nephews of William Edward Burnsyde, a stoker from Western Australia who was 21 years old when he was lost in *Sydney*. Their mother, who was William's sister, was so affected by the death of her brother that she named one son Edward after him and another Sydney after the ship. This was the second time I heard this same story, which made me wonder whether across Australia there was a whole generation of boys named Sydney after the events of November 1941.

As expected the funeral service was a beautiful and moving event attended by invited dignitaries and hundreds of relatives who were all given a Royal Australian Navy bereavement pin to wear in recognition of their special status. John delivered his speech with impeccable timing, considering what a challenge it was to encapsulate the ship's active and notable history into just five minutes. Afterwards more relatives came up to me to express their appreciation for what we had done and to tell the stories of the loved ones they lost. Every possible relation was present: wife, brother, sister, daughter, son, niece, nephew and assorted grandchildren. What struck me most was how each of them felt personally connected to the unknown sailor. While they were all curious to know who he actually was, virtually every relative I spoke to was just as happy that his identity wasn't revealed so they could continue to believe he belonged to them.

The sunset service at Geraldton's *Sydney* memorial at the top of Mount Scott was timed in keeping with the start of the action between the ships. It also made for a beautiful setting with the Dome of Souls in the foreground against a backdrop of clear blue sky that later gave way to light grey clouds tinged with hues of pink and purple. There was seating for a thousand people, half reserved for relatives, but the crowds filling the carpark to overflow, suggested the total number was at least double that. The commemorations started with a pre-service parade of veterans led by Tom Fisher and his fellow shipmates who had actually served in *Sydney*, followed by a prayer led by Father Brenton Taylor and the reading of the official messages, which were all heartfelt tributes to *Sydney* and the service of her men.

The traditional laying of wreaths was accompanied by a reading of the names of *Sydney*'s 645 souls by navy, army and air force cadets and Geraldton schoolchildren who lined the path up to the Dome. After the audience was treated to a beautiful rendition of the 'Naval Hymn' sung by an exceptional female vocalist and the RAN band, a lone bugler blared out the 'Last Post' and 'Reveille'. The minute of silence that followed was especially still, it seemed everyone was deep in thought and prayer. A fly-past by RAAF aircraft marked the end of the service and the start of a walk of remembrance in which family members were invited to lay floral tributes to their own relatives whose name was etched into the black granite wall that framed the Dome. By the end of the evening the central floor beneath the Dome where a bronze propeller sits was awash with poppies and colourful wreaths, many including photographs of the men and personal messages of remembrance.

Hundreds of miles away, over the site of *Sydney*'s silent hull, 280 more relatives were guests of the RAN for a service conducted from the platform deck of HMAS *Manoora*. In attendance with *Manoora* was the fourth Royal Australian Navy warship to proudly bear the name *Sydney*. The fast frigate added to the occasion by giving

Above: Relatives of those who died; (top) William Burnsyde's nephews and (bottom) Percy Willis's granddaughters.

her predecessor a full 21-gun salute. More wreaths were laid on the sea, as well as the ashes of several people who requested that their last remains be scattered at sea over the site of the wreck once it was found.

To cap the day off there was one more event that evening to mark the launch of the FSF Virtual Memorial. The memorial was a web-based concept designed by Richard Sojka that enabled families to contribute photographs and stories about the men they lost.[7] I had returned to Geraldton for exactly this reason: to hear more about the men whose sacrifice inspired so much love and a nation's commitment to never forget them.

The experience I will remember most, however, came later at the Returned Service League club where I met the family of Percy John Christian Willis, who was one of *Sydney*'s oldest and most experienced sailors. Percy was a plumber first class and it was he who repaired *Sydney*'s funnel after it was holed by a shell in the famous action with the *Bartolomeo Colleoni*. Like all his shipmates Percy returned to Australia a 'Hero of the Seas' and was feted at a party and dance in his honour at Campbelltown's Town Hall. Percy's death was a huge blow to his wife and family of four children.

Percy was a remarkable man whose life and service continued to touch his family long after he was gone. Making the trip across the country from New South Wales with his daughter Edna, now aged 84 years, were his five granddaughters and their husbands and two great-granddaughters. The long journey was like a family pilgrimage to the Mount Scott Memorial, which they couldn't wait to see and as his granddaughter Janet described, 'We found his name on the wall and just had to run our fingers along his name just I think to say we have found him, and we know where he is.' They carried with them an extraordinary diary written by Percy of his time on board, which covered some of *Sydney*'s most famous exploits. I was humbled to have been given a copy of the diary by Janet, and absolutely delighted to see that Percy, like me, loved to fish.

A final thought for *Sydney*'s men

The FSF expedition I had the privilege to lead that found the wrecks of *Kormoran* and *Sydney* was an amazing experience for me and a remarkable achievement for the scores of people directly and indirectly involved in laying the groundwork for and mounting the expedition. While the most important objective for Ted Graham, Don Pridmore, Bob Trotter, Keith Rowe, Glenys McDonald and their countless supporters was to provide answers to the questions posed by relatives, it has to be expected

that the results of the expedition and the evidence it generated will reignite and intensify the debates that have alternately simmered and boiled over through the years. More books will be written to be added to the nearly two dozen that already exist on the subject, and it is likely that new theories about the battle or the conduct of either Detmers or Burnett will spring forth as well.

While the objective of achieving closure may not appear to sit well in an environment where debate is intensifying, the nature of the debate will most certainly have been transformed by the location and filming of the wrecks. Gone will be the rancorous arguments about northern or southern search boxes, underwater or above-water torpedoes, Japanese submarines, the machine-gunning of survivors in lifeboats and dozens of similar conjectures that polarised opinion and prevented a serious search from being mounted for literally decades. Whatever subjects are debated in the future, at least now there will be a substantial body of hard evidence to inform people and to counter mindless speculation.

For those who decide to study and make sense of the events of 19 November 1941, and in the process attempt to apportion responsibility for the loss of *Sydney*, they would do well to heed the following caution against adopting a judgmental stance.

> *For those who pick over the bones of other people's disasters, it often seems incredible that these warnings and human failures, seemingly so obvious in retrospect, should have gone unnoticed at the time. Being blessed with both uninvolvement and hindsight, it is a great temptation for retrospective observers to slip into a censorious frame of mind and to wonder at how these people could have been so blind, arrogant, ignorant or reckless…*[8]

Lastly, for the relatives whose overriding interest has always been about the memory of *Sydney*'s men and their selfless sacrifice, they will forever be safe in the absolute knowledge of where the wrecks and their loved ones lie. For them the debate is over. Australia's greatest maritime mystery has been solved.

GLOSSARY

•••

ASDIC	a British anti-submarine detection system that was a precursor of the modern sonar		**HSK**	*Hilfskreuzer* (auxiliary cruiser)
			HT	Hired Transport
C-in-C	Commander-in-Chief		*Kriegsmarine*	German Navy
CO	Commanding Officer		**NAA**	National Archives of Australia
CWR	Central War Room		**POW**	Prisoner of War
DCT	Director Control Tower		**RAAF**	Royal Australian Air Force
DNOWA	District Naval Officer Western Australia		**RACAS**	Rear Admiral Commanding the Australian Squadron
DNI	Director of Naval Intelligence		**RAN**	Royal Australian Navy
ETA	Estimated Time of Arrival		**RANVR**	Royal Australian Navy Volunteer Reserve
FRUMEL	Fleet Radio Unit Melbourne		**RN**	Royal Navy
FSF	Finding *Sydney* Foundation		**ROV**	Remotely Operated Vehicle
G	Golf Time — GMT plus seven hours (the time kept by *Kormoran*)		**SUPSALV**	Supervisor of Salvage (US Navy)
GMT	Greenwich Mean Time		**UNESCO**	United Nations Educational, Scientific and Cultural Organisation
H	Hotel (Fremantle) Time — GMT plus eight hours		**WA**	West Australian
HACS	High-Angle Control Station		**WTB**	Watertight Bulkhead
HMA3S	HMAS Sydney Search Pty Ltd		**W&A**	Williamson and Associates
HMAS	His Majesty's Australian Ship		**W/T**	Wireless Telegraphy
HMI	Hydrargyrum Medium-Arc Iodide (lights)		**Z**	Zulu or Z Time (also known as Greenwich Mean Time)

Previous page: A photograph of the crew on the deck of the Sydney *taken in July, 1940.*

SEARCH TEAMS

•••

Side-Scan Sonar Search Team

1. David Mearns, Search Director
2. Rob Bruinsma, Client Representative
3. John Perryman, Senior Naval Historical Officer
4. Glenys McDonald, Observer
5. Art Wright, Sonar Party Chief
6. Jeff Koch, Watch Leader
7. Carter Le, Sonar Engineer
8. Brian Bunge, Sonar Technician
9. Michael Kelly, Data Analyst
10. Kelly Curtis, Data Processor
11. Phil Colvin, Winch Technician
12. Bill Heather, Winch Technician
13. Nigel Meikle, Senior Surveyor
14. Stephen Bagnell, Survey Technician
15. Blair Cliffe, Master
16. Rupert Saville, Chief Officer
17. Graham Cann, 2nd Mate
18. Patrick Wildermoth, Chief Engineer
19. Sydney Villanueva, 2nd Engineer
20. Howard Sarmiento, 3rd Engineer
21. Nelson Largo, Motorman
22. Graeme Luckie, Electrician
23. Louis Jacomos, Integrated Rating
24. Dennis Hicks, Integrated Rating
25. Luke Harris, Integrated Rating
26. Peter Morgan, Cook
27. Joseph Larsen, Assistant Cook
28. Ashley Kelly, Steward
29. Matthew Kelley, Director
30. Ullrich Krafzik, Camerman
31. Chistopher MacGregor, Soundman

ROV Investigation Team

1. David Mearns, Search Director
2. Rob Bruinsma, Client Representative
3. John Perryman, Senior Naval Historical Officer
4. Glenys McDonald, Observer
5. Mack McCarthy, Observer
6. Simon Hall, ROV Supervisor
7. David Norton, ROV Supervisor
8. Bruce Burman, ROV Technician
9. Deane Glazebrook, ROV Technician
10. Peter Skinner, ROV Technician
11. Brett Murray, ROV Technician
12. Kaamil Douglas, ROV Engineer
13. Brian Bunge, Sonar Technician
14. Michael Kelly, Data Analyst
15. Nigel Meikle, Senior Surveyor
16. Johannes Van Rooyen, Survey Technician
17. John Spooner, Electrical Engineer
18. Deland Van Wieringen, Master
19. John Barnard, Chief Officer
20. Peter Sedgwick, 2nd Mate
21. Chistensen Preben, Chief Engineer
22. Howard Sarmiento, 2nd Engineer
23. Sydney Villanueva, 3rd Engineer
24. Nelson Largo, Motorman
25. Robert McBride, Integrated Rating
26. Neil Anderson, Integrated Rating
27. Geoff Rickets, Integrated Rating
28. Joanne Ham, Cook
29. Lesie Perso, Assistant Cook
30. Sonia Sovor, Steward
31. Matthew Kelley, Director
32. Ullrich Krafzik, Camerman
33. Chistopher MacGregor, Soundman

ENDNOTES

•••

Prologue

1 W.H. (John) Ross, *Lucky Ross, The Autobiography of a RAN Officer — 1934–1951*, Hesperian Press, Carlisle, Western Australia, 1994.

2 G.H. Gill, *Australia in the War of 1939–1945, Royal Australian Navy 1939–1942*, Vol. 1, Australian War Memorial, Canberra, 1957.

3 Admiral of the Fleet, Viscount Cunningham of Hyndhope, *A Sailor's Odyssey*, Hutchinson & Co., London, 1951.

4 Ibid.

5 Ibid.

6 *Battle Summary — No. 2, Mediterranean Operations — Action off Cape Spada (Crete) 19th July, 1940*, Training and Staff Duties Division (Historical Section) Naval Staff, Admiralty, SW1 (T.S.D.211/42).

7 Gregory P. Gilbert, *Papers in Australian Maritime Affairs No. 17, Australian Naval Personalities*, Sea Power Centre — Australia, Canberra, 2006.

8 Vice-Admiral Sir John Collins, *As Luck Would Have It: The Reminiscences of an Australian Sailor*, Angus & Robertson, Sydney, 1965.

9 Letter, Commanding Officer, HMAS *Sydney*, SO253/456, 6 October 1941, Naval History Section, Sea Power Centre — Australia.

10 Combined Operations Intelligence Centre, Daily Summary, Serial No. DS/116, 7 October 1941.

Introduction

1 National Archives of Australia (Melbourne), MP 1185/8, 2026/19/6, *Loss of HMAS* Sydney, Report on interrogation of survivors of *Kormoran* by F. B. Eldridge.

2 G.H. Gill, *Australia in the War of 1939–1945, Royal Australian Navy 1939–1942*, Vol. 1, Australian War Memorial, Canberra, 1957.

3 Joint Standing Committee on Foreign Affairs, Defence and Trade, *Report on the Loss of HMAS* Sydney, Parliament of the Commonwealth of Australia, Canberra, 1998.

4 M. Montgomery, *Who Sank the* Sydney?, Leo Cooper and Secker & Warburg, London, England, 1983.

5 The rank of *Fregattenkapitän* in the German Navy is equivalent to a commander.

6 German Navy.

7 Bundesarchiv/Militärarchive, Freiburg, Germany: RMD 4/601, Heft 10, Operation und Taktik, Auswertungen wichtiger Ereignisse des Seekrieges. Die Fahrt des Hilfskreuzers 'Schiff 41' ('Kormoran'). A translated version of this document can be found in the Public Records Office: ADM 1/18899, Operation and Tactics, Evaluation of Important Events in the Naval War, Book 10. The voyage of the auxiliary cruiser 'Ship 41' ('Kormoran').

8 Because Allied warships were always painted grey, Detmers and his officers jokingly referred to them as ships of the 'grey funnel' line.

9 National Archives of Australia (Melbourne), B6121, 165K, *Translation of Diaries*.

10 T. Frame, *HMAS* Sydney *— Loss & Controversy*, Hodder & Stoughton, Rydalmere, NSW, 1993.

11 Four Chinese seamen taken prisoner after *Kormoran* sank the British steamer *Eurylochus* on 29 January 1941 agreed to join *Kormoran* working as paid laundrymen.

12 Detmers created at least four different accounts of the action with *Sydney*. What is believed to be the original account was started in 1942 and was kept hidden in a Cassel's German and English dictionary.

His final account was his book *Hilfskreuzer Kormoran*, published in 1959. The account depicted in this Introduction draws primarily from all these sources.

13 Interview with Heinz Messerschmidt, Altenholz, Germany, 2008.

14 T. Detmers & J. Brennecke, *Hilfskreuzer Kormoran*, Koehlers Verlagsesellschaft, Munich, Germany, 1959.

15 Personal communication with John Perryman.

16 *Sydney*'s crow's-nest was higher than *Kormoran*'s telescopic mast, thus *Sydney* had a slight advantage in being able to sight the raider before being sighted herself.

17 'NNJ' was an international signal that meant 'YOU SHOULD MAKE YOUR SIGNAL LETTERS'.

18 According to official sources, the maximum range of *Sydney*'s 6-inch guns was 25,480 yards at an elevation angle of 45°. However, in actions in the Mediterranean, the longest range the guns ever opened fire at was 22,000 yards. In comparison, the maximum range of *Kormoran*'s World War I-era 15-cm guns was 20,120 yards at an elevation angle of 30°, and the longest range they were ever fired at in action was less than 12,000 yards.

19 *Kormoran* was keeping time in Zone G (Golf), which was GMT plus seven hours, whereas *Sydney* and Western Australia were keeping time in Zone H (GMT plus eight hours). As the account in this Introduction is based on German sources, all times quoted here are in Zone G time.

20 These 'QQQQ' signals were heard by Geraldton Radio and the tug *UCO*.

21 Interview with Heinz Messerschmidt, Altenholz, Germany, 2008.

22 Ibid.

23 The Allied procedure for challenging a suspect ship was to signal with the inner two letters of that vessel's secret call sign, whereupon the suspect ship was to signal back with the outer two letters of the secret call sign. The secret call sign for the *Straat Malakka* was IIKP. Apparently *Sydney* signalled IK to the *Kormoran*, which only confused Ahlbach and Detmers, because they knew nothing of this procedure nor did they obviously know the secret call sign for the *Straat Malakka*. When *Kormoran* failed to reply to this challenge for their secret call sign, *Sydney* then signalled them to hoist their secret signal letters.

24 Interview with Baron Reinhold von Malapert, Santigao Chile, 2006.

25 Report of Lieutenant Commander Rycroft's interrogation of *Kormoran* survivors, dated 30 November 1941.

26 National Archives of Australia (Melbourne), B121, 164M Kormoron *(Raider No. 41)* — *German AMC* — *Interrogation of Survivors*.

27 *Kormoran* was converted from the merchant ship *Steiermarck,* formerly of the Hamburg–America Line (HAPAG). She was the eighth *Hilfskreuzer* (raider) converted, and thus was designated HSK8, but operationally the German Navy referred to her as Schiff (Ship) 41, while to the Allied navies she was Raider G.

28 Because of his accurate and decisive shooting during the action, Fend was the only crewman who received the Iron Cross First Class, while all others received the Iron Cross Second Class. Detmers reportedly said to Fend: 'I hereby award you the Iron Cross, First Class, for your bravery and excellent gunnery. It was marvellous shooting and I am proud of you.'

29 Personal communication with Heinz Messerschmidt, 2008.

30 B. Winter, *H.M.A.S.* Sydney — *Fact, Fantasy and Fraud*, Boolarong Publications, Brisbane, Australia, 1984.

31 *Kormoran*'s engine room log was also found hidden in the Cassel's German and English dictionary.

32 Two hundred and eighty kg is the lightest warhead for an early G7a torpedo. The Germans apparently issued torpedoes with heavier warheads during the war, and if *Kormoran* was resupplied with one of these torpedoes the warhead could be as heavy as 430 kg.

33 Detmers put the total of 15-cm shells fired at 550.

34 B. Winter, op. cit., p. 143.

Chapter 1

1   There is uncertainty about the exact number of men who were on board *Kormoran* at the time of the battle, and also about the exact number of men who survived and made it safely to land. The figure of 399 men on board is supported by a list of the entire ship's company put together by Captain Detmers. Other sources put the total number of men at 400; however, it appears that this figure does not take into account the man (Hans Hofmann) who was killed in an accident on board and was buried at sea on 3 July before the action with *Sydney*. Various documents and sources place the number of survivors at between 315 and 319 men. Although apparently 320 men were able to get away from *Kormoran* alive, one German survivor (Rudolfe Loesche), who was in the lifeboat that was eventually recovered by *Yandra*, died as a result of his burn injuries and was buried at sea, while another unidentified German survivor who was in the lifeboat picked up by the *Koolinda* apparently died as a result of drinking sea water, and according to the other survivors was thrown overboard. The final figure of 318 survivors is supported by documents created by Captain Detmers. Much of the confusion stems from how the three Chinese prisoners-turned-laundrymen were factored into the total number of survivors. One of the Chinese laundrymen who was in Detmer's lifeboat, which was recovered by *Centaur*, signed on with the ship and thus avoided being counted as a survivor.

2   Written correspondence with Kurt Meder, 2008. meder was one of the 26 *Kormoran* crew in the life raft recovered by *Aquitania*.

3   National Archives of Australia (Melbourne), B6121, 164M, Kormoran *(Raider No. 41) 'G'* — *German AMC* — *Interrogation of Survivors*.

4   Written correspondence with Kurt Meder, 2008.

5   National Archives of Australia (Melbourne), B6121, 165P, Sydney-Kormoran *(Raider No. 41) Action Signals etc. 1941–1945*.

6   National Archives of Australia (Melbourne), MP1185/8, 2026/3/453 and B6121, 164L, Kormoron *(Raider No. 41) 'G'* — *German AMC*.

7   *Sydney* escorted HT *Zealandia* to the Sunda Strait, handing over the escort to HMAS *Durban* on 17 November in position 7° 56' South 104° 40' East and was returning to Fremantle with an ETA of PM Thursday 20 November.

8   *Trocas* was a Shell tanker that was on a voyage from Palembang, Sumatra, to Fremantle when it recovered the 25 German sailors from the drifting life raft.

9   Confidential message from DNOWA to (AC) NB on 24 November at 1540Z.

10 Imperial War Museum, 69/18/1, Diary of Admiral Sir J. Crace.

11 Secret message from DNOWA to (AC) NB on 24 November at 1700Z.

12 Secret message from Admiralty to (AC) NB and C-in-C China on 25 November at 1120Z.

13 Message from DNOWA to (AC) NB on 25 November at 1935Z.

14 *No Survivors*, 50th Anniversary Commemorative Issue, booklet published by West Australian Newspapers Ltd, Perth, WA.

15 Detmers's statement that *Sydney* missed with two torpedoes conflicts with his written account, created at a later date, in which he states that *Sydney* fired a full spread of four torpedoes.

16 Detmers had already been awarded the Iron Cross First Class.

17 Australian War Memorial, 124 4/224, *Loss of HMAS Sydney*.

18 B. Winter, *H.M.A.S.* Sydney — *Fact, Fantasy and Fraud*, Boolarong Publications, Brisbane, Australia, 1984.

19 Bundesarchiv-Militärachiv, 7-30.

20 P. Schmalenbach, *German Raiders* — *A History of Auxiliary Cruisers of the German Navy 1895–1945*, Patrick Stephens, Cambridge, 1979.

21 The interrogation team consisted of Admiral J. G. Crace, RACAS, Lieutenant Commander James Lumley Rycroft, RANVR, Captain Charles Farquhar-Smith, DNOWA, Commander Victor Ramage, Commander

Emile F.V. Dechaineux, DOD, Commander Salm, Royal Netherlands Navy. Messrs Lobstein, Frankel, Van Dahl, and Holtham also provided important and valuable assistance as interpreters.

22 National Archives of Australia (Melbourne), B6121, 164M Kormoron *(Raider No. 41) 'G' — German AMC — Interrogation of Survivors.*

23 National Archives of Australia (Melbourne), MP1049/5, 2026/19/6, *Interrogation of German Survivors ex Raider* Kormoron.

24 Dechaineux also served as CO of HMAS *Warramunga* in 1942 and CO of HMAS *Australia* in 1944, where he was killed on 9 March when a Japanese dive-bomber struck his ship.

25 M.J. Hehir, Submission to the Parliament of Australia Inquiry into the Circumstances of the Sinking of HMAS *Sydney*, Vol. 6, pp. 1133-1139, Canberra, February 1998.

26 The private diary of Captain John Hehir for January 1942, as provided and translated by his daughter Maria J. Hehir.

27 B. Winter, op. cit.

28 H. Kevin has been mistakenly identified by some authors as a man. In fact, Mrs Hermaine Kevin was a woman.

29 Public Records Office, ADM 199-736 and National Archives of Australia (Melbourne), MP 1185/8, 2026/19/6, *Loss of HMAS* Sydney, Report by F. B. Eldridge on Interrogation of Survivors of *Kormoron*.

30 National Archives of Australia (Melbourne), B6121, 164M Kormoron *(Raider No. 41) 'G' — German AMC — Interrogation of Survivors.*

31 G.H. Gill, *Australia in the War of 1939–1945, Royal Australian Navy 1939–1942*, Vol. 1, Australian War Memorial, Canberra, 1957.

32 M. Montgomery, *Who Sank the* Sydney?, Leo Cooper and Secker & Warburg, London, England, 1983, pp. 198–9.

33 B. Winter, op. cit. The author is now known as Barbara Poniewerski.

34 T. Frame, *HMAS Sydney — Loss & Controversy*, Hodder & Stoughton, Rydalmere, NSW, 1993, p. 224.

35 Ibid., p. 217.

36 Ibid., p. 225.

Chapter 2

1 H. Pretterebner, *Der Fall Lucona*, Verlags GmbH, 1987.

2 There were also two wives on board *Derbyshire*, making the total number killed 44.

3 An excellent book on the controversy surrounding the loss of *Derbyshire* is *A Ship Too Far*, by D. Ramwell and T. Madge, Hodder & Stoughton, London, 1992.

4 *Liverpool Daily Post*.

5 In August 1992 Eastport International was purchased by the oilfield services provider Oceaneering International and was renamed Oceaneering Technologies (OTECH).

6 Dr W.J. Gould, *Currents in the Region of Loss of MV* Derbyshire, Institute of Oceanographic Sciences Contract Report, Surrey, UK, 1992.

7 MV *Derbyshire* Surveys, UK/EC Assessors' Report, UK Department of the Environment, Transport and the Regions, London, 1998.

8 The Hon. Mr Justice Colman, *Report of the Re-Opened Formal Investigation into the Loss of the MV* Derbyshire, in the High Court of Justice (Admiralty Court), UK Department of the Environment, Transport and the Regions, London, 2000.

9 R. D. Ballard, *The Discovery of the Bismarck*, Hodder & Stoughton, London, 1990.

10 David Mearns and R. White, Hood *and* Bismarck*, the Deep-Sea Discovery of an Epic Battle*, Channel 4 Books, London, 2001.

Chapter 3

1 The *West Australian*, 28 March 1998.

2 PerthNow, online article dated 17 March 2008.

3 Defence Media Release dated 14 June 2002.

4 Royal Australian Navy, Sea Power Centre — Australia,

HMAS Sydney *II, Proceedings of the Wreck Location Seminar*, 16 November 2001.

5   Peter Hore was a member of the Archival Record Workshop committee, along with Wes Olson (chair), Mr Richard Goldsmith and Commander Geoff Vickridge, RANR.

6   National Archives of Australia (Melbourne), B5823, *Detmers's Diary — Account of Action between* Kormoron *and* Sydney, *Decode and Translations*.

7   US National Archives and Records Service, *Guides to the Microfilmed Records of the German Navy, 1850–1945*, Washington, DC, 1984.

8   Ibid.

9   I. G. Aylen, 'Recollections of Assault Unit No. 30', *Naval Review*, Vol. 65, No. 4, October 1977, p. 320.

10   All the documents found in the box labelled *Kormoran* are posted on the RAN Sea Power Centre website: wwwnavy.gov.au/HMAS_Sydney_and_KORMORAN_DOCUMENTS.

11   National Archives of Australia (Sydney), SP551/1, Bundle 528, *Log Books of HMAS* Sydney *1940–1941*.

12   *Sydney*'s June and October transits followed virtually the same course (162°) in the area of 26° South.

13   Detmers recorded the action report in the dictionary under the letter B and the engine room log under the letter M, presumably in keeping with the German words *Brücke* (Bridge) and *Maschine* (Engine), respectively.

14   The coded account was a notebook and not a diary.

15   The independent researcher Robert W. O'Hara was also hired to make a fresh transcription of the decoded account and to compare this to the original FRUMEL transcription. A number of minor, insignificant discrepancies were found.

16   P. Hore & D.L. Mearns, 'HMAS Sydney — An End to the Controversy', *Naval Historical Review*, Vol. 24, No. 4, December 2003.

17   Heinz Messerschmidt also acquired a Cassell's dictionary in early 1942 whilst detained in the Murchison POW camp. Messerschmidt was able to purchase the dictionary by ordering it from a Mr Moody of the YMCA, who regularly visited the camp to tend to prisoner requests. The dictionary was purchased in Melbourne by Moody on behalf of Messerschmidt and hand-delivered to him at the camp. Detmers most likely acquired his dictionary in the same way. The personal diary of Dr Siebelt Habben confiscated from him on his transfer from Murchison to Dhurringile in May 1943 shows that the YMCA was delivering German books and medical periodicals as early as 6 January 1942 (National Archives of Australia, MP385/7, 53/101/178).

18   *Book 10* was one in a series of 'Operations and Tactics' reports on the activities of auxiliary cruisers. The original *Book 10* on the Voyage of *Kormoran* can be found in the Bundesarchiv/Militärarchiv (RMD 4/601). English translations of *Book 10* can be found in the Public Records Office (ADM 1–18899) and National Archives of Australia (B6121/164N).

19   The sheer volume of information that Dr Habben relayed to the German Navy have led some researchers to conclude that Habben carried a written copy of Detmers's action report out of Australia. However, Dr Habben's son has confirmed that his father was made by Detmers to memorise the action report. In the months before his repatriation, Habben had his personal diary confiscated and presumably this would have made him reluctant to carry a written account out of POW camp when it was likely he would be searched.

20   Royal Australian Navy, Sea Power Centre, *HMAS Sydney II, The Cruiser and the Controversy in the Archives of the United Kingdom*, edited by Captain Peter Hore, Royal Navy, Defence Publishing Service, Canberra, 2001, pp. 132–3.

21   In a personal communication, Michael Montgomery states that he was sent the Bunjes, Detmers, Diebitsch and von Malapert material by the Naval Historical Branch, but no mention was made of the Jurgensen, Thurow, Heinz, Hartmann or Noll material.

22   In March 2000 Peter Meyer, the son of *Kormoran*'s navigator, the late Henry Meyer, donated six family photographs to the Western Australian Maritime

Museum. On the back of the photographs were pencilled notes that Meyer had written during the journey he made in the same lifeboat with Rheinhold von Malapert. The notes included similar, and in some cases identical navigation and weather information as that found in Malapert's lifeboat diary, which virtually proved that the two men shared their notes with each other.

23 Warren and Lindsay's discoveries were made by a device invented and operated by Lindsay called the Knight Direct Location System (KDLS). There has been no satisfactory explanation or publication that proves the KDLS device and its principle of detection.

24 For a full discussion of the SPC workshop and its results see: http ://www.navy.gov.au/SUMMARY_ OF_HMAS_SYDNEY_%28II%29_AND KORMORAN_–_LIFEBOAT_WORKSHOP

Chapter 4

1 M. McCarthy, 2007, *A Précis of Search-related Events Leading up to the Commencement of the HMAS* Sydney *Search*, Report, Department of Maritime Archaeology, Western Australian Maritime Museum, No. 230.

2 D. McDonald, 2004, The Journey of Two Lifeboats — An Examination of the Voyages of KAPT LT Meyer and KAPT LT Von Malapert 19–25 Nov 1941, unpublished manuscript, original December 2003, revised February 2004.

3 A. Allen and J. Plourde, *Review of Leeway: Field Experiments and Implementation*, Technical Report No. CG-D-08-99, US Coast Guard Research and Development Center, 1999.

4 G. McDonald, *Seeking the* Sydney*: A Quest for Truth*, University of Western Australia Press, 2005.

5 Personal letter from Maria J. Hehir dated 3 June 2004.

6 One of the recommendations of the 1998 Parliamentary Inquiry on the loss of HMAS *Sydney* was that the Australian Government should match public donations, on a dollar for dollar basis, up to a total of $2 million.

7 The 645 lost in *Sydney* were comprised of men from every state in Australia and from the UK.

8 Baron Reinhold von Malapert died in Santiago on 22 April 2007, aged 93. Peter Hore wrote his obituary in the *Telegraph* newspaper.

9 The original reference regarding the 'QQQQ' signal was a Navy Office message delivered by hand from the South Western Area Command Headquarters to the Central War Room. The time and date of the message was 0630Z-0645Z (GMT) 27 November (National Archives of Australia, MP 1587/1 165P). The same message was also recorded in the RAAF War Diary on the same date but timed at 0748Z (Australian War Memorial 64 0/2).

10 G. McDonald, Australia's Forgotten Son: Summary of Evidence on the Burial Site of the Body at Christmas Island, unpublished manuscript, 2006.

11 The optimum weather window at the northern search location is generally between November and April.

Chapter 5

1 The following three papers were in M. McCarthy & K. Kirsner (compilers) Papers from the HMAS *Sydney* Forum, Fremantle 21–23 November, 1991, Report — Department of Maritime Archaeology, No. 52: Courtney, 1991, Report on the Meteorological Conditions near 26°S 111°E for 17–28 November 1941; R. Southern, 1991, Climatology of Weather Conditions, WA Coast November, 1941; R. Steedman, and M. McCormack, 1991, Backtracking the Lifeboats and Floats — a Metocean view.

2 The deepest depth in the world's oceans, at 10,876 metres, can be found in the Marianas trench.

3 G. Kinder, *Ship of Gold in the Deep Blue Sea*, Atlantic Monthly Press, New York, 1998.

4 The three sources of wind data are: QuikSCAT, a satellite-based measuring system operated by NASA's Jet Propulsion Laboratory; NCEP-DOE Reanalysis

2, a numerical forecast system provided by NOAA's Earth System Research Laboratory; and LAPS, a regional numerical forecast model provided by the Australian Bureau of Meteorology.

Chapter 6

1   www.findingsydney.com

Chapter 7

1   The geographic coordinates for a position at sea during World War II are generally expressed in degrees and decimal minutes. For example, the actual sinking position of *Kormoran* would be written as 26 degrees 05.8 minutes South and 111 degrees 04.6 minutes East. Kim Kirsner and John Dunn found that out of a total of 45 different reports by the German survivors, nineteen reported the position as 26°S 111°E, which is obviously an abbreviated position.

2   Although Detmers and Meyer were unable to fully remember *Kormoran*'s longitude, I was able to make an adjustment for this uncertainty, when establishing my search box for *Kormoran*, by using the longitude (111°15' E) heard by Geraldton radio when they received *Kormoran*'s 'QQQQ' wireless signal at 1705(G).

3   National Archives of Australia (Melbourne), B6121, 164M, Kormoran *(Raider No. 41) 'G' — German AMC — Interrogation of Survivors.*

4   The Finding Sydney Foundation was the charitable foundation given the money by the government to conduct the search. The HMA3S was the company conducting the search on behalf of the FSF. While the directors are the same for both the FSF and HMA3S, the two organisations were separate and had separate functions. The FSF was created in 2003 and HMA3S in 2001.

5   The signal 'BRAVO HOTEL TACK ALPHA DELTA TWO EIGHT' is a request to splice the mainbrace, which in the Royal Navy during the days of sail power was the order for a double issue of rum for someone who spliced the heaviest lines holding the main sail. It later became traditional to splice the mainbrace before a battle, after victory or for a job well done under difficult conditions. Presently the order to splice the mainbrace is heavily restricted.

Chapter 8

1   HMI (hydrargyrum medium-arc iodide) is a type of high-quality light which uses an arc lamp instead of an incandescent bulb to produce light. It is very expensive and typically used in film and broadcast television production work. HMI lights require an electronic or magnetic ballast to provide the ignition pulse and regulate the arc. The main advantages of HMI lights are that they are three to four times more efficient than tungsten-halogen lights so they use less power and run cooler, and they run at a colour temperature of around 5600°K (normal daylight temperature), which provides superior light quality.

Chapter 9

1   *Sydney*'s BL Mark XXIII 6-inch twin gun turrets had a maximum depression angle of -5°. The safety depression gear was a mechanism that physically prevented the gun barrels from being depressed below the maximum angle of -5°. Because the position of 'X' turret was higher than that of 'Y' turret, the gun crew might have needed the lower angle in order to score hits on *Kormoran*.

2   Counting from the stem of *Sydney*'s bow this was the seventh watertight bulkhead.

3   *Kormoran* was fitted with two fixed-angle underwater tubes for firing a single torpedo from either the port or starboard sides of the ship. The use of the underwater tube in firing a torpedo would be less conspicuous than firing a torpedo from the twin

tubes fixed to the main deck because there it was easier to see the torpedo splash as it entered the water. Some people believe *Kormoran* used its underwater torpedo in conjunction with a signal to surrender to defeat *Sydney*.

4 *Kormoran*'s gunnery officer Fritz Skeries put the range between the ships at 1,500 metres. In this case *Sydney* would have to have been about ten boat lengths astern of *Kormoran* in order to be hit by an underwater torpedo.

5 The nearly perfect symmetry of the shell hole and surrounding circle where the turret's paint has been blown away by the shell impact indicates that the trajectory of this shell was very close to a straight 90° angle.

6 In order to safely fire her underwater torpedoes, *Kormoran* had to either be stopped or moving very slowly at a speed no more than 3 knots. Consequently, *Kormoran* only fired its underwater torpedoes twice in previous actions: once as a test during the vessel's sea trials and once as a trial combined with an above-deck torpedo to dispatch the British merchant vessel *Craftsman*, which stubbornly refused to sink.

7 Skeries testified that *Sydney*'s 'A' and 'B' turrets were put out of action by their third and fourth salvos, and that 'B' turret was blown up by their tenth salvo.

8 Although Detmers and Skeries refer to the firing of salvos, *Kormoran* did not possess a central firing control system, as each of the 15-cm guns were fired independently and as rapidly as possible by their respective gun crews. Range and target information was initially provided to the gun crews by Skeries, but thereafter the gun crews had no difficulty in finding and hitting their assigned targets.

9 In *H.M.A.S. Sydney — Fact, Fantasy and Fraud*, B. Winter lists the following warships as having suffered total loss of life when sinking: HMS *Black Prince*, HMS *Defence*, HMS *Good Hope*, HMS *Monmouth*, SMS *Pommern*, and SMS *Scharnhorst*.

10 During the examination of Michael Montgomery on 12 December 2007, Commander Jack Rush, QC, acting as counsel assisting the Commission of Inquiry into the Loss of HMAS *Sydney* II, referred to 47 15-cm shell hits on *Sydney*'s starboard side and just a little fewer on the port side.

11 It took the crew of *Arethusa* six hours to control the single fire caused by the torpedo and a further six hours to extinguish it completely.

12 The loss of electrical supply to the steering motors might also explain why *Sydney* suddenly veered to port after the torpedo strike and moved behind *Kormoran*. This manoeuvre was tactically unsound as it closed the firing arcs for 'X' and 'Y' turrets, which had only just resumed their fire and begun to hit the raider with good effect, but in the end it may have been unintentional.

Chapter 10

1 Bundesarchiv/Militärarachiv, W-04-11730.

2 The diver Innes McCartney discovered the *Komet* in the English Channel on 4 July 2006, lying at a depth of 70 metres. The wreck is broken in two halves and heavily encrusted with marine growth, which is obscuring much of the ship's architecture.

3 Bundesarchiv/Militärarachiv, RM-100-176.

4 As testified by Fritz Englemann on 8 July 2008 to the Cole Commission of Inquiry into the Loss of HMAS *Sydney* II.

5 Personal memoir of *Kormoran*'s torpedo officer Joachim Greter.

6 Bundesarchiv/Militärarachiv, RM-100-137.

7 Personal memoir of *Kormoran*'s torpedo officer Joachim Greter.

8 Based on construction drawings, the break in *Kormoran*'s 164-metre-long hull is approximately 83 metres from the bow.

9 As testified by Fritz Kummerer on 4 July 2008 to the Cole Commission of Inquiry into the Loss of HMAS *Sydney* II. There was some confusion in Mr Kummerer's interview whether the lifts were raised hydraulically or pneumatically.

Epilogue

1   Admiralty policy during the war was that Boards of Inquiry were to be held to investigate the loss or damage to HM ships other than small craft by enemy action. Boards of Inquiry were held for the losses of HMAS *Perth* and *Canberra* and for the damage of HMAS *Hobart*, the sister ship of *Sydney*.

2   M. Buckland, et al., *Report on Technical Aspects of the Sinking of HMAS Sydney and HSK Kormoran*, Marine Platforms Division, Defence Science and Technology Organisation, Victoria, 2009.

3   In a letter dated 6 October 1941 to the Rear Admiral Commanding Australian Squadron, Captain Burnett raised the possibility that a target-like structure that *Sydney* found floating about 40 nautical miles away from Christmas Island had been dropped by a raider.

4   As testified by Tom Fisher on 23 June 2008 to the Cole Commission of Inquiry into the Loss of HMAS *Sydney* II. Fisher's testimony indicated that Burnett's warning at Sunday divisions happened in mid-October, after he had written to the RACAS raising the possibility that a raider dropped the suspect target they found.

5   National Archives of Australia (Melbourne), MP1049/5, 2028/2/508.

6   As per the witness statement of Heinz Messerschmidt on 11 July 2008 to the Cole Commission of Inquiry into the Loss of HMAS *Sydney* II. Numerous other German accounts describe seeing men dressed in white aprons and hats believed to be cooks watching from the waist of *Sydney*.

7   www.sydneymemorial.com

8   James Reason, *Human Error*, Cambridge University Press, Cambridge, England 1990.

ACKNOWLEDGEMENTS

•••

First and foremost, I would like to thank my wife, Sarah, for her love and support, without which this book and my involvement in the search would have not been possible.

The search for *Sydney*, and the truth behind her loss, was a collaborative undertaking by countless people spread over a period covering several decades. A list of everyone involved would run to many more pages than I have at my disposal, and I am sure it would still inadvertently omit scores of people whose contributions behind the scenes I am personally unaware of.

It would be remiss of me, however, not to acknowledge the Commonwealth, West Australian and New South Wales governments, which put up the bulk of the funds for the search; the individuals and companies who also generously donated funds for the search; the Royal Australian Navy for its total commitment to the success of the search; the German Government for granting me permission to film the wreck of *Kormoran*; and the directors of the Finding *Sydney* Foundation (FSF), past and present, for their hard work in making the search a reality.

Vice Admiral Chris Ritchie was Chief of the Navy when I and the FSF were independently lobbying the RAN to support a search for the wrecks. His intervention and bold decision to reverse the RAN's negative stance about a search was fundamentally important in gaining necessary political support. About the same time, Marty Grogan and John Francis were instrumental in getting the membership of the HMAS *Sydney* Association to enthusiastically support my proposal for a search. Without this early and crucial support, I doubt a search would ever have gotten off the ground.

The research I used to find the wrecks grew out of a collaborative effort between me, Peter Hore, Wes Olson and Barbara Poniewierski that was stimulated and encouraged by Mack McCarthy. All three had written excellent books and collectively unearthed an enormous amount of background material that gave me the springboard to focus my work on the question of location. Peter shared with me the somewhat unpopular burden of proving Detmers's veracity and did the lion's share of work in deciphering his various accounts. A decade earlier Barbara blazed the trail for both of us by making the vitally important discovery of Detmers's dictionary. Barbara is a first-class researcher and historian and deserves enormous credit for her early work, which has more than stood the test of time and intense scrutiny. Wes is another of the unsung heroes, who from the very first day I contacted him right through to the present has been amazingly generous with his research, ideas and sound advice. Wes wasn't with us on board the *Geosounder*, but he definitely shares in our success.

I gained valuable insights into the mind of Captain Detmers and the operation of *Kormoran* by talking to and corresponding with the last surviving German members of her crew and some close relations. For that I am deeply indebted to Detmers's nephew Dr Hans-Günther Jantzen, Heinz Messerschmidt, Baron von Malapert (deceased), Dr Habben's son, Dr Redelf Habben, Joachim von Gösseln and Kurt Meder. I have always felt that a mark of truth of the German accounts was the extent to which my requests for information from these men were met with complete openness and a willingness to do whatever they could to help me find the wrecks.

My own research in the German Federal Archives was expertly assisted by Sebastian Remus and I am equally grateful to Axel Salander of Ince and Co. for providing his firm's services in the translation of torpedo officer Greter's personal account of the action.

Archival research is the lifeblood of my profession, which I could not practise without free and unfettered access to historical records. I am most grateful to the following archives for providing such access and to the named individuals for their assistance beyond the call of duty: Dr David Stevens of the RAN Sea Power Centre; Chris Page and Kate Tildesley of the UK Naval Historical Branch; Dr Diether Schmidt formerly of the Peter Tamm Institute now known as the Internationales Maritimes Museum Hamburg; Steve Stuckey of the National Archives of Australia; Mack McCarthy of the Western Australian Maritime Museum; the UK Public Records Office in Kew; the Imperial War Museum in London; the Australian War Memorial in Canberra and the Bundesarchiv in Freiburg, Germany.

I have enjoyed a long and spirited correspondence with a large number of researchers and mostly benefited from the experience. Michael Montgomery is the best example of a researcher, who despite disagreeing with me about many things, never let these differences get in the way of our relationship and was always helpful in answering questions and providing important documents. Other researchers and individuals who over the years offered me information and their opinions included Graham Anderson, Betty Daly-King, James Eagles, Tom Fisher, John Francis, Jochen Franke, Peter Grage, Maria Hehir, George Jackson, David Kennedy, Dr. Kim Kirsner, Dr John MacArthur, Commander David McDonald, Ean McDonald, Glenys McDonald, Phil Shepherd, Bruce Teede, Alaistair Templeton, and most energetically of all, Warren Whittaker.

True to her word, Margaret Gee has been more than just my book agent. Because of her father's history in surviving the sinking of HMAS *Perth* just a few months after the loss of *Sydney*, Margaret had a visceral connection with the story and encouraged me to write it with the same passion and depth of feeling. My sincere thanks also go out to all those at HarperCollins who worked so hard to produce a book that lived up to the considerable expectations we set ourselves: publisher Amruta Slee, layout artist Matt Stanton, and editors Neil Thomas and Mary Rennie.

Lastly, but certainly not least, I would like to thank John Perryman for his friendship and for writing the wonderful introduction, which is as fine a tribute to the history of HMAS *Sydney* as I could have ever hoped. As with the search, John has been beside me every step of the way and this book has been much improved by his review of the manuscript and suggestion of photographs. The only other words I can think of to express my immense respect and appreciation of John's role in the search for *Sydney* are: Alpha Delta Two Eight.

DAVID MEARNS

PICTURE CREDITS

•••

Images courtesy of Australian Bureau of Meteorology:
Pages 138 and 173

Images courtesy of Wikimedia Commons (Public Domain):
Pages 65 (top) and 75

Images courtesy of Sea Power Centre:
Pages 6, 7 (top & bottom), 8, 21 (top), 36, 52, 60, 182, 194 (middle), 196 and 206

Images courtesy of Sea Power Centre (Taylor Family):
Pages 15 and 30

Images courtesy of Sea Power Centre (Kim Hay collection):
Page 47

Image courtesy of John Broadhead & Fred Woodward:
Page 32

Image courtesy of Mark Corcoran:
Page 105

Images courtesy of National Archives of Australia:
Page 59 (Public Domain)

Images courtesy of Newspix:
Page 81 (00396897) (left)

Maps created by Tom Coulson, Encompass Graphics:
Page 91, 96 and 229

CGI model of the HMAS *Sydney,* by Thomas Schmid,. Please note, these models are not shown in their war time colours.

Images on pages 184, 185, 186, 188, 191, 199 (& inset), 200, 202, 204, 209 (top), 219, 221 and 223 are mosaics which have been put together from multiple consecutive photographs.

During the publication of this book all efforts have been made by the publisher to locate the original source of the images on page 21 (top), 94 and 164. If you have any information regarding these images, please don't hesitate to contact HarperCollins Publishers.

INDEX

• • •